FOODSERVICE FOR THE EXTENDED CARE FACILITY

FOODSERVICE FOR THE EXTENDED CARE FACILITY

LENDAL H. KOTSCHEVAR, PH. D.

Jule Wilkinson, Editor

CBI Publishing Company, Inc.
51 Sleeper Street, Boston, Massachusetts 02210

Printing(last digit): 9 8 7 6

ISBN 0-8436-0548-0

Library of Congress Catalog Card. No. 72-75295

Printed in the United States of America

To my mother

TABLE OF CONTENTS

LIST OF TABLES

LIST OF ILLUSTRATIONS

PREFACE

My mother has been a resident in a nursing home for a long time. If there were nothing else, this would make me have an interest in seeing that maximum care is given to those entrusted to nursing homes. But, there is another reason. There is a great need today for information on how to operate foodservices more efficiently in small extended care facilities so that these facilities can render the service they must in our health care program.

The time also has come for higher professional standards to be applied in these foodservice programs. The extended care industry has grown rapidly from a small casual effort until today it is a large and significant part of our health care program. The extended care industry must now consolidate its position and improve its standards.

A small health facility is often at a serious disadvantage in providing adequate nutrition for its residents. It prepares a limited number of meals, too few to make efficiency possible. Yet, the provision of an adequate diet and meals that satisfy is essential to the residents.

To meet these needs, the small health facility must incur higher costs than are required of a facility which produces more meals and can afford to have a large professional staff and many workers. It is important that those in charge of administering public funds for the support of small facilities recognize this problem. The cost of health care has risen dramatically within the last several decades; however, the extended care industry has not shared equally in obtaining adequate payment for these increased costs.

There are many problems in feeding those who live in extended care facilities. The problems are enumerated in this text and an attempt has been made to point out the best solutions. The food served to the resident is as essential to his happiness and welfare as the medical and nursing care he needs. This must be recognized. The foodservice department is not just a "service" department, only there to fill people up, but is a highly significant part of the health care program.

The foodservice department must also become a professionally organized, oriented and operated department. Quantity food production, even for a few individuals in a facility, is not the same as cooking food at home. The whole organization of planning, producing and serving meals in such a facility is a complex process requiring a staff trained to do the job.

Serving good food is not enough; the food must also meet nutritional and medical requirements. To do this requires people who not only know how to plan, produce and administer diets but who can also weave these dietary requirements into a complex meal-producing system so that nutritional needs are met without reducing the satisfaction provided by the foods served.

Any author must be truly indebted to a number of people who help in the compilation and writing of a book. Many of these will go unnamed but to them I give my sincere thanks. I am especially indebted to Mrs. Iris Lochner, a pioneer consulting dietitian of great competence, who has been an innovator and a leader and who has done much to bring recognition of what a professional dietitian can do in serving a small health facility. She has counseled me in the planning and writing of this book, giving me much from her experiences. Throughout the book one will note forms and other items to assist in achieving a better operation that she has given me. I am also immeasurably indebted to Mrs. Frank Z. Pirkey who has also pioneered in this field and has contributed much from her tremendous experience with consulting dietitians. She has loaned me valuable background materials and also has counseled me throughout the planning and writing of this book. And, to Miss Cynthia Bishop of the State of Texas, a great friend, I owe a lot because I have so liberally borrowed from her diet manual and other vast treasures of information she has compiled. Without these 3 great dietitians and individuals, I could not have written this book.

The author is also grateful to Dr. C. G. King and Mrs. Iris Lochner for their reading of the chapters on menu planning and nutrition and to Mrs. Frank Z. Pirkey for her reading of the chapters on management, menu planning and nutrition. He is also grateful to Miss Anne Claire Donovan of the Hill-Burton Division of the U. S. Dept. of Health, Education and Welfare for her counsel and suggestions relating to Chapter X: Layout and Design. Since the feeding of residents in long term institutions is still a developing area, it was desired that the best authorities in these areas review the material before publication for suggestions and comments. The participation of these highly respected individuals should in no way be interpreted as responsibility for any of the content presented in these chapters. The responsibility is solely that of the author. However, their assistance made it possible to make the material more pertinent, accurate and helpful. And, to Mrs. Jule Wilkinson, my editor, I owe special thanks for carrying the mass of detail needed in editing rough copy to its finished state. She has contributed so much I feel it is her book as much as mine.

Lendal H. Kotschevar, Ph. D.

I: HEALTH CARE AND THE EXTENDED CARE FACILITY

INTRODUCTION

FOOD AND PEOPLE Food is essential to life from its beginning to end; how well we eat has much to do with how well we live. Food is also important psychologically. Eating gives pleasure, creating a satiety value denoted by the comfort, satisfaction and peacefulness that comes after eating. There is even pleasure in anticipating food as well as in tasting and eating it. Additionally, food can play an important part in giving us social activity; we enjoy eating with others. Good social interaction with others at meal time increases an individual's food intake and improves his nutrition and "psychological and social health."[1] Eating can also consume time and, for many, this time is the most enjoyable of the day.

Important as food is to the normal person, food and its role are far more important to the ill, aged or handicapped. It is more critical to their well-being and health. Slight nutritional imbalances may result in serious health changes which would not occur in a normal person under the same mild stress. Ailments once thought caused by physical infirmities are now being traced more and more to nutritional causes. Vague, non-specific symptoms formerly attributed to circulatory problems, such as "weakness, mild paralysis, depression, confusion or irritability are now more often found to be the result of a poor vitamin intake or a poor absorption of the vitamins consumed."[2]

The social activity occurring around food can also be extremely important to the ill or aged. Besides giving enjoyment from social contact, food can draw them to others. Even the silent and bedridden individuals become more socially expansive at meal times with roommates they hardly recognize at other times. This contact through food may be as important to their well-

[1]"Nutrition and Aging." *The Gerontologist,* (Autumn, 1969) p. 42.
[2]Ibid.

being as food itself, for this may be the only time they are in touch with their environment.

Food's satiety value is also extremely important to them. As life's pleasures narrow, those remaining become more important and are more valued. The comfort and peace food gives can have a soothing, almost narcotic effect on an anxious, restless individual. Even though one loses some of his sense of taste, the repetition of an habitual function such as eating can give a sense of security.

And, lastly, in discussing why food is important to the ill and aged, in a long day of inactivity, looking forward to the next meal and then spending time eating it may help shorten the day and provide something to do. It can be very helpful just as a "time killer."

FOOD AND THE HEALTH FACILITY

The health facility that cares for the ill or aged must realize that a good food program is essential for adequate care and the facility must give food proper emphasis in its care program. A failure to do this may negate all other efforts to provide needed care. All the values food can give—nutritional, psychological and social—must be utilized to a maximum degree.

To the facility itself, having an adequate and efficient foodservice is important because of the dollars it demands, the number of staff that must be committed to it and the attention that management must devote to it. Unless such a department is operated efficiently, high costs and very unsatisfactory results are obtained.

Most extended care facilities are small and usually find it very difficult to provide the financing, personnel and other resources needed to establish a desirable food program. Operating a foodservice department is not easy in *any* health facility. Even a large operation with better physical facilities, professional personnel and more adequate financing has trouble. The smaller facility, without such professional capability and handicapped by a lack of other important factors, finds the job more difficult.

Unfortunately, the burden of operating a small department is much the same as operating a large one. A small operation cannot eliminate many things just because it is small. It is as necessary and takes as long to fill in a fire inspection report or an accident report in a small unit as in a large one.

The small unit must plan a menu which probably takes as long and as much skill—if not more—than planning one for a larger unit. The same time-demanding steps also must be taken in ordering food, storing, preparing and serving it.

Personnel can be specialized in large units and do a limited number of tasks, thus increasing efficiency. In the small operation, one person must do a wide variety of jobs and the benefits of the division of labor and specialization are lost because this is so. For these reasons, and others, the small foodservice operation must try harder to have an adequate foodservice program.

More research has been done and information published on the operation of the large dietary department than the small one. True, many of the procedures are the same for both and what has been done for the larger can be applied to the smaller, after some modification. But, the small operation, because of its low meal volume and lack of professional and trained personnel, has special problems. We have not done much, either, to build information on how they can be solved. Neither has as much time and attention been devoted to the problems of feeding individuals under long time care and this has not helped the small facility. We have somehow overlooked foodservices in extended care facilities until suddenly we realized that we had many such facilities and they needed assistance.

Because of a lack of information and the need for assistance, this text has been prepared. Emphasis is upon problems encountered in the small health facility. A wide range of subjects had to be covered and, to avoid a book of greater length, some items lack detail. Important ones, however, have had more treatment in depth.

THE LONG TERM CARE INDUSTRY

**A NEW LOOK
IN HEALTH CARE**
Our health service industry has been one of the fastest growing of our industries. It will soon overtake the foodservice industry which is now fourth in size but will then drop to fifth. Today, about $75.4 billion or 7.4% of our gross national product is spent per year for health care; in 1955, it was around $40 billion. Each person in 1971 spent $358 for health care, up $31 from 1970. Health costs rose in 1971 over 11%, the lowest annual gain in 5 years. The government's outlays for health rose 14% and private costs increased 9%. About 40% of the public spending was because of a 25% increase in Medicaid costs. At this rate of growth, health costs should about double in 8 to 9 years.

At the present time we are drawing on public funds for over 38% of our care costs; third parties (government, private health insurance, philanthropy and others) pay 63% of the health bill, 87% of hospital bills and 61% of physicians' bills. Hospital care is the largest expenditure and increased 14% in 1971 for a total cost of $29.6 billion. Private health insurance benefit payments jumped 15% in 1971, reaching $16.6 billion. The increasing cost of health care is causing increasing concern in many areas and there is a growing feeling that we must give more attention to monitoring and controlling these costs to slow their rate of growth.*

As our population has increased, we have had to increase the amount of health services available but this has not been the most significant reason for the substantial growth noted in the industry. It has been stimulated also because we are extending the use and scope of our health care programs. More people needing care get it. We are also providing more adequate care which pushes up requirements.

Good health in our populace is needed to have a vigorous and productive society, to best promote our economy, our welfare and to further important national programs. We have been surprised to find we do not have a healthy society; there are significant lacks and we have not been able to contribute to a maximum national effort because of them. For instance, men in 17 countries of the world live longer than they do in this country; their span of productive work is also greater. While we have more financial and other resources and better medical facilities than many countries, we lack performance. Our high rejection rate of men for the Armed Services is also of concern. Other countries lead us also in reducing problems during birth and post-natal care.

Today, health in this country is a matter of national concern and no longer one considered solely private and individual nor one to be supported completely from private funds. As a result, we are emphasizing health as a national problem and are committing considerable public resources toward building a program that will cover *all* individuals regardless of income, race or creed. And, while this cost is staggering—especially in future projections—it

*The material in this section is taken mostly from *National Health Expenditures,* 1929-71, reprinted from the *Social Security Bulletin,* January, 1972, U. S. Department of HEW, Washington, D. C., 1972, authored by Dorothy P. Price and Barbara S. Cooper.

may be low when compared both with needs and with the benefits obtained in having a more productive and healthy society.

Many agree the question is not whether we can afford to expand our health programs but whether we can afford *not* to. Authorities have pointed out that illness, low productivity, accidents, welfare and other hidden costs arising because of poor health may be costing us more than the contemplated program.

This changing concept and emphasis in our national health picture has significant implications for the mode of operation and growth of the extended health care industry.

HEALTH CARE INSTITUTIONS While most health care takes place under clinical conditions with the patient going and coming from his home for this care, another very important adjunct occurs in institutions such as hospitals, nursing homes, convalescent centers and related facilities where the individual stays to receive care. We have over 1.7 million beds in such institutions in this country and they are constantly increasing. It is estimated we need nearly 100,000 more beds in general hospitals and over 175,000 more in long-term care institutions. About 230,000 beds in our general hospitals and 250,000 in extended care facilities need modernization. This is 40% of our total beds. To bring our health care facilities, such as hospitals, long-term care institutions, outpatient facilities, public health centers and rehabilitation facilities, to a proper level of modernization is estimated to cost over $12 billion. By 1973, it is expected we will have nearly 900,000 general hospital beds and nearly a million in long-term care institutions.*

Health care institutions where the patients stay to receive treatment divide into two groups. The first contains the intensive-care facility usually found in hospitals. These tend to be large, have well trained staffs and are well equipped so they can provide highly specialized medical treatment. They have been well supported from public, private and philanthropic funds. This group has been a part of our health care program for a long time and is today well recognized and integrated into it. These may also be called short-term facilities because they care for individuals for a short time. Individuals requiring less care and who must receive such care over a long period of time will return to their homes or go to an institution providing less intensive but longer term care.

*See preceding page.

The other group of health care institutions provides long-term care. They vary from those providing only housing accommodations or bed and board to those that give considerable medical and skilled nursing care. Grouped together, the term "extended care facilities" seems to fit them best. Medical care will not be the main purpose for the existence of these units. Few provide intensive care or give complex medical treatment; they lack the staffs, facilities and equipment for this. Instead, the emphasis will be on living care rather than on medical care.

In 1961, those giving personal care and assistance were 48% of all extended care facilities; 42% gave skilled nursing care and 10% residential care only. Today, because of the trend to add registered and licensed practical nurses on staffs, a majority give skilled nursing care. In fact, the industry is emerging as one in which skilled nursing care units will be largely characteristic of this group.

The establishment and growth of extended care facilities has not been as well defined as that of the short-term, intensive care units. Until recently, extended care facilities were not closely related to our medical programs and had little recognition, use, sponsorship or support from them. The industry grew more or less "like Topsy." Originally, many were started in converted homes or buildings that could be adapted for use for such an institution. The average size was small, around 25 beds; they had limited facilities for the care needed; few gave skilled nursing care although the occupants may have needed such care.

Many of these facilities were poor farms or county homes supported meagerly from public or philanthropic funds. Few of the occupants had money of their own for their care. Here the aged, afflicted, indigent or handicapped lived under very sparse conditions. For a long time, these were units which had as their main purpose the keeping of such people isolated from a society that felt little responsibility for them.

Table 1-1—POPULATION PROJECTIONS, 1970 AND 1980

Year	Total Population (millions)	Total Over 65 (millions)	Percent in Various Age Groups			
			Under 19	20 to 44	45 to 64	Over 65
1970	214	20.0	40.4%	19.7%	30.5%	9.4%
1980	260	24.5	41.9%	17.0%	31.6%	9.4%

Adapted from the U. S. Dept of HEW's *HEW Trends* and *HEW Indicators,* 1962

EXTENDED CARE FACILITIES
AND THEIR RECENT GROWTH*

But, things have changed. The number of extended care facilities, their occupants and quality of care have increased materially. In 1900, 4% of our population, or 3.1 million individuals, were over 65 years of age; today 20 million, or 9%, are. This is one of every 10 Americans. By 1980, we expect 24½ million people, or 9% of our population, still to be over 65 years of age.** These factors, plus a feeling of social responsibility, has brought about a new industry.

A few statistics may serve to indicate how the extended care facility industry has grown. The number of beds increased over 100% from 1960 to 1970, employment over 130% and care expenditures over 400%. The industry is now estimated to have nearly 1¼ million beds with an occupancy rate of nearly 86%. Over 90% of these beds are in nursing homes or convalescent centers.

Over $3.6 billion per year is spent for extended care in this country, over half of which comes from public funds, largely Medicare or Medicaid. (Medicare is a federally financed health insurance program under which most individuals over 65, and some others, are covered, regardless of economic condition. Medicaid is a joint federal-state program of medical assistance giving care to those who cannot afford it, regardless of age.)

Today, more than 40% of all beds in all types of health institutions are in the extended care facility group. The number of extended care facilities has not increased much; in 1961, we had around 23,000 and today we have about the same number. The total has not increased because as new units were built about the same number of old units, most of them quite small, discontinued operation, largely because they were unable to operate economically or were unable to meet higher standards of care required for certification. In 1969, a unit averaged about 42 beds; today, the average new facility has about 70 beds; about half the beds in licensed nursing homes now are in units built in the last 5 years.

Most of the units are privately owned; voluntary nonprofit (church related or other) and public units make up only about 10% of the total. There

*Most of these data come from *Health Care Facilities, Existing and Needed,* Hill-Burton State Plan Data as of January 1, 1969, U. S. Department of HEW, HEW Publication No. (HSM) 72-4004, 1972
**We are adding around 350,000 people over 65 to our population each year. In the year 2000, we estimate we will have 30.6 million over 65, 5% or more of whom (around 1½ million) will be in long-term care institutions.

is a definite trend in the industry for the proprietary units to be a part of a multiple unit organization or a corporation rather than the single family-owned unit.

A gradual upgrading in care, operation, staffing, facilities and other factors has occurred in the industry in the last several decades. Upgrading has been pushed at a slower pace than growth to allow an emerging industry to adjust slowly to improved standards. The industry was too much tied to its past and too limited in funds and operational knowledge to push this too fast.

In 1962, the Department of HEW reported only 32% of the existing beds met acceptable standards. While today a much larger percentage does, continued upgrading is needed before completely satisfactory conditions will exist. Up to now, many submarginal or marginal facilities have operated through certification by waiver, a method allowing operation providing standards are raised as quickly as possible. This procedure will become less and less common in the future.

One of the most significant changes occurring in the industry has been in its management. Today, a large number of units are managed by individuals who work for ownership and who have had professional training and experience for their positions. This management is younger; it is also more aggressive and imaginative and alert in meeting the needs of health care for residents. It is active in health care associations and in representing the industry's needs in legislation. Most state and federal regulations today require that administrators of these facilities have such qualifications.

Both the state and federal governments have initiated training programs to upgrade and to provide personnel for the industry and it is not unreasonable to expect that soon standards and certification may be established for all types of personnel, in addition to the nursing and medical staffs, in extended care facilities. Such upgrading would be consistent with our national health aims and would bring *all* extended care workers into a more equitable status. Without meeting such standards, foodservice workers can never expect to receive the recognition they seek.

National and state associations of extended care facilities have been strong supporters of upgrading. Management has also. A strong stimulus to upgrade has occurred through the requirement that facilities built with federal or other public funds must meet high standards of construction and operation thereafter. States, through licensure, have also been able to stimulate upgrading. The federal government has been effective in enforcing standards with those facilities that participate in the Medicare, Medicaid and other public assistance programs.*

Undoubtedly, this upgrading has worked a hardship on many small units, forcing some to discontinue operation but, if the industry is to give the care required and take its proper place in our national health structure, this upgrading is required and must continue.

THE FUTURE While the industry is perhaps still in a metamorphic stage between its past and future, there is evidence that it is reaching certain stages of maturity. Probably its most rapid growth is over—there is overgrowth in some areas and occupancy rates are generally dropping. Many facilities report they no longer have waiting lists.

Nevertheless, the industry, based on population growth, should increase 15 to 20% in the next decade; however, its growth will undoubtedly be greater than this because the scope of the programs should also expand, making more people eligible for care. Also, we have only begun to construct facilities to attract the more affluent individuals who need such care. Elaborate retirement centers with all types of housing, lodging and care facilities, some resembling clubs more than care centers, are becoming more common. It is estimated that we need in long-term care facilities 4 beds per 100 individuals 65 or over or 3.9 beds for each 1000 of total population in this country. By 1980, these figures could go as high as 5 beds per 100, 65 or over, or 4.8 per 1000 of our population.

While, today, over 90% in these facilities are 65 or over, this percentage should drop. There is a trend in some states to move individuals not requiring intensive care from state hospitals to proprietary units. In California, for instance, the number of state hospitals caring for such individuals is being drastically reduced as the aged, chronically ill, mentally handicapped or others, requiring care that can be provided by private institutions, are moved out.

Employment will increase in the industry. The present ratio of about 2½ residents to each person in nursing services personnel is expected to drop

*See "Conditions of Participation: Extended Care Facilities—Regulations," *Federal Health Insurance for the Aged,* U. S. Dept of HEW, Social Security Administration, HIR-11 (2-68). Also, conditions relating to the foodservice program in this treatise appear in the Appendix of this book.

to 2 or less. The U. S. Dept. of Labor estimates that the number employed in the industry by 1980 will increase over 1970 by 50%; about ¾ million will be working in the industry, approximately 13% in the dietary department. Expenditures for care will continue to grow faster than the industry. Upgrading will continue. The average facility size will increase materially; this is being done to meet health care needs and reduce costs. Establishing extended care facilities to care for the members of religious organizations, unions or fraternal organizations will become more popular.

Public expenditures for health care in extended care facilities will increase, especially those of the federal government. Costs will increase out of proportion to the rise in income of those needing care; the balance will usually come from public services. About 50% of the aged couples in 1980 are expected to have incomes of less than $3000 per year and slightly over 86% of the unmarried aged are expected to have incomes of less than $2000 per year. With care costs running at least $3500 a year now, the inadequacy of these incomes for such care is evident. A recent study stated, "using various measures of income adequacy, it was found that little or no improvement in the adequacy of aged income . . . can be expected relative to the rising incomes of the rest of the U. S. population."*

We can expect considerable expansion of health services into the community. Home care will be given by hospitals and other health facilities to individuals who need more care than can be provided by outpatient services but do not especially need the care that can be provided within the facility. Home care is not a substitute for facility care but will fill a vacuum that presently exists in our health care program.

There is a need also for a type of care called "ambulant care." Frequently this type of care can be given in the facility or in clinics but at times the medical team may have to travel outside its environs to serve those needing such care adequately. Educational programs on self-care also will be developed by these facilities.

There will also be a significant advance in preventative health care. Instead of waiting until individuals are ill and the cost increased and the problem aggravated, health care facilities will utilize their resources to check and take care of health problems before they occur. In perhaps 50 years, we may

*These statistics and the quotation come from Schulz, James H., *The Economic Status of Retired Aged in 1980,* Research Report No. 24, U. S. Dept. of HEW, Office of Research and Statistics, (HEW 8-68), 1968.

not recognize the health facilities then in existence in comparison with what we have now. Undoubtedly, health care facilities will tend more and more to come together in conglomerates so a greater amount of specialization can occur and the facilities of each be used to build a better total health care program. In such growth, the extended care facility will become an ever increasingly important unit in the health care field.

THE EXTENDED CARE FACILITY RESIDENT

THE INDIVIDUAL NEEDING CARE The most important factor in extended care is the individual. And, while he will not be normal, he may be quite normal for his group. Nine out of 10 in a health care facility are over 65. The average age is frequently 80 years! At 65, the life expectancy for a white male is 12.9 years and for non-white males, 12.6; for white females it is 16.3 years and for non-white females, 15.5.

There are two chances to one the individual is a female. Most individuals will be in the facility because they have no other place to live or because they cannot receive the care they need at home. They will usually be ill or have physical impairments. Half will need assistance in walking and another fourth will not walk at all; about 35% will be incontinent either by bladder or bowel or both.* Half will be confused all or part of the time. Ailments such as diabetes, senility, paralysis, mental illness, fractures, arthritis, tumors, etc. will be common and many will have more than one of these. Individuals over 65 have twice the health problems that others do and their length of illness is 2½ times that of a normal individual.

Most feel isolated and about a third feel no one has any concern or interest in what they eat or the quality of food they get; this will usually be the most frequent complaint heard about the food. From 15 to 25% will need special diets; diabetic and low-salt diets will be the most common. Obesity diets will also be needed frequently. A number of residents will have problems that require not only one but more than one type diet.

Most will be in a state of malnutrition, the signs of which may not be clear-cut nor evident but may show up as secondary symptoms such as apathy,

*U. S. Dept. HEW, Public Health Service. *Nursing Homes and Related Facilities, Fact Book,* No. 930 F4. Washington, D. C.: Government Printing Office, 1963.

depression, suspiciousness or delusion. We know it is possible to starve nerve cells to a point where they function poorly or not at all. We call this PCM (protein-carbohydrate-malnutrition) and poor emotional or mental functioning associated with senility can be an evidence of this.*

Improved memory and mood in older adults have taken place when they have received adequate diets. Many will have had a long history of inadequate food intake and we should know on entry what the diet has been in the distant past as well as recently; we may have to correct more for these past deficiencies than for the recent ones.

Odd, rigidly fixed food habits will be common and many will follow food fads. Most will lack knowledge of what an adequate diet is. Frequently, opinions on diet and nutrition will be erroneous and contribute to a poor food intake. Around 20% will not like milk; 11% will dislike eggs and 9%, meat. Religious, cultural or other beliefs will color ideas on food. All these factors will increase the problems of serving an adequate diet and providing meal satisfaction. These all incorporate a challenge that must be met by the foodservice department.

One of the most difficult things to do is to change food habits, especially in the infirm, aged or handicapped. Authorities who have studied the problem say it is easier to change other living modes, even religions, than to change the food habits of people.**

Foodservice personnel will usually find that *mild* modification of an habitual diet, so as not to bring about objection to the change, is a better way to win co-operation than making significant changes and then attempting to rationalize them to the individual. We can also do much to circumvent problems. For instance, milk need not be consumed in a recognizable liquid form to make a diet adequate in it. There are substitutes or milk can be in the diet in non-recognizable forms.

Before an individual learns, he must understand and some time spent in gaining the understanding of a resident may help. Of course, the resident must be fairly rational. Extended care residents many times will find leaders whom

*Most of the information in this section comes from "Aging and Nutrition," *The Gerontologist,* Washington, D. C. (1969), p. 27.
**Burgess, A. and Dean, R. F. A. (eds.), *Malnutrition and Food Habits,* (New York: Macmillan, 1962), p. 76.

they will blindly follow. Thus, spending time with the leaders to get them to change may induce change in a number of others.

Special promotion of items scheduled for a meal may help. The fanfare and attention may bring about expectations which can culminate in a trial and then change. A well thought out "lesson plan" should be made previous to such promotion. Obtaining successful experiences through the use of encouragement, compliments and rewards is another way.

Every resident will also need individual study and attention to his dietary needs. An interview form should be prepared to check on needs when an individual enters. Get all the facts. The reason given for non-food acceptance may not be the correct one, although completely believed to be by the resident. Lonesomeness, a feeling of rejection, being away from a familiar environment or other factors may cause food rejection. Food is something that helps acclimate us to our environment and a dissatisfaction with the environment can also cause us to reject food.

We learn early in life to tie our emotions to food. When we are babies, we cry when we are hungry. Psychologists have hypothesized that mother-love may be based on the fact that the mother feeds the child. Later, we learn to submerge this crying or emotional upset associated with food. But, when we come upon stress or lose our ability to control our emotions, we revert back to those basic stimuli which we exhibited as infants. Thus, we can expect complaints many times when residents are disturbed even though the food is good.

Adults in hospitals are apt to reflect the stress of their illness in food criticism. College students during exam times frequently register a high number of food complaints. Food becomes the whipping boy for other dissatisfaction. This is one of the crosses we in foodservice have to bear. However, it is comforting to know that our crosses are becoming fewer. Food quality in many facilities has improved considerably from past standards and, as this occurs, complaints decrease.

The lack of teeth, poorly fitting dentures or other problems in mastication or salivation may deter eating or cause a change to undesirable foods, such as a soft, carbohydrate diet lacking in protein and other nutrients. Or, digestive problems such as the lack of gastric juices, esophagus disorders or intestinal malfunctions may be the cause of a poor food intake.

Finding the real problem and then doing something about it may do much to improve the dietary intakes of individuals. Many residents earn a reputation of being "finicky" eaters. They will eat only certain foods. Very often this is a reaction against poor food selection for the resident or poor food preparation by the foodservices. Frequently, the list of food items residents "won't eat" exists only in the minds of some foodservice employees who want to take the easy way out and do not meet the challenge.

But, after everything possible has been done, we may find we are still fighting a losing battle. There is a point at which many aged, ill or infirm people go into negative nutritional balance in spite of all we can do. Perhaps we do not know enough yet about why this happens or how it can be prevented. But, when this time comes, we still can do much to reduce the impact of an inadequate diet by using all the skills and knowledge we have available. The human body adjusts remarkably to nutritional stress and, if we are able to reduce the deficiency to a minimum, we can delay for a long time adverse reactions to it. If we can even maintain a *fairly* adequate intake, we can achieve a great deal even though we can't win.

We can build on what is accepted. For instance, if liquid foods are tolerated, then packing these with highly nutritional components is recommended. If bread is eaten, add as much soy flour, dry milk and other nutrients as it will hold and still retain quality for acceptance. A maximum number of nutrients should be sought always in the small amount of food accepted. Liquid whole milk that can be fortified with dry, non-fat milk solids is an example. (It is recommended that a physician's order for this be obtained, since some states stupidly do not permit the use of dry milk as a beverage without such an order.)

EPILOGUE

The operation of a foodservice in a health facility is always a challenge. There are many interesting facets and functions to capture one's interest. Planning the layout and equipping it is an important task and, after this, getting the department staffed and operating smoothly can be another challenge. There is always a need to improve certain functions and upgrade standards.

A foodservice department is always functioning on a dynamic basis. Things are always on the move. If one enters into the spirit of things, there is little chance for boredom. Meal planning, buying, storing, pre-preparation, production, service and clean-up are a never-ending series of on-going functions to be performed.

Operating a foodservice is not like operating a home kitchen; it is more like operating a factory. Raw materials are processed into finished products for consumption. Workers in foodservice have more of a chance to create than in any other department in a health facility. Most other departments do not manufacture their own items but use those they buy. They have little chance to take raw materials and end up with something they have created that will be of great benefit to those they serve.

Workers employed in an extended health care facility should be aware that they are doing important work in our national health program. It is an area in which there has been tremendous, challenging development. Continued growth and change will occur. This change will require flexibility, adaptability and individual growth. One can gain much satisfaction in working in a situation in which he knows he is important. Much satisfaction can also be gained in knowing the foodservice department is extremely important to the nutritional, social and psychological well-being of the facility's residents. Food, frequently to those people, is as important as the medicines and drugs administered by the medical and nursing staffs. Actually, the foodservice department is an important member of the medical team and should be given such recognition. It is a professional area of the greatest importance.

Additional Bibliography*

Butler, R. N. "The Life Review," B. Neugarten, ed. *Middle Age and Aging.*
    Chicago: University of Chicago Press, 1968.
Moore, H. B. "The Meaning of Food," *American Journal of Nutrition,* Vol.
    V, 1966, pp. 77-82.
Oklahoma State Dept. of Health. *Demonstration of Nutritional, Occupation-
    al, Recreational and Social Service Training Programs in Nursing Homes,*
    Community Health Services Project 38-3. Oklahoma City, Okla.: Okla-
    homa State Dept. of Health, 1965.
Pelcovits, Jeanette, and Holmes, Douglas. *Aging,* U. S. Dept. of Health, Edu-
    cation and Welfare, AOA Publication 143, Washington, D. C.: Govern-
    ment Printing Office, 1970.
Riley, M. W., and Foner, A. "Aging and Society," *An Inventory of Research
    Standards, I.* New York: Russell Sage Foundation, 1968.
Skillman, T. G.; Homivi, G. J.; and May, C. "Nutrition and the Aged," *Geri-
    atrics, XV,* (Spring, 1960), pp. 464-472.
U. S. Dept. of Labor. *Nursing Homes and Related Health Care Facilities,*
    Industry Manpower Surveys, No. 116. Washington, D. C.: Government
    Printing Office, 1969.

---

*In addition, consult references noted in the body of the text in this chapter.

II: MANAGEMENT, SUPERVISION AND PERSONNEL

MANAGEMENT

WHAT IS MANAGEMENT? Management is defined as the achievement of goals through people. However, without the assistance of personnel, management seldom arrives at its objectives. About 10% of the time, management deals with technical problems and the remaining 90%, with personnel.

Management has the overall responsibility for directing an organization of people. It must do this so as to achieve maximum efficiency and economy of operation with minimum effort. Since each individual in an organization has his own goals, management must see that these also are attained at the same time that management's goals are being pursued. With this in mind, an astute management directs the organization so that management goals and those of the workers coincide as much as possible.

Organization

We have used the word "organization" without defining it. A common definition is "a group of individuals working together toward a common goal." Such a group must work within a system where each individual has a well-defined job to do. Jobs are also co-ordinated to achieve maximum results from a minimum of effort. Each individual in an organization should know clearly what his function is in the organization and should have the necessary authority and responsibility to get his job done.

The relationship of positions in an organization is frequently shown by means of a chart. (See Fig. 2-1). This will usually show the following:
1. The positions in the organization
2. The relationship of positions to each other
3. How the positions are integrated and co-ordinated
4. The flow of authority and responsibility
5. Lines of communication.

In large health organizations, this chart will show the overall organization of the facility but each department will also need its own chart showing organization within the department.

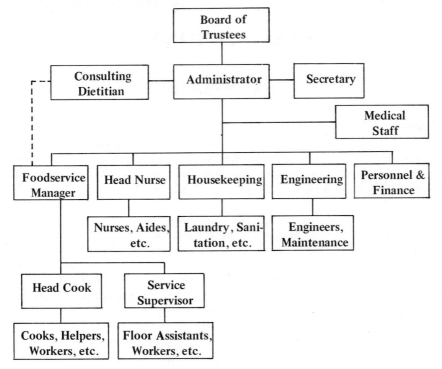

Fig. 2-1.   *An organization chart which might exist for a fairly large extended care facility.   Line authority and responsibility are exerted through the board of trustees and administrator to the heads of departments shown here as foodservice, nursing, housekeeping and engineering—there could be others. Detail is shown only for the supervisors and others in the foodservice department. The head cook is in charge of other cooks, bakers, helpers, etc. In this organization the service supervisor has equal authority with the head cook and is in charge of delivery of trays, the service of food, etc. The consulting dietitian is shown in a staff position responsible to the administrator. The dotted line from consulting dietitian to the foodservice manager indicates co-ordination but no line of authority over this position.   The consulting dietitian must work through the administrator who exerts authority over the foodservice manager. As the chart indicates, the secretary and medical staff exert no line authority.*

Line, Functional and Staff Organizations

An organization chart can show three types of positions: line, functional and staff. In a line organization, authority flows from the top positions down through the workers, each individual being responsible to the person above him. Communication moves up and down the lines of authority. Communication can also go across from one line to another between individuals of equal authority in the organization.

Normally, a top position should have no more than 4 to 5 individuals reporting to it and mid-management and supervisor levels no more than 7 to 15.

Staff positions exert no line authority. They are established to furnish advice to line positions. Thus, a consulting dietitian is in a staff position, responsible to the manager or administrator of the health facility unless otherwise designated. Advice and recommendations are made to the administrator/manager who, in turn, considers them. If he wishes, he will then transfer them as an order down to others in the line organization.

A functional position is one where the position covers a function in the operation. Thus, the function of foodservice may be covered by a foodservice manager or dietitian who has authority over all foodservice workers but also exerts authority over some of the nursing staff because they deliver food to the residents. Normally, small organizations do not use functional positions; line organizations are most suitable for these organizations with staff positions used for certain specialized needs.

Authority and Responsibility

There are four levels of authority and responsibility in an organization. These are (1) top management, (2) mid-management, (3) supervisory and (4) worker. It is said that management plans and directs action; supervisors create action and workers act. While many workers are not expected to exert authority over another individual, since they are at the bottom of the organization line, they do have the responsibility to perform the job assigned to them and also should have the requisite authority to discharge that responsibility. Management must be sure that authority and responsibility in positions are balanced.

In a line organization, authority and responsibility may be delegated to others in the operation. Top management has the responsibility for seeing that jobs are delegated properly and that the necessary authority and responsibility to perform the task are given to the person who must perform it. It is necessary that the person to whom the job is delegated know what is delegated, know how to perform the job and be capable of performing it.

While the person delegating the job must be sure the necessary authority and responsibility are given to do the job, this person himself can never escape final responsibility for the way the job is done. An individual who fails to do a delegated job can be blamed for his failure but the person who has delegated the job also shares in the blame. In a line organization, top management has complete responsibility for all the actions of subordinates. By the same token, in the line organization each person in the line also shares responsibility for the actions of those beneath him.

There are several points at which problems arise in organizations and it may be advisable to re-emphasize these even though they have been covered previously in the discussion on management:

1. *STAFF INDIVIDUALS MUST NOT EXERT LINE AUTHORITY.* Line people know staff individuals do not have the authority to give orders or direct actions and they resent the interference when it occurs.

2. *DELEGATION MUST BE DONE PROPERLY.* Be sure a delegated job can and will be done properly; because a job is delegated does not mean the individual delegating the job escapes responsibility for the way it is done.

3. *THE FLOW OF AUTHORITY MUST BE ALONG LINES OF COMMAND.* One department head cannot give orders to another department head of equal rank; the head of nursing cannot give orders to the head of the foodservice department. The request for an order must be transferred up to an individual having authority over both departments and then passed down by that individual. On occasion, communication and agreement can occur straight across lines between individuals of equal rank but this can only be done by mutual agreement.

4. *NO PERSON, UNLESS IN A FUNCTIONAL POSITION, SHOULD HAVE TWO BOSSES.*

5. *AN INDIVIDUAL IN HIGHER AUTHORITY SHOULD NOT BY-PASS OTHERS BELOW HIM IN GIVING ORDERS.* Thus, an assistant administrator should not by-pass the foodservice manager in giving orders to a cook. If he does, the foodservice manager loses authority and responsibility.

6. *LIKEWISE, AN INDIVIDUAL SHOULD NOT BY-PASS AN IM-MEDIATE SUPERIOR AND GO TO AN INDIVIDUAL OF HIGHER AUTHORITY.* In some cases, it can be done by mutual agreement between the individual and the superior or if the individual wishes to protest some matter of disagreement with the superior, he may go over the superior to higher authority. Avenues for protest to higher authority should *always* be open. No person should ever feel he has no one to whom he can go with a problem other than the person to whom he is immediately responsible.

The Functions of Management

To manage properly, management must perform certain functions. These usually revolve around 1) planning, 2) organizing, 3) directing, 4) co-ordinating, 5) controlling, 6) communicating and 7) decision making. These cover the main management functions. Terms such as "actuating" or "forecasting" may be used to indicate what might seem to be other management functions, however, these are largely the "directing" and "planning" indicated in the above list of functions.

1. *PLANNING.* Management's success will be closely tied to the success of its planning. Planning is said to be thinking through the actions needed to achieve a goal. It requires the use of judgment and discretion in deciding what or which actions will be most effective. Planning establishes a guide for achieving goals. Planning for major management problems should not be delegated. Planning together among those who will be responsible for the work done is recommended, however. Managers, supervisors and even workers should help to plan work they must do.

There are two types of plans: immediate and long-range. Immediate plans must be made to assure that a condition, situation or problem is acted upon at once or soon. Routine short-range planning such as menu planning or purchasing is oftentimes done periodically and frequently top management or even mid-management is not concerned with it. Long-range planning should provide guidance for a long period; such plans are usually concerned with the achievement of the objectives of the organization. Long-range planners must perform the function of forecasting and preparing for eventualities. Alternative plans should also be considered so that, if conditions arise in which the original plan cannot be followed, another avenue to the goal is possible.

To develop a plan, first consider the goals or the need. Understand the essential factors required to complete the plan and the sequence in which these will occur. Know what resources are available to carry out the plan.

Then, formulate the plan, being sure to have all the facts needed to establish each step.

Consult others affected by the plan and get their ideas. Written plans are more easily understood and inadequacies will become more evident. Be sure those who will be responsible for putting the plan into effect understand it, know the sequence of steps and are capable of doing the job. Finally, follow up on the progress of plans after they are put into action.

2. *ORGANIZING.* Work in a health facility or a foodservice department must be systematized and organized so it is done efficiently and with the least effort and cost. Individuals should be assigned tasks which they are capable of doing and understand how to do. A sign of poor organization may be:

  a. Strain in personnel relationships
  b. Responsibility without authority
  c. Individual action without team work
  d. Failures in communication and misunderstandings
  e. Inefficient use of resources
  f. Poor planning and decision making
  g. Lack of control by management.

3. *DIRECTING.* Management direction is a difficult task but it is essential if an operation is to be led to its goals. A lack of direction leads to poor performance, poor morale and chaotic, frustrating working conditions. Direction must come from a strong leader who can direct in a fair, kindly manner but who knows where he is going and where others should be going.

Commands or orders by a stern, forceful, aggressive individual may offend and result in failure to achieve objectives. A soft approach or an attempt to win may do the same. A firm, strong approach coupled with fairness usually works. Workers do better under such individuals. They sense the sureness of direction and are encouraged to follow.

Individuals should not be directed by orders or commands, except in unusual circumstances; commands should be used only to secure quick compliance or to enforce required authority. A request is a much more desirable directive because it assumes a willingness to comply and makes the employee feel more important. Another way of giving direction is by suggestion which may imply an order. This is frequently used when an employee knows what to do. It may, however, be misunderstood or disregarded.

Directions should be clear and understood. Oral directions are common and cover routine matters. They usually are general instructions on a subject and tell an individual what to do and how to do it.

Written orders should be established to cover policy, work standards, safety measures, plans or similar matters. These may be rules, regulations, policies, instructions or operating procedures given for guidance. They are usually quite specific. Or, they may be written directives with the purpose of communicating, to a specific person or group, information on a specific subject. They usually set forth the actions required.

4. *CO-ORDINATING.* The co-ordination function in management is the process of seeing that events occur at the proper time to insure smooth operation, harmonious relationships and efficient performance. Good co-ordination depends on good planning and organization. It also requires good control so events move in their proper sequence. The major tool of co-ordination is a schedule plan. Materials, workers and equipment must be brought together at the right time. The plan must be coupled with co-operation, action and accomplishment.

Co-ordination must occur not only within a department but also between departments. The foodservice department frequently can co-operate with medical services so as to co-ordinate food service and medical services, thus achieving maximum results in health care.

5. *CONTROL.* Control is not solely the authority to enforce or restrict action. It is also the ability to control resources so main goals are achieved. It means that needs are recognized and adequate provision is made to satisfy them.

Good control is achieved when waste is minimized and resources are still adequately allocated to provide for needs. Good control requires that standards be established so performance can be evaluated. Standards that provide a measure of quality, quantity or nutritional adequacy for food are needed in foodservices. Other standards that relate to work procedures, timing and the organization of work are also required. Proper supervision is a necessary adjunct to good control.

It is possible to over-control. Employees must not feel that they are completely controlled in everything they do; actually they should feel they are more guided than controlled. Over-control can result in a loss of efficiency and can bring about confusion, duplication, unnecessary work and poor quality products.

Good production control assures that work processes are properly maintained at an efficient level. It should eliminate inefficiency, waste and other losses. Work reports, accomplishment records and a work simplification program can assist in improving production control. Workers should be motivated to achieve standards of quality and quantity. Unless standards are established and quality and quantity checks made throughout the production process, good production control cannot be achieved.

6. *COMMUNICATING.* To bring about a mutual understanding and appreciation between management and employees on the goals of the organization and how to achieve them, communication is necessary. Communication involves sending out, receiving and understanding signals representing ideas. The same idea as the one the sender had in mind should occur to the receiver when he receives the signal. It takes skill to do this. Words do not mean the same thing to everyone and other communication signals may also get different responses from different individuals. The spoken word and the written word are the most important ways of communicating.

One of the best ways to achieve good communication is through good listening. Listening is active work; it cannot be a passive, automatic response. A good manager gives his full attention to the person talking, concentrating on what he hears. He knows he can think two or three times faster than the person he is listening to can talk, but the good listener keeps his mind focused on what is being said. He may use the extra time, as he waits for speech to catch up with his thoughts, for evaluating or being sure he is understanding what he hears. He becomes involved; if he does not understand, he asks questions.

Listening should be done objectively and not with prejudice, moodiness or attitudes that change the meaning of what is being said. Employees stop talking to a boss that can't listen. Soon such an individual may find himself isolated from his employees because they've given up trying to tell him anything.

It also takes preparation to be effective when telling something to another person. Use plain, simple words; speak slowly and use voice inflections and gestures that lend emphasis and clarity to what is being said. Do not use generalities when you can be specific. Do not talk down to listeners nor show anger or dislike. Make sure the listener has understood. Do not try to be adamant in situations where there may be a difference of opinion. Choose words carefully. Although the speaker may not be aware of it, some words can sound inflammatory or bluntly contradictory even though the speaker may not have this intent.

Communication requires that one keep informed and take time to read and study written materials relating to organizational matters. Reading, like talking, should be done with full attention. Training can improve reading speed, comprehension and understanding.

The ability to write effectively is another talent that does not just come with birth. It is learned by hard application and study. The most common faults in writing are a lack of clarity and a failure to write at a level required for best understanding.

The art of interviewing is an important part of communicating. A good interview is a two-way exchange of information. Before starting an interview, set up a plan for it; establish what the objectives are, what the interviewee is to be told and how the interview will be conducted. A part of the interview may be having the interviewee answer questions on a form. This is usually done before the verbal part of the interview.

Interviewing is much like teaching. The person interviewed must be put at ease. The person interviewing should be well informed, know where he is going and quickly build a good rapport between himself and the interviewee. While some notes may be written during the interview, too much note writing may not promote a good interview. Compile the information needed after the interview.

7. *DECISION MAKING.* The decisions made by management reflect managerial ability. Decision making and planning are perhaps the two most important functions performed by management.

A decision is an attempt to set forth a plan that will solve a problem. Good decisions are seldom made on the spur of the moment although decisions too often are made in just that way. Decision making should come after obtaining the facts and then weighing them. It is not always a one-man process; others may assist in it. If others help to make a decision, they are more apt to agree with it and act more effectively when they are asked to carry it out.

Decision making should be based on the scientific method, which is:

1. State the problem clearly
2. Get the facts
3. Analyze them
4. Develop possible solutions
5. Select a solution; hold others as possible alternatives
6. Apply a solution
7. Verify the correctness by observation.

Decision making improves with practice. Eventually making the better decision becomes almost automatic. It is not always possible to make the *best* decision but if decision making is done properly, the one selected will be far better than one resulting from an improper approach. Success in decision making depends upon the application of the decision and the follow up or verification of it.

Some individuals are afraid to make decisions, fearing criticism or trouble. Others are afraid they may make a mistake. It is said, "The turtle never makes headway until he sticks his neck out" and this is also true of the decision maker.

Span of Control

The number of people a manager or supervisor can manage or have report to him is limited. Top management should not have more than 4 or 5 individuals reporting to it and the supervisor's limit is from 7 to 15.

The span of control one person can exercise over others will depend upon conditions; this must be watched carefully in setting up an organization. If one has too few people to exercise authority over, he may have too little to do and he may then interfere with others in doing their work. The job also will have few challenges and he may leave it. Too many people to supervise may lead to inadequate supervision, poor performance, overwork, frustration, inefficiency and job dissatisfaction.

The number in one's span of control must be guided by the complexity of the assignment and the difficulty of controlling individuals and conditions. Span of control may be increased by good delegation of authority. A good operation with maximum performance results when management studies the specific situations within the organization and assigns positions and responsibilities on this basis. This is not done without facts, consultation and then good assignment. The span of control exercised by individuals should be frequently reviewed because, as conditions change, the span of control may also have to change.

Policies and Procedures

To properly guide a health facility, procedures and policies should be succinctly stated so all will know how the operation is to run. These procedures and policies can be stated in a manual. Accreditation authorities, recognizing the importance of a good set of policies and procedures, will use a manual stating these as one guide in evaluating a facility for accreditation. But, even if this were not done, every health facility should have a manual to guide it in controlling the organization and directing it toward its goals.

Policy and procedure manuals help prevent misunderstandings and indicate how the facility should function. The *why* and *what* should be included. These manuals promote teamwork, consistency and give a continuity of administration and performance. Job orientation is quicker if employees read and understand the manual. The manual can act as a guide in establishing standards and measures for evaluating performance. It can save time and make it possible to keep the facility up-to-date. Quick communication of vital information is possible through it.

Two types of manuals are needed: one stating general policies and procedures for the entire facility and another for each department covering policies and procedures affecting the department.

The facility's overall manual should cover goals, general policy, administrative directives, inter-departmental policies and procedures plus matters that relate to all employees, indicating authorizations, budgetary and fiscal controls, capital expenditures, payroll allocations, etc.

A policy is a plan or directive for action telling *what* to do, while a procedure is a summary of the steps necessary to achieve the action, indicating *how* to do it. A policy is an overall rule, not a routine, casual regulation. The facility's manual usually stresses policy while the departmental manual stresses procedures.

The departmental manual complements the general manual; it should not repeat or duplicate the material in the general manual but should be consistent with it and differ from it only when some specific procedure or policy must be changed for departmental operation. The manuals should be consistent with rules of the government or other regulatory bodies. They should be widely distributed and understood by employees.

A manual is usually divided into two parts. The first part covers introductory material while the second discusses specific policies and procedures. The introductory material will frequently contain the philosophy of the facility or department, the principles or accepted truths which act as guidelines for departmental or facility operation and perhaps a creed which may include major standards and the mission. These serve as a broad framework into which policies and procedures are later woven in the second part. The manual should be well organized into subject areas and logically developed so the information is easily located. Policies and procedures may be mixed together or separated into various subject areas.

Top management should be consulted during formulation of a department manual although departmental authorities may set it up and do the writing. Whoever does the manual should know the department and the facility thoroughly. Assistance from top management, the consulting dietitian and others can be given. It is often advisable in large departments to form a committee to work on the manual. Frequent consultation is required with other department heads so co-ordination of activities is achieved. For instance, before meal hours are established, nursing should be consulted.

Ideas for the manual can come from various sources. Top management may suggest some. A number of rules, regulations or administrative actions exist although they may not be in writing. Assemble these, write them up and then later classify them for inclusion. Ideas may also come from manuals of other facilities or departments. Check the files as well for notices, memorandums and other information from administrative sources. If the department manual repeats material from the general manual, rephrase it to suit the department's needs.

Use one style of presentation, separating main headings into subject areas with sub-heads below covering material belonging to this main subject area. The number of main areas and sub-headings will depend upon the size of the department and the scope of operation. If the department is a large one, the major headings may be 1) department organization, 2) personnel, 3) public relations, 4) resident nutrition and diets, 5) foodservice, 6) food production and 7) controls and accountability. Sub-headings might be as follows under 4) resident nutrition and diets: "Policy 1: General diet management,

Policy 2: Implementing and cancelling diet orders, etc." If necessary, sub-headings may be introduced under sub-headings. Date all policies.

There should be one policy per page, set up with good spacing and short paragraphs. Use a concise style. Make statements in short sentences or even in incomplete sentences. Understanding is increased when graphs, charts, examples, forms or form numbers are used. Use action verbs. Have a table of contents and a good index. The manual should be prepared first in rough draft for discussion with a committee, fellow workers, department heads or management. It can then be typed in somewhat final form and once more critiqued.

Usually the departmental manual is a loose leaf binder containing 8½ by 11 in. sheets of a good grade of bond paper, 20 lb. weight, with reinforced edges. The manual should be typed. It is preferable to duplicate a large number so each employee can have one. The minimum made should be three, one to be kept in the department office, one on the department bulletin board and another with management. Keep a record of those having manuals.

No manual is ever finished. It is a viable thing, changing constantly. Review, critique and revise it frequently. The individual responsible for this is usually the department head. Before changing items, discuss changes with top management. Test and, if they work, incorporate them into the manual. Sample randomly and often to see if the manual is achieving the desired results and to see if there are weak areas requiring change or revision.*

STAFFING

MANAGEMENT OF THE FOODSERVICE DEPARTMENT A small health facility's foodservice may be managed by a cook, owner or administrator. In larger units, a part-time manager or dietitian** may do

---

*The material discussing policy and procedure manuals comes largely from three articles in *HOSPITALS,* the Journal of the American Hospital Association. These are "Developing Policy and Procedure Manuals," by Ben Carlisle, Parts 1 and 2, Vol. 43, April, 1969 and May, 1969 and "Writing a Policy and Procedure Manual for the Dietary Department," by Kay Boles, Vol. 42, Nov., 1968.

**"Dietitian" as used in this book means a dietitian registered under the American Dietetic Association.

this or a foodservice supervisor may manage. In very large facilities, a full time manager or dietitian will be used.

Federal standards require that an individual of professional competence be responsible for or be consulted on the operation of the foodservice. This can be a dietitian or an individual having a baccalaureate degree either in nutrition or in institution, hotel or restaurant management providing nutrition is taught in the curriculum. Small health facilities may satisfy this federal requirement for professional management by retaining a part-time or consulting professional person, usually a dietitian.

The Consulting Dietitian

The position of a consulting dietitian differs from that of a part-time manager. The consulting dietitian is in a staff position while the manager is in a line position. The consulting dietitian is retained by management and reports to it. She has no line authority and issues no orders. She gives her recommendations to top management. If management then wishes, the recommendations are transferred as orders to the foodservice department. A line individual in the foodservice department then implements these orders. The consulting dietitian must maintain very close relationships with the foodservice and other departments because the acceptance of her recommendations will be largely conditioned by such a relationship.

The consulting dietitian is used to assure that diet orders and other dietary matters are properly controlled and that the foodservice department functions adequately. She may also plan menus, prepare diet manuals, select or prepare recipes, participate in training programs, recommend procedures and policies, establish staffing requirements or procedures for accounting or financial control and set up adequate plans for serving, purchasing or preparing food. In addition to working with the facility administrator and foodservice staff, the consulting dietitian may have to maintain close contact with the medical and nursing staffs, other departments of the facility and even some of the residents or their families.

The consulting dietitian should spend at least 8 hours a month at the facility; double this amount of time is recommended. She may visit a facility only once a month—more frequently if conditions demand it. Because she is not at the facility much of the time, she should make it possible for responsible individuals to reach her to consult on foodservice matters. An answering service is recommended. It is also necessary that she be thorough in her visits and go over all matters requiring her attention, handling them in a satisfactory manner. She should leave very definite plans and procedures for the time she is away so things function properly during her absence. This takes good organizational ability.

The administrator of the facility may have had little previous experience in working with a dietitian and may not know what services she can render. The consulting dietitian has the responsibility of educating the administrator on what her services can do for the facility. A consulting dietitian will usually be only as good as the administrator lets her be. One of her most important jobs is to win strong support from the administrator for the dietary department and its program. This may take time and perseverance. Food is usually more important in a small health facility than in a hospital and this must be realized by the administrator. The consulting dietitian can be more effectively utilized by the administrator if:

1. He sees that the consulting dietitian becomes well acquainted with the facility, its philosophy of care, financial limitations and other factors which increase understanding of operational problems.

2. They confer on all important matters, agreeing on a course of action and presenting a common front.

3. He considers her a highly important professional staff member and utilizes her to the fullest degree.

4. He uses her to work with nursing in establishing feeding routines and to build respect for the foodservice department and its goals, encouraging cooperation and giving status to the department.

5. He evaluates his foodservice in terms of how much nutrition and health care he is buying for his dollars. (A properly nourished resident has fewer care problems, is more sociable and is a better advertisement for the facility.)

6. He strongly supports a training program in the foodservice department and sees that in-service programs continue at times other than when the dietitian is there.

7. He appreciates the role of nutrition and gives strong encouragement to the residents to eat properly and to learn to eat new foods.

8. He encourages special attention to the residents' needs but he should discourage catering to whims and avoid turning the kitchen into a short order cafe.

9. He encourages a balance of staffing so all shifts in the foodservice department are staffed with some skilled and experienced personnel.

10. He allocates sufficient resources to operate the department.

The consulting dietitian is a distinct type of dietitian just as the therapeutic and the administrative dietitian are. The consulting dietitian has recently come into the health care field. Her talents must cover a wide range: she must be strong in administration, business and personnel and equally strong in nutrition. She must have excellent organizational ability and be able to work well with people. There is a need for special educational programs which prepare the dietitian for consulting work. Undoubtedly, these will come in the future.

In retaining a consulting dietitian, the facility should make a distinction between the professional dietitian and one who takes one or two facilities and treats the job as a casual part-time one. The consulting dietitian should have a minimum of five years of strong administrative experience. She should fit the facility's needs and not require the facility to fit into hers. She should be strong in teaching and training.

Information about clients should be treated confidentially just as it is in the medical and legal professions. She must have a high standard of ethics. Costs and financing of an extended-care facility should be understood and she should adjust her professional thinking to a long-term care situation rather than that of an intensive-care facility where she may have received part of her experience.

She should appeal to people quickly and win their respect and confidence. The cultivation of professional contacts with the nursing and medical staffs is required to build in them a confidence in her and her program so the foodservice can provide the care it should.

"Socializing" with clients or employees of a facility should be avoided. The consulting dietitian is better off if she can establish her social life away from her consultancy. Gifts should not be given or received. A small contribution, however, to a "gift pot" to purchase flowers or other items, or the giving of a gift on a special occasion to the foodservice manager or others with whom she works closely, may be authorized.

The consulting dietitian should realize that she belongs to the foodservice department and that its employees are apt to be slightly unwilling to share her with others. Many times, it is the consulting dietitian who gives these employees their first impression of what a registered dietitian is and who gives them their first professional recognition in the facility. She is theirs and they will often jealously claim her.

Good health and stamina are required. Besides hard work done under pressure, there are long drives and long hours. There is little time to relax and take it easy. As soon as one visit is over, she must be off to another facility and handle its problems. It is wise to carry a list of doctors and dentists available in places she travels to—even a list of hairdressers may be useful.

The consulting dietitian is a motivator and must be a master at feeding proper doses of ego-building remarks and compliments to those whom she must motivate. She must be able to spot, build and motivate leaders. Patience and foresight are required. Sometimes, she may "twiddle her thumbs" on a problem for a long time but she must be ready when the proper opportunity comes to do something about it. She must never build barriers for herself or anyone else. Paths must always be left open.

She must not take disappointments personally but instead react to them as a professional. If she fails in one goal, she must go on to the next. One experienced consulting dietitian who has been extremely successful has said, "A consulting dietitian has to have the self-confidence of a politician; the tact, diplomacy and patience (and firmness at times) of a mediator at the Paris peace talks; the imagination and creativeness of an Escoffier, tempered with the modest ability to cook good ham-hocks and beans; the endurance of the turtle (and shell sometimes) and the lasting quality of a camel."

It is essential that a consulting dietitian keep up in her profession. New rules and regulations in the health care field are also constantly appearing; as changes occur, they should be known. It is important that the facilities she serves keep above standards. Plans should be made in advance to meet new standards. It is easier to meet stricter standards if standards have been raised slowly ahead of the required time of implementation. Those health facilities that had already started to raise standards were able to implement the standards imposed by Medicare and Title XIX very easily.

The consulting dietitian should know something about pharmacology so she can work better with nursing and medical services. Much can be done to co-ordinate the foodservice program into their programs. For instance, it is not unusual for facilities to administer mecurial diuretics on a given day. On this day it is wise to place orange juice or other juices, broth soups and other liquids on the menu. Some foods and medications do not go well together and planning by the dietitian should avoid their combination.

The contract salary should be sufficient to cover all fees and charges. Remuneration may be 1½ times that paid a professional dietitian working in a regular position. This is because the consulting dietitian maintains herself and her car. She draws no Social Security, no vacation pay, no sickness or health benefits, no workmen's compensation and even pays her own way to meetings and conventions.

The position is also very demanding, requiring a high degree of professional talent as well as business acumen. She must invest in books, films, professional societies, etc. It is desirable that she design and invest in her own printed forms. She should carry adequate life, accident and income insurance.

Most consulting dietitians charge a flat fee sufficient to take care of telephone calls, film rentals, per diem, mileage and other expenses. She should not allow a health facility to use her only to assist it in becoming accredited or in obtaining public funds, but rather she should be a functioning staff member making a contribution to the health care of the residents. If this is not the case, she should resign. The contract should be made for a year with a 30-day escape clause for both parties.

If, after the first six months, she does not feel the climate is conducive to a desirable level of operation, she should give notice of contract cancellation, indicating the reasons why. It is also possible for a consulting dietitian to reach a stalemate after two or three years of work with the facility. If this happens, she should evaluate the situation and possibly pick a successor. If both parties know the contract rests squarely on the satisfactory performance of both, communication is improved and performance is apt to be better. Some consulting dietitians require the contract to specify that at least one employee of the foodservice department, and preferably two, be enrolled in the foodservice supervisor's course.

Not all consulting dietitians can design the same type of program or give the same type of service. Each must be changed to suit special needs of the facility, give the best solutions to problems and render the type of professional assistance required. There are few common patterns. However, enough information and experience has been gained by consulting dietitians by this time to give some guidelines.

The consulting dietitian should not do the purchasing but she should establish the procedures, standards and other criteria needed to do this. She may advise on specifications and even recommend the quality or brand of an item to use. She should be consulted on equipment, even small items such as paring knives.

Some consulting dietitians are bothered by the fact that the owner of a facility takes food home from the facility but, taxwise, the owner is allowed to have his own and his family's meals. It is, therefore, recommended that an account be set up for this and the cost of these foods be charged to this account. Or, a flat fee per month can be established and this deducted from the cost of food for the facility.

Many standards may not be adequate in the facility when the consulting dietitian is retained. It is extremely important that a program be established for improving these. She should not impose her standards on the facility but study the facility and establish the standard needed. It is wise not to set standards too high at first and even though the standard set may be under that desired, it could be an important goal to achieve that standard before establishing a higher one. There is danger that as the consulting dietitian wins confidence and respect her standards may be automatically adopted. This may not be the best solution for the facility and she should watch to see that this does not happen.

It is best for the consulting dietitian not to get involved in employee selection. She is there for only a short time while others must work with the employee for much longer periods and, therefore, others should be more influential in deciding with whom they work. She may at times advise on a selection. Many consulting dietitians recommend that workers employed in the facility indicate before employment a willingness to take in-service training or even outside course work.

Many long-term care facilities have limited financial and other resources and the consulting dietitian should know this. She should be completely conversant with the problems of financing and the need for making a profit. She should, however, strongly oppose shorting the residents on food or food standards to increase profit and should resign if she cannot convince management of the folly of such a policy. The consulting dietitian should recognize that the administrator has to keep a large number of individuals satisfied and at the same time meet costs. He may be torn between feeding adequately and feeding poorly, using the savings to defray other expenses. The consulting dietitian should attempt to dissuade him from lowering standards.

In a health facility, the dietitian is the authority on nutritional health care, just as the head nurse is on nursing care, the engineer on mechanical maintenance and the head pharmacologist on drug formulation. The food-service supervisor or cook-manager who heads up the kitchen staff is the head of the dietary department in the small facility. This employee needs to be given adequate training and status to function with other department heads.

The consulting dietitian should not arrive too early at the facility on visits because everyone may be busy and she can accomplish little. If her visit can be timed when most foodservice workers are on duty, this is advisable. It is difficult to plan too far in advance for visits but tentative dates can be made ahead. Usually it is possible to make firm dates about a month in advance. The facility should be advised of these dates.

Arriving early may be advisable if the dietitian wishes to observe some early morning practices or meet someone not on shift at later hours. On the day of the visit, the head of the foodservice department should be free to confer with the consulting dietitian as soon as she arrives. They should briefly go over all matters of importance that have occurred since the last visit to bring the dietitian up to date on all developments. It is advisable for the manager to keep a diary for quick recall of items.

After this briefing, the dietitian should visit the administrator and discuss problems with him and gain his views. Next, the head nurse may be contacted to discuss any matters needing common review. A return can then be made to the foodservices to discuss developments in more depth. Students may be allowed to participate in some of these sessions for preceptoring. It may be wise to lunch with the foodservice staff; this will make the visit a little less formal and also give more time to go over the situations that need discussion.

Right after lunch, most foodservice workers will have work that must be done so the dietitian should make other visits. All residents cannot be visited but pressing cases or those needing special attention may require a call at this time. New residents may also be contacted to ascertain problems.

A good preventive maintenance program for equipment and facilities should be set up for the foodservice department and the consulting dietitian may profitably spend this time checking with the engineer or individual charged with responsibility for this program.

Later, when more of the foodservice staff are less busy, an in-service training program may be given by the dietitian. When that is concluded she should then complete her consultation with the foodservice manager and take up any matters with individual workers—these workers should be encouraged to keep a record of problems or questions they might have. The dietitian should get all problems solved at this time as well as set up the program to be followed until her next visit.

With this accomplished, she should then complete her report and have it typed, giving a copy to the foodservice manager and the administrator. (One experienced dietitian has said, "Reports must be compiled carefully to be significant to the facility yet they should not be revelations that tell inspectors where to look for skeletons.")

The report should be discussed with the manager and administrator. A memorandum should be kept of these discussions indicating what was discussed, agreements, etc. (Figure 2-2 shows one form used by one consulting dietitian for such a report.) The consulting dietitian should also make a note of items requiring follow-up on her part, making sure this includes any programs or tasks assigned to individual employees. It is entirely possible for such a visit to take 8 hours or more. She should not be a clock watcher.

The Foodservice Manager

The foodservice manager usually reports to the administrator or his assistant but there are also other forms of line organization. The manager of the foodservice department may be called the foodservice supervisor or even cook-manager. Normally, this position has responsibility for:

1. Budgeting, maintaining the budget and keeping adequate food and other controls.
2. Maintaining proper records for meal counts, employee time, other costs or records.
3. Directing and scheduling foodservice personnel.
4. Purchasing equipment, supplies and food; receiving food and supplies.
5. Planning menus.
6. Supervising food production.
7. Maintaining liaison with the administrator and other departments.
8. Establishing standards for safety, sanitation, food quality, etc.
9. Maintaining proper personnel records.

DATE_____

FACILITY_____

REPORT OF DIETARY CONSULTANT

TIME:

NEXT VISIT:

REVIEW OF FOODSERVICE/PREPARATION:

Conference with Foodservice Supervisor:
    Yes   No

Recommendations and Discussion:

Purchasing Review:

Sanitation:

Personnel Review:

THERAPEUTIC ASPECTS OF FOODSERVICE:

Menu Review   Yes   No

Recommendations:

Specific Action on Nutritional Problems:

CONFERENCE WITH PHYSICIANS:
    Yes   No

IN-SERVICE TRAINING:

Time: See In-Service Sheet (attached)

PRECEPTORSHIP:

Recommendations:

POLICIES AND PROCEDURES ACTION:

CONFERENCE WITH DIRECTOR OF NURSING:

     Yes   No

CONFERENCE WITH ADMINISTRATOR:

     Yes   No

NEXT TRIP:

Consultant Dietitian

Attach additional specific items to this sheet.

Fig. 2-2. *A form used by one consulting dietitian for a visit report. Courtesy Mrs. Iris Lochner, R. D., Food Systems Design, Oklahoma City, Okla.*

10. Planning.

11. Training.

12. Maintaining a standardized set of recipes.

13. Making floor visits and maintaining liaison with the residents.

14. Seeing that a proper maintenance program is established and operated.

15. Dietary management as instructed by the consulting dietitian or other competent authority.

16. Establishing policies and procedures for departmental operation.

17. Forecasting needs.

18. Compiling reports required for the foodservice department.

19. Performing other management functions as required.

The kind of responsibility assigned to the foodservice manager varies with the facility. In some cases, records and other clerical work may be done by a clerk, secretary or by the accounting department. If purchasing is done through a central purchasing office or by the administration, only the definition of quantities and quality needed for production will be required from the manager. If the nursing staff, instead of the foodservice, serves the food to residents, the responsibility for overseeing this is not the manager's. If there is an accounting department that maintains personnel and financial records, this work too will be minimized. It could be the consulting dietitian who plans the menus, establishes purchasing requirements and sets up diets, relieving the manager of this work. It is important that the manager have time for whatever paper work is required.

In larger organizations, the manager of foodservice will have assistance in some of these matters. A food production supervisor may be responsible for the production of food, scheduling employees, food withdrawals, some ordering and other delegated tasks. She may also be manager in the manager's absence.

In addition, the larger organization may have a service supervisor responsible for: setting up resident's trays; dishwashing; maintenance of foodservice and dining areas, and the serving of food. Diet records and the supervision of diets may also be the responsibility of this individual. Since she maintains contact with the residents, she may also make visits to them to check on diets, how well they eat, etc. She will probably have equal status to the food production supervisor and both of them will report to the foodservice manager.

Head Cook

The head cook is responsible for organizing food production and for cooking some of the food, usually the most important dishes. She sees that foods are prepared in a manner which preserves nutrients and produces a high quality product. The maintenance of safety and sanitation standards may be her responsibility. Some other functions assigned to the head cook may be: seeing that equipment in the cooking area is used and maintained properly; directing others in the food production area; setting up requirements for menu items and even ordering some foods; supervising the portioning and service of food; acting as manager when the cook-manager is not there. She may have some record-keeping responsibilities and have to do some training.

Assistant Cook

The assistant cook is concerned with the cooking of food and its pre-preparation. She can act for the head cook in her absence. The assistant cook's work may be divided between one or more assistants, each assuming responsibility for specific menu items. Some may specialize in cooking only items such as meats, vegetables, etc.

An assistant cook may be in charge of a special production section such as the bakeshop, pantry, etc. She will use standardized recipes and be responsible for the quality and quantity of food prepared. Some modified diet items may be prepared by her. The work area and equipment must be properly maintained. She may direct helpers. Good sanitation, safety and food handling procedures are her responsibility.

Other Foodservice Workers

The kitchen may use cook's or other helpers. If the tasks are those of the head or assistant cook, the work will be done in their section. Helpers may also prepare vegetables, salads, wash pots and pans, wash dishes and do other assigned cleaning or other tasks. They usually work under the direction of the head cook or her assistants. Some foodservice workers may work in the foodservice sections or dining areas. Here they may dish food, clean or do other tasks. Janitorial and sanitation tasks will usually be done by janitors or porters but, if not by them, these workers may do them.

Larger facilities may have clerical workers in the department. Their work may be assigned by the manager and the work done in the foodservice office. Typing of menus, keeping records, files or schedules, typing letters or reports, requisitions or orders or doing other general clerical duties might be among their assigned tasks. However, when the worker is in another office, this individual may not be responsible to the foodservice manager.

SUPERVISION

The foodservice manager in a small facility may partly manage and partly supervise. In the line organization, a supervisor stands between management and the worker and may participate in some of management's functions but at a different level of responsibility.

Supervisors must plan, organize, co-ordinate, direct, communicate, control and make decisions. Careful planning, good organization, clear directions and proper controls must be practiced just as they are in management but at the supervisory level.

A supervisor must be able to promote harmony and team work. He must be creative, a good teacher and work well with people. A consistent attitude of fairness, friendliness and firmness is required. Since supervisors work closely with those they supervise, a good example is required. Enthusiasm and optimism are needed. Planning ahead is required so work proceeds on schedule. A good supervisor works to make working conditions as favorable as possible. He will commend good work and take prompt action to correct problems and misunderstandings.

PERSONNEL

The worker is an extremely important person in the organization and today we do everything possible to develop his potential to the maximum.

Manpower

A health facility has many assets: cash, inventory, furniture and furnishings, drugs, etc. It may even count good will as an asset and list it with a value. Few, however, look upon manpower as an asset or list it as such. Yet, it is one of the most valued assets of the facility. Without it, the facility could not operate. Further, what we have in manpower largely controls what we can do. Our human resources depend largely upon what kind of workers are available on the labor market plus what we can do to improve them after they join the organization. Properly handled, manpower can grow in value and yield a large return for the investment we make in it. Or, it can decline in value and create operational problems and higher costs.

Building strong assets in manpower begins with employee selection. It is often true that a facility's own employees are its best recruiters. While some nepotism can be allowed, the build-up of too many employees from one family group is not advised.

Advertisements and employment agencies may help to find good workers. Before filling a position, advancement from among the facility's present workers should be considered. Sometimes part-time workers from high schools or schools of higher learning or homemakers may be a solution to a recruitment problem.

Either a physically or mentally handicapped individual can be employed and much success has been achieved with such individuals by many foodservice departments. Mentally handicapped individuals with an IQ rating as low as 60 have been satisfactorily used. Frequently, the physical dexterity of these individuals is high.

A mentally handicapped worker should be put on a job that is simple and highly repetitive. These workers do not do well on jobs that change frequently in work patterns. Once trained, however, they become very loyal and dependable employees.

The personnel file of the facility is its manpower inventory. This should contain:

1. Personnel data such as name, age, address, pay rate, date of hiring, training given, education, etc.

2. Performance or evaluation ratings taken periodically

3. Potential for development, indicating promotability, career goals, training needs, future contributions, etc.

Few files contain information on the potential worth of the employee but more should. Every facility should give time and attention to planning for manpower needs, both for quantity and for quality. Someone should know who is training for other positions and plans should be made for replacements, especially in key positions, long before the need arises.

Personnel files should be studied to indicate problems relating to specific personnel. For instance, why is an individual with high potential being kept so long on the same job? Why was an individual passed over in a promotion? An employee may presently lack certain potential skills but plans should be made to develop them if this is considered feasible. In addition, employees may lack certain attributes needed in their current jobs yet they may have other qualifications which make them of value in other positions or make it worthwhile to develop capabilities they are now lacking. Many times it is wise to ask, "Can an employee who has lost potential be salvaged?" The personnel file should contain this information.

Job Specifications

Every position in a facility should have a job specification. This is a summary of the type of individual required to fill a certain position and indicates the sex, education, skill, experience, age, etc. required for it. Job specifications should be kept in a bound notebook or a file, one specification to a sheet or card. The specification should list all factors needed to fill the position and is usually based on the job description. The job specification should include information about the advantages and disadvantages of the job. During the employee interview, factors covered by the specification should be discussed with the employee. The job specification should be used as a measure to determine whether the prospective employee fits the job.

Orienting the Employee

A new employee has much to learn, not only about his job but about his fellow workers, his supervisors, managers and the facility. Helping to introduce the employee to these factors will do much to bring him to full performance and increase his job satisfaction, thereby reducing employee turnover.

Employees should be selected after they have completed an application for employment and have had a personal interview. In larger operations, an employment or personnel officer may conduct the original negotiations but it is also advisable to have the manager of the foodservice make the final decision. The following information should be given an employee, either in written form, or while discussing the job with the employee:

a. Wage or salary
   1. Pay rate   3. Deductions; fill out W-2 form
   2. Time of first check   4. Overtime regulations
b. Working hours and days off
c. Leave
   1. Sick   3. Accrual
   2. Annual

   d. Fringe benefits
      1. Insurance   5. Health, safety, incentives or
      2. Retirement   other programs
      3. Educational development   6. Legal assistance
      4. Employee activities   7. Meals or the use of foodservice
                                        facilities
   e. Duties and responsibilities of the position from the job description
      (The employee should get a copy of the job description.)
   f. The facility's mission and goals
   g. Promotion
      1. Chances for wage or salary   3. Employee evaluating and rating
         increases
      2. Advancement
   h. Health and physical requirements
      1. Health card to work in foodservice
      2. Other requirements
   i. Introduction to other workers, supervisors and the facility with a
      tour of the entire facility.

It is recommended that a check list be prepared to use in acquainting
the employee with his work, fellow workers, supervisors and the facility.
Orientation is seldom completed in an hour, a day or a week. The employee
should get settled in his job before too much is thrown at him. Giving information in small bits gives a better chance for retention.

Job Descriptions

   Perhaps one of the most valuable tools for co-ordinating management
and worker performance is the job description. This describes what is done
and usually does so in considerable detail. To prepare a job description, a job
analysis is made. This is usually a rough statement by the employee outlining
what he does on the job; it may even be written by the employee. Management and supervisors go over the analysis and put it into the desired form,
wording it to fit their pattern. When the analysis is acceptable to them, they
go over it with the employee to be sure it is correct.

   Every position should have a job description. It indicates to the employee what his job is and how it is done. Management and supervisors will
find job descriptions useful tools in studying positions, consolidating work

assignments, scheduling, etc. To management, the job description serves as a means of communication that gives them an understanding of the work to be covered.

Each employee should be given a copy of his job description when he is introduced to his job. A file of job descriptions should be kept in the department manager's office and in the facility's main office as well. Copies may also be kept in the personnel office. They should be reviewed frequently and revised to suit changes. A job description should contain: the purpose of the job; the job described; the specific functions of the job; the work load and the qualifications needed to fill the job. Fig. 2-3 (facing page) is an example of a job description.

Job Evaluations

Every employee has the right to know what management thinks of his efforts. He must know for reasons of security, recognition and a feeling that he is of worth to the organization; these are powerful stimuli to job satisfaction and employee productivity. Pay raises or promotion may be based on the evaluation given an employee. Management has the responsibility of keeping employees informed of their job evaluations. Too many times employees are either uninformed or only informed by silent implication. A definite statement is much more desirable in bringing about good employee relations.

Management or supervisors should establish performance standards to measure the work of employees. These may be precise or general. A precise standard* may be the performance of so many units of work in a given time. This is seldom used in health services, the general type of standard being more suitable to work done in foodservice in health care facilities.

A standard establishes a benchmark to measure factors to see if they are equal to, below, or above, the standard. A general and rather loose work standard might be one that describes work that is acceptable or is not acceptable. Standards can be established according to duties to be performed such as washing dishes, mopping floors, cooking, etc. Or, a standard may cover work behavior or the traits displayed, such as accuracy, productivity, judgment, dependability, co-operativeness, etc.

---

*Such a precise standard might be: "Set up 4 trays per minute," or "Prepare the breakfast in 1½ hours." A general standard may be "operate the dish-machine in a satisfactory manner," etc.

Fig. 2-3—JOB DESCRIPTION

Job Classification: Head Cook   Department: Food Service
Job Code: 2.26.32   Date: 5 August 1972

 I.   Job summary:

      Supervises food production area

      Prepares meat or main dishes, soups and gravies and sauces; should know vegetable cookery

      Supervises assistant cooks and helpers in food production

      Responsible for safety, sanitation and equipment maintenance in area

 II.   Performance requirements:

      Job knowledge: Plan own work schedule and schedules of those under her; know basic principles of quantity food production, sanitation, safety and the maintenance of equipment in her area; must be able to participate in some training of those under her

      Mental ability: Intelligent, alert; able to do required mathematical calculations in changing recipes, estimating quantities required, portioning food and checking requisitions, orders or inventories

      Dexterity and Accuracy: Able to manipulate the tools and utensils needed; accurate in weighing and measuring foods and in portioning servings.

      Standards: High ethical standards; able to quickly win respect from others; good health and ability to do work

 III.   Supervision:

      Under supervision of foodservice manager

      Supervises assistant cooks and helpers working in food production

 IV.   Career Ladder

      Can be promoted from assistant cook, head pantry worker or head vegetable worker

      Can be promoted to foodservice supervisor but must take foodservice supervisor course

 V.   Minimum requirements:

      Experience: At least three years in one of above positions, one year of which must have been in facility

      Education: At least eighth grade and preferably has had a course in food production, sanitation and safety or perhaps the foodservice supervisor's course; vocational or technical training desirable; must understand and speak English well; must be able to spell and write well.

      Preferred sex and age: Female, 24 to 55 years of age

Fig. 2-3. *A job description for a head cook.*

It is wise to start with a few good standards and expand them as rapidly as possible. The employees involved should be allowed to assist in the development of these. A standard of performance should be reasonable, attainable and acceptable to the employee.

Performance evaluation is the mechanics of measuring an employee's performance against standards. It should be done by someone who knows the job, although others not as well versed may also participate. The other person is desirable because it gives a check.

Evaluations are best based on a rating scale that indicates the degree of performance under a factor to be rated. For instance, if under the factor of dependability, a 2 is given on a numeral scale of 1 to 5, this would indicate marginal performance in dependability, with 1 indicating unsatisfactory; 2, marginal; 3, acceptable; 4, above average; and 5, excellent.

Such a rating should be based on specific data; for instance, the employee given a marginal rating for dependability may have been late for work 3 times, had 1 unauthorized absence and several failures to show dependability on the job. The health facility should establish the various traits or factors used for rating employees.

Evaluations should be discussed privately with employees and while evaluations should be made periodically, special evaluations may be made from time to time to suit special needs. A performance evaluation review with an employee is a critical one. The employee should not feel he is being criticized but the review should be a discussion in which the manager or supervisor and the worker get to know each other better and develop an agreed program on how to assist the worker in achieving his goals and in achieving a more satisfactory performance.

Before the evaluation interview, the manager or supervisor should go over the job, the standards and the facts compiled on the performance record. The objectives to be achieved in the discussion should be established: the employee should be told how well he has progressed; his strong points and major assets; areas for improvement and plans to assist him in improvement.

There should be a scheduled time and place for the interview and the employee should be advised in advance. Sometimes the appraisal is given the employee several days in advance so he can study it. It is not wise to pick a time when the employee has just made a serious deviation from established standards. Allow adequate time to elapse and then conduct the discussion in private.

Open the discussion with a friendly remark and do not appear rushed or exhibit a "Let's get it over with" attitude. If the employee has not seen the appraisal, let him. Begin with positive factors, being sincere in praise. Avoid generalities; be specific. Discuss negative findings in a positive manner; let the employee know you are trying to help him. Avoid negative criticism. Warnings and negative findings should be based on documented facts. If a warning is necessary, give it so there is no mistake that it is a warning. It is wise to let employees know when an incident occurs that it will be used later in evaluating performance.

The employee should talk and discuss his expectations, hopes and other matters. It should not just be a discussion of management's point of view. Encourage the employee to give his side of the story. Be sure to indicate future needs for development and the assistance that will be given. Management should let the employee know it has an interest in his progress and job satisfaction.

In closing the discussion, the points covered should be quickly summarized and the employee given any last chance to say anything he wishes. After the discussion, make notes on the appraisal sheet on anything that needs recording. Then check later to see that matters discussed in the meeting are being taken care of properly and the employee knows they are.

DIETARY SERVICE—PERSONNEL RATING SHEET

Facility _____   Employee _____

Date of Rating _____   Job Title _____

<u>Instruction</u>:   Check the value which best applies

PERSONAL ATTRIBUTES	Most of the Time	Usually	Some of the Time	Never	Comments
A. Attitudes					
1. Dependable					
2. Accepts responsibility					
3. Accepts criticism well					
4. Requires minimal supervision					
5. Good working attitudes toward residents, visitors, and co-workers					
6. Profits by mistakes					
7. Gives effort to work					
8. Abides by department and facility's policies and procedures					
9. Loyal to job and supervisor					
10. Enthusiastic and shows initiative					
11. Reacts well to unexpected requirements					
B. Personal Appearance					
1. Appropriate dress: Clean and neat					

2. Cooperates with facility's health program						
C. Punctuality						
1. Reports on and off duty on time						
2. Adheres to rules re: meals and coffee breaks						
WORK HABITS						
A. Quality						
1. Organizes duties well						
2. Accurate about work						
3. Maintains standards of food production and sanitation						
4. Judgment in knowing tasks that require guidance						
5. Accepts resident as a person						
6. Observes safety rules						
B. Quantity						
1. Significant amount of work accomplished in time period						
2. Economy of supplies and motion						
C. Ability						
1. Uses good judgment						
2. Rapid learner						
3. Follows directions						
4. Sufficient job knowledge						
5. Applies knowledge to work						

Additional Comments:

(cont.)

DIETARY SERVICE–PERSONNEL RATING SHEET (cont.)

Employee _____ Job Title_____

TERMINATION INFORMATION: Would you rehire?   _____

Employed from _____ until _____

Reason for Termination: _____

Reason for Evaluation: _____

IN-SERVICE TRAINING ATTENDANCE
Total number of classes   Total number of
conducted this period_____   classes attended___ % of Attendance____

Date 19	Subject	Time	Instructor

Number of days absent during evaluation period _____ Number of days ill_____
Number of vacation days in evaluation period   _____Number of holidays_____
Date of Evaluation Interview _____

_____   _____
    Employee's signature   Rater's signature and title

Employee's Comments:

Fig. 2-4. *The rating sheet on pp. 52-54 is an example of how employees can be rated. It is used to record the employee's training progress and other personnel information. Each facility, however, should compile its own rating sheet to suit its own needs. Courtesy Mrs. Iris Lochner, R. D., Food Systems Design, Oklahoma City, Okla.*

Employee Motivation

Every employee takes a job because he wants something from it. This may not be money. Some women take jobs because they are lonesome at home and find the social activity on the job satisfying. Employees may not always realize the real reason why they want to work and may give reasons that they think are valid but that are not the real ones. Employee needs will vary but most will revolve around:

1. Food, drink, shelter and medical services.
2. Security.
3. A feeling of belonging (companionship).
4. Recognition.
5. A feeling the job done is worthwhile.
6. Desire for activity and new experiences.

These are not necessarily listed in the order of importance they may have for all employees. Once the basic needs listed in No. 1 are satisfied, factors other than money quickly become more important. A worker who has basic needs satisfied without pay may not work at all for the money, feeling that other factors are much more important than No. 1. It should be recognized that, except for No. 1, the other factors need not cost the operation any money.

It is management's job to see that employee needs are satisfied. If they are not, it is most likely that the goals of management will not be satisfied either. Employees who do not get what they want from a job, leave it. An employee who is dissatisfied because he feels others think his job is not worthwhile will not quickly brighten up and exhibit high morale if he is offered more pay. However, a feeling that management and others think his contribution is important will bring about a change. Employees lose a sense of security when they suffer from unfair decisions, discrimination, slights or a failure to appreciate their efforts.

Frustration in an employee is evidenced by: 1) aggression toward others; 2) substitution of highly personal goals for those of the group or of the operation; 3) rationalization of failure or denial that he really wanted the goal he cannot achieve; 4) delusions, such as saying "My superior has it in for me;" 5) negativism that makes the individual oppose others and what they want him to do; 6) fantasy or day dreaming during which fanciful thinking which he enjoys in his imagination is substituted for concern about his lot; 7) identification with others; 8) repression or denying that frustration does exist or 9) regression, which is a retreat from reality.

Employees are motivated when management creates an atmosphere in which motivation is nourished. A genuine feeling of mutual respect and appreciation between management and the worker can do much to build a desire to do one's best.

An employee who feels that management is trying to do something for him and to develop him as a whole person is a better prospect for motivation than one who feels that management is interested in building skills and knowledge solely for the benefit of the operation. Motivation is something that is not generated by the employees. Management must sow the seeds for motivation.

EMPLOYEE COUNSELING   One of the most important parts of management's or a supervisor's job will be counseling or advising employees. To do this adequately, it is necessary to form a habit of listening attentively and politely, letting the employee freely express his ideas. The counselor should be open-minded, fair, calm, patient, sympathetic and respect the employee's opinions.

Empathy is a term that describes a feeling of togetherness (actually it means the transfer of our emotional feelings to an external object) and there is empathy when an employee is allowed to unburden himself to a person who understands and can help him. This experience is something an employee often needs. The counselor should listen without bias and be open-minded.

Exploring ways to establish a plan that will correct the employee's problem will not only help to bring about a solution but will build confidence in the employee. Management should recognize troubles before they become problems for employees. Using the scientific method to analyze and solve problems is a good technique to recommend to those who must counsel and advise employees.

DISCIPLINARY ACTION   The return an employee must make for having a job is adequate work performance and acceptable conduct. At times, it may be necessary to take punitive action against an employee because of a failure to meet the required standards in these two areas. The action taken will depend upon the gravity of the situation and the circumstances surrounding it. First offenses should not merit as severe an action as repeated ones. Good management should spot potential trouble before it occurs and thereby reduce the number of times when disciplinary action is required.

No disciplinary action should be taken until there are facts to support the need for it. There should be a record compiled. Actions should not occur because of prejudice, anger, or for personal reasons. In the case of grave offenses, it may be necessary to prepare a report to the personnel office or top management.

The facts should be studied and a course of action decided on after discussing the matter with top management, if need be. The matter should next be discussed with the employee, being sure to listen to his side of the story. In deciding the action to take, all the facts should be weighed and then the action decided.

It is helpful if there is a guide to indicate what type of action should be taken in certain cases. Usually it is desirable to have these listed in the policy and procedures manual. If possible, employees worth retaining should be salvaged. Warnings, reprimands, suspension for a period, all can be used instead of separation from the job; punish adequately but try not to destroy the employee's worth to the organization.

Foodservice operations frequently have high turnover rates—the national average for the foodservice industry is 10.8 positions out of every 100 positions each year, compared with the national average for all industry of 4.3.

Turnover is costly. Training a new employee has been estimated as costing about 8% of his yearly wage. Dismissals should, therefore, be avoided, if possible. Interviews with employees who are leaving are recommended. These may reveal factors to management that they may not know about but that are leading to employee dissatisfaction and job termination. Some reasons for leaving may be easily explained such as when a husband is being transferred to another area and his wife is quitting to go with him. However, keeping a record is recommended; indicate whether the reason for the termination is the employee, fellow workers, supervisors, management, the department or the facility. Indicating what might have been done to avoid the job separation is also recommended.

There are usually standard procedures to follow when an employee is separated. Forms must be filled out, personnel and accounting may have to be notified and, in some cases, a severance notice, indicating the reason for dismissal from or for leaving the job, may have to be completed. Usually each facility has its own method and this, of course, should be followed.

TRAINING   The day an employee comes to work, his
                                  value to the organization should begin to
grow. Growth should occur both in technical and social areas. The first leads
to job proficiency while the second leads to the development of an individual
who can take more responsibility; improve his ability to get along with fellow
workers; become a better team worker, and a promoter of morale and loyalty.
Neither technical nor social growth comes to an employee without assistance.
Although the consulting dietitian usually is in charge of training of foodservice personnel, both supervisors and management should make such growth
possible and establish programs to improve both technical and social growth.

Galileo once said, "You cannot teach a man anything; you can only help
him find it within himself." Growth must be encouraged by creating expectations in an employee and a confidence that he can learn and improve. Understanding is needed if one is to learn. Perhaps learning can be achieved by repetition but if an employee gains an understanding of what is to be learned, he
learns more surely and quickly. Put emphasis in training on the "why."

Learning results when a change occurs either in attitude, knowledge,
skills or in goals. Change develops an individual while habit inhibits growth.
Let employees know that attaining knowledge and skill or an aptitude to master the next job level is not the only reward he can gain from his job. Be sure
you make these other rewards available.

Teaching social growth is frequently not done formally. It is done more
often by example; by developing good working conditions; by working with
employees to help them achieve their own personal goals and by encouraging
self-teaching within a group. An employee gains added satisfaction when he
realizes he has developed not only better job proficiency but has also become
a more valued member of the team, or has gained greater recognition and security within the organization, or greater responsibility and authority, or
more potential for advancement.

Training programs should be established that answer employees' needs.
These can be estimated by a study of the employee or by checking the job description. Whether the employee is capable of learning what is required must
also be decided so as not to build false hopes. Employees should be told what
will be required and the changes that will have to occur. Complete approval
on the planned program should be secured from the employee. He should
know also what help will be given and what part he must play in the program.

DATE_____ FACILITY_____

DIETARY IN-SERVICE TRAINING

TIME:
SUBJECT: PURPOSE:
AUDIO-VISUAL MATERIAL
LESSON PLAN:
POINTS AND ACTION TAKEN AS RESULT OF CLASS DISCUSSION:
ATTENDING:

_____

Consultant Dietitian

Fig. 2-5. *A form used for setting up a lesson plan for training. Courtesy Mrs. Iris Lochner, R. D., Food Systems Design, Oklahoma City, Okla.*

Instructors must prepare to teach and also prepare the employee to learn. No training session should occur until the trainer has listed the objectives of the session, the method of instruction, the teaching materials required and the amount of outside work and progress required of the trainee. Normally, such a plan is called the lesson plan. Teaching should be in small segments with a learning pace set that suits the ability of the learner. Proper preparation of the student-employee requires that he be motivated, establish goals, know how to study and be at ease for learning.

Frequently the best learning is done in a natural setting, preferably an area where the employee or group may work. The time selected should be one in which both the teacher and the learner can devote full attention to the task.

Utilize work materials from the area. Written materials, audio-visual materials and other items should be pre-assembled, if required. Indicate in the lesson plan where these will be used. If you wish, utilize the services of others. For instance, the local public health inspector might be used to give a short talk on the part the Public Health Service plays in assuring that adequate sanitation occurs in food substances and in foodservice operations. There are many films, slides and other useful teaching materials that can be obtained just for the asking.

The lecture method is the most simple teaching method. It is effective in introducing new materials and in summarizing materials covered. It can be used with large groups and with other methods of instruction. Lecturing allows one to present a large number of ideas within a short period of time. Its defect is that one can't be sure the student is learning because he does not become involved. While lecturing is the simplest way to teach, it is not necessarily the most effective one.

Discussion or conference sessions are good methods of learning. They allow the trainee to express ideas, to pool his knowledge with others and to develop learning based on his own thinking. Such sessions stimulate interest and encourage a critical evaluation of ideas. These methods also allow the trainer an opportunity to ascertain if the trainee is learning and to find out what his weak spots are. These methods are time consuming and it takes skill to make them work.

Demonstration is a technique in which the instructor shows and tells and it is related to the discussion or conference techniques. It is best suited to teaching the employee how to do a job or for on-the-job learning. It can utilize the normal work area and materials. Demonstration puts theory into practice and permits immediate application of what is learned. Because sight is used in this learning situation, learning may be faster and better. The instructor also has a better chance to correct faulty practices and habits and gain an accurate estimate of the employee's progress.

To show-and-tell, follow the steps of instruction listed above, first, preparing the learner to learn, putting him at ease and then explaining and showing how the job is done. Check carefully to see that the job is explained in a step-by-step manner—but not always in the same sequence as the work is done if learning is facilitated by presenting material in a different order. Stress points to be emphasized and those which, if missed, will mean the job will not be done.

It is frequently helpful in the lesson plan to underline important points. Encourage questions and ask questions frequently to check learning. Be sure to stress the "why" of the job. This helps to improve the learner's understanding of what he sees and hears. After completing the teaching, it may be advisable to repeat. Then, ask the trainee or trainees to do the job, explaining it as they go along as you have done. Ask questions that require a "why" answer.

Frequently, in an operation, time cannot be found to give lessons and the employee must get his information through self-study. If this is the case, be sure to have frequent checks and conferences to see if the learning is progressing and to clear up any difficult points. Self-study requires that the instructor put in a good deal of time in preparing materials for study and in setting up the lessons. Time will also be required for conferring with the student afterwards. If a group is to be taught, this may be an efficient way to teach, using a sort of tutorial method in which each student sets his own pace of learning. Have frequent conferences to check on learning and progress. Programmed learning is a process of self-study in which the learner studies material and then makes his own checks, to see if he has learned and understood, before he moves on to further learning. This helps to give the student a chance to evaluate before moving on.

Do not attempt to teach too much. Understand also the ability of the individual or group to learn. Suit the pace and difficulty of the learning to these limitations. Be sure the basics are taught first. Do not start your teaching by introducing advanced concepts first. Thus, one cannot teach how to extend an inventory unless the individual knows multiplication and other basic arithmetic. Be sure the material to be learned has value and is meaningful. Unless the student feels it is, learning will not occur.

A facility's foodservice should set up training programs to cover mastering the knowledge and skills needed to work in a job. At least two employees and one individual in administration should take the food supervisor's course. All employees in foodservice may need certain courses such as sanitation, safety, etc. Special courses should be taken by employees who need training in one area for a particular job. While training programs from outside organizations or educational groups are helpful, often the facility has such specific requirements that the training program must be designed around them. The consulting dietitian should keep records of employee training and progress. She should retain a copy of this and see that the facility also has a record in the personnel files.

It is anticipated that state and federal training programs will become more common and these will be offered locally so employees need not travel far to take them. These will usually be good courses given by good instructors and apply directly to conditions in the area. When this occurs, perhaps the individual facility will not need to put as much time into training programs.

Wages

The Fair Labor Standards Act requires that hospitals and nursing homes primarily engaged in the care of the sick, the aged, the mentally ill or defectives residing in a facility, pay not less than $1.60 per hour for labor, with meals and lodging customarily furnished as part of the wage. Executive, administrative and professional employees are exempt from the Act.

Non-exempt employees in hospitals must be paid not less than 1½ times their regular pay for all hours worked in excess of 40 hr per week (48 hr in nursing homes) *unless there is an understanding arrived at before the work is performed* that a fixed work period of 14 consecutive days is accepted in lieu of the 7-day work week.   If such an agreement exists, 1½ times the regular rate of pay is required for any excess over 80 hr worked in the 14-day period, or any hours worked over 8 in any 1 day during such a period. If a nursing home fails to pay 1½ times the regular rate for any time over 48 hr during a week, overtime for work over 40 hr per week must be paid. When by law or the nature of the work, uniforms must be worn, no part of the cost of the uniform or its maintenance may be charged to the employee, if the charge reduces the wage below the minimum wage level. Equal pay must be paid for equal work regardless of sex. Individuals on a temporary job or a trainee for the first month may be exempt from some of the Act's provisions. No discrimination because of age, color, race or religion may occur.

The minimum age for employment is 16, but minors 14 and 15 years old may be employed outside of school hours but not after 7 p. m. or before 7 a. m. (7 a. m. to 9 p. m. June 1 through Labor Day). The limit of work for minors is 3 hr in any 1 day or a total of 18 hr per school week. Eight hours can be worked on non-school days or 40 hr in any 1 non-school week. If state laws regarding child labor are more strict than federal requirements, the state requirements must be observed.

Accurate records of earnings, hours worked and other data covering the time an employee works must be maintained as outlined in Regulations, Part 516 of the Act. Labor notices must be posted where employees can see them. For the Act to apply, a facility must employ over 25 people or be engaged in interstate commerce. Recent rulings have indicated that any business doing over $200,000 in business annually is in interstate commerce regardless of whether or not interstate trade occurs.

Operations should know that if provisions of the Act on discrimination, equal pay, etc. are in violation, the pay of one individual cannot be lowered to correct the discriminatory practice. The pay of those discriminated against must be raised instead. Labor organizations cannot force an operation to violate the equal pay provision.

There is a 2 year statute of limitations for violations, with the exception that in the case of willful violations the statute of limitations is 3 years. This means that 2 or 3 years after a violation has occurred, the provisions of the Act cannot be used against the violator. Because local or state regulations may be different from the federal Act, and because interpretations of the Act have varied depending upon local conditions, a facility should check to see exactly what the regulations are in its own area and what the interpretations are as well.[1]

Employees' wage records should be maintained indicating the date and time, wages paid, deductions made, days off, including time off on holidays, vacations, etc.

---

[1] U. S. Department of Labor. "Hospitals and Nursing Homes under the Fair Labor Standards Act as Amended in 1966," WHPC No. 1165, November 1966.

JOB CLASSIFICATION It is important that a health facility set up a classification for jobs, placing jobs within specific categories depending on the knowledge, skill, pay, responsibility, etc. required to fill each.

Workers receive different wage rates based on the work done. Wages may also differ according to type of work; dangerous work usually merits more pay; hours that are not as desirable usually result in higher pay. In the future, in health facilities, unions will participate in establishing job classifications and wage scales. However, if a facility has a long established system, unions usually do not interfere with it. It is far better that a facility set up its own system than to have a union do it. Job descriptions are helpful in setting up a job classification system. The U. S. Department of Labor has established job classifications which are helpful in setting up classifications in foodservice and making job assignments.

Good classification, even in a small operation, will produce higher employee morale and job efficiency. The following advantages usually result when classifications are established:

1. Employees get equal pay for equal types of work or work, which although different, requires about the same degree of experience, skill, ability or knowledge.

2. Jobs that differ in danger, hours, or those with other undesirable factors are recognized and usually earn higher pay.

3. An orderly arrangement of job assignments and organization in the departments of the facility is promoted.

4. Selecting employees for specific jobs is assisted.

5. Guidelines for evaluating employee work are made available.

6. Training needs can be identified.

7. Understanding between management, supervisors and workers is promoted.

LEGAL RESPONSIBILITY OF WORKERS Employees are only legally responsible for their acts if personally at fault. They should understand that negligence on their part or an intentional act, or injury to another because of willfulness or carelessness, may make them responsible. A tort liability (civil wrong) resulting in injury to a resident or other individual arising from negligence or a failure to protect from injury by an employee is usually the responsibility of the facility and not the employee, since it is assumed that the facility can control the actions of its employees. A facility has corporate responsibility in this case.

Willful or intentional negligence may change this, however, and the employee may bear the responsibility. At times, although this does not often occur, a health facility can ask an employee to indemnify it for costs it must pay because of an act of the employee.

An employee is not responsible for contracts made for the facility when acting within granted authority but, if a contract is made outside of this authority, then the employee is responsible. For instance, if an employee, authorized to purchase food from vendors, is not granted authority to contract for orders over $100 but does so, the employee may be held responsible. This is why a good delineation of duties and responsibilities is needed in job descriptions and why the authority and responsibility granted in a line organization needs to be spelled out carefully.

State, charitable, federal or other government organizations may be exempted from liability provisions but the trend in court decisions is to make them less so. It is wise to check and see exactly what tort or other liability your organization has and also what liability employees who work for the facility have. A health facility can sue a vendor who sells goods knowing that the items are not suitable for the purpose intended.

In almost all states, workers are protected by a law called "workmen's compensation." This is a type of insurance that is paid to the worker in case of injury or other factors which cause the worker to lose time on the job.

Managers and supervisors establishing policies and procedures must be sure that these are consistent with state and federal regulations such as child labor, working hours, Fair Labor Standards Act, etc. The management of the facility is responsible for licensing to operate and for seeing that all regulations relating to Public Health and other factors are complied with. Safety codes must also be complied with. A manager can be held legally responsible if he allows an individual who should not be working to work or allows conditions, or contributes to conditions, violating regulations. This is frequently not known by administrators.

The provisions of the Fair Labor Standards Act and other regulations that apply to the facility must be complied with. State regulations must also be met. State laws take precedence over federal laws only if the regulations of the state laws are more strict than those of the federal government. Any health facility receiving federal funds must comply with the provisions of the Civil Rights Act, Title IV. It must periodically file an assurance of compliance on Form 441 with the U. S. Department of Health, Education and Welfare.

A health facility must provide a safe working place and safe conditions for employees and it can be held responsible for negligence in the care of the premises or in maintaining the facility, its equipment or other factors. Toilets and washrooms must be furnished employees. Other regulations also must be met and management should ascertain what these are.

Complaints by employees on labor practices are usually handled by the Wage and Hour Division of the U. S. Dept. of Labor. A Compliance Officer investigates complaints and has the right to ask to see the payroll and employment records and also to conduct private interviews with employees. Information he receives from records or employees must be treated as confidential. The Officer must indicate to the facility whether his investigation has or has not revealed any violations.

His investigation may cover minimum wage, overtime, discrimination in age, color, race, religion, equal pay or any other area where federal authorities have jurisdiction. If a violation is found, an employee may bring suit to recover back pay, an additional sum up to the amount of the back pay, plus attorney's fees and court costs. Or, the federal government may bring suit at the written request of the employee. Or, the Secretary of Labor of the U. S. Dept. of Labor may obtain a court injunction restraining the operation against whom the complaint was filed from continuing violation, including withholding of proper minimum wage or overtime compensation. If the violation is considered willful, criminal proceedings may be taken against the operation.*

Inspections

Federal, state and local authorities will from time to time make inspections of the health facility to check on adequacy of procedures and health care. These are also made to certify and license the operation. Different forms are used. Table 2-1, pp. 68-80, indicates the type of investigation that might be made of the foodservice.

*The material in this discussion on legal responsibilities comes mainly from "Legal Aspects," Vol. IV of Administrative Aspects, HEW Public Health Services, No. 930-G-3. Government Printing Office, 1966.

Additional Bibliography*

Aitken, Edith T. "Guidelines for Employing a Dietary Consultant," manuscript, no address or date.

Balsey, Marie. "Workshop Focuses on Consultation Techniques." *Hospitals, XXXIX.* (Feb. 1965)

Gerletti, John D.; Crawford, C. C.; and Perkins, D. J. *Nursing Home Administration.* Downey, Calif.: Attending Staff Association, 1961.

Jernigan, Anna K. "What a Part-Time Dietary Consultant Can Do." *Hospitals, XXXX.* (Oct. 1966)

Lochner, Iris, R. D. Personal communication and notes, Oklahoma City, Okla.: 1971.

McQuillan, Florence L. *Fundamentals of Nursing Home Administration.* Philadelphia, Pa.: W. B. Saunders, 1967.

Pirkey, Mrs. Frank Z. *Effective Consultation,* notes and workshop book used for consulting dietitian workshop at Mercy Hospital, Denver, Col., Oct. 6-7, 1969.

Ranch, Margaret. "Food Service in a Small Nursing Home," *Nursing Home Administration, X,* No. 6. (Nov.-Dec. 1966)

Robinson, Wilma F. "The Dietitian's Role in Nursing Homes and Related Facilities," *Journal,* American Dietetic Assn., LI, No. 2. (1967)

(NOTE: Conditions of Participation for Extended Care Facilities, 1966, appearing in the Appendix of this book covers matters relating to organization, policies and procedures, etc. for the dietary department. The reader should also consult this.)

*These references are excellent materials in addition to those cited in the body of the text of the second chapter.

Table 2-1–SURVEY OF FOODSERVICE DEPARTMENT

Date _____

Facility _____

Address _____ Phone _____

Licensed number of beds _____ Rate of occupancy _____

Administrator_____ Phone_____

Foodservice Supervisor _____ Phone _____

Qualifications/Training _____

Dietary Personnel _____ Full Time _____ Part Time _____ Relief _____

Employee	Position	Hours	Days Off

See back of page for additional employees

Chief of Staff: Medical Staff:

Director of Nurses:

Office Manager:
Board of Directors meets _____ Medical Staff meets _____
Has there been a Consultant Dietitian previously? Yes _____ No _____
    List, if answer is yes:

    Attach copies of last twelve consultations if possible.
    Attach any copy of requests for corrective action in Dietary Services
      which may have been reported for Medicare, Title XIX, or JCAH.

Facility _____ Date _____ Page 2

I. FACILITIES

A. Review of physical layout of dietary department in rough sketch on back of page. Comment on:

(1). Size in relation to number of meals served:

(2). General cleanliness and ease of cleaning:

(3). Adequacy of lighting:

(4). Location in relation to: Dining Room/Cafeteria

    Delivery   Dish cleaning

    Storage   Patient area

B. Food Preparation Equipment: Give model, brand, size and general condition of:

(1). Range(s):	(7). Food Mixer(s):
(2). Oven(s): Calibrated? (3). Other cooking equipment:	(8). Blender(s):
	(9). Food grinder(s):
(4). Refrigerator(s): Visible thermometers?	(10). Meat slicer:
(5). Freezer(s): Visible thermometers?	(11). Other equipment:
(6). Other refrigeration:	

(cont.)

SURVEY OF FOODSERVICE DEPARTMENT (cont.)

Facility _____ Date _____ Page 3

C.　Food Serving Equipment: Give model, brand, size and general condition of:

(1). Hot Food Holding:	(5). Size tray used:
(2). Cold Food Holding:	(6). Method of covering tray in transporting to patient area:
(3). Method of delivery of trays:	
(4). Method of serving patients in Dining Room:	(7). Pocket thermometers for Dietary to check holding temperatures?

D.　Food Storage:

　　(1). Dry storage: Dry or staple food items stored off the floor _____inches.

　　　　Room is well ventilated? _____

　　　　Not subject to sewage or waste water backflow, or contamination by condensation, leakage, rodents or vermin? Comments:

　　　　Describe shelving:　　　　　　　Describe organization:

　　　　Could spacing arrangement be made more efficient?

　　　　Containers for bulk items:

　　(2). Condition of food on hand and cleanliness of area:

　　(3). Storage of Housekeeping Supplies and detergents for dishes:

E.　Dining Room/Cafeteria

　　(1). Adequate seating and convenient arrangement:

　　(2). Who is responsible for housekeeping?

　　(3). Provisions for feeding patients?　employees?　guests?

Facility _____ Date _____ Page 4

F.   Other comments:

    (1). Is general layout of the department well-planned?

    (2). Who is responsible for heavy cleaning?

    (3). Air conditioning and ventilation adequate?

    (4). Is there a "janitor's closet" available to the kitchen area?

    (5). Chilled water drinking fountain in kitchen?

    (6). Handwashing facilities including hot and cold water, soap, and individual towels, preferably paper (or air dryers), provided in kitchen area?

    (7). Office space or available desk/filing cabinet for keeping records? Storage for recipe books, periodicals?

II. MEAL PLANNING

A.   Responsibility for planning menus is assigned to _____

    (1). Planned in advance how far? If cycle is used, how many weeks?

    (2). Is a menu conference held?   Are worksheets made from menu?

    (3). Menus filed for minimum of 30 days?

    (4). Are changes, substitutions and the reason for the change recorded to show menu as served?

    (5). How are modified diet menus planned?

       Comments:

    (6). Describe nourishment system:

III.   FOOD PURCHASING SYSTEMS

A.   Person responsible for procurement _____

B.   Sources of supply: Meats:

      Produce: Dairy:

      Eggs: Staples:

      Bakery: Non-food:

      Local grocery stores and method of purchasing:

C.   Who is responsible for receiving, inspection or merchandise?

(cont.)

SURVEY OF FOODSERVICE DEPARTMENT (cont.)

Facility _____ Date _____ Page 5

- D. If non-profit, are commodities used?

- E. Is an inventory system used?

- F. What records are maintained of food and non-food items purchased? How long are records stored?

- G. Describe method of determining food costs:

- H. What communication is there between Dietary and Administration concerning food cost, budget, limits on amounts to be purchased?

IV. FOOD PREPARATION
- A. How well are the menus followed? Who decides on changes and substitutions?

- B. Food tasted prior to serving each meal?

- C. Are tally sheets used to communicate the amount to be prepared?

- D. Portions: Small____Regular____ Large_____?

- E. Who supervises food preparation when Foodservice Supervisor is off duty?

- F. Are standardized recipes used and easily available? Attach form if one is used.

- G. List quantity recipe books in use:

  Other sources:

- H. Production forecast properly?

- I. Describe preparation of foods for modified diets:

- J. Control of left-over items:

Facility _____ Date _____ Page 6

    K.   Foods purchased from the menu and available for preparation?

    L.   Food handled properly by cooks?   storeroom?   bakers?
          cafeteria personnel?   aides or waitresses?   dietitians?

V.   FOODSERVICE
    A.   Equipment for foodservice: Adequacy, condition and cleanliness
         of any permanentware: Adequate serving utensils?

    B.   Adequate choice of food on cafeteria line? At proper temperature?

    C.   Foodservice to patients at:

    D.   Are employees served?   Cost handled:

         Coffee breaks?   Cost handled:

    E.   Any special policies concerning employee meals:

    F.   Approximate number of employees served daily:

    G.   Describe policy for feeding patients' guests in patient rooms or
         Dining Room/Cafeteria:

         Other methods of feeding the public:

    H.   Rate of service satisfactory?

    I.   Attractive dining room?   Adequately staffed?   Adequate
         equipment?

VI. MODIFIED DIET CONSIDERATION
    A.   What is the method of communication between Dietary and the
         Medical Staff?

    B.   Does a designated Dietary Employee(s) contact patients routinely?
                                         (cont.)

SURVEY OF FOODSERVICE DEPARTMENT (cont.)

Facility_____ Date_____ Page 7

    C.   Is there an effort made to make menus acceptable to both patients and personnel? Is a selective menu used? Selection on modified diets?

    D.   Describe method of making modified diet menus acceptable.

    E.   Who gives discharge diet instructions to the patients?
        (Attach copies of forms used, if possible).

    F.   Method of ordering diets for patients and recording preferences:

    G.   Describe how patient's diet orders and food intake are recorded:

    H.   Attach copy of meal census form. Does it reflect adequately the information needed for determining % of modified diets served?

    I.   Most commonly ordered modified diets:

    J.   Do the medical staff have any of their own diets? Describe. What kind of diet instruction sheets do they use in their offices?

    K.   Do tray cards denote necessary information? Describe:

    L.   Officially designated diet manual and date of publication:
        Is there a record in the Staff minutes that it was agreed that the manual was to be used? Date:

    M.   Are copies available in Dietary?_____Nurses Station(s)?_____
        Library?_____

VII. DISHWASHING FACILITIES
    A.   If dishmachine is used, model:

        Adequate racks in good condition?

        Storage of racks between meals?

    B.   If three compartment sink is used, are procedures followed for correct sterilization? What disinfectant method is used?

Facility _____ Date _____ Page 8

    C.   Sterilization of cooking utensils and storage between uses?

    D.   Detergents/cleaning agents used:

        Dishes:
        Pots and Pans:
        Work surfaces:
        Other areas:

    E.   Is machine routinely checked by a qualified person? Who? Are records of inspection filed? Where?

    F.   Soap dispenser in use?   Wetting agent used?

    G.   Thermometers or gauges in use? Are they working?

        Temperatures checked: Wash cycle_____   Rinse cycle_____

        Pot and Pan sink_____   Is booster used?

    H.   How are soiled dishes handled?

        (1). Is soiled dish area separate from rest of kitchen area?

        (2). How are soiled dishes returned from patient area? From dining room/cafeteria?

        (3). How is clean permanent ware stored between uses?

    I.   Describe procedure for isolation trays:

    J.   How many disposables are used and how are they handled?

    K.   Are cultures taken routinely and records maintained? Who takes the cultures? Where are records maintained?

VIII. FOOD DISPOSAL AND GARBAGE

    A.   Mechanical disposal(s):   Locations:

    B.   Waste not disposed of by mechanical means is kept in leak-proof non-absorbent containers with close fitting covers and disposed _____.

(cont.)

SURVEY OF FOODSERVICE DEPARTMENT (cont.)

Facility_____ Date _____ Page 9

Containers are thoroughly cleaned inside and out each time emptied? Plastic liners or equal in use?

C.　Method of disposal of trash/garbage from grounds?

D.　Is there adequate separation of food supplies and trash/garbage?

E.　Is anything such as "dog food" removed from the facility?

IX.　FOODSERVICE SANITATION
A.　Is there a local health department:
Are health cards required locally?

B.　Do Dietary employees attend annual Food Handlers' Courses?
Date of last class:

C.　Are physical examinations required of new employees before reporting to duty?

D.　Are routine food handlers' exams given every six months?_____
annually?_____

E.　Routine checks made by local sanitarian?
Date of last report:　　　　　　　Where are these filed?

F.　Are uniforms of a specific kind required for all dietary employees?

Are lockers provided?　　　　Employees' restroom(s) clean?

Location of restroom(s):

G.　Is employee smoking in kitchen controlled?

H.　Is unauthorized traffic in kitchen controlled?

I.　Are disposable plastic gloves used for food service?

J.　Provisions for water at patients' bedside?
Who sterilizes permanent carafes and glasses?

K.　Do employee policies reflect control over people having symptoms of communicable diseases or open infected wounds so they do not work?

Facility_____ Date _____ Page 10

X. DIETARY MANAGEMENT

    A. Does the Foodservice Supervisor have full responsibility and authority for the Dietary Department? Explain organization:

    B. How and by whom are employees' schedules written and posted? (Attach copy of staffing pattern). How are holidays and vacations assigned?

    C. List books (other than recipe books) and periodicals available and in use:

    D. Are job descriptions written and accurate? Attach copies, if possible.

    E. Does each employee have a work schedule for the position worked?

    F. Is there an on-going program of in-service training? Are classes also conducted for non-dietary personnel?

    G. Have personnel, particularly the Foodservice Supervisor and her relief, attended special training in food preparation and service. List workshops, conferences, etc., for the past 12 months:

    H. Are there written policies and procedures and are they in use?

    I. What is the best time for in-service training?_____

XI. WRITTEN POLICIES AND PROCEDURES (should include the following points):

    A. Purpose of the Dietary Department

    B. Organization Chart

    C. Budget (allocation for personnel, food, non-food, equipment)

    D. Dietary operating cost records

    E. Menu planning

(cont.)

SURVEY OF FOODSERVICE DEPARTMENT (cont.)

Facility_____ Date _____ Page 11

    F.   Modified diets

    G.   Meal and nourishment services

    H.   Purchasing and storage

    I.   Food preparation and service

    J.   Housekeeping, sanitation and safety

    K.   In-service training

XII. PERSONNEL
    A.   Employees in uniform?_____

    B.   Caps or hairnets?_____

    C.   Clean and neat?_____.

    D.   Satisfactory work schedules?_____

    E.   Health cards?_____

    F.   Vacations and holidays: Scheduled?_____ Activated?_____

    G.   Employees well trained?_____

    H.   Labor turnover: Low?_____ High?_____

    I.   Attitudes conducive to good operation?_____

    J.   Work stations covered: Adequately?_____ At all times?_____

XIII. CONTROL
    A.   Reports up to date?_____

    B.   Food cost at proper level?_____

    C.   Payroll cost at proper level?_____

Facility _____ Date _____ Page 12

    D.   Expenses at proper level?_____

    E.   Expenses written up as received?_____

    F.   Food written up as received?_____

    G.   Standard food specification?_____

    H.   Adequate food stock?_____

    I.   Storeroom overstocked?_____

XIV. PATIENT SERVICE OR OTHER SERVICE
    A.   Meals on schedule?_____

    B.   Food at proper temperature?_____

    C.   Trays attractive?_____

    D.   Plates garnished?_____

    E.   Menus followed?_____

    F.   Best selection to private patients?_____

    G.   Special diet residents visited on satisfactory schedule?_____

    H.   Problems reported?_____

    I.   Problems solved?_____

    J.   Manager or dietitian observing and correcting loading of trays?___

    K.   Time element from line-up to service: Satisfactory?_____
        Unsatisfactory?_____

    L.   Adequate tableware supply?_____

(cont.)

SURVEY OF FOODSERVICE DEPARTMENT (cont.)

Facility _____ Date _____ Page 13

    M.   Trucks loaded to allow efficient service on floors? _____

    N.   Normal percentage of selective menus being returned? _____

    O.   S & S Diet Manuals available per contract? _____

XV. GENERAL
    A.   Good cooperation with other departments? _____

    B.   Daily Reports delivered to Administrator? _____

    C.   Did you talk with Administrator? _____

    D.   Remarks: _____
                  _____

MAJOR PROBLEM AREAS DISCUSSED

RECOMMENDATIONS FOR PLANNED IMPROVEMENTS IN
    DIETARY SERVICES

Survey by _____ Reviewed with _____

Courtesy Mrs. Iris Lochner, R. D., Food Systems Design, Oklahoma City, Okla.

III: FOODSERVICE CONTROLS

COST CONTROLS　　　　　　　　To control means to keep things going according to plan. In foodservice there are many things that need control: among them are quality, time, sanitation and costs. Nearly 20% of an extended-care facility's budget goes for foodservice, so cost control *is* important. Adequate control must occur to avoid waste, gain maximum benefits and prevent over-expenditures.

A cost can be controlled better if its existence, cause and magnitude are known. Cost information can come from the accounting department, foodservice records, recipe costing, market prices, food yield studies, etc. But having such information does not control; it merely informs. After we get the information, we must do something about it. Unless we are informed, action usually is not taken. The first thing to be done in cost control, then, is to set up a good information system.

Budgeting

Cost control is improved if we estimate costs ahead and use the estimated figures as a guide in controlling costs. Normally, we would want to have the final cost equal this estimate. If costs appear to be running ahead of the estimate, we can take action to control them before final costs are committed. Often it is just as bad to have costs go under estimates as to go over them, since this may mean poor performance or inadequate standards. Normally, a cost estimate is called a *budgeted* figure and a number of such estimates grouped together to show all costs is called a *budget*.

It is important that management realize the need to establish good, realistic budget estimates and know that to make such estimates adequate records must be maintained. Good records and their prompt interpretation will indicate what proper costs are. Unless this can be done, good cost control is not achieved. The information must also be available in time for control to be exerted.

Cost control systems vary with the type of operation but they are essential to every type of foodservice.

THE BUDGET. A budget is a financial plan for operation during a specified period. The foodservice budget should conform in format to the budget of the facility. It will be second in total dollars required, with only the nursing services budget exceeding it.

Besides 20% of the dollars, the foodservice department will take about 18% of the facility's labor hours.* Labor is usually a significant part of the budget and must be carefully controlled.

The budget indicates where dollars are committed as well as how much money is committed. Estimates should be based on past experience and expected future operating conditions. They must be realistic and should not take into account the hopes of the estimator. If it becomes clear that a budget does not reflect actual conditions, it should be changed unless conditions which should be changed—waste, inefficiency or other controllable factors—are changing projections. If that is the case, correct the disturbing factors. This is why a budget is set up—to act as a guide to, and a measure of, the operation's effectiveness. It is a weather vane to tell management when controls must be implemented.

Employees of a facility should be aware that a budget is not easily changed. An upward revision of an estimate may mean that dollars must be taken from valuable reserves, contingency funds or from the operating funds of other departments. In this situation charges to residents may have to be increased as well to take care of increased costs.

All departments have a strong obligation to meet costs imposed by a budget, but a budget should not be used as a means of beating down costs. The budget should allocate the funds needed to meet standards. If expenditures can be reduced below budgeted amounts without lowering standards, the department has an obligation to do so. Waste should not be permitted.

---

*Hospital Administrative Services, Dec. 31, 1968, of the Am. Hospital Assoc., listed other costs in percentages as: Daily Services (nursing, etc.) 38%, Special Services 4.6%, Laundry and Linen 3.7%, Housekeeping 4.5%, Plant and Maintenance 6%, General Administration 8%, Employee Health and Welfare 3.2%, Other Operating Expenses 1.8%, Depreciation 6%, Rent in Lieu of Depreciation 4%, Taxes, etc. ½% and Miscellaneous 2%.

A rough approximation of the percent of dollars allowed in a small health facility's budget are:

Wages and Salaries, with taxes and fringe benefits	40%	Dishes, Glasses, Silverware, etc.*	1½%
Food	45%	Heat, Light, Power, Water*	2-4%
Supplies	2-4%	Employee Meals	2-4%
Operation and Maintenance	2-4%	Capital Expenditures	2-4%
Laundry and Uniforms*	2-4%	Miscellaneous	1%

*These may be allocated differently or consolidated with other items.

A budget may also provide for major capital outlays, remodeling, building repair or new construction. Equipment replacement should be included; equipment over 10 years old should be checked for replacement. Include under Miscellaneous such items as certification or licenses, travel, education or training. A contingency or reserve fund should be set up in the budget.

A foodservice budget for a year's operation might appear as follows:

Wages and salaries		$ 74,000
Social Security, benefits, etc.		9,500
Food		112,000
Services:		
Laundry	$2,200	
Utilities	1,120	
Telephone	240	
Pest control	150	
Garbage removal	800	
Miscellaneous	200	
		4,700
Supplies:		
Cleaning	$2,240	
Paper	960	
Dishes, etc.	1,800	
Office	400	
Miscellaneous	200	
		5,600
Maintenance and repair		1,600
Equipment replacement		1,500
Education, travel, etc.		800
Contingency		700
Total		$210,410

Budgets vary with each facility; the preceding budget was for a large extended-care facility with 350 residents; $600 per year was allocated per resident for foodservice. Space costs, janitorial, accounting, stenographic, clerical and some other costs were picked up in the main facility budget.

SOME STANDARD
ACCOUNTING PRACTICES

We have few precedents for standardizing some accounting methods in health facilities. Many of the practices used today come from commercial foodservice customs; the Internal Revenue Service, for the most part, has gone along with these when applied to health facility accounting. Some of these commercial practices are:

1) Heat, light, water and other utility costs are usually considered an operation cost and not a rent or occupancy cost. Ice is not considered a food cost but rather a supply cost, even if it is made in the kitchen and a large part of the ice is used there. If nursing services uses some of the ice, the cost can be prorated, based on the amount used.

2) Employee benefits (Social Security, insurance, welfare funds, etc.) are separated from labor costs. These may be segregated as follows:

Social Security taxes	Workmen's compensation insurance
Federal insurance	premiums
Federal unemployment	Welfare plan payments
State unemployment	Accident and health insurance premiums
State health insurance	Hospitalization, Blue Cross, Blue Shield
Pension fund	Group insurance premiums
Social insurance	Etc.

Employee educational expense, travel, recreation and cost of credit union or awards and prizes may also be included under this.

3) Space occupied by the foodservice department in commercial areas is charged off at from 5 to 15% of sales, the higher percentage applying when utilities, heat, light, etc. are furnished. Occupancy charges to foodservice are usually not made in health facilities.

4) Utility charges would cover cost of fuel; lights; electric light bulbs; water, including softeners, purifiers, etc.; ice and refrigerator supplies; waste removal; engineer's supplies for foodservice, etc. Credits can be deducted from these charges for items furnished by the foodservice department to other departments, as in the case of ice used by the nursing services.

5) Besides not placing occupancy charges against foodservice, management may decide to pick up other indirect or even direct charges and put them

in the general budget. It is wise to allocate legitimate charges to foodservice as much as possible, however, even to the point of prorating taxes, licensing costs, etc., if these could logically be charged against foodservice. Hiding costs by putting them in the general budget does not give management all the information needed to control costs in the foodservice department.

6) Some other general accounting practices in commercial foodservice are: Payroll includes regular salaries and wages, extra wages, overtime, vacation pay, etc. Also, janitor or sanitation wages, service wages, cafeteria labor costs, etc. are charged to the payroll. Fringe benefits are not included.

Employee meals can be shown as a part of employee benefits but they are usually shown separately as an operating expense. If the nursing service passes trays and does other work for foodservice, the time so spent can be charged to foodservice but usually it is not. Clerical, accounting and stenographic work, etc. done outside the department for the foodservice department may be charged to it.

Non-Food and Non-Labor Costs

Costs that are not food or labor are maintained in separate categories. Laundry, uniforms, repair and maintenance, heat, light, power, water, garbage collection, etc. are usually charged under operation and maintenance; this is a direct expense in small operations. Supplies, such as glassware, eating utensils, dishes, paper goods, detergents, light bulbs, soaps, may be similarly lumped together under a supplies account. If more detailed information is desired, these can be separated for study by management. Non-food and non-labor costs are becoming more significant in foodservice. They have risen faster than food and labor costs.

It is usually desirable to have the foodservice department keep its laundry and uniform count separate from other units. A reduction in laundry costs can be made if foodservice installs a small, durable home-type washer and dryer for cleaning rags, dish cloths and towels, drip-dry uniforms, etc. Normally, employees furnish their own uniforms but frequently the facility may launder them.

Repair and maintenance records should be kept. Malfunctioning hot or cold carts, motors, refrigerators and other mechanical equipment can run up big repair bills. It is wise to know how these costs arise and how sizable they can be. A card recording repair and maintenance work for all mechanical equipment can be maintained. This gives a record of such costs and from time to time these can be checked to see if costs are excessive and the equipment should be replaced. If engineers or other non-foodservice employees do repair or maintenance work for the foodservice department, the time and material costs should be charged to foodservice.

Separate heat, light and water meters for foodservice are not apt to exist. If management wants to make charges for these, they must be estimated. In commercial foodservice, these costs are about 4% of total costs. So, if 4% of the foodservice budget is allocated, the difference between allocation and actual cost should not be too great. All equipment has a rated use for energy and if hours of operation are equated to this, a good estimate of energy use can be made.

Other data used in estimating utility usage are: If utility usage is not wasteful, it takes about 0.33 Kwh (kilowatthour) of electricity or about 1.8 cu ft of gas rated at 1000 Btu/cu ft to cook a meal. (Btu stands for a unit of heat called British thermal unit.) Around 60% of the connected load in an all electric kitchen is used for cooking.

About 1 gal of water is used for each meal that is prepared, 60% of which is hot water. It takes about 1000 Btu of gas (about 1 cu ft) to raise 1 gal of water $120^{\circ}F$ (i. e., from 40° to $160^{\circ}F$); thus, if 200 meals are prepared, 200 gal of water would be used, 60% of which, or 120 gal, is hot water. Raising 120 gal water $120^{\circ}F$ would require 120 cu ft of gas or about 35 Kwh of electricity.*

Whether gas or electricity is least expensive depends upon the basic rate charged for them. Where electricity is low in cost, it usually is the least expensive fuel but where gas is low in cost, it is. It takes 1.65 Btu's of gas to equal a Btu of electricity because of the loss of heat in venting gas. This means that for every Kwh of electricity which gives 3412 Btu's, about 5600 Btu's (about 5.6 cu ft) of gas is needed.

A study in 1968 indicated that a sq ft of building space costs 75¢ per year to maintain, heat, clean, light and amortize. If no janitorial service is provided, the cost is approximately 50¢ per sq ft/year. Since costs have risen since then, a dining area and kitchen of 800 sq ft might cost about $700 a year to maintain, including interest and mortgage payments, etc.

---

*120 gal of water is approx. 1000 lb; if raised $120^{\circ}F$, it uses 120,000 Btu of heat (1 Btu for every pound raised $1^{\circ}F$) and at 3412 Btu/Kwh of electricity this would mean 35 Kwh would be required.

The cost of glassware, dishes and silverware usually runs about 1½% of total foodservice costs. Thus, if a foodservice budgets $100,000 for total costs, $1500 is about right in the budget to cover glassware, dishes and silverware. This cost is usually considered a direct operating cost and not part of repair and maintenance costs. The inventory value of these items is usually calculated as 50% of the last price. Reserves are carried at 100%. About 1/10th of the value of small tools and of other small equipment such as pots, pans, etc. can be depreciated at this rate; this rate can also be used to calculate replacement costs.

The same charge may be reasonable for stoves, ovens, mixers, etc. but more durable equipment such as stainless steel sinks, tables, etc. may be better charged off in 15 to 20 years.

Because of their high rate of perishability, rubber scrapers, linens, etc. should be charged off as supplies. For the same reason, small tools and utensils are charged off as supplies, unless held in reserve. Uniforms, laundry, dishes, silverware, etc. that go into direct use are charged as an operating expense; fuel, cleaning supplies, etc. are also a direct cost. About 2% of the total budget is spent for cleaning supplies, soaps and detergents. The cost of paper goods varies with usage.

EMPLOYEE MEALS Employee meals may be recorded by having employees sign on a sheet or by issuing meal tickets which are picked up as the employee comes for a meal. Or, a meal count estimate can be made from the payroll; if an employee works 21 days and is entitled to two meals a day, a charge is made for 42 meals. Unless a record is kept of employees' meals, it is difficult to estimate the cost of the residents' meals.

In a sales tax state, meals sold to employees may be taxed, especially if they pay cash for them. Meals are usually considered fringe benefits and a part of operating expense and not a sale. These are logically a part of labor cost. Such meals are considered to be a part of conditions of employment, served for the convenience of the employer and not the employee. They are not indicated as employee income for income tax purposes but for federal unemployment and retirement tax purposes are considered as wages. If in doubt, employers should check with federal authorities on how to make meal charges in a health facility.

The method of calculating the cost of employee meals may vary. A value may be established based a) on actual costs, b) on past experience, c) on the standard charge used by many foodservice operations in the area or d) on an arbitrary amount established by the facility. Most facilities do not recover total costs for meals but subsidize a part of them. Normally, at least food costs and a part or all of the labor costs (at least direct labor costs) are included in the charge. Where a separate dining room is operated for employees, meal charges may be based on actual costs.

Resident Food Costs

To obtain the meal cost for residents, the estimated cost of food for employees' meals is deducted from the total food cost. Resident and employee food costs together are called "gross food cost" or "cost of food consumed." Frequently, 50% of the total meal charge for an employee meal is considered food. If this percentage is used, the food cost calculation for 681 employee meals charged at 70¢ each would be shown by accounting as:

Beginning inventory		$ 380.00
Add:		
Food purchases for period	$3520.00	
Delivery, etc.	55.00	
		3575.00
Total		$3955.00
Deduct:		
Ending inventory		420.00
Gross food cost or cost of food consumed		$3535.00
Deduct:		
681 employee meals @ 70¢ ÷ 50%		$ 238.35
Resident meal cost or cost of food sold		$3296.65

If 15,000 resident meals are served in our example and the cost of food sold is $3296.65, the cost of food per resident meal would be calculated: $3296.65 ÷ 15,000 = 21.9¢. Table 3-1 shows three methods that accountants

Table 3-1—FOOD COST CALCULATION

Method A: Beginning inventory		$1600.00
Add:		
Food purchases for period	$6750.00	
Shipping, delivery, etc.	65.00	6815.00
Total		$8415.00
Deduct:		
Ending inventory		1755.00
Cost of food consumed		$6660.00
Method B: Beginning inventory		$1300.00
Purchases including delivery, etc.		3250.00
Total		$4550.00
Less:		
Issues, requisitions, etc.		3175.00
Total		$1375.00
Ending inventory		1325.34
Shortage		$ 49.66
Method C: Beginning inventory		$ 300.00
Direct food purchases, etc.	$3500.00	
Storeroom issues	3225.00	6725.00
Total		$7025.00
Less:		
Ending inventory		430.00
Cost of food consumed		$6595.00

use to calculate the cost of food. Method "B" is good when a check is desired on withdrawals from storeroom supplies.

Meal Costs

As noted, food is about 50% of all costs in extended care facilities; in commercial foodservice, it is about 35%. Other costs, such as labor, utilities, supplies, etc., must be added to the food cost to get a total cost for meals. If these other costs in the example above were $3500, plus gross food cost of

$3535.00, the total cost of all meals for residents and employees would be $7035 ($3500 + $3535). The average meal cost for both resident's and employee's meals would be about 44.9¢ ($7035 ÷ 15,681 meals). If we want to learn the cost of resident meals only, we deduct the estimated cost of employee meals (681 meals x 70¢ = $476.70) from total cost of meals, $7035, which gives us $6558.30. The average cost of resident meals would be $6558.30 ÷ 15,000 or about 43.7¢.

LABOR CONTROL[1]

The increasing cost of labor, frequently higher than food costs today, makes it necessary to budget labor use carefully. Adequate labor is needed to get the work done but an excess can cause not only a waste of dollars but may even interfere with the quality of the food produced and employee job satisfaction.

Budgetary estimates for salary and wages should be based on the number and type of employees. Such estimates are determined by work load and type of work. Hours of operation are also a factor; for instance, no more than 14 hr should be allowed between the evening meal and breakfast and not more than 10 hr between breakfast and the evening meal. The foodservice should operate over a continuous 12-hr period each day. These are recommendations made by federal and other authorities.

Labor in the budget may be allocated on the basis of experience, but this may not provide a safeguard in instances where past labor use has been excessive; past mistakes may only be perpetuated. It is said that "If one cannot learn from the past, one is bound to repeat it." However, *good* experience can be helpful in determining labor and other requirements and should be used.

Another method of calculating the labor budget for a cafeteria has been established by Johnson.[2] He developed the formula $Y = 2.99 + 0.82X$, where Y equals the number of employees needed and X equals the thousands of

[1]Hartman, Jane. "Proper Budgeting Aids Food Service Planning." *Modern Hospitals,* June, 1969.

[2]Johnson, John F. "A Statistical Analysis of the Relationship between the Number of Meals Served and the Number of Employees in 171 Cafeterias." Master's Thesis, University of Chicago, School of Business, 1950.

meals served per month. Thus, if a facility serves 9000 meals a month, 10.37 employees are needed (Y = 2.99 + 0.82 x 9 = 10.37). Because of the tray deliveries, diet preparation and other increased labor requirements in a health facility, Y = 2.99 + .9X is a better formula to use. This would give 11.09 employees as the answer in our example above (Y = 2.99 + (.9 x 9) = 11.09).

The employees on the payroll will exceed the number of positions allowed; 7-day-a-week positions require 56 hr/week for coverage. If one employee works 40 hr, 16 hr must be covered by someone else. Thus it takes 1.4 employees to cover a 7-day-a-week position. This does not provide for sick leave or holidays; many workers work only about 232 days a year or about 67% of the working days. This usually means that 1.5 to 1.6 workers must be on the payroll for every position requiring daily coverage. For 5-day-a week positions, extra coverage is not usually needed unless the position is filled on vacations, during sick leave, etc. In this case, 1.1 workers is allowed for each position.

Another method of allocating labor—on the basis of the number of meals produced and served per labor hour, can be used. Extended-care facilities produce about 5 meals for every hour of labor.[1] On this basis, an operation serving 15,000 meals a month should use 3000 labor hr on the payroll (15,000 ÷ 5). If there are 30 days in the month, 100 hr per day can be budgeted or 12½ workers (including managerial, clerical, janitorial or others) can be working an 8-hr day.

If the number of meals served per day or month is known, the labor hours to be budgeted can easily be calculated on the basis of this reasoning. For instance, if employee or resident meals average 350 per day, multiply this by 30 days in a month to obtain 10,500 meals/month and, if the facility wants to average six meals per labor hr, this allows 1750 payroll hr or slightly over 58 hr per day (10,500 ÷ 6 = 1750) in a 30-day month. This should be the maximum number of hours used.

It is also recommended that labor hours also be broken down by shift or by worker. For instance, if a facility serving 127,750 meals a year allows 1

---

[1]HAS of the American Hospital Association reports that large hospitals with over 500 beds produce 3 meals for every hour of labor used; large state hospitals produce 11.6; clubs and hotels, 1¾; restaurants, around 3; school foodservices, 13; and college dormitories, 11. The amount of service given with meals and other factors are influential in establishing the number of meals produced per hr of labor.

labor hr for every 6 meals, the number of allowed hours per year is 21,292 (127,750 ÷ 6 = 21,292) or 1774 hours per month (21,292 ÷ 12 = 1774) or 59.2 hr per day (1774 ÷ 30 = 59.1). We may divide these monthly hours between workers as follows:

Cook-manager	162	Kitchen helpers and foodservice	1037
First cook	244	Clerical assistance	26
Assistant cook	275	Accounting	16
Consulting dietitian	16	Total	1776

The total hours allowed per year, month or day can be multiplied by the average hourly pay of foodservice workers to arrive at a dollar figure for budgeting. Fringe benefits usually are 15% or more of labor cost and these benefits should be estimated and put into the budget.

Table 3-2 indicates how a foodservice might set up a labor budget based on an allowance of 1776 hr per month producing 6 meals per labor hr. A 15% fringe benefit is added to the total.

It is important in allocating positions to maintain proper balance between skilled and non-skilled jobs. Too many skilled workers indicates non-

Table 3-2—LABOR BUDGET

Position	Number to Position	Hr/mo.	$/hr	Wage/mo. ($)	Wage/yr. ($)
Cook-manager	1.0	162	2.45	396.90	4762.80
First cook	1.5	244	2.10	512.40	6148.80
Assistant cook	1.7	275	2.00	550.00	6600.00
Kitchen helpers & service workers	6.4	1037	1.80	1866.60	22,399.20
Consulting dietitian	1.0	16	6.25	100.00	1200.00
Clerical	1.0	26	2.00	52.00	624.00
Accounting	1.0	16	3.50	56.00	672.00
Total		1776		3533.90	42,406.80
Fringe benefits 15%				530.08	6,361.02
Total				4063.98	48,767.82

skilled work is being done by them; too many non-skilled workers means inefficiency and poor quality food.

Using Table 3-3, the percentage of hours and dollars can be compared between skilled and non-skilled workers. It is evident from this comparison that skilled workers, omitting management, are putting in 30% of the hours and are taking slightly over 30% of the dollars. Unskilled workers are using 59% of the hours and receive 53% of the dollars. This is usually the normal distribution.

Management, including the consulting dietitian, takes about 10% of the time and is paid 14% of the dollars. This is not unreasonable; experience has shown that from 6% to 20% can be paid for management and the operation will remain efficient and profitable.

Adequate space and equipment should be provided for the individual who keeps the data for the foodservice operation. For this activity, a small desk or table should be available, preferably in a separate room but, if this is not available, then, in a quiet corner of the kitchen or dining room. Spindles, clipboards, drawers and filing space are needed. An adding machine or calculator may be useful also, and a typewriter.

If much of the accounting, clerical, stenographic or other work is done in other offices, the equipment needs will be minimal. The work done by the foodservice staff will also depend upon the competence of the foodservice staff to do it. Time to do the work should be allocated. Frequently, this work requires one day a week.

Table 3-3—A COMPARISON OF DOLLARS AND HOURS USED BY VARIOUS POSITIONS

Position	Percent Hours	Percent Dollars
Cook-manager	9.1	11.2
First cook	13.7	14.5
Assistant cooks	15.5	15.6
Helpers, etc.	58.3	52.8
Consulting dietitian	.9	2.8
Clerical	1.5	1.5
Accounting	.9	1.6
	99.9	100.0

Scheduling

Three types of work schedules may be used. One schedule will show days off, vacations and days on duty. Another will indicate the position and the hours worked; it may also indicate the number of days worked per week as well as the relief assignments for positions when regular workers are off. The third type of schedule will indicate the food production plans. Each is important if efficiency is to be maintained and proper job assignments are to be made.

The proper quantity of labor, with the workers having the requisite skill to do the work, must be assigned to jobs. An excess or an inadequate amount can hamper operation, increase costs and decrease quality. To schedule properly, one needs to know how long it takes to do a job. One should not assign too much or too little. Employees can appear busy when they are actually stretching out the work.

Pre-preparation is very important. Workers must have things prepared ahead and the production schedule should assure proper pre-preparation so that material to work with is at hand as needed. Also, idle or "down" time can be used for pre-preparation.

It is wise to have certain jobs reserved for the hours not needed for the day's production. For instance, cleaning jobs, or jobs such as grinding dry bread into crumbs, can be saved to take up slack time. Flexibility in assignment should also be practiced so workers can be transferred from one type of work to another. The schedules should be co-ordinated with menu planning, purchasing and storage of foods used.

In assigning day's off, some type of rotation should be used so the same workers do not work every week-end. In specific cases, some workers may never work a week-end while in others they may work every week-end, in either case because that is the scheduling they prefer. It is wise to set up the schedule—showing days on and off, vacations, etc., several months in advance or at the least, one month in advance. Vacation time can be agreed upon with management even earlier than that.

A simple method of setting up such a schedule is to put the worker's name on the left hand side and then indicate, by numbers of the month or days of the week, the times the worker will be on the job. Dates or days omitted indicate days off or an "O" indicates "off." Figure 3-1 shows the headings that might be used for such a chart.

SCHEDULE FOR DAY S OFF

Worker																				

Worker	1	2	3	4	5	6	7	8	9	10	11	12	13	14	15	16	17	18	19	20 etc.
Baker				0	0						0	0						0	0	
Collins	0	0						0	0						0	0				
Darr			0	0					0	0					0	0				

Days of the Month Assigned (an "0" indicates off)

Fig. 3-1. *A chart indicating days on and off. Vacations could be shown by a long line of "0's" to show time off.*

Fig. 3-2 is a line chart showing job assignment and hours worked. Other types of schedules are possible. For instance, the worker's name may be listed and the hours of work placed immediately after it. A line graph is helpful, however, in showing when the maximum amount of labor is on hand and whether it coincides with the heaviest point of production and service. This chart, and any others used, should be co-ordinated with the labor budget so the proper amount of labor is used. (See Fig. 3-2, p. 96.)

A production schedule controls production. It usually shows:

1. Period covered
2. Work to be done
3. Who does the work
4. Amount to produce
5. Recipe to use
6. Portion size
7. Meal or time for completion
8. Run-out time (in pay or staff cafeterias)
9. Comments
10. Slack time assignment

For instance, a production schedule might be set up as shown in Fig. 3-3, p. 97. It gives specific information to workers for various jobs.

LINE SCHEDULE

Position	Worker*	Relief for	Days/Week	Hours
Cook-mgr.	A		5	
First cook	B		5	
Asst. Cook	C		5	
Kitchen helper	F		5	
Kitchen helper**	G		5	
Kitchen helper	H		5	
Kitchen helper**	I		5	
Food service	J		5	
Night janitor	L		5	
RELIEF POSITIONS				
Cook-mgr.	D	(A)	3	
First cook	D	(B)	2	
Asst. Cook	E	(C)	2	
Kitchen helper	E	(F)	2	
Kitchen helper	E	(G)	1	
Food service	K	(H)	2	
Kitchen helper	K	(I)	2	
Night janitor	M	(L)	2	

*Workers' names would replace the letters under actual conditions.

**Also assists on floor delivery of foods.

Fig. 3-2. *A line schedule showing hours of work for a facility serving approximately 400 meals a day. The letter in parenthesis after the relief worker's initial indicates the worker relieved.*

PRODUCTION SCHEDULE

Production Schedule, Wednesday, Sept. 20, 1972

Meal and Menu Item	Worker	Amount	Portions	Comments
Breakfast				
Tomato juice	F	12 46-oz	87	6 oz; do Tues. pm
Pineapple juice	F	1 No. 10	12	6 oz; do Tues. pm
Prunes	F	3 No. 2½'s	16	3 prunes; do Tues. pm
Oatmeal (R-1)	B	4 gal	60	1 c cooked
Dry cereals	F	(Assorted)		Send to floors
French toast (B-18)	B	84 orders	3 half slices	
Sirup	G	84 orders	1 packet	
Butter	G	84 pats		
Coffee (G-2)	G	4 gal	60	Send in thermos pitchers
Milk	F	138 ½-pts		
Special diets	B	check diet chart		

OTHER ASSIGNMENTS

Cleaning: Refrigerators 1 and 3 and storeroom
Pre-prep: Wash lettuce and separate leaves for dinner salads
Peel 40 lb AP potatoes for dinner
Make cream sauce for croquettes for Thursday (2 gal) C-11 recipe
Pick over split peas for Thursday lunch soup
Take chicken meat and turkey meat from bones stored in refrigerator 2.
Check dressings and make up those low in quantity

Lunch				
Turkey-Chix shortcake (A-7)	B	7 gal	147	6 oz
Cornbread for shortcake etc.	A	3 12x20 pans 2-in. sq		Turkey over cornbread

Fig. 3-3. *The above indicates a production schedule that might be set up for a small nursing home facility. R-1, B-18, etc. indicate recipe to use.*

WORK SCHEDULE BY ASSIGNMENT

Date

Assistant Cook	**Cook's Helper**
Duties	**Duties**
Make coffee and hot cereal	Put ice into bins
Prepare main breakfast item	Put water into steam table
Help with dinner preparation	Cut butter or margarine
Set up salads & desserts for lunch	Set up breakfast trays
Check Kardex for modified diets	Help dish up breakfast
Prepare special modified diet items	Take breakfast carts to floors
Help dish up breakfast	Wash pots and pans
Take breakfast carts to floors	Set up lunch trays
Help on lunch and dinner work	Help set up cafeteria
See that cafeteria is set up	Assist cooks
Help dish up lunch	Do pots and pans
Help clean dining room	Help dish up lunch
Clean:	Take carts at lunch to floors
Coffee pots Monday	Do vegetable and salad preparation
Teapots Tuesday	Wash pots and pans
Kettles Wednesday	Do tray set ups for dinner
Floor carts Thursday	Help assistant cook on cleaning
Ice boxes Friday	
Walk-in Saturday	
Cook's section Sunday	

Fig. 3-4. *The above job assignment schedule can be posted near the sign-in sheet. Such a reminder is helpful if jobs are rotated, if workers are new or if a relief worker is on. Courtesy Mrs. Iris Lochner, R. D., Food Systems Design, Oklahoma City, Okla.*

FOOD CONTROL　　　　　　　　　　Food must be controlled not only because of the dollars it costs but also be-
cause of the importance of supplying nutritional requirements. Most small
health facilities will have limited dollars and these must be made to purchase
a sufficient amount of food to maintain health.

Some facilities control food by allowing a specified amount of various
foods per resident within a period. This is frequently called a ration allowance
and allows foods to be purchased in sufficient quantities to give adequate nutrition. The mental hospitals of the states of California and New York are on
such an allowance. The California allowance is based on the basic low cost
plan of the USDA[1] except that it allows slightly more meat to give the diet
more palatability.

Other facilities allow a certain amount in dollars for food. The menu is
planned within this restraint with food selected to meet nutritional requirements. Unless someone who knows nutrition plans the menu, however, the
foods selected may fail to adequately provide a balanced diet. Also, unless
the dollars allowed are sufficient to purchase the required food, nutritional
needs will not be met.

Hartman[2] has suggested an approach which has merit. It allocates funds
on the basis of 17 specific food groups in amounts sufficient to meet nutritional needs. This method brings "foods of similar nutritional and money values together" which simplifies budgetary calculations. It also tends to insure
adequate nutrition and makes possible a greater variety of foods. The amounts
of food in the 17 groups can be established either on the economy low cost,
low cost, basic low cost, moderate cost or liberal cost plans of the USDA.

These USDA plans are based on weekly food allowances, but extended
care facilities find it better to change this to a monthly allowance. About 10¢
per month should be added to the basic cost to defray the cost of leavening
agents, spices and seasonings, etc. If food served the residents is also served
to employees or others who eat at the facility, the allowance can be extended
to include them. If not, then separate calculations must be made on the

---

[1]U. S. Department of Agriculture. *Family Food Budgeting.* Home and Garden Bulletin, No. 94. November, 1969 or Home Economics Research Report
No. 35
[2]Hartman, Jane. "Proper Budgeting Aids Food Service Planning." *Modern
Hospitals,* June, 1969.

amount budgeted for employee meals. This cost is added to the food cost for resident meals to obtain a total food allowance. If employees do not eat a full three meals, the total number of meals consumed by employees can be divided by three to get a close approximation of the number of meals to include. Table 3-5 indicates how the type of control suggested by Hartman might be achieved. It is based largely upon the USDA's basic low cost plan.

The allowance in Table 3-5 is lower in amounts of sugar and fat than is found in normal American diets but authorities agree sugar and fat intake is usually too high anyway in the average diet. Sugar and fat are frequently consumed at the expense of other foods that would give a better nutritional yield.

The USDA food plans differ in allowances for men and women over 75 years. For instance, men are allowed per week 3¼ lb meat, 10 oz of the sugar group, 3¼ lb of the cereal group and 4½ lb of other vegetables. Women are allowed respectively 2½ lb, 6 oz, 2 lb and 3 lb. Table 3-5 allows respectively 2.9 lb, 8 oz, 2¼ lb and 3½ lb. Thus, if a facility is composed of a large group of men, the allowance might have to be raised but if women outnumber men, the allowance might have to be lowered. Per week, the basic USDA low cost plan allows men 6 eggs, 2¼ lb potatoes and 8 oz of fat but women are allowed 5 eggs, 1¼ lb of potatoes and 4 oz of fat for the same period.

The food allowance in Table 3-5 is based on AP (as purchased) weights. The meat calculation is based on a normal amount of boneless, low, medium and high bone cuts. The egg allowance is slightly below the USDA recommendation but since so many elderly individuals may not be able to have eggs in the diet in any quantity, this is reduced here. The grain allowance is based on dry cereals and flour; count 1½ lb (20 slices of bread) as 1 lb of flour—a slice of bread would, therefore, equal about 3/4 oz flour. Cereal foods should either be whole grain or enriched.

Dry non-fat milk is substituted for half of the day's liquid milk for economy reasons. Other equivalents of 1 c of liquid milk can be: ½ c evaporated milk; 1½ oz cheddar-type processed cheese; 10 oz creamed cottage cheese and 1½ c ice cream.

Tomatoes are high in ascorbic acid and are, therefore, included separately. One medium tomato, ½ c canned or 4 oz of tomato juice is considered a serving. An ounce of concentrated fruit juice is equivalent to 4 oz of juice. Lemons, tangerines, grapefruit, cantaloupes and other fruits high in ascorbic

Table 3-4—FOOD AND DOLLAR ALLOWANCE PLAN

Food Group	Allowance AP/ Day*	Lb/Resident/Mo.	Av. Unit Price/Lb in Area**	Cost/Resident/Mo.
Meat, fish and poultry	6 1/2 oz raw	12.30	$0.80	$9.840
Eggs	3/4 egg	3.15	0.30	.945
Milk, liquid	1/2 pt (1 c)	15.00	0.22	3.300
Milk, non-fat, dry***	1/3 c instant	1.80	0.48	.864
Margarine	1/2 oz (1 T)	.60	0.22	.132
Other fats	2/3 oz (1 1/2 T)	1.50	0.34	.510
Sugar, jam, sirup, etc	1 oz (1 1/2 T)	2.20	0.14	.308
Grains or cereals	5 oz	9.00	0.16	1.440
Dry legumes, nuts, etc.	1/2 oz	1.00	0.26	.260
Vegetables, yellow or green leafy	2 oz	4.00	0.28	1.120
Tomatoes	1 oz	2.00	0.32	.640
Fruit, citrus group	2 oz	4.00	0.30	1.200
Fruit, non-citrus	4 oz	8.00	0.28	2.240
Fruit, dried	2/3 oz	1.25	0.40	.600
Potatoes	5 oz	9.00	0.06	.540
Other vegetables	4 oz	8.00	0.24	1.920
Coffee	1/2 oz (2 T)	1.00	0.80	.800
Tea	.05 oz (2 t)	.15	1.60	.240
Miscellaneous				.100
		83.00 lb		$26.999

*AP = as purchased. **These prices are hypothetical and used for illustrative purposes only. ***Use in cooking.

acid may be put on the menu in place of orange juice and meet the citrus type fruit requirement.*

The prices given here are hypothetical to show how the calculations are made. An average price will have to be established for meats, sugar group, flour group, etc. This can be done by checking purchase orders and obtaining an average price for the group. It should be done for the area in which the facility is located; since prices may change from season to season, adjustments may have to be made.

In this calculation, the monthly cost of food per resident is $26.999, which would be approximately $324 per year. The USDA estimated, in March 1969, that the basic low cost plan per year would cost $323.80 for men and $275.60 for women or about $300 per individual. Therefore, the estimate made in Table 3-5 is perhaps too low for 1973. A more realistic figure would probably be $340 or more per year.

Operations seeking to provide food for less than this are probably not meeting nutritional needs, unless the economy plan or its equivalent is being followed. If these more stringent plans were followed, one *might* provide adequate food in 1972 for about $300 per year per person, or from around 82¢ per day.

PURCHASE AND   The value of foods and supplies
STORAGE CONTROL   ordered and held in storage is sub-
stantial and proper procedures must be established in ordering, receiving, storing and accounting for them.

Normally, a facility will have a standard procedure for ordering items. Special purchase or order forms may be used with 4 copies usually prepared. The forms should give the order number, the date, the quality and quantity of merchandise, price quoted including terms, shipping instructions and the vendor's name and, perhaps, address. The original should be approved by the proper authority and then be sent to the vendor. A copy goes to the accounting office. Two are retained by the foodservice department, one to be filed under the name of the vendor and the other under purchases pending.

When the goods arrive at the facility, the receiver picks up the order

---

*The reader should also refer to the chapters dealing with nutrition requirements and menu planning for further information on how to obtain balanced diets.

from the purchases pending file and inspects the goods for quality, quantity, etc. A record may be made on the purchase pending order copy, indicating the date received, quality, quantity, balance due if full shipment is not received, etc. A signed delivery slip is also attached to the order. This is then sent to the accounting office after routing it through the foodservice department office.

Some operations may wish to keep a different type of purchase receiving record. This could be a sheet on which the desired information is recorded with the purchase pending order sheet and the signed delivery slip attached. Periodically, this sheet is sent to the foodservice office and then on to the accounting office. The receiver should date all packages received by marking the date on the packing case. Items should then be delivered to the production center, if needed at once, or they can be put into storage. A distribution record should also be kept.

Blind receiving is a method in which the vendor is instructed not to put price, quality or quantity on the delivery slip. The receiver at the facility then must put down the quantity received and the quality. Price is not put down. This method of blind receiving is used to prevent the receiver from automatically accepting both the quantity and quality shown on the delivery slip without checking.

Do not allow milkmen, bread delivery men, coffee salesmen, etc. to enter the facility, check supplies and then leave an order, without having a check made on the amount delivered. Individuals receiving orders should be capable of receiving them. This might mean the manager has to check item quality although the rest of the recording could be done by other personnel. Cooks or other workers should not sign for deliveries without checking them.

PRODUCTION USE RECORDS

Foods and supplies used will come either via direct deliveries or from storeroom stocks. Direct deliveries are usually recorded upon receipt. Storeroom items should be issued by requisition which lists the quantity desired, unit size, name of the item, unit price, total amount, with special notations added. Unit price and total amount can be added later by the accounting office.

In small facilities, requisitions may not be used; instead, withdrawals may be recorded on a sheet of paper placed on a clipboard near the storage area door. The name of the item, unit size and the amount should be listed. This sheet is changed daily. The food production schedule for the day can be

DAILY FOOD AND MEAL COST RECORD

Date _10 Jan 72_

	Costs		Budgeted	
	Today	To Date	Today	To Date
Total day's purchases	$51.28			
Less those sent to storeroom	$22.60			
Total direct purchases	$28.68	$310.62		
Storeroom issues	$46.23	$1190.80		
Cost of food consumed	$74.91	$1501.42	$78.40	$1449.56
Number of meals served	280	5177		
Food cost per meal	$.26½	$.29	$.28	$.28

used to organize withdrawals. It is good to withdraw all items needed for a meal or the day at one time.

The cost of direct purchases can be added to requisition costs to obtain the daily cost of food. Some facilities may wish to keep a record of their costs plus other data. The form used might be something like the one above.

INVENTORIES   The quantity of items in storage or on hand needs to be known if a foodservice is to operate efficiently. This information and the value of these items must be known if accurate costs of operation are to be compiled. For a small operation, just going to the storeroom and sighting items may be sufficient to inform management that the production needs for a specified period are on hand or need to be ordered. However, for calculating costs, a physical inventory is needed.

A physical inventory is an actual count of the quantities of food and supplies on hand. To facilitate the taking of a physical inventory, the storeroom should have an established arrangement that does not change and the inventory form should coincide with the arrangement so that one does not have to hunt around for each item. A physical inventory will list the name of the item, unit size and number of units on hand. Prices will be added later and extended into totals by the foodservice department or the accounting department, or prices can be duplicated onto the forms along with the names of the items and the unit sizes, leaving only the quantity to be written in. If prices are subject to change, however, this may not be advisable since the last price received is usually the one used. If items are listed, leave space for new items to be written in.

Frequently, a perpetual inventory is maintained. This is a method in which the quantity of items as received and put into storage are recorded on a card, with one card supplied for each item. The total of the item on hand is also shown. As items are withdrawn from storage, they are deducted from the total. Thus, one can tell without going to the storeroom what the status is on various items.

The perpetual inventory card may also indicate the price of the item and also low stock levels at which reordering should be done. Maximum amounts to store may also be shown. Some cards carry further information such as order number, date received, location in storage, etc.

For a small institution, it is frequently easier to "sight" items than to keep a perpetual inventory. But, if an inventory is not kept, then some method for indicating minimum and maximum stock levels of items is needed so ordering is done at the proper time. These levels are usually established on the basis of experience, time between ordering and delivery, etc.

An example of a perpetual inventory card follows; maximum and minimum levels of inventory are indicated below:

Item: **Brand:**

Date	Size or Unit	Amount Received	Cost/ Unit	Total Cost	Amount Used	Cost Out	Balance on Hand
On Hand			$1.00				18 No. 10's
8/7	No. 10	2 cs	$1.00	$12.00			30 No. 10's
8/15					3 No. 10	$3.00	27 No. 10's
8/16					6 No. 10	6.00	21 No. 10's
8/20					8 No. 10	8.00	13 No. 10's
8/24	No. 10	2 cs	$1.05				25 No. 10's
8/26					2 No. 10	2.10	23 No. 10's

Maximum: 6 cs or 26 No. 10's   Minimum: 2 cs or 12 No. 10's

Inventories should also be maintained of supplies, small and large equipment, etc. The equipment inventories may be taken once or twice a year and checked against the last one taken, to ascertain losses, etc. The value of the equipment inventories is usually calculated by accounting, the same as is done for inventories of foods and supplies.

TIME RECORDS   Some type of record of employee time on the job must be maintained. This may be a time clock provided for health facility personnel and located near the locker rooms, although it is preferable to have this at a place where it can be supervised.

In small operations, employees may sign in and out on a sheet of paper kept for this purpose. Some responsible individual should verify and sign the record. It is especially important that hourly time records be checked and verified. Deductions and pay calculations are usually not handled by the foodservice department.

MISCELLANEOUS RECORDS   Some facilities feel it is worthwhile to precost menus. This can be done quickly if the standardized recipes are costed. Precosting can alert management to the possibility that costs may be going above those desired. However, when the time of employees is limited and much other more pressing work is to be done, facilities do not feel this expenditure is worthwhile. If there are other dependable checks on costs, this may be true. Otherwise, consideration should be given by management to this type of cost control.

The foodservice department should set up a standardized list of portions for the foods it serves and this record should be set up in an area where employees can see it. The proper portioning tools and equipment should be available to make it possible to portion foods according to this schedule.

Food production records may be maintained to give valuable information for purchasing, cost analysis or quality control. It is helpful to a buyer to know how well items perform in production and service. The amount of shrink or loss in pre-preparation or cooking may be recorded for this purpose. It is also helpful in calculating costs of food served. Future purchases can be refined on the basis of the information.

Data on quality or acceptability may lead to better purchasing or production techniques. It does not take too much effort to jot down data which later can be extremely valuable to management. However, some instruction and training may be needed at first to assure getting the right information.

SUMMARY Management must make a decision on how much time and effort is needed and how much information must be obtained to maintain proper controls. Certainly, in a small facility, a minimum expenditure of time, effort and dollars is required. Sometimes data can cost more than it is worth. On the other hand, it may help to save a great deal.

Management may at times think cost information is too involved or too costly and that is can be dispensed with, but experience has shown some type of cost control it needed in even the smallest facility. Information is needed if controls are to be implemented. It is recommended that the simplest, most effective system needed to give adequate control be established. This means that management must give a considerable amount of thought and time to planning and setting up the system. No one else can do it.

Additional Bibliography*

American Hospital Association. *HAS Reports.* Chicago: no date.
National Restaurant Association. *Uniform System of Accounts,* 3rd ed. Chicago: by N. R. A., 1530 N. Lake Shore Blvd. 60611, 1958.
U. S. Dept. of Agriculture. *Family Food Budgeting,* Home and Garden Bulletin, No. 74. Washington, D. C.: Government Printing Office, 1969.
West, B. B.; Wood, LeVelle; and Shugart, G. *Food Service in Institutions.* New York: John S. Wiley, 1966.

————

*In addition to those cited in the text of this chapter.

IV: NUTRITION

Methuselah ate what he found on his plate
And never as people do now.
Nor did he note, the calorie count
He ate it because it was chow.
He wasn't disturbed as at dinner he sat
Devouring a roast or a pie
To think it was lacking in granular fat
Or a couple of vitamins shy.
He cheerfully chewed each species of food
Unmindful of trouble or fears
Lest his health may be hurt
By some fancy dessert,
And he lived over 900 years. —Author unknown

INTRODUCTION

In spite of what Methuselah thought, what we eat *has* much to do with how healthy we are. Everything in our bodies has come from food. If we have not eaten in our lifetime as well as we could, our bodies have not functioned as well as they could. We also may have more health problems because we have not eaten correctly.

At times, for health reasons, we may have to control what individuals eat; we say they are "on a diet." Most people don't like diets because they can't eat everything they want. A diet is a denial program. The challenge is to emphasize acceptable things that *can* be eaten and make the dieter miss the other things as little as possible. Positive attitudes, imagination and ingenuity on the part of the staff, when applied to modifications of a normal diet, can do much to bridge the "golly-awful-diet gap."

This chapter is written for those that must make diets *work*, not just plan them.* In many long term care facilities, the consulting dietitian or other

---

*See also the chapter on menu planning; that chapter and this one are at times very closely related in the area of nutrition and diets.

individual responsible for planning diets will be at the facility for short periods of time. Some other individual at the facility, therefore, must be trained to handle problems of diet when the one who plans the diets is not there. The person who provides the food for diets must act through guides left by the consulting dietitian. This chapter is written to give some background information to help in using such guides.

Only a physician can prescribe a diet and only a dietitian or other competent person can plan or interpret one. The nursing staff, foodservice employees, relatives and others are not considered competent. The physician should not only specify the diet but also should review the restrictions and limitations pertaining to it plus other information needed to assure that the correct diet is provided. For instance, in a diabetic diet the amount of carbohydrate, the number of calories and, perhaps, grams of protein and fat should be specified.

It is especially important to establish specific names for diets and to use this terminology consistently. Diet orders should be revised once a month by the dietitian, with the foodservice manager and head nurse noting progress, therapeutic feeding problems, etc., to provide the dietitian with background as to how the diet is working. Federally-funded programs require that residents receive this kind of individual attention to diet needs.

Most government-funded contracts under Title XIX (Medicaid) require that diet histories be maintained. This can be done by keeping a diet record on the back of a diet card. (See diet cards in Fig. 5-4, Chapter V, or use a form shown in Fig. 4-1 (p. 109a) putting dietary information on the back.) The procedures outlined in Fig. 4-2 (p. 109b) indicate government requirements for handling diet orders, etc. Also, in the Appendix are to be found the recommended "Guidelines for Therapeutic Dietitians on Recording in Patient's Records," Standard IV for Dietetic Services in the Joint Commission on Accreditation of Hospitals' Manual plus some generally recommended procedures for handling dietary information matters. The physician's diet order should be on the resident's medical record and transferred to the foodservice department on a standard form. Facilities can purchase standard forms on which to maintain diet histories.

A competent person with adequate dietary training should translate the doctor's diet order from the standard form to the individual resident's record, indicating foods allowed or restricted, amounts to be served and how to serve them. Also, likes and dislikes and other individual needs should be outlined.

HOW TO HANDLE DIETARY RECORDS

Fig. 4-1—FORM FOR DIET RECORD

ROOM: 101   NAME: Mr. Peters   DIET: 1500 calorie diet

BREAKFAST	DINNER	SUPPER	DISLIKES
½ cup Orange Juice 1 Egg 1 slice of Toast 1 slice of Bacon *or* 1 tsp Oleo ½ cup of Milk Coffee, Tea— any amount	3 oz Cooked meat, poultry or fish ½ cup Potatoes, Rice, Macaroni and the like A vegetables—any amount ½ cup B vegetables 1 serving of Fruit 1 slice of Bread 1 tsp Oleo Coffee, Tea—any amount	2 oz Cooked meat, poultry, fish or meat substitute 2 slices of Bread *or* ½ cup Potatoes, Rice, Macaroni and the like *and* 1 slice of Bread A vegetables—any amount 1 tsp Oleo ½ cup Milk Coffee, Tea—any amount	
			LIKES
			BEDTIME: 1 cup Milk or Buttermilk 5 Saltines *or* 1 serving of cereal

(NOTE: Please record on the back acceptance of the above meal indicating any significant information in view of the patient's diet, etc.)

Fig. 4-1. *A standard diet card used by many health facilities on which it is common to note on the back significant information relating to the resident's response to his diet. Data from this may then be recorded "in strict chronological order in the Progress Notes Section of the resident's medical record." (See further information on this also in the Appendix.)*

GOVERNMENT REQUIREMENTS FOR
HANDLING DIET ORDERS

Federal regulations for Skilled Nursing Homes with respect to Medical Assistance under Title XIX, popularly known as Medicaid state:

"Procedures are established and regularly followed which assure that the serving of meals to patients for whom special or restricted diets have been medically prescribed is supervised and their acceptance by the patient is observed and recorded in the patient's medical record."

In the regulations for Hospitals participating in Medicare there is a requirement that:

"The dietitian correlates and integrates the dietary aspects of patient care with the patient's chart through such methods as patient instruction and recording diet histories and participates appropriately in ward rounds and conferences, sharing specialized knowledge with others of the medical team."

Regulations do not require any special forms—generally one of three procedures is followed.

1. The Dietetic Service has its own special form on which it records diet histories, instructions, and relevant information.
2. The dietitian uses a regular Consultation Form, just as staff or consultants from other departments of the facility use.
3. The dietitian integrates pertinent information in strict chronological order in the "Progress Notes" Section of the patient's medical record.

Fig. 4-2. *The above is taken from a private communication from Charlotte E. Smith, Nutrition Consultant, the U. S. Department of Health, Education and Welfare that outlines some of the common federal requirements for handling diet orders and procedures. (Also, see the Appendix for further details on how to handle dietary information.)*

Physicians periodically should review diet orders and the progress of the resident on them. Diet orders should be renewed about once a month if they are to be continued. The physician should initial and date the renewal. Only a physician can discontinue a diet; if a diet is to be discontinued, the discontinuance order should be signed and dated by the physician.

Prescribing a diet is like prescribing medicine. But, filling the diet order is not quite like filling a drug prescription. A complex series of steps must occur to produce and serve the food. It is not in bottles ready to mix or hand out ready-made.

The dietitian interpreting the diet order must have a great deal of knowledge and experience in food preparation, purchasing, management, personnel, etc. She must have a college degree for which she took many scientific courses to prepare her for this job. After receiving her degree, she has also had to spend time in an internship learning a lot more about her profession. She is a professional person heading up a highly important section of the health care team.

FOOD NUTRIENT GROUPS   From foods we get these five major groups of nutrients: 1) carbohydrates, 2) proteins, 3) fats, 4) vitamins and 5) minerals. We need two other things from food to maintain life: 6) water and 7) residue or bulk.* While alcohol is not considered a food, it must be recognized as a source of calories and may lead to excess body fat. Some few alcoholic beverages contribute a small quantity of nutrients but this contribution is never very important nutritionally. However, alcohol can act as a medication in some geriatric problems.

A food usually gives more than one of these seven groups. A cereal gives carbohydrate, protein, minerals, vitamins and residue. An apple gives carbohydrate, vitamins, minerals, a trace of protein and bulk.

Some foods furnish only one nutrient; for instance, salad oil gives only fat or granulated sugar gives only carbohydrate. We select foods because of the nutrients they yield if we want a balanced diet. We can eat a lot of some foods and get very few nutrients; such foods are called "empty nutrient foods." Lists of foods (see Table 5-7) are frequently given that indicate how much of each food we should consume daily.

---

*Sometimes referred to as roughage.

1) Carbohydrates

Our bodies burn carbohydrates to give warmth and energy. The substance burned is glucose, a sugar; it burns in our bodies somewhat as wood burns in air. All carbohydrates must be changed to glucose in the body before we can burn them. As is true for a wood fire, oxygen is needed for this burning. The oxygen for burning glucose is carried from the lungs by the blood to points where it combines with the hydrogen or carbon of the glucose to produce heat or energy. Just as the wood fire leaves a residue of ashes, this "body-burning" process also leaves a residue; it is the carbon dioxide exhaled by the lungs and the water which is used by the body or expelled as urine or perspiration.

Sugars, starches, syrups and many candies are practically all carbohydrate. Cereals, breads, macaroni and rice are high in carbohydrates. Dried beans and peas are higher in protein but also contain considerable starch. The body converts the carbohydrates in foods to glucose. If we eat more carbohydrates than we need for heat or energy, the body changes them into fat and stores the fat.

A gram (which is about ¼ tsp of water) of carbohydrate produces 4 calories of heat or energy. Thus, 1 T of sugar, 12 grams, will give about 50 kilocalories because sugar is pure carbohydrate. Protein or fat can furnish calories also. The body uses fat or protein for heat or energy, if it lacks carbohydrate.

If we exhaust our supplies of carbohydrate, fat and protein, we die from starvation. This takes a long time usually because we carry considerable reserves of food substances in our bodies. Normally, we store about 12 oz of carbohydrate, or about 1500 calories, which will run the body for about 12 to 13 hr, if we are not too active. After that, we start to use fat and protein reserves.

From 50 to 60% of our calories each day should come from carbohydrates but Americans do not eat this much on the average. We like our calories instead from fats and proteins which may not be as desirable. Diabetics must get a substantial amount of their calories from fats and proteins because they can handle only a limited amount of carbohydrates, but this must be adjusted to assure the best utilization of the foods they can have.

THE FATTENING POWER OF FOOD. The fattening qualities of food are often misunderstood. Faddists profit a good deal because of this misunderstanding. About a $½ billion a year is spent on diet foods, most of which are unnecessary. About $100 million is spent for fake reducing aids. Many diet pills are only vitamins, salt, soda or fillers. Some may be dangerous.

To some people sugar, cereal, starch, potatoes and other starchy foods are like dirty words, to be avoided; these food items are avoided because they are fattening—*not true*. Other foods are equally or more fattening. A pure gram of carbohydrate gives 4 calories; protein, 4; fat, 9 and alcohol, 7. (The fewer the calories, the lower the fattening power.)

Protein and carbohydrate have less than half the fattening power of fat and slightly more than half the fattening power of alcohol. A 4-oz baked potato gives 85 calories but the same amount of lean, cooked chicken breast, thought non-fattening by many, is 166 calories. Some think that the bread in pizza is fattening—*not so*—or at least not as fattening as the topping. A slice of bread has 64 calories; put butter on it and it has 164 calories. We can eat a fairly large quantity of food, not get fat and have a good diet; it's all in knowing what to select. It is also true that eating very little food can be fattening and provide a poor diet.

When we burn body fat, we lose water. Body fat contains a potential of 20 to 50% water. So, if we burn 9000 calories of fat*, we can lose from ½ to 2 lb of water. Salt helps hold water in the body. If in weight-reduction we reduce salt intake, the water lost in burned body fat leaves the body more quickly and makes us happier because we see we are losing weight.

It is considered safe for a normal person to lose up to 1½ lb per week but long-term care individuals should perhaps not lose more than ½ lb per week unless they are either quite healthy and active or it is medically necessary.

Most people reach normal weight between their 25th and 30th year. There should be little gain after this. An excess of 100 calories a day over needs gives a weight gain of about 10 lb per year.

One out of 5 people in our country is overweight. Good evidence exists that obese (fat) people do not live as long as leaner ones; they also have more health problems. Men, 20% or more overweight, have a higher death rate than those who are of normal weight or are slightly underweight. Animals fed a restricted diet may live longer than those fed too generously. In

*If there are 9 calories in a gram of fat, then we have lost 1000 grams or slightly over 2 lb of fat in addition to this water which is freed when fat is burned.

one test, rats, fed so little food they were moderately stunted, lived twice as long as those fed a rich diet. This should not, however, be taken to mean we should not have an adequate intake of food. It only means that excesses in eating can do us harm.

All carbohydrates should not be eliminated from the diet because we are apt to substitute other foods giving us more calories. We need carbohydrate to balance the use of protein and fat. If fats are burned without carbohydrate being used in the process, incomplete burning occurs, leaving harmful residues called ketones. Too many of these can bring about a condition called ketosis which may put us into a coma and cause death. Ketosis is always a danger in diabetics because they tend to burn fat when low on carbohydrate. A person trying to reduce who is burning a lot of body fat because of a poorly planned diet can develop ketosis.

Burning fat or protein in place of carbohydrate also increases the cost of the diet. Carbohydrates spare proteins because protein is not burned for energy if carbohydrates are available. Proteins burned in the body in place of carbohydrate are changed to glucose by a process called "deaminization."

Diets high in simple sugars are now thought to be harmful. There is some tie-up between simple sugars and the development of arteriosclerosis problems. Simple sugars such as honey, sirups, granulated or brown sugar are thought to be less efficient in helping to metabolize fats and proteins in the body than the more complex carbohydrates such as starch, flour, potatoes, etc. and, because we are eating such a high percentage of refined sugars, some authorities feel we are encouraging the development of arteriosclerosis and related problems.

Too much carbohydrate in a diet may tend to eliminate other needed protective foods. Elderly individuals tolerate carbohydrate foods better than foods high in other substances and for this reason may like a "tea and toast" regime. Fats, proteins and bulky vegetables and fruits take more time to digest and the elderly may find such digestive activity distasteful. They prefer something easier to digest. This is where imagination and ingenuity are needed to prepare the protective foods needed in a form acceptable to the geriatric person.

HOW MANY CALORIES? We need calories to move, work, breathe, to keep the heart beating and to continue other body functions. If we do nothing, it takes from 1000 to 1400 calories a day to run the body and, if we serve just a basic diet, we can run up 1000 to 1200 calories. We call this minimum amount the *basal metabolic requirement*. While this varies in individuals, elderly people or bed patients probably require less calories than normal ones.

If we are active, we about double our energy needs over our basic metabolic rate. Body composition, its shape and size, sex, age, race, temperament and even climate influence our caloric needs. Fat insulates the body and reduces the heat loss. This reduces calories needed. A skinny, tall person loses more heat than a fat, short one. The bigger the body in surface and weight, the more calories it needs. Women need about 8% fewer calories than men.

As we age, the body slows down; both metabolic activity as well as amount of action drop and so our calorie needs drop. Older men need about 20% fewer calories than younger ones and older women, 10% less than younger women. A change in activity, body size or body composition changes caloric needs; soft, flabby muscles need less than firm, vital ones. As a result, some extended care residents may have extremely low caloric requirements.

The requirement for other nutrients does not drop as age increases. Many extended-care residents need as high or higher vitamin and mineral intakes as younger individuals. They do not need the calories, however. If extended-care residents "eat like birds," they are only showing the need for fewer calories but this does not mean that they also need fewer nutrients. The challenge is to get all the nutrients needed into the small quantity of food they eat. Diets for these individuals should provide a large quantity of protective foods.

A slightly active man, 55 years or older, 5 ft 7 in. tall, weighing 154 lb, living in a temperate climate, needs about 2400 calories a day and a 128-lb woman, 55 years old, 5 ft 2 in. tall, needs about 1700 calories per day. Because of inaction, bed-ridden or wheelchair residents need much fewer calories.

DIABETICS. About 2% of our population is diabetic today; soon it may be 5%. Overweight and advancing age seem to predispose people to diabetes; two-thirds of diabetics are over 40 and 9 out of 10 are overweight.

A diabetic usually is a person who does not have enough insulin to burn up the glucose in the blood. If too much is present, it is excreted in the urine. There are a number of tests that can be made to ascertain if a person is a diabetic. Some are quite simple.

A diabetic has a low threshhold for sugar. This sugar threshhold is much like a dam holding water back, except that it holds sugar back in the blood and keeps it from spilling over into the urine. A high threshhold gives good storage capacity for blood sugar, a low one a low capacity. In a diabetic, the threshhold is low and only a small quantity can be held in the blood. When the blood has more than this, it spills over the dam and is lost. Normal people have a threshhold that holds enough glucose to give adequate energy and heat. Drugs can be given, such as insulin, to raise the threshhold. An individual who fatigues quickly and drinks a lot of water can be suspected of being a diabetic. Excess appetite and weight can also be indicators.

If a diabetic converts too much body fat too rapidly for heat or energy, ketosis can develop. Ketosis is an acid condition in the body which, as was noted earlier, can cause one to go into a coma and die. A diabetic with a slight ketosis or a person dieting for weight reduction may have a breath smelling like nail polish (bad breath.) This odor is caused by the large number of "ketones" and acetones exhaled.

2) Protein

Nitrogen is the key element in protein. To burn protein, nitrogen factors must be removed—deaminized—and we get rid of these nitrogen substances via the urine. Deaminization takes time and so, when the body burns protein, the energy release is slower. Thus, one who eats a lot of protein and burns a large share will have a long, slow energy release. This is very helpful to a diabetic. A diabetic tends to use up the glucose coming from carbohydrate foods rather quickly and then turns to other substances for energy. Protein, since it lasts longer, helps provide the diabetic with energy over a longer period of time. This is also why we sometimes try to feed a diabetic more frequently, each time giving the diabetic some small amount of carbohydrate and protein food. It is preferable to use natural means in assisting diabetics and not depend entirely upon drugs to do the job.

Some residents may have difficulty in metabolizing protein and also in eliminating waste nitrogen products. Some with kidney problems, high blood pressure, etc. may not handle waste protein substances but still need an adequate amount of high quality protein. If they do not get it, they cannot live. When protein must be limited in diets, we give the protein that can be consumed in foods with as good a protein as we can include, such as milk, eggs, meat, fish, poultry and other animal foods having what we call high "biological value."

Proteins build body tissues, muscles, blood, hormones, etc. To do this, they must be what we call complete proteins. Proteins are made up of a large number of *amino acids*. The body uses some 26 different amino acids to keep it going, to build tissues, etc. But, only 8 to 10 amino acids must come in the food we eat; we can get the others by manufacturing them from protein substances in our foods.

The 8 or 10 amino acids we must eat in our food are called *essential* amino acids. If a food we eat contains all of these essential amino acids in adequate quantity, we say the protein is *complete*. If some of these essential amino acids are missing or are contained in extremely low amounts, we say the protein is incomplete. Animal proteins, except gelatin, generally are complete. Some nut and legume proteins are complete enough to support normal life but do not have as high a biological value as animal proteins.

If we combine cereal proteins with nuts or legumes, we can get a fairly good ratio of essential amino acids. This is why the Chinese do well with their rice and soy beans (legumes). The people of the Nile have lived since the time of the Pharoahs, or before, on rice and legumes or wheat and legumes. Few vegetable proteins are complete but soy beans have a complete protein; many new food items high in soy are becoming popular on the market. Half the protein from animal sources and half from other foods is generally a good balance in a diet. Low cost protein foods, such as non-fat milk, cottage cheese, fish, hamburger, chicken and soy beans, can be used to reduce costs yet give a complete protein. A brown bread and baked bean meal or a peanut butter sandwich gives a complete protein. We can do well if only 15% of our calories come from proteins, if they are fairly complete proteins.

Another fact to note about proteins is that all the essential amino acids are used more efficiently when consumed in the same meal. One cannot take some essential amino acids at one meal and then the remainder of those needed at another meal and hope to get efficient utilization. All should be consumed at the same time.

3) Fat

Fat is needed for essential body functions and also for protective padding around body organs. Food containing fat stays in the stomach longer, thus delaying hunger pangs; this gives such food a satiety value. After an all carbohydrate breakfast we are soon hungry but when some fat is eaten with it, the onset of hunger is delayed. Fat takes the longest time to be broken down into heat or energy in the body. Like proteins, this helps in a diabetic diet.

In this country about 45% of our calories come from fat, but it would be better if only 35% did. In 1938, we got 38% of our calories from fats; older people should have less fat in their diets than younger ones. Butterfat, meat, mayonnaise, nuts and oils are high in fat; cereals and legumes are low in it. Cooked lean meat, trimmed of all visible fat will still have from 5 to 10% fat.

Some residents may have difficulty in digesting fat because it is retained in the stomach longer or because they have difficulty in digesting it in the intestines; this is especially true of those with gall bladder problems. Fats may be restricted in the diet and those allowed will be highly emulsified or easily emulsified in digestion. To reduce fats in foods, cook them in a Teflon pan. No fried foods are allowed those on a low fat diet. The vitamin A and vitamin D content in the diet may have to be watched if butter or margarine are restricted.

Hardening of the arteries (arteriosclerosis) and heart disease may be associated with hard fatty products that deposit and clog up the arteries. One of these products is cholesterol. It is high in some fats, egg yolks, shellfish, fat fish, fat meat, cream and butter. A loss of memory, mental degeneration, strokes, heart failure, blood clotting and other arterial malfunctions can result if too much waxy, fatty material is deposited in the arteries.

Diabetes and arteriosclerosis frequently come together. Most diabetics have high blood cholesterol. From 60 to 70% of women diabetics have heart conditions and/or high blood pressure. The body normally manufactures as much cholesterol as is needed. However, high levels can often be reduced when calories are reduced and we allow only a limited quantity of cholesterol-containing foods in the diet. There is enough evidence for a strong recommendation that *saturated* fats be restricted in the diets of some people.

Hard fats, usually those from animals, dairy products, coconut, etc., are called "saturated" because they are less reactive chemically. Other softer, more liquid fats are what we call *unsaturated*. These would be fish oils, safflower oil, cottonseed oil, soy oil, corn oil and peanut oil. These can help to keep excess cholesterol from the bloodstream. Highly unsaturated fats are called *poly-unsaturated*. Poly-unsaturated fats are best in a diet that must emphasize unsaturated fats; check labels to see what kind of fats products contain.

Some vegetable oils called unsaturated can be made into a saturated fat by a process called *hydrogenation*. If a label says *hardened vegetable oils* or *hydrogenated vegetable oils,* one can almost be sure that while they were probably unsaturated at one point, by hardening or hydrogenation they've been made into saturated fats. The hard or highly saturated fats should be restricted in a diet that must be low in saturated fats.

4) Vitamins

Vitamins are organic compounds needed by all individuals for proper functioning of the body, good appetite and optimal mental and emotional stability. A vitamin, like all essential nutrients, assists in carrying out essential functions in the body. Individuals over 55 are said to require the following amounts per day:

Table 4-1—VITAMINS—REQUIRED AMOUNTS

Vitamin	Quantity Needed Per Day	
	Male	Female
A	5000 IU*	5000 IU*
D	**	**
E	30 IU*	30 IU*
C (ascorbic acid)	60 mg	55 mg
Folic acid (folacin)	0.4 mg	0.4 mg
Pantothentic acid	**	**
Niacin	14 mg	10 mg
Riboflavin (B_2)	1.7 mg	1.5 mg
Thiamine (B_1)	1.2 mg	0.9 mg
Pyrodoxine (B_6)	2.0 mg	2.0 mg
B_{12}	6 u g***	6 u g***
Biotin	**	**

*An International Unit is equal to a USP unit.
**No quantity established; vitamin K (not listed here) is needed but we do not know in what quantity; it is usually in good supply in a balanced diet
***microgram or a millionth of a gram.

The functions of vitamins in the body are frequently interrelated and, if one is lacking, then others in plentiful supply may not be able to function.

VITAMIN A. Vitamin A is needed for good vision; a lack of it may cause night blindness or, if the lack is severe, complete blindness. Vitamin A is involved in protein synthesis, tissue repair, maintenance and growth.

The skin may become quite dry and horny if vitamin A is lacking. Xerophthalmia, a dryness of the eye, also results when vitamin A is lacking.

Vitamin A is fat soluble and found in animal fats such as cod liver oil, liver, egg yolk and butter. A number of foods contain the vitamin A precursor* called carotene. The carotenes are yellow pigmented substances, some of which the body changes into vitamin A. They are plentiful in yellow pigmented vegetables, such as carrots, sweet potatoes, squash, or in green vegetables, such as broccoli, string beans, etc.

We can store vitamin A in our bodies; this makes it possible to consume a plentiful supply on one day which will be sufficient to last for several more days. An excess of vitamin A can do harm. If too much is taken, hemorrhages start under the skin, the hair thins, the joints become inflamed and skin lesions form. Vitamin A and the carotenes are fairly stable and are only slowly destroyed in storage or cooking.

VITAMIN D. Another stable, fat soluble vitamin is vitamin D. It is found in fish liver oils, cream, butter, eggs, etc. It can also be made in our bodies by the action of the sun's ultra-violet rays. We can manufacture vitamin D by radiating foods containing certain fats with ultra-violet rays. An individual with dark or black skin manufactures less vitamin D than others with fairer skins. (Some now think vitamin D may be more a hormone than a vitamin.)

Vitamin D is needed for proper utilization of phosphorus and calcium and, although no requirement of quantity needed has been established for older people, it is quite possible a lack can result in insufficient calcium and phosphorus being deposited in the skeletal system. Children lacking vitamin D develop rickets. Again, too much can be taken and the body can store it.

VITAMINS E AND K. Vitamin E is essential for smooth muscle functioning. In human beings it seems to be effective as an antioxidant of fats, and other body substances. It may be helpful in circulatory problems and in utilizing amino acids. Vitamin K helps the blood to coagulate. Absorption of vitamin K may be impaired if the gall bladder does not supply enough or good enough bile salts to emulsify fats containing vitamin K. Excess aspirin or sulfa drugs interfere with the blood coagulating properties of vitamin K. Both vitamins E and K are oil soluble and are fairly stable. Usually our

---

*Precursor means "something that comes before."

foods furnish all we need of them. It is possible that microorganisms can manufacture vitamin K in our intestinal tracts.

A growing interest in vitamin E is developing in nutritional circles although, as yet, there is little evidence that vitamin E plays roles in human nutrition other than those described above. Vitamin E has been found to be essential to the metabolism of unsaturated fatty acids and as the intake of unsaturated fatty acids increases so must the intake of vitamin E. However, foods high in unsaturated fatty acids also carry a liberal supply of the vitamin so there is little danger of a shortage in the body for this metabolic purpose. Claims that vitamin E may be effective in reducing problems in sclerosis, nephritis, diabetes, hypertension or the heart have not been substantiated and administration for these purposes may be harmful to the individual.*

THE B-VITAMINS. The B-vitamin group, or B-complex, once was thought to be one vitamin. Because what we thought was one turned out to be a group, we designate them sometimes as B_1, thiamine; B_2, riboflavin; etc. They are all water-soluble and most are not very stable, especially thiamine and B_6.

Thiamine. Vitamin B_1, or thiamine, is needed to develop a good appetite, to burn carbohydrates and for good nerve functioning. If we do not have enough, we develop a disease called beriberi, a condition typified in part by constipation and tenderness of the calf muscles. Good sources of thiamine are whole-grain cereals, enriched cereals, yeast, meats—especially pork and liver—legumes and milk. Since the quantity of thiamine one needs is governed by the amount of carbohydrates burned, the quantity needed is less as carbohydrates are reduced.

Thiamine is not very stable. Alkalies quickly destroy it; heat can also. It is water soluble and so can be easily leached from foods. It is plentiful in the drip that flows from thawed meat because of this solubility. Cook foods as quickly as possible to preserve the vitamin, preferably in a slightly acid medium. No soda should be added to the cooking water when cooking vegetables, since soda develops an alkaline reaction. This means avoiding the addition of soda to keep vegetables green or to make dry beans or other legumes

---

*From an article by Robert E. Hodges, M. D., and Roslyn Alfin-Slater, Ph. D., for *Nutrack* of the American Heart Assn., January, 1972.

cook more quickly.* Thiamine cannot be stored in the body so each day we should consume what we need.

Riboflavin. Another of the B-complex, riboflavin or B_2, is water soluble and can be destroyed by sunlight. For this reason, some glass milk containers are tinted to stop the entrance of the sun's rays which would destroy the riboflavin. Riboflavin is important in developing energy in the body. If the body lacks riboflavin, tiny sores appear in the skin, especially at the corners of the mouth; the eyelids will also become inflamed and sore. Some people on unwise weight reduction programs can show this deficiency. This vitamin is plentiful in milk, cheese, eggs, meats and whole-grain cereals or enriched cereals.

Niacin. A lack of niacin can cause pellagra, a disease evidenced by skin sores in the same place on the left and right sides of the body, diarrhea, mental deterioration and even death. Niacin is important in developing energy and combines with thiamine and riboflavin to do this.

Niacin is plentiful in nuts, especially peanuts, brewer's yeast, meats and enriched cereals. The body can manufacture it from tryptophan, an amino acid. Milk is a good source of niacin. Niacin is rather stable to heat but quite water-soluble. We try to avoid leaching it out in the preparation and cooking of foods. So, we keep foods as whole as possible and don't soak them for long periods of time. Using the liquid from vegetables and meat drippings for soups, gravies, etc., helps get back some of these lost nutrients.

Other B-Complex Vitamins. The remaining B-vitamins, B_6, (pyridoxine), B_{12}, folic acid, biotin and pantothentic acid are needed in small quantities by human beings but how much is needed of some of them, we do not as yet know.

It is thought that some of the physiological problems of the aged and chronically ill may be caused by a low intake, poor absorption or poor utilization of B_6, B_{12} and folic acid. Pyridoxine (B_6) is important in protein metabolism and in converting tryptophan to niacin. It is also involved in the metabolism of some fatty substances. B_{12} is found in most of our foods but is plentiful in fish, poultry, meat, cereals, dairy products, soy beans, nuts and organ meats. Brewer's yeast is extremely high in it. The body can also manufacture it if given the proper materials.

*In some areas the cooking water may be so hard that a *very* small amount (a touch) of vinegar, lemon juice or cream of tartar may be recommended.

Folic acid is found in leafy (foliage) type vegetables as well as liver, legumes, yeast, asparagus and broccoli. It is important in cell functioning and in blood formation. A lack of folic acid affects the oxygen-carrying power of the blood. The vitamin is helpful in some anemias. There is reason to believe that some physiological malfunctions in the elderly, such as mild paralysis, fatigue, weakness, etc., may be caused by a lack of folic acid or vitamin B_{12}.

Pantothentic acid is found in plentiful supply in the same foods in which pyridoxine is high. It is important in body metabolic processes. It supports the nervous system and is involved in the function of the adrenal glands and in body oxidations. Some think it may prevent hair from becoming gray but probably it does not.

VITAMIN C. Scurvy, a disease once common in sailors because they were unable to get fresh fruit or vegetables, is caused by a lack of ascorbic acid or vitamin C.* This vitamin is plentiful in citrus fruits, tomato juice, cabbage, many fresh berries and will be in good supply in bean sprouts, broccoli, cauliflower, fresh leafy greens, melons, turnips, rutabagas, kohlrabi, okra, onions, parsnips, fresh peas, peppers, persimmons, pimientos, fresh pineapple, potatoes, rhubarb and spinach.

Vitamin C is one of the most perishable vitamins. It oxidizes easily; a pitcher of orange juice left in a refrigerator overnight will lose very little, however, because it is acid and low in oxidizing enzymes. Mincing vegetables finely quickly results in oxidation. Cooking foods in lots of water encourages leaching of the vitamin. Heating destroys it when exposed to air or copper equipment, especially if the food is cooked in an alkaline medium. (Soda, again, is effective in destroying it if added to the cooking water.) Because the body cannot store large quantities of it, one should receive an adequate amount each day.

Ascorbic acid is important in the formation and maintenance of tissue, bones, teeth and blood. Cuts and wounds of individuals low in ascorbic acid heal with difficulty. Vitamins A and C seem to work together closely and a lack of one of them in the diet may hamper the functioning of the other.

---

*The British sailor became known as "limey" because of a regulation that all British ships had to carry limes on board to ward off scurvy. Limes and other citrus fruits are high in vitamin C.

5) Minerals

In general, minerals help to regulate the body or are important substances in the muscle tissues, body fluids or other body structures. In addition, they help maintain the correct acid-base ratio in the body, regulate fluid (osmotic) pressure, help the blood to clot and promote nerve impulse transfer. Elderly people sometimes have difficulty in absorbing minerals even if they are plentiful in the diet. Therefore, their diets should contain maximum quantities of them.

The body needs a number of minerals. While we know it needs specific quantities of some, we are not sure about the need for others. Some, needed in minute quantities, we call "trace" minerals.

CALCIUM AND PHOSPHORUS. Adults need 0.8 grams a day each of phosphorus and calcium. Both are important in maintaining a proper acid-base ratio, in keeping up the bones and teeth and in promoting many body functions. Calcium helps maintain good muscle tone, helps the blood to clot, the heart to beat rhythmically and the nervous system to function.

Phosphorus, among many functions, maintains normal muscle functioning, it is vital to the metabolism of carbohydrate, fat and protein. It is a part of the activity of enzymes and vitamins, brain and nerve functioning and cell metabolism. To assure an adequate amount of these two minerals, a pint of milk or its equivalent should be consumed daily.

Meat and other protein-rich foods are good sources of phosphorus. Cereals and legumes are also. Leafy vegetables contain calcium but, because of their fiber, may hamper its absorption. Some foods, such as spinach, beets, chard and rhubarb, contain oxalic acid which also interferes with the absorption of calcium.

Many residents lack calcium and phosphorus either because they do not get enough in their diets, they absorb it poorly, fail to retain it or are just too inactive to absorb and utilize it. As an individual ages, his bones become brittle. Softening (osteomalacia) or the decrease of bone substance and an increase of bone porosity (osteoporosis) are also common bone problems.

Bone fractures are common and dangerous and once a bone breaks, it mends poorly. It is, therefore, important that the diet contain enough calcium and phosphorus. Even then, we may not be successful in getting residents to consume enough to prevent slow deterioration. Residents may avoid milk and other foods high in calcium and phosphorus because they think they cause intestinal difficulties or constipation, although they seldom do. However, some adults may not retain the digestive enzymes to utilize milk sugar. The use of substantial quantities of dry, non-fat milk in foods such as soups, bakery products, etc. can solve many dislikes without requiring direct attack. Also, the use of other foods giving good amounts of these minerals can help. Some substitutes for milk are:

Table 4-2—MILK EQUIVALENTS

Food Item	% Of a Pt Of Milk	Fat Adjustment In Diet Use
1 oz cheddar, Swiss or similar cheese	.40	1 t less
1 oz cream cheese type:		
Neufchatel, 25% fat	.03	1 t less
Philadelphia, 35% fat	.03	1½ t less
5 oz cottage cheese	.20	none
5 oz non-fat cottage cheese	.20	add ¼ t
½ c ice cream, 10% fat	.15	1 t less
½ c sherbet, 4% fat	.06	none

IRON AND COPPER. Most extended care residents will have poor blood (anemia) either because of poor iron absorption or low dietary intake. Other causes might be a lack of vitamins, a chronic blood loss or a failure to manufacture enough blood cells in the bone marrow. About 1/10th of the iron consumed by young, active adults is absorbed; less is absorbed by extended care residents.

Green, leafy vegetables; meat; egg yolk; molasses; prunes and other dried fruits; whole-grain cereals and legumes are good sources of iron. Organ meats are high in iron; milk and dairy products are not, but what they do contain is well absorbed.

The diet should supply about 10 mg (mg = milligrams or 1/1000th of a gram) of iron a day. This is not a great amount but it is extremely important. Seeing that some iron-rich food is served daily usually assures an adequate supply. The following foods will supply the listed milligrams of iron:

1 pt milk	1.0 mg	½ c rolled oats	1.0 mg
1 egg	1.5 mg	¼ c raisins	1.0 mg

4 oz prune juice	1.5 mg	3 oz ground beef	2.3 mg
½ c Swiss chard	3.1 mg	¾ c bean soup	3.0 mg
1 oz 40% Bran Flakes	1.8 mg	1½ oz cooked beef liver	6.5 mg
Slice whole wheat bread	0.9 mg	1½ oz cooked pork liver	13.0 mg

Copper is also important for manufacturing good blood. Usually it is plentiful in the diet. A copper deficiency in elderly individuals can cause a loss of calcium and phosphorus and increased bone fragility.

SODIUM. The body's reserves of bases (alkalies) are largely made up of sodium. These reserves help maintain a proper acid-base balance. Sodium is necessary also for good muscle tone and contraction. It is associated with tissue and fluid functions of the body. A sodium deficiency causes severe fatigue and even illness. Salt tablets (common salt is sodium chloride) may correct this loss but should be used only on doctor's orders.

Sodium may have to be restricted for some cases of edema or high blood pressure or kidney diseases. Only small quantities of table salt are allowed in a 1000 mg sodium diet, about ¼ t per day. No salt is permitted in diets for 250 or 500 mg of sodium per day.

Many foods contain fairly large quantities of sodium such as beets, carrots or celery. Baking soda or baking powder contain large quantities. So do catsup, Worcestershire sauce, pickles, dry cereals, gravy, soup bases, bakery mixes and so forth. Many dried fruits and some dried vegetables, such as potatoes, are bleached with sodium sulfite. Some fish flesh is high in sodium and some frozen or fresh fish may be lightly salted to help preserve it.

Read labels of processed foods for their salt content. Canned vegetables and a number of frozen vegetables usually contain about 1% salt. A salt brine is used to test for the maturity of peas, lima beans, etc. for canning or freezing. The mature ones sink to the bottom. This treatment may add so much salt the vegetables cannot be used in low sodium diets.*

Even drugs, such as alkalizers, laxatives, headache remedies, etc., may have to be avoided. Where drinking water contains a high quantity of sodium, distilled water may have to be prescribed. Do not use ice made from water high in sodium. If a quart of water contains 20 mg or more of sodium, the

---

*Some processed foods may also have sugar added in packing and these may not be used for diabetic diets.

use of distilled water for drinking and cooking may be required for 1000 mg, 250 or 500 mg diets. Water softeners may increase the sodium content of water. Consult your local Heart Association, Health Department or local water department on the sodium content of local water.

Upon receipt of a physician's request, a local Heart Association will provide copies of the following booklets: *Your Mild Sodium Restricted Diet, Your 1000 Milligram Sodium Restricted Diet* and *Your 500 Milligram Sodium Restricted Diet.*

A mildly restricted sodium diet allows about 2500 mg of sodium per day. Some salt can be used for food preparation but the shaker is not on the tray. Usually, the advice is "use a very small amount." But, even with this, some foods with high sodium content must be avoided. Note the salt content of some foods as given in Table 4-3.

For a 1000 mg sodium restricted diet, food is prepared without salt; milk and meat are restricted to reduce the sodium intake. This may make the protein intake low. This can be corrected by using foods high in protein but low in salt such as soy flour, soy products, legumes or cereals cooked without salt. A diet of 500 mg of sodium per day or less requires that some foods high in natural sodium be eliminated and meat and milk must be curtailed somewhat. Such a diet is difficult to maintain for an extended period.

Sodium-free baking powders are obtainable. Potassium bicarbonate can be used in place of baking soda (sodium bicarbonate.) A single-acting, non-sodium baking powder can also be made using 6 oz potassium bicarbonate, 1¼ oz tartaric acid (cream of tartar), 8 oz potassium bi-tartrate and 4 oz cornstarch.* Use this as a single-acting baking powder, adding it late in the mixing of many products and stirring or manipulating the dough or batter as little as possible after this addition. In quantity work, this is used in a ratio of 1½ oz to every oz of double-acting baking powder; in small quantity, 1½ t for every t of double-acting baking powder.

Salt substitutes may be used only on doctor's orders because some contain sodium. Some artificial sweeteners do also. Plain saccharin, a sweetener, has a sodium base; special saccharins do not. Some meat tenderizers are high in sodium. Potassium substances are not good substitutes because those with kidney problems may not have a lot of potassium.

---

*Gram measurements would be, respectively: 159, 30, 225 and 112.

Table 4-3
APPROXIMATE SODIUM CONTENT OF SOME FOODS*

About 500 mg Sodium

1 oz (15) 2-in. potato chips
¾ t monosodium glutamate
¼ t (scant) table salt
Average serving cooked cereal, rice,
    macaroni product, hominy, etc.
    cooked with salt
3 oz canned salmon or sardines
2 oz canned cornbeef hash
½ slice fried bacon or 1 frankfurter

1½ pork sausages or 1½ oz ham
½ c drained sauerkraut
¾ c cornflakes or other prepared salted
    cereal (check label)
220 mg sodium per qt water
1½ T salted butter or margarine
2 T mayonnaise
2 ½-in. slices white bread
2 2-in. square salted crackers

About 250 mg Sodium

2 c milk or buttermilk
2 large olives
1 small pretzel
½ c canned or regularly seasoned
    beets, carrots, spinach, celery,
    kale or white turnips
3 oz raw kidneys
½ t catsup or chili sauce

1 oz (scant) canned crab or shrimp
½ c baked beans with pork
1 c canned peas or lima beans
1½ T dry brewer's yeast
120 mg sodium per qt water
1 small pat butter or margarine
    (salted)
1 slice bread

About 200 mg Sodium

½ c regularly seasoned or
    canned vegetables
6 oz (2 small servings) unsalted
    cooked beef or hamburger

2½ eggs
3 canned asparagus spears
100 mg sodium per qt water

About 50 mg Sodium

2 T cocoa
2 egg yolks
4 oz cooked unsalted halibut
½ c flavored gelatin dessert
½ c frozen dessert

1 T light or whipping cream
10 medium size raw oysters
2 medium chicken livers
1 artichoke
50 mg sodium per qt water

---

*Values taken from *Nutritional Data*, H. J. Heinz Co., 5th edition, 1963.

If there is competent supervision of food preparation and diet planning, few special low-sodium foods need be purchased, although low-sodium bread, rolls or crackers and some prepared cereals may have to be. Some bakery goods contain sodium propionate, a softener and mold retarder; but calcium propionate can be substituted to do the same thing. It may be necessary to use some low-salt canned or frozen vegetables and juices, low-salt tuna or salmon, etc. for 1000 mg or lower, sodium-controlled diets.

On labels, the word "dietetic" is not enough; the words "low sodium" or "salt-free" should appear. When preparing foods in quantity, omit salt; then, remove the salt-free portions and salt the remainder. Poach eggs in non-salted water for low salt diets but you can add 1 T of vinegar per gal of water to assist in getting a higher quality egg. Special desserts may have to be prepared. For 1000 mg sodium diets or less, do not use commercial gelatin desserts but make these from plain gelatin or sodium-free gelatin desserts.

Wise use of seasonings—a very large number are permitted—will do much to cover the lack of salt. There are many aids available to help plan interesting taste treats on these diets. Milk and eggs used in cooking or baking should be counted in calculating the sodium content of 1000 mg or lower low-sodium diets. A special dialyzed milk, low in sodium, can be obtained for use on the very low level of restriction of sodium.

IODINE. Thyroxin from the thyroid gland is an important hormone in controlling the speed or metabolic rate at which the body operates. It contains considerable iodine. If the body lacks iodine, the thyroid gland overworks trying to produce enough thyroxin and it may become enlarged, a condition called *simple goiter.*

Most soils have enough iodine in them to give adequate quantities in the drinking water but in the north mid-central (Great Lakes basin) and northwestern states the drinking water lacks iodine and this area is called the "goiter belt." By using iodized salt, this lack can be made up. Seafoods and fish from the sea have a high quantity of iodine in them. In a salt-free diet in the goiter belt, iodine may be given under medical orders.

POTASSIUM. As noted, potassium is one of the minerals important in maintaining the proper electrolyte or acid-base ratio in the body. Recent research has indicated that a potassium deficiency in older people may be more common than suspected. When potassium is lacking, the individual will have a marked lassitude, accompanied by diarrhea and a decreased food intake. Potassium helps the nerves and muscles to function. Meats, their juices and broths, are high in potassium. Potassium is fairly well distributed in most foods but legumes, cereals, nuts, dried fruits and molasses will have a higher amount than most foods.

When individuals take diuretics, even mild ones, the potassium level in the body needs to be watched because a diuretic eliminates minerals other than sodium from the body. Too low a potassium level in the body may cause cardiac problems and even heart arrests.

MISCELLANEOUS MINERALS. There are a number of minerals that may be required in the body, some only in trace quantities. There are others in foods but we do not know their function, if any, in the body or how much of them we need. Since most of these are liberally supplied in a well balanced diet, there is usually little need to see that they are included.

Magnesium is important in maintaining important body functions. It aids bone formation and is important in the utilization of amino acids. Sulfur is a significant substance in several of the amino acids and in some other body substances. Zinc can be a poison if taken in too great a quantity but in minute amounts it is important in maintaining metabolic reactions and in the functioning of the pancreas.

Fluorine is important in the formation of teeth and perhaps in their maintenance. It helps to create a larger, stronger, harder dental crystal in the teeth, making them last longer and become more resistant to decay. Molybdenum is required in enzyme systems. Chromium is also essential. Aluminum, silicon and bromine are probably used by the body in small amounts but just how is not known. Similarly, arsenic, nickel, boron and selenium are metals that may have a function in the body. Selenium and molybdenum can be toxic if taken in too great a quantity.

ACID-BASE BALANCE. To survive, our bodies must maintain an acid-base ratio close to neutral. An excess of either acid or base (alkali) can cause severe illness and even death. The body maintains its neutrality through bringing up reserves of either alkaline or acid substances whenever the acid-base ratio may be disturbed.

Some parts of the body are acid or alkaline. The stomach is acid. After it empties its contents into the small intestine, the acid is neutralized and the food mixture becomes alkaline; bile salts are largely the alkaline neutralizing substances. Later, in the colon, the mixture becomes neutral. Largely calcium, sodium, potassium or magnesium substances are used when we must neutralize an acid; sulfur, phosphorus or chlorine substances are used when we must neutralize an alkali in the body.

Many acid foods such as fruit juices from apples, oranges, lemons, etc. become alkaline in the body. Meats and protein-rich foods, such as legumes and others, become acid in the body. What we eat usually tends to balance out between acid and alkaline. Buffers can also be used by the body to absorb either an alkali or acid substance and prevent it from acting chemically in the body. Such buffers may be blood or other protein substances, bicarbonates or phosphates.

Normally, the body has little difficulty in maintaining a good acid-base balance and we need not concern ourselves with the problem. As one authority states, "It is fortunate the body has the ability to resist most efforts of the uninformed to tamper with the pH of its fluids,"* (pH refers to the acid or alkaline condition in the body.) It is only when a diabetic develops ketosis or someone, through renal difficulties, develops an excess acidity in the body that a real problem develops and we must do something about it. There

---

Nutritional Data, H. J. Heinz Co., 5th edition, 1963.

are sometimes a lot of false notions current among residents on the acid-base condition of the body; these may be sufficient to restrict the intake of certain foods which they need.

6) Fluids

Water is necessary to maintain life. Our bodies are about two-thirds water; there is about 10 lb of water in the blood. Fluids transport substances needed by the body and most body reactions take place in them. Water also regulates the body temperature when we sweat. As sweat evaporates, it absorbs heat, thus cooling the body. Liquid is needed in the intestines to promote proper motility and intestinal activity.

From 6 to 8 glasses of water, or their equivalent in fluids, should be taken per day. Beverages, soups, moist foods, fruits or other foods can furnish the needed liquid. We should expel from 1 to 1½ qt of urine in a 24-hr period. Extended care residents may not consume enough water, especially if dinner is at 5 pm or earlier and fluids are not given again until morning. Watch nursing staffs because they like to restrict evening fluids to avoid bed-wetting. An excess of fluids, however, does not aid in flushing out toxic substances but the kidneys do a better job if they have a plentiful rather than a restricted supply of water.

We use much more water in our bodies than we consume. The stomach alone uses about 2 qt per day. In addition to the fluids we consume, the body manufactures fluids in metabolic processes such as when we burn carbohydrate. Digestive materials in the small intestine must be quite fluid but when they move into the colon (the large intestine) a lot of this excess is removed and reused. We lose water when we exhale or sweat. The main loss is in the urine. The urine contains from 2% to 4% solids which are waste products.

7) Residue or Bulk

We need a certain amount of roughage or residue to promote digestion and eliminate waste products as feces. Bulk or residue is largely a complex carbohydrate called cellulose. Human beings cannot digest cellulose but cows, horses and other ruminants can. If cellulose is not present in our food, the amount of residue in the colon is so small constipation occurs. Normally, there is little danger of residue causing digestive distress, especially if foods are properly cooked. Too much residue can cause distress, however. For instance, too much bran or other roughage can irritate the intestinal walls. A normal, well-balanced diet usually contains an adequate amount of bulky substances.

8) Alcohol

Ethyl alcohol is a substance closely related to carbohydrates and fats. It can be burned in the body just as they are burned. Pure alcohol (100% or 200 proof) gives 7 calories of heat or energy per gram; 2 oz of 80 proof whiskey (40%) will give 168 calories or nearly as much as a baked potato with a pat of butter. Normally, the caloric value of non-sweet alcoholic spirits is equal per oz to the numerical value of the proof; for instance, an ounce of 100 proof spirit yields about 100 calories. This rule does not apply to wines, beers, ales, etc. that are of lower proof.

A physician may prescribe an alcoholic beverage. This may be for psychological reasons or to stimulate the appetite, to relax the individual or to promote blood circulation in the capillary system. Alcohol helps to enlarge the small capillaries, allowing more blood to flow into them.

For some individuals alcohol can be harmful and must be avoided. It can raise blood pressure or irritate the kidneys, etc. Some elderly or chronically ill individuals have a very limited capacity to oxidize alcohol. Normally, when given as a medication, an alcoholic beverage should be diluted and sipped slowly. Pure alcohol is a poison. However, alcohol 95% pure or less can be diluted and consumed. The proof of an alcoholic spirit is always twice that of percent alcohol. Thus, a 100-proof spirit is 50% alcohol. Table 4-4 gives the calories in some alcoholic beverages.

Table 4-4—CALORIES IN SOME ALCOHOLIC BEVERAGES

Beverage	Calories	Beverage	Calories
Beer or ale, 8 oz glass	115	Dry dinner wine, 3 oz	80
Sweet liqueurs, 1 oz	75	Sherry, 3 oz	85
Brandy, 70 proof, 1 oz	60	Sweet wine, 3 oz	120 to 150
Eggnog	338	Champagne, 3½ oz	90
Gin, rum, whiskey,		Hard cider, 6 oz	75
80 to 86 proof,	120	Dry martini, 4 oz	200
1½ oz or jigger			

Additional Bibliography

American Heart Assoc. *Sodium Restricted Diets.* New York: American Heart Assoc., 1966.

Cooper, L. F., et al. *Nutrition in Health and Disease.* Philadelphia: Lippincott, 1963.

National Academy of Sciences. *Sodium Restricted Diets: The Rationale, Complications and Practical Aspects of Their Use.* Publication 325. Washington, D. C.: National Academy of Sciences, no date.

New York State Department of Social Welfare. *Diets for Use in Homes for the Aged, Public Homes and Private Proprietary Homes for Adults.* Albany, N. Y.: N. Y. State Dept. of Social Welfare, 1964.

Proudfit, F. T., and Robinson, C. H. *Normal and Therapeutic Nutrition.* New York: Macmillan, 1961.

Turner, D. *Handbook of Diet Therapy.* Chicago: American Dietetic Assoc., 1965.

V: MENU PLANNING

"Now learn what and how great benefits a temperate diet will bring along with it. In the first place you will enjoy good health."–Horace

THE MENU A menu is a planned order for production. It is a document around which all the functions of the foodservice department will revolve. In addition, what the menu contains will have much to do with the morale, health and satisfaction of the facility's residents.

A menu for a facility should list menu items; when they are to be ready; in what amount and the methods to use as well as the recipe. If it lists who is to do the work, it can take the place of a production schedule. A menu should be planned with consideration for what labor is available, its skill, the equipment available, space, cost, nutritional requirements, quality standards, type of service and, most important, those who eat the food. The menu sets into motion a complex series of events, from calculation of the kinds and quantity of food needed, its purchase, receipt, storage, withdrawal, preparation, service through cleanup. Functions of the foodservice department must be tied in with menu production. Employees must be on the job when needed; equipment must be available and not tied up. Storage, production, service, sanitation and other procedures must also be co-ordinated.

Menu Mechanics

A menu takes time and skill to prepare. There are many factors to be considered. Enough time, freedom from fatigue and quiet are needed so one can concentrate on this important task. A desk and the proper tools should be available. One large sheet of paper, 12 x 17 in. for a 7-day menu or a 12 x 21 in. for a 10-day menu, makes it possible to see on one sheet of paper all the meals planned for the period. Allow a column for each day where meals of the day and the items served can be listed.

Plan the menu at least 1 week ahead of production and preferably 3 or 4 weeks before. This assures the best planning, quality and cost control. The planner can start with Sunday or Monday or any day of the week. Many like Sunday because it is a day in which emphasis on the meals may be given. Others prefer to start with Monday because this is usually the first day of the week when everyone will probably be on the job.

A good menu takes knowledge, imagination, creativity and artistry to plan. One must have an excellent sense for food combinations which, although original, are not so original as to "turn residents off." A planning committee may be used, made up of some members of the nursing staff and others who might be helpful. Menu suggestions can also come from residents.

Good menu planning tools are needed. A menu reminder file listing special occasions, holidays and other important events to be observed should be maintained. Birthdays of residents might be remembered, or, a day of the month may be set aside for a special birthday party for those having a birthday that month. A menu diary, indicating past acceptance of menus, amount prepared, amount of food carried over, weather, day, etc., is helpful. This diary can be a file of past menus with notations on them.

There are other lists that can be helpful such as foods to serve, portion costs, good food combinations, special foods for special occasions, etc. The recommended daily dietary allowances should also be available. (See Table 5-1.) The menus of other facilities or those in foodservice publications can be used as guides, if changed to suit the specific needs of the facility.

Start planning a menu after first checking and listing carry-over items that may need to be used and then work these into the menu as early as possible. Keep in mind factors such as dietary needs, those who cannot feed themselves, etc. Figures 5-1 and 5-2 are check lists that can be helpful in menu planning.

Table 5-1–RECOMMENDED DAILY DIETARY ALLOWANCES

AGE AND SEX	Weight Kg. (lb)	Height cm. (in.)	Calories	Protein Gm.	Calcium Gm.	Iron mg.	Vitamin A I.U.	Thiamine mg.	Riboflavin mg.	Niacin mg.	Vitamin E I.U.	Vitamin C mg.
MEN												
25 years	65 (143)	170 (67)	2800	65	0.8	12	5000	1.6	1.7	18		60
45 years	65 (143)	170 (67)	2600	65	0.8	12	5000	1.5	1.7	17		60
65 years	65 (143)	170 (67)	2400	65	0.8	12	5000	1.3	1.7	14		60
WOMEN												
25 years	55 (121)	157 (62)	2000	55	0.8	12	5000	1.2	1.5	13		55
45 years	55 (121)	157 (62)	2000	55	0.8	12	5000	1.1	1.5	13		55
65 years	55 (121)	157 (62)	1700	55	0.8	12	5000	1.0	1.5	13		55
Pregnancy (3rd trimester)			Add 400	65	1.5	15	6000	1.5	1.8	15	400	60
Lactation (850 ml. milk daily)			Add 1000	75	2.0	15	8000	1.5	2.0	20	400	60
INFANTS												
1 to 3 months	6 (13)	60 (24)	Kg. x 120	Kg. x 3.5	0.6	6	1500	0.3	0.4	5	400	35
4 to 9 months	9 (20)	70 (28)	Kg. x 110	Kg. x 3.5	0.8	6	1500	0.4	0.5	7	400	35
10 months to 1 year	10 (22)	75 (30)	Kg. x 100	Kg. x 3.5	1.0	6	1500	0.5	0.6	8	400	35
1 to 3 years	12 (27)	87 (34)	1200	25	1.0	7	2000	0.6	0.7	8	400	40
4 to 6 years	18 (40)	109 (43)	1600	30	1.0	8	2500	0.8	0.8	11	400	40
7 to 9 years	27 (59)	129 (51)	2000	40	1.0	10	3500	1.0	1.2	15	400	40
BOYS												
10 to 12 years	35 (78)	144 (57)	2500	45	1.2	12	4500	1.3	1.3	17	400	40
13 to 15 years	49 (108)	163 (64)	3000	60	1.4	15	5000	1.4	1.5	18	400	55
16 to 20 years	63 (139)	175 (69)	2800	60	1.4	15	5000	1.4	1.6	18	400	60
GIRLS												
10 to 12 years	36 (79)	144 (57)	2300	50	1.2	12	4500	1.2	1.3	15	400	40
13 to 15 years	49 (108)	160 (63)	2400	55	1.3	15	5000	1.2	1.4	16	400	50
16 to 20 years	54 (120)	162 (64)	2200	55	1.3	15	5000	1.0	1.5	18	400	55

CHECK LIST FOR REGULAR MENUS

Referring to our Policy and Procedure on menu planning, check your menu for these items:

CLOSE YOUR EYES AND IMAGINE HOW EACH MEAL WILL APPEAR ON THE TABLE OR TRAY

		S	M	T	W	T	F	S
	If your answer is "Yes" to the question, mark in the box:							
1.	Is the menu suitable to our guests' age and condition?							
2.	Are foods planned according to our guests' eating habits?							
3.	Have you considered the climate and season?							
4.	Then check for contrast in:							
	A. Flavor:							
	i. Tart and sweet foods							
	ii. Mild and highly seasoned foods							
	iii. Light and heavy foods							
	iv. Acid and bland foods							
	v. Starchy foods (like corn and potatoes in one meal)							
	vi. Same type of flavors in same day							
	B. Color							
	C. Shape and form							
	D. Temperature							
	E. Texture							
	F. Method of preparation							
	G. Variety and did you have the same food on the same day a week ago?							
5.	Does the menu fit the way we serve our guests?							
6.	Is the menu planned for good distribution of labor required?							
	A. Planned for pre-preparation?							
	B. Will you have time to maintain our cleaning schedule?							
	C. Planned to use each cook's skills to best advantage?							
	D. Does it require too much last-minute preparation?							
7.	In planning for use of equipment, have you:							
	A. Enough oven space? Can you dovetail temperatures?							
	B. Enough refrigeration, such as room to defrost meats?							
	C. Enough range-top space?							
	D. Planned to use other equipment such as mixer, blender?							
	E. The correct cooking/serving containers and utensils?							

(cont.)

CHECK LIST FOR REGULAR MENUS (cont.)

If your answer is "Yes" to the question, mark in the box.

	S	M	T	W	T	F	S
8. What about the cost? Did you plan and think of:							
A. What portion-size you will use and what it costs?							
B. What is in season and most economical to use?							
C. What "convenience foods" are economical of labor and money?							
D. What "left-overs" could be incorporated?							
9. Will the food items needed be available in time for preparation?							
A. Do we have enough storage space for what we will need?							
10. Do we have recipes available? Does the cook have access to them?							
11. Did you include a new recipe once this week?							
12. Have you any special event or holiday this week? Plan for it?							
13. Have you filled out the Menu Planning Check List from the Oklahoma State Health Department to check the Basic Four? Attach it and this sheet to the back of this week's menu.							
14. Can this day's menu be easily modified for modified diets without an excessive amount of additional labor?							

Name of Facility _____ Written by _____

Date or Cycle of Menus _____ Menu conference with _____

Approved by _____

Date checked _____

Fig. 5-1. *The menu after checking against such a list will be far better planned than if menus are not checked by this or in a similar way. Courtesy Mrs. Iris Lochner, R. D., Food Systems Design, Oklahoma City, Okla.*

MENU PLANNING CHECK LIST

	S	M	T	W	T	F	S	Total

VEGETABLES AND FRUITS

Dark green or deep yellow vegetable or fruit or equivalent sources (e. g. liver) of vitamin A; 4 or more servings per week.

1 serving is equivalent to ½ c broccoli, chard, collards, cress, kale, spinach, turnip greens, or other dark green leaves, carrots, pumpkin, sweet potato, winter squash or five apricot halves or ½ medium cantaloupe.

Citrus fruit or equivalent sources of vitamin C; 1 serving per day. (Vitamin C cannot be stored – must be in diet every day.)

1 serving is equivalent to ½ grapefruit, 1 medium orange, ½ cantaloupe, ½ c strawberries or ½ c orange, grapefruit or blended orange and grapefruit juice.

½ serving is equivalent to 1 wedge honeydew, 1 tangerine or ½ c tangerine juice, ½ c tomato juice or cooked tomato, 1 medium raw tomato, ½ c broccoli, Brussels sprouts, raw cabbage, collards, kale, mustard greens, spinach or turnip greens.

Potato and other vegetables and fruits – 2 to 3 servings daily to make a total of four servings. With the above fruits and vegetables, should be distributed throughout the 3 meals.

1 serving is equivalent to ½ c of vegetable or fruit, or a usual serving such as one medium apple, banana, peach or potato.

MILK

Milk, fluid whole, skim, buttermilk or equivalent – 2 c daily for adults, 4 c daily for children.

½ c is equivalent to ¼ c undiluted evaporated milk, 2 T non-fat dry milk, *1 thick slice cheddar cheese, ½ c custard or milk pudding, 1 serving cream soup made with milk, 1 serving milk used on cereal.

¼ c milk is equivalent to ½ c ice cream, *1 thin slice cheddar cheese, *½ c cottage cheese.

(cont.)

MENU PLANNING CHECK LIST (cont.)

MEAT AND OTHER PROTEIN FOODS

Meat, poultry, fish or protein equivalent—5 oz (cooked weight) per day used in the dinner and supper.

1 oz is equivalent to 1 oz of lean beef, veal, lamb, pork, poultry, fish, seafood or variety meats such as liver, heart, or kidney, 1 frankfurter, 1 thick slice luncheon meat, *1 thick slice of cheese, *¼ c cottage cheese, ½ c dried beans or dried peas, 2 T peanut butter.

Eggs—4 or more per week.

BREAD AND CEREALS

Bread and cereals, whole grained or enriched—4 or more servings per day.

1 serving is equivalent to 1 slice of bread, 1 roll, muffin, or biscuit, 1 oz ready to eat cereal, ½ to ¾ c cooked cereal, cornmeal, grits, rice, macaroni, noodles or spaghetti.

OTHER FOODS

Butter or fortified margarine—3 or more t per day used as a spread or in cooking.

Is there meat or another protein food (above) in each dinner and supper?

Is there at least one serving of a fruit and/or vegetable in each meal?

*If serving of cheddar or cottage cheese is being counted as a milk equivalent, it should not also be counted as a meat equivalent.

Institution _____ Dates of Menus _____

Date checked _____ By _____

Fig. 5-2. *The above check list is recommended by the Oklahoma State Dept. of Health in checking menus.*

DIETARY REVIEW

Consultant Report

Patient _____

Diet Order _____

Date _____

Doctor _____

Method of Feeding _____

Dentures _____

Self-help feeding devices _____

Other Problems _____

19___	Weight	Action Taken/Comments/Suggestions	Professional Reviewer

Fig. 5-3. *The record maintained by the consultant on a resident's diet and other information of importance. Courtesy Mrs. Iris Lochner, R. D., Food Systems Design, Oklahoma City, Okla.*

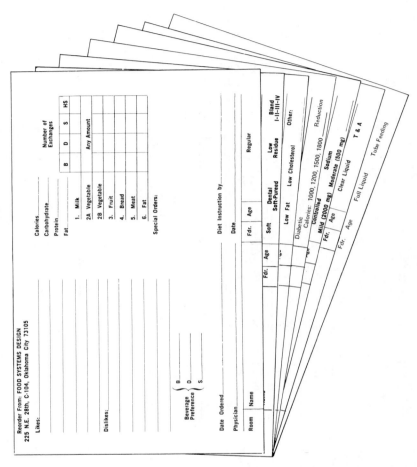

Fig. 5-4. *A group of diet cards maintained on residents. Each card is a different color. They are all alike except at the lower right hand corner where the type of diet is indicated. Some cards require that the specific type of diet be circled. Courtesy Mrs. Iris Lochner, Food Systems Design, Oklahoma City, Okla.*

THE MEAL PLAN   A menu is based on a meal plan which indicates the number of meals served per day and the types of foods served. The most normal meal plan is 3 meals a day with the heaviest meal at dinner. (See Table 5-2). In this plan about 25% of the day's calories come at breakfast, 33% at lunch and the remainder (42%) at dinner; or, the heavy meal, about 42% of the calories for the day, can be at noon with a light supper, 33% of the calories, served at night. If the supper is light, a snack may be served in the evening to reduce the long period between the light dinner and breakfast.

Table 5-2—THE 3-MEAL PLAN

Breakfast	**Lunch***	**Dinner**
Juice or fruit	Soup	Meat or main dish
Cereal and milk	Sandwich or protein food	Vegetables (2), one is
Egg, meat with toast	or substantial salad	frequently a potato
or coffee cake, hot	Bread, if not in sandwich	or other starchy
cakes, Danish pastry,	Margarine or butter	food
etc.	Dessert	Salad
Margarine or butter	Beverage	Bread
Beverage		Margarine or butter
		Dessert
(Jam, jelly, sirup or		Beverage
other additions can		
be made depending		
on the type of food		
served.)		

NOTE: About 25% of the calories are served at breakfast, 33% at noon and 42% at dinner. There is usually a 10-hr time span between breakfast and dinner.

*The foods on the lunch may be varied considerably; for instance, a light main dish could be substituted for the soup and sandwich.

A fairly heavy dinner is more usual in family meal patterns and residents are said to rest better and require less sedation if the heavy meals come late in the day.* However, some residents, such as those with cardiac problems, may do better if the heaviest meal is at noon. The nursing staff may also have more workers on at noon to handle the heavy meal than will be available later in the day.

Most residents, especially those coming from rural settings, will be used to fairly substantial breakfasts. Those with family backgrounds from northern Europe will eat a heavier breakfast than those who follow the light breakfast pattern of France, Spain and southern Europe. A diabetic may need more frequent feedings during the day than 3 meals, especially if he takes a long acting insulin. To give more meals we may use a 4-Meal or a 5-Meal plan depending upon the resident's needs. Residents may absorb nutrients better, have fewer digestive problems and feel better if they have lighter and more frequent meals.

In a 4-meal plan, a light continental breakfast is served around 7:00 am. About 10:30 am, a substantial brunch is served and at 3:30 pm, the main meal is served with a supper coming in the evening.

In the 5-meal plan, there is a continental breakfast around 7:00 am, a brunch about 10:00 am, a light snack about 12:30 or 1:00 pm, the main meal at 3:00 or 4:00 pm and a light snack sometime between 6:30 and 8:00 pm. These meal times may be varied. (See Tables 5-3 and 5-4).

Before a change is made to either a 4-meal or 5-meal plan, the medical and nursing staffs and others concerned should be consulted and the plan discussed *thoroughly*. Go over the timing of meals, type of foods to be served, advantages and disadvantages and what changes in routine will have to be made. Omit nothing. Be frank and candid. It is better to have open discussion with disagreement at this time than later when the plan goes into effect. A failure to completely cover all matters may cause the plan to fail.

Full support from all concerned must be secured. Management should strongly back the plan and indicate its backing to the facility. If support is not gained from all quarters, the plan should be dropped. These plans fail in-

---

*This pattern may be changing; we are becoming used to the mid-morning and mid-afternoon coffee break and a TV snack in the evening giving us a 6- rather than a 3-meal a day schedule.

Table 5-3—THE 4-MEAL PLAN

Breakfast	Brunch	Main Meal	Supper*
Juice or fruit	Main dish	Main dish	Soup
Cereal and milk	Vegetable	Vegetables (2),	½ Sandwich
Bread item	Salad	1 starchy	Dessert
Margarine or butter	Bread	Salad	Beverage
Beverage	Margarine or butter	Bread	
		Margarine or butter	
		Beverage	
		Dessert	

EXAMPLE OF 4-MEAL PLAN

Orange juice	Creamed chicken omelet	Lamb fricassee with dumpling	Cream of potato soup
Bran flakes and raisins	Carrots, buttered	Minted fresh peas	Toasted cheese and ham sandwich (½)
Milk	Diced tomatoes with French dressing	Orange gelatin salad, mayonnaise	Baked apple
Butterhorn	Bread	Whole wheat bread	Milk
Coffee, cream and sugar	Margarine	Margarine	
	Milk	Tea with lemon	

*The foods on the supper may be varied considerably; for instance, a light main dish could be substituted for the soup and sandwich.

Table 5-4—THE 5-MEAL PLAN

Breakfast	Brunch	Dinner	Supper	Evening Snack
Juice or fruit	Main dish	Main dish	Soup	Sandwich or Pastry
Cereal and milk	Vegetable	2 vegetables	Dessert	Beverage
Bread item	Bread	Salad	Beverage	
Margarine or butter	Margarine or butter	Bread		
Beverage	Beverage	Margarine or butter		
		Dessert		
		Beverage		

EXAMPLE OF 5-MEAL PLAN

Breakfast	Brunch	Dinner	Supper	Evening Snack
Tomato juice	Ham fondue	Grilled cube steak	Vegetable-rice soup	Graham crackers
Farina and milk	Hash brown potatoes	Corn pudding	Crackers	Fresh apple
Cinnamon rolls	Toast and jelly	Glazed carrots	Melon cup	Milk
Margarine	Margarine	Cole slaw, boiled dressing		
Coffee	Coffee or milk	Raspberry tapioca cream pudding		
		Iced tea with lemon		

frequently, but, if they do, one of the most common causes of failure is inadequate planning or a failure to gain full support from the staff. Support should come not only in planning but heavily in the early stages of implementation.

Changes in the routines of the nursing and the medical staff may be required but once made are liked. Doctors find they can make early rounds without interfering with breakfast. Early morning care is also not disturbed and afterwards the resident can have a substantial meal and not a snack. Some residents may wish to sleep longer and not eat as early. Yet, when they awaken, they want a substantial meal. With the 4-meal or 5-meal plan this can be done. While the nursing staff may have to pass more meal trays, they will have less nourishments to give. While it is thought that residents may not like the plan because it changes eating patterns, experience shows that where the plan is well set up beforehand and implemented well, residents do not object. One group of small nursing homes on the 5-meal plan had only one complaint in five years. If the plan is implemented, a cereal, frequently hot, should be given with breakfast. If it is not, then no matter what is served, it is not breakfast for many.

Besides being better for the residents, these plans help the foodservice department. Only one shift is needed to prepare cooked meals; a skeleton crew can prepare the early morning and late evening menus. The use of paper goods increases. It has also been found that more sugar and fat are consumed because sweet rolls, cookies, cakes or similar items may be served more frequently for breakfast or late snacks. Placing a toaster on a snack cart and making toast close to the room can help to reduce the frequency of serving richer bread products. If the caloric content is not watched with these plans, residents may gain more weight than desirable.

**VARIETY AND INTEREST
IN MENU OFFERINGS**

Most residents in extended care facilities are there for a long term. This makes it necessary to plan meals differently than for those who may be in an acute care unit. Manu planners must introduce enough variety and interest to avoid a feeling of monotony and repetition, but not too much variety and interest.

Most residents will have rather limited food experiences and prefer old favorites, providing they do not come too often. They usually lack a desire to explore. Something new to them may be an old favorite dressed in a new form. Nevertheless, a menu should offer a new food occasionally. Never put two new foods on the menu on the same meal or even on the same day—perhaps not in the same week.

Introducing variety is not a matter of serving foods out of season. Variety can also be obtained by using contrasts of color, flavor, textures, temperatures and form. Originality tempered with judgment produces variety. Menu terms can help sell foods but if the resident does not see the menu, then one has to merchandise with tray presentation, excellent food and special touches.

If there is a fairly large ambulatory population that can participate in some social activities, blend the menu in with these. For instance, have a luncheon club or dinner club menu once a month. Let them play bridge or pinochle afterwards. Or, have hobby activities. The social director, by enlisting some local talent, can have a cabaret after the dinner. A square dance or an indoor picnic can be good fun. Interest in a social event coupled with food not only raises the acceptability of the food at that time but at other times.

Menu Guides

If the planner uses guides as reminders, the menu may be better planned. Some guides are merely lists of foods for the recall of kinds of entrees, salads, desserts, vegetables, etc. Another type may indicate preferences in order of rank. A list indicating the frequency for serving some dishes is also helpful. (See Tables 5-5 and 5-6).

Table 5-5—FOOD PREFERENCE LIST
(in order of preference)

Entrees

Roast chicken	Meat or chicken pies	Macaroni or spaghetti dishes
Roast beef	Stews	Hot meat sandwiches
Fried chicken	Fricassees	Stuffed peppers
Baked ham	Creamed meat dishes	Croquettes
Pork chops	Meat loaf	Chop suey or chow mein
Roast lamb	Liver	Ravioli
Roast veal	Meat patties	Hot dogs
Roast pork	Fried fish	Sweetbreads

Vegetables and Starchy Foods

Green beans	Spinach	Artichokes
Carrots	Squash, winter	Eggplant
Peas	Broccoli	Whole kernel corn
Rice	Stewed tomatoes	Onions
Potatoes	Cabbage	Succotash
Asparagus	Cauliflower	Brussels sprouts
Beets	Creamed corn	Parsnips
Fresh tomatoes	Lima beans	Turnips
Mixed vegetables	Succotash	Dried beans

Salads

Molded gelatin or aspic	Fresh fruit	Mixed vegetable
Cottage cheese and fruit	Canned fruit	Carrot and raisin or date
Potato	Tomato	Cole slaw
	Seafood	Red bean and onion
	Fresh green	

Soups

Chicken noodle	Thick vegetable	Broths
Beef rice	Cream of tomato	Cream soups

The above list was adapted from one used by Mannings, Inc. in a foodservice operated in a nursing home.

Table 5-6—FREQUENCY SELECTION GUIDE

Meal	Times/ week	Possible Selections
BREAKFAST		
*Fruit or juice**		
Citrus	3	Tangerine, orange, grapefruit, etc. or their blends
Tomato juice	1	Or blends high in tomato; serve two times per week and one less citrus, if desired
Other juices	1	Apricot, pineapple, apple, grape, prune, carrot, etc.
Stewed, fresh, canned or frozen fruit	2	Prunes, plums, pears, pineapple, berries, peaches, bananas, applesauce, mixed fruit, melon, papaya, apricots, etc.
Cereals		
Dry	3	Cornflakes, wheat flakes, puffed, etc.
Hot or cooked	4	Farina, oatmeal, cornmeal, cracked wheat, rice, etc.
Main dishes		
Egg, one	3	Poached, fried, scrambled, shirred, French toast, etc.
Bacon, two	1	Use Canadian bacon or ham occasionally, if cost permits
Sausage, 2 oz	1	For alternates, use hash, creamed chipped beef, etc.
Hot cakes (2)	1	Alternates can be buckwheat cakes, cornmeal, etc.
Other hot breads	1	Coffee cake, muffins, sweet rolls, etc.
Beverages		
Coffee	ad lib	
Tea	ad lib	Try iced tea occasionally
Lemonade or punch		Introduce these for variety, to increase fluid intake and to increase ascorbic acid intake
Milk	7	For beverage but also use non-fat dry milk for cooking, cocoa, etc.

*A serving would be 4 oz juice, half grapefruit or 1/3 c, etc.

Meal	Times/ week	Possible Selections
BREAKFAST (cont.)		
Breads		
Toast (2 slices)	4	Use variety breads; serve with butter or margarine
Biscuits (2)	2	Vary these with orange, cheese or other biscuits
Other bread	1	Cornbread, Sally Lunn, steamed breads, etc.
LUNCH MAIN DISHES		
Soups (1 c)	2 to 4	Vary between cream, chowder, mixed vegetable, broth, etc.
Entree (4-6 oz)	2	Creamed tuna, macaroni and cheese, creole lima beans, chicken or turkey and noodles, baked beans, cold plates, hot meat sandwich, croquettes, etc.
Sandwich	2 to 4	Combine soup or salad; if alone, make it substantial; vary by using open-face, hot dog, hamburger, toasted or grilled, etc.
Salads	2 to 4	Fruit or gelatin, lettuce and tomato, cottage cheese, mixed vegetable, tossed green, radishes, vegetable stocks, cooked vegetable, potato, carrot and nut, Waldorf or more substantial ones with meat, etc.
OTHER LUNCH FOODS		
Vegetables	2	Use to complete nutritional needs, to accompany entrees or otherwise complete a meal; consult dinner vegetable list
Desserts	3	Cookies, bars, cake, puddings (cream, fruit, gelatin, etc.) custards, bread pudding
Fruit	3	Canned, frozen, fresh or dried

(cont.)

Table 5-6–FREQUENCY SELECTION GUIDE (cont.)

Meal	Times/ week	Possible Selections
OTHER LUNCH FOODS (cont.)		
Frozen dessert	1	Ice cream, sherbet, iced milk, etc.
Beverages	7	Use breakfast list; allow for substitutes, as yoghurt, buttermilk, eggnog, etc.
Bread and spread	7	Omit if sandwich served; ½ to 1 slice/portion; all cereal products should be whole grain or enriched
DINNER MAIN DISHES		
Meat (3 oz)*		
Beef	2	Pot roast, Swiss steak, braised ribs, cube steak, ground, hash, boiled, meat loaf, pot pie, meat balls, stew, etc.
Lamb or veal	1	Chop, cutlet, roast, stew, patty, etc.
Chicken or turkey	1	Roast, fried, a la King, pot pie, hash, croquettes, etc.
Pork or ham	1	Chop, roast or baked, cutlet, creamed, a la King, croquettes, ham loaf, curried, etc.
Fish	1	Poached, fried, creamed, baked, a la King, loaf, etc.
Extender dish	1	Meat and noodles, beans, macaroni products, omelet, cheese dishes, tamale pie, chili con carne, weiners and sauerkraut, creamed meats, eggs, chop suey or chow mein, etc.
OTHER DINNER FOODS		
Potatoes or Starchy Foods		
Potatoes (4 oz)	5	Mashed, steamed, boiled, riced, escalloped, au gratin, baked, French fried, American (raw) fried, hash browns, cakes, creamed, etc.
Rice, macaroni, etc.	2	Use appropriately with the main dish

Meal	Times/ week	Possible Selections
OTHER DINNER FOODS (cont.)		
Vegetables (½ c)	7	Creamed corn, kernel corn, carrots, turnips, rutabagas, kohlrabi, egg-plant, tomatoes, tomatoes and egg-plant, creamed vegetables, fried or boiled or creamed onions, sauer-kraut, dandelion, turnip, spinach, kale or other greens, peas, beans, cabbage, red cabbage and apples, stewed celery, winter or summer squash, okra, beets, hominy, salsi-fy, asparagus, broccoli, Brussels sprouts, parsnips, etc.; vary between canned, fresh, frozen or dried; vary preparation also
Salads (½ to ¾ c)	7	Vary from gelatin, fruit, vegetable, etc.
Desserts	4	Use lunch list but add baked fruit, whips, bettys, cobblers, regular and deep dish pies, steamed puddings, shortcakes, crisps, etc.
Fruit	2	Fresh, stewed, frozen or canned
Frozen	1 or 2	Ices, sherbets, ice cream; if served twice, delete one dessert in the week
Bread and spread	7	Variety breads, 1 or 2 slices, or rolls or biscuits
Miscellaneous	ad lib	At times introduce a fruit cup, cock-tail, canape, soup or juice and omit vegetable or salad.

---

*Substitute liver or organ meats occasionally. Do not rigidly follow any plan such as the one outlined here. For instance, for a Sunday supper have French toast and sausage, or for other dinners, try hot cakes filled with hot apple-sauce and topped with sour cream. Variations such as this break monotony.

MENU PLANNING PROCEDURES   In planning menus, main
dish items should be se-
lected first and then other foods which complement them. Traditional combinations may be followed; applesauce goes well with pork because it is tart
which helps to mask the fattiness of pork; mint sauce or a grilled pineapple
ring helps tone down the strong flavor of lamb; cranberries help to soften the
sulfury, pungent flavor of turkey.

Contrasts are good, providing they are not shocking. Flavor contrasts
should be carefully made; blend bland flavors with strong; tart, with sweet;
bitter, with mild. A strong meat or vegetable should be complemented with
mild flavored foods.

Modification of flavor is also good, such as mashing rutabagas and Irish
potatoes together. A cream sauce masks the flavor of a strong vegetable. Do
not use a vegetable from the onion family and one from the cabbage family
at the same meal. They are both strongly flavored products.

Color contrasts can increase acceptability. Avoid an all-white plate of
foods or an all-brown group of foods. Gain color through the use of a variety
of colored fruits and vegetables selected because of their color contribution.

Textures are also important. They are responsible for the heaviness or
lightness of the foods presented. For best effect, a heavy soup should be followed by a light entree and dessert. Heavy dinners can be started with a light
broth. Contrasting soft with crisp foods gives a desirable texture contrast. In
an extended care facility, many soft foods must be served but a crisp cracker
or toast, or some other food that can be masticated but gives a sense of crispness, should be used. Salads can give a crisp quality and lettuce can be included on many soft diets.

The serving of foods of similar texture at the same meal should be
avoided. For instance, perhaps a gravy should be avoided when a creamed
vegetable is on the menu.

Plan for contrast in temperatures and form of foods to be served. A
plate of food looks more attractive if all the foods on it have different shapes
and forms. Try also to achieve a difference in the height of foods on the plate.
Even on a cafeteria counter doing this can assist in giving a feeling of difference.

Keep meals simple; a meal with a lot of items tends to confuse residents.

When they developed their food tastes and habits, food patterns were different, so don't be bothered if they do not like the same foods you do. Work within their limitations.

These individuals usually had a better diet than we have. A survey of nutritional deficiencies in American diets in 1955 and 1965 indicated that, in spite of higher incomes, we ate more poorly in 1965 than in 1955. In 1938, our diets averaged about 35% of calories from fats; today, it is 45% or more. And, while they may have consumed more carbohydrates and less vegetables and fruits, they also consumed less sugars.

COST In menu planning the costs must be worked out, just as the required nutrients are. It is usually recommended that low cost menus follow the low cost food plans of the USDA; these plans were discussed under budgeting in Chapter 3. The quantities of food allowed in these plans assure nutritional adequacy for either economy, moderate or liberal menu plans.

Establish as a guide an allowed cost per resident per year, per month, per week, per day, per meal or per menu item as needed. Table 5-7 indicates how a guide may be set up to indicate the approximate costs of some items. Similar lists can be prepared for vegetables, desserts, etc. However, it is necessary to vary from this to achieve a good menu. A meal or portion costing more than the average can be adjusted by adding one costing less. It is much more important that a menu planner know the cost per portion than the cost per pound.

Menu Cost Control

It is important to start planning the menu by selecting the most expensive main items for the main meals for the period. If Pot Roast of Beef on Sunday, Baked Pork Chops on Wednesday and Broiled Red Snapper on Friday average out 25¢ per item, select four lesser cost items for the remaining dinners such as Hamburger Stroganoff with Noodles (15¢), Baked Cheese and Tomato Omelet (14¢), Ham a la King on Cornbread (15¢) and Roast Beef Hash (17¢); this will bring the average cost per dinner entree to slightly less than 20¢. If your limit is 20¢, then you've made it.

Next, select the most expensive main dishes for the second heaviest meal, similarly balancing them with less expensive ones and checking their suitability with the items selected previously for the main meals. After this, select the most expensive main items for breakfasts, averaging costs and mak-

Table 5-7—ENTREE COST LIST

6¢ or less	7 to 8¢	9 to 12¢
Shirred egg	Shepherd's pie	Lamb fricassee,
Carrot and weiner slices	Stuffed cabbage roll	dumplings
in tomato sauce	Italian spaghetti	Baked chicken livers
Scrambled eggs and ham	Fish croquettes	Fish sticks (2) or
Baked rice and cheese	Ravioli	poached cod
Creamed eggs and ham	Chicken croquettes	Stuffed frankfurter
Creamed codfish and peas	Fish or turkey croquettes	Weiners and kraut
Egg cutlet	Chop suey or chow mein	Cold cuts, two slices
Chicken giblet pie	Fish stew	Beef hash
Welsh rarebit	Baked beans and weiners	Meat loaf
Macaroni and cheese	Cheese souffle	Stuffed peppers
Macaroni, bacon and	Baked cheese and	Hamburger steak
tomato casserole	tomato omelet	Salisbury steak
Spanish rice	Tuna pie	Spaghetti, meat balls
Tuna fish a la King	Ham and eggs a la King	Lasagne and meat
Poached egg	Chili con carne	Lamb patty
Cottage cheese loaf	Hamburger and noodles	Sausage patties
Vegetable plate	Baked chicken and rice	Chicken or turkey and
Vegetable pie		noodles
		Baked heart and dressing
		Beef hamburger stew

13 to 16¢	16 to 20¢	21 to 25¢
Fried cod	Swiss steak	Roast beef
Fish sticks (3)	Pork chop	Roast pork
Beef or lamb stew	Baked ham	Roast veal
Braised or baked liver	Cube steak	Roast leg of lamb
Beef stroganoff	Pot roast	Small sirloin steak
Beef pie	Roast turkey	(tenderized)
Fried chicken	Braised shortribs	Veal steak
Chicken fricassee	Boiled beef	Veal cutlet
Creamed ham and	Roast shoulder lamb	Ham steak
mushrooms	Braised beef tips	
Boiled fresh or cured	Shish-kabob	
tongue	Cornbeef and cabbage	
Shoulder pork or lamb	Boiled dinner	
chops		
Turkey-broccoli casserole		
Beef bird		
Breaded pork steak		

NOTE: These are 1969 prices. Prices will also vary according to regions. Use this list as an example only, compiling your own costs from your recipes.

ing sure that the selections go with the other items that have been chosen.

The planner can then go back and select the foods that go best with the main dishes. Skill, knowledge and experience is required to do this well. Compromises must be made between costs, nutritional requirements and acceptability in meeting all the requirements. After all meals have been completed, recheck costs. Such a check might appear for one day:

Breakfast		**Lunch**		**Dinner**	
Applesauce	5¢	Cream of tomato		Creamed chicken in	
Fried cornmeal mush	3¢	soup	6¢	nest of mashed	
Sausage patty	7¢	Crackers (2)	½c	potatoes	16¼¢
Sirup	2¢	Peanut butter and		Broccoli, lemon	
Margarine	½¢	banana sandwich		butter	4½¢
Cocoa or milk	4¢	with bacon-		Cranberry-nut	
Coffee	2½¢	flavored soy bits	4½¢	muffin	4¢
		Custard cup	6¢	Margarine	½¢
		Tea with lemon	2¢	Molded cottage	
				cheese, diced	
				orange salad,	
				mayonnaise	6¢
				Chocolate ice	
				cream	5¢
				Tea or lemonade	2¢
Total	23¢		19¢		38¼¢

Total cost for day 80¼¢; budgeted, 85¢.

It is wise to be under the budgeted amount because somehow costs always go higher. Note that in the example given, milk is served only once, to reduce costs, but the diet is high in milk solids used in cooking. This menu is purposely soft and even the nuts may have to be left out of the muffins for some. The broccoli also might have to be minced. Many frozen minced or chopped vegetables are available.

Market Prices

The planner should keep market prices in mind. There are certain times when foods are less costly than others. For instance, the following are usually highest and lowest in price at these times:

Food Item	**High in Price**	**Low in Price**
Eggs	Aug—Nov	Feb—June
Turkeys	July—Aug	Nov—Feb
Beef	July—Sept	Dec—Apr
Pork	June—Sept	Oct—May
Fish	Oct—Nov	Apr—Sept

Prices differ according to geographic area and also according to market conditions. It is not unusual to see prices for some foods high when they should be at their lowest in price. For instance, a heavy freeze in Florida during the height of the citrus season may mean high prices when normally they are low. The USDA publishes a list of plentiful foods for a given period in newspapers and trade journals; you can also subscribe to it at no cost.

Labor and Equipment

To control costs, one must watch that menu items do not take too much labor and that work is simplified. Pot Roast on Sunday can be cooked in sufficient quantity for hot beef sandwiches on Tuesday if it is stored properly. A balance in equipment use should be achieved; some equipment should not be overloaded and other pieces not used.

Most small health facilities operate on limited funds. Many patients or residents will have modest incomes. Cost of health care is a big problem to them and also to the facility. Economy must be practiced and this text has been written from that standpoint. Table 5-8 indicates the approximate types and amounts of food to serve each day.

There are some facilities, however, that have residents who are able to afford a more expensive standard of living and such individuals, even though they reside in a facility which attempts to meet the standard they can afford, may not be the most easy to care for. Aging and ill health are no respectors of incomes and these individuals frequently need as much care as those who have less money.

Having an adequate income is no assurance one will have used it to maintain a high standard of life. Instead, it may prove to be a factor in helping to bring about poorer health; investigations have shown that high income families often eat more poorly from a nutritional standpoint than those with moderate or low incomes. They may eat richer foods and fewer protective foods. Many people in these circumstances will have to reduce in body weight when they enter the facility. They also may not be amenable to other dietary restrictions; since they have had what they wanted all their lives and feel they have the money to afford what they want in old age, they may not be willing to modify their wants and many, from all levels of income have known nothing but poorly prepared food all their lives. A lifetime habit of eating unpalatable, overcooked food can increase considerably the problem of gaining acceptance for good nourishing food.

Table 5-8–DAILY RECOMMENDED AMOUNTS OF FOOD
(approximately 1800 calories)

Food Group	Amount/Day	Approximate Equivalents	Good Sources of	
Milk	1 pt (2 c)	1 pt liquid, 1 pt buttermilk, 1 c evaporated, 2/3 c non-fat dry instant, 1-1/2 lb cottage cheese, 3 c ice cream or frozen dessert containing milk, 3 oz cheddar type cheese	Protein, Vitamin A, Thiamine, Vitamin D	Riboflavin, Calcium, Phosphorus
Meat and Egg*	5 4-oz portions, clean, cooked meat	A portion is 4 oz cooked meat, fish, poultry or 1 medium egg; 1 oz cheddar-type cheese or 1/4 c cottage cheese; beans or other legumes may be a substitute occasionally.	Protein, Iron, Iodine (fish)	Vitamin A, Thiamine, Riboflavin, Other B-complex vitamins
Vegetable and Fruit	6 portions, 1/2 c each	Dark green or deep yellow vegetable every other day; citrus or equivalent daily; remainder other vegetables or fruits	Carbohydrates, Vitamin A, Thiamine, Iron	Vitamin C, Riboflavin, Calcium
Bread, Cereal, Potato or Legume	6 portions	Portion equals: 1 slice bread, 5 saltines (2 in. sq) 1/2 c cooked cereal, 3/4 c dry cereal, 1/2 c cooked rice or macaroni product, 4 oz white potato, 2 oz (1/4 c) sweet potato; 1/2 c corn, cooked dried beans or other legume; if additional meat portion added, deduct one from this group	Carbohydrates, Vitamin A, Riboflavin, Calcium	Protein, Thiamine, Vitamin C, Iron
Fats and Sweets**	1T (3 t) fat; 1 T sugar, jam, jelly, etc.	Butter, margarine, oil or shortening for fats; sweets may also be puddings, cakes, cookies or frozen desserts	Fats, Carbohydrates	Vitamin A and D in butter or margarine

*If more meat or egg is desired, add another portion and deduct a portion from the bread, cereal, potato or legume group; use fortified or whole grain cereals. Serve eggs three times a week.

**The amounts in this row allow for 250 calories approx.; if additional calories can be added, these foods may be increased. The protein should be supplemented with meat, fish, poultry, eggs or milk products.

If the rules of the game are followed as outlined in this text, a low cost menu will be every bit as adequate nutritionally as one planned on a more liberal budget and also will be nearly as acceptable. It may be easier to plan a low cost menu that is adequate nutritionally than a more liberal one because some restrictions help, rather than hinder, the planning of balanced meals. Menu planners may be challenged in planning higher cost meals that must meet dietary restraints because so many foods they could use may not be allowed.

A table for a liberal diabetic diet is presented in the Appendix. It does not consider cost but follows fairly well the dietary restrictions for a diabetic who responds fairly well to drug supplements for the diabetic condition.

MODIFIED DIET PLANNING*   All modified diets should be based as much as possible on the general menu for the facility. Five or six modified diets will usually be required: 1) calorie and carbohydrate restriction for the diabetic or just calorie restriction for a weight-reduction diet; 2) fat restriction; 3) sodium restriction; 4) soft, bland or mechanically soft; and for some facilities, 5) low fiber and 6) liquid. The diet manual of the facility may contain other diets which will occasionally be needed. When a diet is prescribed, it should be followed closely just as an order for medication is followed.

Use a 12 x 17 in. sheet of paper divided into columns for each of the diets that must be planned plus an additional column. Write the general menu in the first column. In the second column, plan the diabetic and low calorie diets. In the next, put the low fat diet, then the low sodium, next the soft, bland or mechanically soft, using the remaining columns for the other diets that must be planned. If a different order is desired, it can be set up to suit the need. Always work into each diet from the general menu, making as few changes as possible.

Another method used in planning modified diets is to put the general diet for a day in the first column and then put the various diets in rows beneath it. Tables 5-9 and 5-11 show this method and Table 5-10 shows the first method described.

_____

*See also Chapter IV.

Table 5-9 —GENERAL AND MODIFIED DIETS

Breakfast	Lunch	Dinner	Mid-morn snack	Evening snack	Type diet
Prune j	Cr chicken	Cube steak	None	None	Normal
Oatmeal	Rice	M potatoes			
Milk, 4 oz	Sli toms	Gravy			
Scr eggs	Fr Dr	But spinach			
Toast (2)	Bread and	Let and may			
Marg	marg	Roll, marg			
Coffee	Fruit cup	Slic oranges			
	Milk	Vanilla wafer			
		Milk			
Tom j	Same as	Cube steak	non-fat	milk shake	Diabetic
Oatmeal	normal,	Spinach	milk		or low-
	no marg	Carrots			cal
		Let, plain			

Table 5-10 –GENERAL AND MODIFIED DIETS

Normal	Diabetic Low-cal	Low fat	Low Sodium	Soft, etc.	Low residue	Liquid
BREAKFAST:						
Prune j	Tom juice	Prune j	Prune j	Prune j	Tomato j	Prune j
Oatmeal	Same	Same	Salt free	Strained	Strained	Gruel
Milk, 4 oz	Same	Low-fat	Milk, 4 oz	Milk, 4 oz	Milk, 4 oz	Milk
Scr eggs	Same	Minced veal	No salt	Scr eggs	Scr eggs	Hi-cal eggnog
Toast (2)	Same	Toast	Salt free	Toast (2)	Toast (2)	
Margarine	Omit	Omit	Salt free	Margarine	Margarine	
Coffee	Same	Same	Coffee	Coffee	Coffee	
LUNCH:						
Cr chicken	Same	Sliced chix	Salt free	Cr chicken	Same	Hi-pro drink
Rice	Same	Same	Saft free	Rice	Rice	Tomato j
Sli toms	Same	Same	Sli toms	Stewed tom	Pureed beets	Soft ice cream
Fr Dr	No-cal Fr Dr	No-cal Fr Dr	Fr Dr, SF			with marsh-
Roll, marg	No marg	Roll, no marg	Salt free	Roll, marg	Roll, marg	mallow sauce
Fruit cup	Same	Same	Same	Baked apple*	Baked apple*	
Milk	Low-fat	Low-fat	Milk	Milk	Milk	Milk

Morning snack for diabetics, low calorie, low fat, soft and liquid diets: 8 oz non-fat milk. Evening snack for diabetics: milk shake; low sodium: orange juice; liquid: orange juice. Many diabetic diets could include margarine or butter, if not low-calorie. *No peel.

(cont.)

Normal	Diabetic- Low-cal	Low fat	Low Sodium	Soft, etc.	Low residue	Liquid
DINNER:						
Cube steak	Same	Poached cod	Salt free	Broiled hamb	Broiled hamb	Hi-pro pine-apple milk shake
M potatoes	Carrots	M potatoes	Salt free	M potatoes	M potatoes	Orange j
Gravy	Omit	Carrots	Salt free	Gravy	Gravy	
But Spinach	No butter	No butter	Salt free	Chopped	Pureed Spin.	
Lettuce, may	No-cal Dr	No-cal Dr	Fr Dr, SF	Same**	Same**	
Rolls, marg	Roll (1)	No marg	Salt free	Same	Same	
Sli orange	Same	Sli orange	Sli orange	Orange sherbet	Orange sherbet	
Milk	Low-fat	Low-fat	Milk	Milk	Milk	

Evening snack for diabetics: milk shake; low sodium: orange juice; liquid: orange juice. Many diabetics could include margarine or butter, if not low calorie.

**Pear and cottage cheese salad for those who cannot tolerate lettuce.

Table 5-11 –MODIFIED DIETS FROM A GENERAL MENU

General Diet

SUNDAY

BREAKFAST
Baked half apple stuffed with dates
Farina, (1/2 c)
Milk, 4 oz
Poached egg
Toast (2)
Margarine or butter (2)
Strawberry jam, 2 T
Coffee or tea
Sugar and cream

LUNCH
Vegetable soup, 6 oz
Crackers (2)
Chicken a la King, 6 oz, on steamed brown rice (1/2 c)
Diced pear in lime gelatin salad, 1/3 c, on chopped lettuce, mayonnaise, 1 T
Bread (1)
Butter or margarine (1)
Prune whip, 1/2 c, custard sauce, 2 T
Milk, coffee or tea
Sugar and cream

DINNER
Hot or cold spiced tomato juice, 4 oz, lemon wedge
Poached cod, 4 oz, caper sauce, 2 T
Boiled potato, med, buttered
Mixed green peas and chopped new green cabbage, buttered, 1/2 c
Carrot-raisin salad, 1/2 c, boiled dressing, 1 T
Hot rolls (2)
Butter or margarine (2)
Ice cream, 4 oz
Coffee, tea or milk
Sugar and cream

Diabetic Low Carbohydrate–Moderate Reducing Diet (1500 cal)

Applesauce, dietetic
Farina, 1/2 c
Milk, 4 oz
Poached egg
Toast (1)
Coffee or tea with evaporated milk, if desired

Vegetable soup, 6 oz, FF
Cracker (1)
Minced chicken, 1/2 c, on steamed brown rice, 1/2 c
Low-cal pears in low-cal lime gelatin (1/3 c) on chopped lettuce
Bread (1)
Fresh orange sections, 1/2 c
Milk, coffee or tea
Evaporated milk, if desired for coffee

Hot or cold spiced tomato juice, 4 oz, lemon wedge
Poached cod, 3 oz, capers only, 1 T
Boiled yellow summer squash
Mixed green peas and chopped new green cabbage, FF, 1/2 c
Carrot salad, 1/2 c, low-cal dressing, 1 T
Hot roll (1)
Butter or margarine (1)
Canteloupe or sliced bananas
Milk, coffee or tea
Evaporated milk, if desired

Low Fat (50 gram) or Low Cholesterol

BREAKFAST
Baked half apple stuffed with dates
Farina, 1/2 c
Non-fat milk, 4 oz
Poached egg or soya ham hash
Toast (2)
Coffee or tea, low fat enrichener, if desired

LUNCH
Vegetable soup, 6 oz, no fat
Crackers (2)
Broiled chicken breast, 6 oz on steamed brown rice, 1/2 c
Diced pear salad, etc., low fat dressing
Bread (2)
Fresh orange sections, 1/2 c
Milk, coffee or tea, low fat enrichener, if desired

DINNER
Hot or cold spiced tomato juice, 4 oz, lemon wedge
Poached cod, 4 oz, capers only, 1 T
Boiled potato, medium
Mixed green peas and chopped new cabbage, 1/2 c*
Carrot-raisin salad, low-cal dressing, 1 T
Hot rolls (2)
Fresh cantaloupe or sliced bananas
Coffee, tea or non-fat milk, low fat enrichener, if desired

Mechanically Soft Diet

Pared half apple stuffed with dates and baked
Farina, 1/2 c
Milk, 4 oz
Poached egg
Toast (2)
Butter or margarine (2)
Coffee or tea
Sugar and cream

Pureed vegetable soup, 6 oz
Crackers (2)
Chicken a la King, 6 oz on steamed brown rice, 1/2 c
Diced pear in lime gelatin, 1/3 c, on chopped lettuce, mayonnaise, 1 T
Bread (1)
Butter or margarine (2)
Prune whip, 1/2 c, custard sauce, 2 T
Milk, coffee or tea
Sugar and cream

Hot or cold tomato juice, 4 oz, lemon wedge
Poached cod, 4 oz, caper sauce, 2 T
Boiled potato, med, buttered
Mixed green peas and chopped new cabbage, buttered
String bean salad, Fr Dressing
Hot rolls (2)
Butter or margarine (2)
Ice cream
Coffee, tea or milk
Sugar and cream

*Substitute with boiled yellow summer squash or plain peas for cardiacs.

(cont.)

Table 5-11—MODIFIED DIETS FROM A GENERAL MENU (cont.)

SUNDAY (cont.)

Soft, Bland or Moderate Low Fiber Diet

BREAKFAST
Applesauce or orange juice
Farina, 1/2 c
Milk, 4 oz
Poached egg
Toast or bread (2)
Butter or margarine (2)
Coffee or tea**
Sugar and cream

LUNCH
Pureed vegetable soup or cream of tomato
  soup, 6 oz
Crackers (2)
Creamed chicken, 6 oz on steamed
  white rice, 1/2 c
Pureed pear in lime gelatin, 1/3 c,
  mayonnaise, 1 T
Bread (1)
Pureed prune pudding, 1/2 c, custard
  sauce, 2 T
Milk, coffee or tea**
Sugar and cream

DINNER
Tomato or apricot juice, 4 oz
Poached cod, 4 oz, lemon butter
Mashed or boiled potato, 5 oz, buttered
Green peas or yellow summer squash,
  buttered***
String bean salad, Fr Dressing or peach and
  cottage cheese, mayonnaise, 1 T
Hot rolls (2)
Butter or margarine (2)
Ice cream
Milk, coffee or tea**

1500 Calorie–Low Sodium Diet (1 gram sodium)

Baked half apple stuffed with dates
Farina, low salt, 1/2 c
Non-fat milk, 4 oz
Poached egg, SF
Toast (1)
SF butter or margarine (1)
Coffee or tea
Sugar and low-cal milk
  for tea or coffee

SF vegetable soup, 6 oz, FF
SF crackers (2)
Minced SF chicken, 1/2 c, on SF steamed
  brown rice, 1/2 c
Diced pear salad, SF dressing on
  lettuce bed
Bread (1)
Fresh orange sections, 1/2 c
Non-fat milk, coffee or tea
Sugar and low-cal milk for tea or coffee

Hot or cold spiced tomato juice, 4 oz, lemon
  wedge
SF poached cod, 3 oz, plain capers
SF mixed green peas and chopped new green
  cabbage, 1/2 c
SF boiled yellow summer squash
Carrot-raisin salad, low-cal dressing, 1 T
Hot roll (1)
SF margarine or butter (1)
Canteloupe or sliced bananas
Milk, coffee or tea
Sugar and low-cal milk for tea or coffee

**tea or coffee must be allowed by doctor
***may have to be pureed and strained for low fiber

Low Calorie and Diabetic Planning

A diabetic diet seeks to control the quantity of carbohydrate and, usually, the calories. If the calories are below 1000 per day, the diet is apt to be inadequate.

THE EXCHANGE METHOD. The exchange method is best used for planning low calorie and diabetic diets. The need in such planning is to limit and space out carbohydrate intake. This method divides foods into six groups: 1) milk, 2) vegetables, 3) fruit, 4) bread, 5) meat and 6) fat. Table 5-12 lists the foods allowed in each of these groups, each group being called a *list*. The vegetable list is divided into 2 groups, an A group which can be served in unlimited quantities and a B group, one of which can usually be served a day because the B vegetables are much higher in carbohydrate than A vegetables.

Each food in a group or list is approximately the equivalent of another in carbohydrate content. Thus, ¼ c cottage cheese is an exchange equal to 1 oz beef, fowl, lamb or veal. Or, all items in the bread list can be exchanged one for the other. If the diet allows 4 bread exchanges, then any 4 of the items in this list can be selected or one item can be repeated 4 times. If the meat exchanges allowed are 6, then any 6 items in the meat exchange can be selected.

Table 5-12—FOOD EXCHANGE LISTS

LIST 1 MILK EXCHANGE
(170 CALORIES)

Milk, whole 1 c
Milk, evaporated 1/2 c
Milk, whole, dry 1/4 c
Buttermilk* 1 c
Low-fat* 1 c
Milk, non-fat, dry* 1/4 c
Diabetic ice cream* 1/2 c

*80 calories

LIST 2 VEGETABLE EXCHANGE**
A Vegetables

Asparagus	Greens:
Broccoli	Mustard
Brussels sprouts	Spinach
Cabbage	Turnip
Cauliflower	Dandelion
Celery	Lettuce
Chicory	Mushrooms
Cucumber	Okra
Escarole	Parsley
Eggplant	Radish
Green pepper	Rhubarb
Greens:	Sauerkraut
Beet	Squash, summer
Chard	String beans
Collard	Tomatoes
Kale	Tomato juice
Watercress	Tossed salad
Poke	

B Vegetables

Beets	Pumpkin or squash
Carrots	Rutabaga
Shelled green	Strained infant B
beans	vegetable, 6 to 7
Green peas	T or 3 to 3-1/2 oz
Mixed vegetables	Turnips
Mixed vegetable	
juice	

LIST 3 FRUIT EXCHANGE
(40 CALORIES)

Fresh, frozen, dried, canned***

Apple juice or cider	1/3 c
Apples	1 small
Applesauce	1/2 c
Apricots, dried	4 halves
Apricots, fresh	2 med
Apricot nectar	1/4 c
Banana, small	1/2
Blueberries	2/3 c
Loganberries	2/3 c
Blackberries	1 c
Boysenberries	1 c
Raspberries	1 c
Strawberries	1 c
Fruit cocktail	1/2 c
Mixed fruit cup	1/2 c
Kadota figs	3 med or 1/3 c
Grapefruit	1/2 small or 1/2 c
Grapefruit juice	1/2 c
Grape juice	1/4 c
Grapes	12
Honeydew melon, medium	1/8
Mango, small	1/2
Nectarine, medium	1
Orange, small	1
Orange juice	1/2 c
Papaya, medium	1/3
Peach, medium	1
Pear, small	1
Pineapple	1/2 c cubes or 2 slices
Pineapple juice	1/3 c
Plums, medium	2
Prunes, medium	2
Raisins	2 T
Tangerine juice	1/2 c
Tangerine, large	1
Watermelon	1 c diced or 3 in. x 1-1/2 in. slice
Cherries	1/3 c
Cantaloupe, 6 in. diam	1/4
Dates	2
Figs, dried, small	1
Figs, fresh, large	2

**Allow all A vegetables desired; allow
1/2 c B vegetables (36 calories)

***All fruit unsweetened or dietetic

LIST 4 BREAD EXCHANGE
(68 CALORIES)

Biscuit, 2 in.	1
Bread, 1/2 in. slice	1
Cereal, cooked	1/2 c
Cereal, dry	3/4 c
Cereal, infant	1/2 c
Cornbread, 1-1/2 x 1-1/2 in.	1
Crackers:	
Graham, 2-1/2 in. sq	2
Oyster	1/2 c
Round, thin	6 to 8
Saltine, 2 in. sq	5
Soda, 2-1/2 in. sq	3
Flour	2 t
Grits, rice, noodles,	
macaroni, etc.	1/2 c
Matzoth, 3/4 in. sq	1
Melba toast	4
Muffin, medium	1
Pancake, 3 in. diam	2
Popcorn	1 c
Ry-Krisp	3
Shredded Wheat, biscuit	2/3
Sponge cake, 1-1/2 in. cube	1

The following can be substituted
for one bread exchange:

Beans, baked	1/4 c	Peas, dried	1/2 c
Beans, dried	1/2 c	Potato, sweet	1/4 c
Corn	1/3 c	Potato, white	5 oz
Parsnips	2/3 c	Potato, white	1/2 c

LIST 5 MEAT EXCHANGE****
(73 CALORIES)

Beef, lamb, liver, pork, veal,	
chicken, turkey or fish	1 oz
Cheddar or American cheese	1 oz
Cottage cheese	1/4 c
Cold cuts, all meat, slice	1
Egg, medium	1
Frankfurter	1
Oysters, shrimp, clams, etc.	5
Peanut butter	2 T
Salmon, tuna, crab,	
lobster, etc.	1/4 c
Sardines, medium	3
Strained infant meats	3 T
	or 2-1/2 oz

****Trim all visible fat; all allowances
boneless; roast, broil or simmer; do not
fry or add thickened sauce or gravy.

LIST 6 FAT EXCHANGE
(45 CALORIES)

Avocado, 4 in.	1/8
Bacon, crisp, slice	1
Butter or margarine	1 t
Cream cheese	1 T
Cream, heavy	1 T
Cream, light	2 T
French dressing	1 T
Half-and-half	1/4 c
Mayonnaise	1 t
Nuts, small	6
Oil or cooking fat	1 t
Olives, small	5

NOTE: None of these allowed
      without physician's
      approval:

Alcoholic beverages	Honey
Beer, wine	Ice cream
Candy	Jam, jelly
Chewing gum	Molasses
Condensed milk	Sorghum
Cookies	Pie or cake
Fried, creamed or	Preserves
escalloped foods	Soft drinks
Fruits in sugar	Sugar
	Sirup

NOTE: Allow any quantity with
      physician's permission:

Bouillon	Pepper
Clear broth	Pickles, dill
Coffee	Pickles, sour
Cranberries,	Rennet tab-
no sugar	lets
Flavor extracts	Saccharin
Gelatin, unsweetened	or other
Lemon	sweeteners,
Meat sauces	spices or
D-Zerta	herbs
A vegetables	Tea
Mustard	Vinegar

(cont.)

A diabetic diet order should indicate the number of exchanges permitted and the planner should neither add nor deduct from this list nor make any other changes.   Allowances approved by the American Dietetic Association and the American Diabetic Association are shown in Table 5-13.   The exchange system is built on the law of averages; the foods actually do vary somewhat in food values but they tend to balance out each other. Problems arise when mixed foods are served. Table 5-14 attempts to indicate some values that may be imputed for some mixed dishes. A dietitian or nutritionist (or one who knows how to use tables of food values) can consult such a table and estimate the various exchanges a mixed dish might yield. Also there are tables for substituting foods. For example, a patient who refuses to drink milk can have 1 fruit, 1 meat and 1 fat added to that meal.

If one receives a diabetic diet order for 1200 calories allowing 125 grams of carbohydrate, 60 grams of protein and 50 grams of fat, we can translate this into a diabetic diet using the exchange system. If we look at Table 5-13, we see that a 1200 calorie diet gives daily allowances of 2 milk exchanges, any amount of A vegetables, a B vegetable exchange, 3 fruit exchanges, 4 bread exchanges, 5 meat exchanges and a fat exchange. The table also indicates a recommended division of these exchanges in a meal plan.

Table 5-13–FOOD EXCHANGES AND FOOD PLANS
FOR DIABETIC OR LOW CALORIE DIETS

Calories	1200	1500	1800	2200	2600	3000
Carbohydrate	125	150	180	220	250	300
Protein	60	70	80	90	115	120
Fat	50	70	80	100	130	145

EXCHANGES:

Breakfast

Fruit	1	1	1	1	1	1
Meat	1	1	1	2	2	2
Bread	1	1	2	2	3	4
Fat		1	2	3	3	4

Milk (If cereal is served as the bread exchange, allow some milk here and deduct later.)

Lunch or Supper

Meat	1	2	2	2	3	3
Bread	1	2	2	3	4	4
A vegetable			Allow any amount			
Fruit	1	1	1	1	1	1
Fat		1	1	2	3	4
Milk	1	1	1	1	1	1

Mid-Afternoon

A vegetable		Allow any amount of A vegetable juice				

Main Meal

Meat	3	3	3	3	3	3
Bread	1	2	2	3	3	5
A vegetable			Allow any amount			
B vegetable	1	1	1	1	1	1
Fruit	1	1	1	2	2	2
Fat	1	1	2	3	4	5

Bed-Time

Milk	1	1	1	1	1	1
Bread	1	1	2	2	2	2
Meat			1	1	2	2
Fat		1	1	1	2	2

NOTE: For a 1000 calorie diet, omit the fat allowance, or, better, serve nonfat milk and retain the 1 fat exchange. If, on any diet, non-fat milk is served completely, allow 4 fat exchanges.

Table 5-14–IMPUTED EXCHANGE VALUES FOR MIXED FOODS

Type Food	Approximate Number of Exchanges*						
	Bread	Fat	Milk	Fruit	B Vege-table	Meat or Egg	Carbo-hydrate
Soup, cream	1/2	1	1				20 gm
Bean, pea, etc. soup					1	1	25 gm
Vegetable soup with cereal product	1/2	1/2			1		15 gm
Meat loaf, balls or other meat with some cereal	1/2	2				3	8 gm
Cheese souffle or fondue	1/2	2	1/2			1	12 gm
Pie, meat or chicken, etc., 2 in. diam biscuit	1-1/2	2				2	50 gm
Breaded meat, 3 oz sauce	1-1/2					3	30 gm
Cream sauce or gravy	1/2	1/2	1/4				10 gm
Cake, angel, plain	1					1	26 gm
Cake, butter, 2 oz, no frosting	1	2	1/10			1/5	30 gm
with butter-cream icing	1	4	1/10			1/5	40 gm
with egg foam icing	1					1/5	40 gm
Cake, pound, 2 oz, plain	1	2				1/5	35 gm
Lemon meringue pie, 1/7 9-in. pie	1	2				1/2	45 gm
Lemon snow pudding						1/4	22 gm
Baked custard		1				2/3	9 gm
Chocolate pudding	1/2	2				1	26 gm
Cup cake, white icing	1	2				1/2	19 gm

*Normal portions; many desserts listed here would not be allowed on a diabetic or low calorie diet; others might be.

Table 5-15—FOOD VALUES FOR EXCHANGE LISTS

Food, one exchange	Carbohydrate gm	Protein gm	Fat gm	Calories
Milk, whole, 8 oz or 1 c	12	8	10	170
Milk, non-fat, 8 oz or 1 c	12	8		80
A vegetable		Negligible in all		
B vegetable	7	2		36
Fruit	10			40
Bread	15	2		68
Meat		7	5	73
Fat			5	45

After checking Table 5-13, we could consult Table 5-12, the exchange lists, and select the following foods to meet these exchange allowances as follows:

Breakfast	**Lunch or Supper**	**Dinner**	**Bedtime**
Orange juice ½ c	Beef sandwich	Baked chicken 3 oz	Milk ¾ c
Poached egg 1	(1 oz beef,	Mashed potato ½ c	Graham
Toast 1	1 slice bread)	String beans ½ c	crackers 2
Coffee*	Sliced tomatoes,	Broccoli ½ c	
Saccharin*	no-cal dressing	½ baked banana	
	Small apple	Coffee or tea*	
	Milk, 1 c	Saccharin*	
	Tea with lemon		

*Allow 2 T of evaporated milk or the equivalent. If non-fat dry milk is served on this menu, allow 2 fat exchanges (2 t) of butter or margarine. The physician must approve the use of saccharin.

Sometimes physicians may use an older method for prescribing a diabetic diet, specifying the amounts of carbohydrate, protein, fat and calories. This must be translated into exchanges. It is not difficult.

To show how this is accomplished for a diet prescribed as 185 grams carbohydrate, 85 grams protein, 80 grams fat and 1800 calories, the following steps can be used to determine the allowed exchanges:

Step 1: Allow 2 milk exchanges, all the unbuttered raw or cooked A vegetables desired, a B vegetable and 3 fruit exchanges.

Table 5-15 shows a milk exchange gives 12 grams carbohydrate. Thus, 2 exchanges give 24 grams. A B vegetable gives 7 grams carbohydrate and 3 fruits, 30 grams; all of which totals 61 grams.

Since meat and fat contain no carbohydrate, the remaining carbohydrate in the diet comes from bread. If a total of 185 grams is allowed and we have 61 grams in the above foods, then we have 124 grams left for bread.

Step 2: Table 5-15 indicates a bread exchange gives 15 grams of carbohydrate; dividing 15 into 124 gives us 8 and this is the number of bread exchanges allowed.

Step 3: Table 5-15 shows milk gives 8 grams of protein and so 2 exchanges give 16. The B vegetable gives 2 grams and the 8 bread exchanges give 16 grams of protein. If we add 16, 2 and 16, we get 34 grams of protein in foods already in the diet and 34 subtracted from 85, the grams of protein allowed in this diet, leaves 51 grams of protein we can get from meat exchanges. Since a meat exchange is 7 grams of protein, 7 divided into 51 gives 7 plus meat exchanges allowed.

Step 4: Two milk exchanges give 20 grams of fat and 7 meat exchanges give 35 grams for a total of 55. The physician allowed 80 grams of fat and if we deduct 55 from 80, we find we have 25 grams of fat left. Each fat exchange is 5 grams and 5 divided into 25 gives 5 fat exchanges allowed.

Thus, we have in exchanges: 2 milk, 1 B vegetable, 3 fruit, 8 bread, 7 protein and 5 fat.

The menu planned from this calculation could be similar to the one that follows:

Food Item	Milk	Fruit	B Vegetable	Bread	Meat	Fat	Calories
BREAKFAST							
½ canned peach		1					40
½ c whole milk	½						85
½ c cooked farina				1			68
2 sl crisp bacon*						2*	90
1 sl toast				1			68
1 t margarine						1	45
coffee**							
MID-MORNING SNACK							
2 graham crackers				1			68
4 oz tomato juice**							
LUNCH							
1¼ c cr asp soup	1			½		½	227
1 whole wheat wafer				½			34
1 c salad greens**							
1 stuffed egg					1	½	93
½ T Fr dressing						½	23
½ c pineapple cubes		1					40
Tea**							
MID-AFTERNOON SNACK							
½ c whole milk	½						85
3 Ry-Krisp				1			68

---

*Bacon is a fat and not a meat exchange. **Allow tea, coffee and A vegetables without restriction.   *(cont.)*

DIABETIC DIET (cont.)

Food Item	Amount of Food and Type Exchange						
	Milk	Fruit	B Vege-table	Bread	Meat	Fat	Calories
DINNER							
Poached cod, 4 oz, lemon wedge					4		292
Steamed potato				1			68
½ c green peas			1				36
½ c coleslaw, no-cal dressing**							
1 slice bread				1			68
½ t margarine						½	23
15 Concord grapes		1					40
Tea**							
EVENING SNACK							
½ c cottage cheese***						2	146
4 Melba toast				1			68
Total	2	3	1	8	7	5	1711

**Allow tea, coffee and A vegetables without restriction. ***If low-fat cottage cheese is used, allow 2 more fat exchanges. (All canned or frozen fruits are sugar free.)

NOTE: It is recommended that inexperienced individuals and even those who have worked considerably with diets avoid using calories as a guide in calculating them. It is preferable to use the exchanges as a guide. This assures a balanced meal pattern which very frequently is not achieved when supervisors and others start following calorie allocations. Calories are given here because the diet restriction in our example is 1800 and this illustrates that we are within the limitation. It should be noted that some few foods with a small caloric content such as salad greens and tomato juice are not shown as possessing calories. They do have calories but in such a limited amount that it is not important to calculate them.

A dietitian can sometimes make substitutions from one exchange group to another. For instance, it was previously noted that there are guides for making substitutions when an individual does not take milk. Or, a B-vegetable is oftentimes called the equivalent of half a bread exchange and so if we want to put more B-vegetables on the menu than one per day, we can do this providing we deduct from the bread exchanges. The rule, however, to make no changes in the allowed exchanges is a good one for the nonprofessional to follow. Always recheck a diabetic or low calorie diet by tabulating the exchanges. Then, make the necessary adjustments. Table 5-16 is an example of a low cost diabetic diet.

Table 5-16—A LOW COST DIABETIC DIET
OF APPROXIMATELY 1800 CALORIES AND 180 GRAMS CARBOHYDRATE

Allowed No. Exchanges		SUNDAY	MONDAY
		Breakfast	**Breakfast**
Fruit	1	Unsweetened orange juice 1/2 c	Diet stewed prunes, 2 30-40 count
Meat	1	FF* scrambled egg, 1	Poached egg, 1
Bread	2	Maltomeal, 1/2 c Toast, 1 slice	Cream of rice, 1/2 c Biscuit, 2 in. diam
Fat	2	Crisp bacon, 1 Margarine, 1 pat	Margarine, 1 pat (use elsewhere)****
Milk	1/4	1/4 c for cereal	1/4 c for cereal
Beverage		(Coffee or tea as desired, no sugar, allow evaporated milk but deduct from milk allowance if freely used)	
		Lunch	**Lunch**
Meat	2	Meat loaf, 2 oz	Lean roast beef, 2 oz
Bread	2	FF mashed pot, 4 oz Bread, 1 slice	8 oz cream of chicken soup Saltines, 5
Veg., 2A		FF green beans, 1/2 c Stewed tomatoes, 1/2 c	FF spinach, 1/2 c, vinegar Crisp celery stick
Fruit	1	Fresh pear**	Fresh peach**
Milk	3/4	3/4 c milk	Lemonade or punch, 1 c
Fat	1	Margarine, 1 pat	(use elsewhere)****
Beverage		(Coffee or tea as desired, no sugar, allow evaporated milk but deduct from milk allowance if freely used)	
		Dinner	**Dinner**
Meat	3	Stewed chicken, 3 oz	FF cod or catfish fillet, 3 oz
Bread	2	FF savory noodles, 1/2 c Plain angelfood, 1/20th***	Baked potato, 4 oz Hot roll, 2 in. diam
Veg., 2A		Shredded lettuce, 3/4 c	Mixed green salad, 3/4 c
Veg., 2B	1	Minted FF peas, 1/2 c	FF beets, grated orange or lemon rind, 1/2 c
Fruit	1	Fresh or diet baked apple, medium	Sliced orange, small
Fat	2	French Dressing, 1 T Margarine, 1 pat	Margarine, 1 pat Mayonnaise, 1 t
Beverage		(Coffee or tea as desired, no sugar, allow evaporated milk but deduct from milk allowance if freely used)	
		Bedtime Snack	**Bedtime Snack**
Milk	1	1 c milk	Buttermilk, 1 c
Bread	2	Saltines, 5 Veg. soup, 1 c	Roast beef (1 oz) sandwich, 2 slices bread, lettuce as desired
Meat	1	Am. cheese, 1 oz	

****See page 181 for explanation.

TUESDAY	WEDNESDAY
Breakfast	**Breakfast**
Diet applesauce, 1/2 c	Tomato juice, 1/2 c
Sausage patty, 1-1/2 oz	Shirred egg, 1
Biscuits, 2 or cornmeal muffins, 2	Total or K flakes, 3/4 c
Margarine, 1 pat	Whole wheat toast, 1
	Margarine, 1 pat
	Crisp bacon, 1 slice
	1/4 c for cereal

(Coffee or tea as desired, no sugar, allow evaporated milk but deduct from milk allowance if freely used)

Lunch	**Lunch**
Broiled beef patty, 2 oz, with FF tomato sauce, 2 T	Beef stew, 2 oz beef with: 1/4 c potato cubes
Whole kernel corn, FF, 1/2 c	
Bread, 1 slice	Bread, 1 slice
Chopped broccoli, FF, 1/2 c	1/2 c 2A vegetables in stew
Coleslaw with raisins, 1/2 c, zero drsg	Sliced cucumber salad, zero dressing
Fresh banana	Fresh grapes, 10, or small orange
1 c milk	3/4 c milk
Margarine, 1 pat	

(Coffee or tea as desired, no sugar, allow evaporated milk but deduct from milk allowance if freely used)

Dinner	**Dinner**
Roast turkey, 3 oz	Baked Pork Cutlet, 3 oz
Sage dressing, FF, 2 oz	Parslied savory rice, 1/2 c
Hot roll, 2 in. diam	Cornbread, 2 in. sq
Carrot sticks, 4 small	Steamed green cabbage, FF, 1/2 c
Eggplant and tomatoes, 1/2 c	Waldorf salad, 1/3 c, boiled dressing
FF stewed onions, 1/2 c	Mashed winter squash, FF, 1/2 c
Diet cranberry sauce, 2 T	Diet sherbet, 1/2 c
None	Mayonnaise, 1 t
	Margarine, 1 pat

(Coffee as desired, no sugar, allow evaporated milk but deduct from milk allowance if freely used)

Bedtime Snack	**Bedtime Snack**
Milk, 1 c	Cream of tomato soup, 1 c
Vanilla ice cream, 4 oz*****	
Gingersnaps, 6 small	Saltines, 5
Peanut butter, 2 T	Sliced weiner in soup

(cont.)

*****See page 181 for explanation.

**Table 5-16–A LOW COST DIABETIC DIET OF APPROXIMATELY
1800 CALORIES AND 180 GRAMS CARBOHYDRATE (cont.)**

**Allowed No.
Exchanges**   THURSDAY

Breakfast

Fruit	1	Sliced oranges, 4
Meat	1	Creamed chipped beef, 1/2 c
Bread	2	on biscuits, 2, 2 in. diam
Fat	2	(use 1 T margarine in beef sauce)
Milk	1/4	1/4 c in beef sauce
Beverage		(Coffee or tea as desired, no sugar, allow evaporated milk but deduct from milk allowance if freely used)

Lunch

Meat	2	Chicken, 1/4 c, and
Bread	2	Noodles, 1/2 c
		Bread, 1 slice
Veg., 2A		Steamed chopped cabbage, 1/2 c
		Tomato slices, 2, zero dressing
Fruit	1	Diet hot cinnamon apples, 1/2 c
Milk	3/4	1/2 c milk (1/2 c in noodles)
Fat	1	Margarine, 1 pat (use in noodles)
Beverage		(Coffee or tea as desired, no sugar, allow evaporated milk but deduct from milk allowance if freely used)

Dinner

Meat	3	Meat balls, 3 oz, baked in cream of mushroom soup
Bread	2	Steamed potato, 4oz
		Bread, 1 slice
Veg., 2A		FF chopped greens, 1/2 c
		Chopped lettuce, 3/4 c
Veg., 2B	1	FF carrots, 1/2 c
Fruit	1	Fresh plums, 2**
Fat	2	French dressing, 1 T
		Margarine, 1 pat
Beverage		(Coffee or tea as desired, no sugar, allow evaporated milk but deduct from milk allowance if freely used)

Bedtime Snack

Milk	1	Milk, 1 c
		Sherbet, 1/3 c
Bread	2	Vanilla wafers 2
Meat	1	Cottage cheese, 1/4 c

FRIDAY

Breakfast
Grapefruit sections, 1/2 c
Soft-cooked egg, 1
Oatmeal, 1/2 c
Toast, 1 slice
Margarine, 1 pat
Crisp bacon, 1 slice

1/4 c for cereal
(Coffee or tea as desired, no sugar, allow evaporated milk but deduct from milk allowance if freely used)

Lunch
Broth with 1/2 c 2A vegetable
Toasted cheese sandwich, 1 oz
  cheese, 2 slices bread
Cherry tomatoes, 3
Pickles, dill, 4 strips
Diced pears in lime Zerta, 1/2 c
3/4 c milk
Omit fat allowance
(Coffee or tea as desired, no sugar, allow evaporated milk but deduct from milk allowance if freely used)

Dinner
Baked ham, lean, 3 oz

Baked yam or sweet potato, small
Biscuit, 1, 2 in. diam
Summer squash, FF, 1/2 c

Raw chopped spinach salad, 3/4 c
FF Lima beans, green, 1/2 c
Diet pineapple, 2 slices
Creamy French dr, 1 T
(Coffee or tea as desired, no sugar, allow evaporated milk but deduct from milk allowance if freely used)

Bedtime Snack
Milk, 1 c

Graham crackers, 4
Peanut butter, 2 T

SATURDAY

Breakfast
Fresh fruit or berries in season, 1/2 c

French toast, 2 slices with diet jelly, 2 T

Margarine, 1 pat
(Use other pat of margarine for French
  toast fried in Teflon pan)

Lunch
Baked cube steak, 2 oz, with FF gravy, 2 T
FF mashed potatoes, 1/2 c
Hard roll, small
Wax beans, 1/2 c
Diced escarole, 3/4 c, zero dressing
Watermelon, 1 c or diet apricots, 2
1 c milk
Margarine, 1 pat

Dinner
Roast chicken, 3 oz

SF escalloped potatoes, 1/2 c
Hot roll, 1
Stewed celery and tomatoes, 1/2 c

Pickled beet salad, 1/2 c

Fresh or canned diet fruit cup, 1/2 c
Mayonnaise, 1 T
Margarine, 1 pat

Bedtime Snack
8 oz cream of mushroom soup

Saltines, 5
Pressed ham loaf, 1 oz

---

*Fat free. **Fresh fruit in season; at other times diet canned, two halves, or equivalent.
***of 9 in. cake. ****Margarine can be used in lunch soup and also lunch margarine
can be used for bedtime snack sandwich. *****Allowed because of no fat at dinner.

(This menu is based largely on one planned by Mrs. Iris Lochner, R. D., with some changes
  made by the author.)

Low Fat Diet Planning

Residents who have liver or gall bladder problems, intestinal disturbances or those who must be on a low cholesterol regime may have fat restricted in the diet. About 50 grams of fat is allowed as a maximum. Some low cholesterol diets may require only the restriction of saturated fats; unsaturated fats may not be restricted. A low fat diet may restrict meat and egg yolk and because of this a low fat diet may be below the recommended levels of thiamine and iron.

For low fat diets, watch fatty gravies or sauces. Use non-fat milk. For low cholesterol diets, use unsaturated spreads. Read labels. If the label says "hydrogenated," forget it; some labels try to fool readers with the word "hardened" but it means "hydrogenated." If the label reads *liquid vegetable oil,* it may be safe. For these diets, only boiled, baked, broiled or poached meat, fish or poultry are recommended. Eliminate fatty meats.

Crackers and many other prepared foods contain saturated fats—usually lard. Eliminate these. If eggs are restricted—which they are frequently—check for eggs in prepared mixtures.

Shellfish are high in cholesterol. Avoid puddings, custards, ice cream, whipped cream, cream, pies, cakes, cookies or other items containing saturated fats or those with a high fat content. Tables 5-17 and 5-18 present a meal plan and sample menu for a low fat diet and foods to allow and avoid. Tables 5-19 and 5-20 set forth the same items for low cholesterol diets.

Tables as guides indicating allowed or unallowed foods are helpful. If the menu has a high number of foods which are not allowed, a considerable amount of special preparation will be required. Good menu planning can reduce this. For instance, if creamed turkey and mushrooms are on the menu, sliced turkey meat can be specified for modified diets and the necessary portions of turkey taken before it is diced and added to the cream sauce.

Table 5-17—LOW FAT MEAL PLAN AND MENU

Meal Plan	Sample Menu	
BREAKFAST		
Citrus fruit	Orange slices	1
Cereal, fortified	Oatmeal	1/2 c
Egg	Poached egg	1
Bread, sliced	Toast	2
Jelly	Apple jelly	1 T
Beverage	Coffee	ad lib
Sugar	Sugar	3 t
Milk, non-fat	Milk, non-fat	1 c
MID-MORNING NOURISHMENT		
Fruit juice	Tomato juice	1/2 c
LUNCH		
Meat or substitute	Veal patty	3 oz
Potato or starch	Baked potato	1
Vegetable	Carrots	1/2 c
Salad	Relish sticks	5
Bread, white	Bread, sliced	2
Dessert	Baked apple	1
Milk, non-fat	Buttermilk	1 c
MID-AFTERNOON NOURISHMENT		
Fruit	Banana, small	1
DINNER		
Meat or substitute	Turkey	3 oz
Potato or starch	Rice	1/2 c
Vegetable	String beans	1/2 c
Salad	Lettuce	1/8 head
Dressing	No-cal	1 T
Bread	Hard roll	1
Margarine	Margarine	1 t
Dessert	Fruit gelatin	1/2 c
Milk, non-fat	Milk, non-fat	1 c
EVENING SNACK		
Crackers	Saltines	5
Milk, non-fat	Milk, non-fat	1 c

(With exception of fat, meats and egg yolks, no measures of foods are necessary; dish standard portions; use no other fat than that listed.)

Adapted from the *Diet Manual*, Board for Texas State Hospitals and Schools, courtesy Cynthia Bishop, R. D.

Table 5-18—LOW FAT DIET
(50 gm fat)

Allowed	Avoid	Allowed	Avoid
BEVERAGES Non-fat milk Buttermilk Carbonated beverages Coffee Tea	Whole milk and beverages made from it; limit eggnogs	**FRUIT JUICES** Orange, grape, grapefruit, pineapple, apricot or their blends Tomato or other vegetable juices	None
CEREALS AND BREADS Bread, enriched or whole wheat Graham crackers Saltine or soda crackers (low fat) Farina Grits Oatmeal Pettijohns Malt-O-Meal Cornflakes Branflakes Special K	Quick breads as: Muffins, hot cakes, biscuits, cornbread, hot rolls, hamburger buns, cinnamon rolls, etc.	**FRUITS** Any fresh, frozen, canned or dry, if tolerated; no cream with any	Raw apples, melons and peelings may cause distress for some
CHEESE Non-fat cottage	All others	**MEAT, FISH AND FOWL** Beef, lamb, liver, chicken, turkey, lean fish, canned salmon or tuna if washed and not over 6 oz per day	Fatty meats as: Pork, ham, sausage, luncheon meats, frankfurters, bologna, spareribs, braunschweiger, etc.
DESSERTS Flavored gelatins Fruit whips Puddings from non-fat milk and egg whites Cocoa in moderation if low fat	Desserts containing whole milk, egg yolk and fat or cream Pies, cakes, cookies, doughnuts, nuts, chocolate	**POTATO OR STARCHY FOODS** White or sweet potatoes Macaroni products Rice, hominy, etc.	All fried or cooked with added fat Add no fat to any starchy foods
EGGS Limited to cooked in shell, poached or scrambled	Fried eggs	**SOUPS** Fat-free soup made from allowed vegetables; use skim milk for those containing milk; fat-free broths with rice or noodles, etc., permitted	Cream soups commercial meat base soups containing fats
FATS Crisp bacon and those allowed by physician; about 3 t of oil or fat allowed per day; 1 crisp bacon equals 1 t fat	Fatty meats, fried foods, gravies and sauces containing fat, butter, margarine		

Allowed	Avoid
SUGARS AND SWEETS	
Jams, jellies, preserves, sugars, honey, sirup, hard candies	Chocolate or sweets with nuts or coco-nut; no fat frostings, etc.
VEGETABLES	
Fresh, frozen canned, dry: Asparagus, beets, carrots, celery, corn, peas, string beans, egg-plant, okra, baby limas, pumpkin, spinach, squash, to-matoes, etc. Lettuce or other greens	No added fat, cream sauce or fried; some may have to avoid cabbage, cucumbers, green or red peppers, onions, radishes, ruta-bagas, sauerkraut, turnips, etc. (See physician.) Avocados
MISCELLANEOUS	
Salt, lemon, parsley, basil, vinegar, flavorings, etc.	Salt pork; some may not tolerate spices or condi-ments.

Adapted from the *Diet Manual,* Board for Texas State Hospitals and Schools, courtesy Cynthia Bishop, R. D.

Table 5-19—LOW CHOLESTEROL DIET

Allowed	Avoid	Allowed	Avoid
BEVERAGES Milk, non-fat Buttermilk, non-fat Carbonated beverages Coffee Tea	Milk, whole and beverages with whole milk and egg yolks; no cream, half-and- half, etc.	**FRUIT JUICES** Allow any desired **FRUITS** Any fresh, frozen, canned or dry	None Avocado
BREAD AND CEREALS Bread or graham or saltine crack- ers Farina, grits, oat- meal, pettijohns, Malto-Meal, etc. Cornflakes, bran- flakes, Special K, etc.	Quick breads as: Muffins, corn- bread, hotcakes, hot rolls, ham- burger buns, cinnamon rolls, biscuits	**MEAT, FISH AND POULTRY** Beef, lean, to 2 oz Chicken, turkey Fish, fresh or frozen, lean types preferred Canned tuna or salmon, washed, not over 4 oz	Fatty meats listed in low fat table; organ meats, shellfish; nothing fried
CHEESE Cottage cheese, non-fat	All others	**POTATO OR STARCH** White potatoes Sweet potatoes Hominy, rice Macaroni prod- ucts	All fried or cooked with added fat Add no fat to any of these
DESSERTS Flavored gelatins Whips made from egg white Puddings made from non-fat milk, egg whites and starch thick- ener	No cakes, pies, or other des- serts contain- ing fat Chocolate, cocoa, coconut, nuts, candies	**SOUPS** Fresh turkey or chicken broths Cream soups from non-fat milk; may be seasoned with unhydrogenated fats	Soups from beef or beef broth; soups made from whole milk
EGGS Egg whites only	Egg yolk, unless allowed by physician	**SUGARS AND SWEETS** Jams, jellies, preserves, mar- malades Sugars, honey, sirups, sorghum or molasses Hard candies	Rich candies, chocolate, coconut, etc.
FATS Corn, cotton- seed, soybean oils, unhydro- genated; pure vegetable un- hydrogenated margarine	Butter, hydro- genated mar- garine, lard, hydrogenated margarine, animal fats, gravies, bacon or bacon fat, dressings with fat, eggs or cheese, etc.		

Allowed	Avoid
VEGETABLES Some strong vege- tables may have to be avoided	No fats, except allowed; no cream sauce containing whole milk, evaporated milk or cream
VEGETABLE JUICES Tomato or any other	Highly spiced juices may bother some
MISCELLANEOUS Spices, garlic, catsup, chili, sauce, pickles, lemon, mustard, vinegars, sac- charin, if allow- ed by physician	Salad dressings containing fat or hydrogenated fats; some spices may have to be avoided

Adapted from the *Diet Manual,* Board for Texas State Hospitals and Schools, courtesy Cynthia Bishop, R. D.

Table 5-20–LOW CHOLESTEROL MEAL PLAN AND MENU

Meal Plan	Sample Menu	
BREAKFAST		
Fruit	Diced canteloupe	1/2 c
Cereal, fortified	Farina	1/2 c
Bread, sliced	Toast	2
Margarine, unhydrogenated	Margarine	2 t
Jelly, jam, etc.	Orange marmalade	1 T
Beverage	Coffee	ad lib
Sugar	Sugar	3 t
Milk, non-fat	Milk, non-fat	8 oz
MID-MORNING NOURISHMENT		
Juice	Carrot juice	4 oz
LUNCH		
Meat or substitute	Roast beef	2 oz
Potato or starch	Baked potato	1
Vegetable	Chopped spinach	1/2 c
Salad	Relish sticks	5
Bread, sliced	Bread	1
Margarine, unhydrogenated	Margarine	2 t
Dessert	Peach halves	2
Milk, non-fat	Cinnamon milk*	8 oz
MID-AFTERNOON NOURISHMENT		
Fruit juice	Orange juice	4 oz
DINNER		
Meat or substitute	Broiled chicken	3 oz
Potato or starch	Rice	1/2 c
Vegetable	Green beans	1/2 c
Salad	Lettuce, lemon	1/8 head
Bread	Hard roll	1
Margarine, unhydrogenated	Margarine	2 t
Dessert	Fruit whip	1/2 c
Milk, non-fat	Buttermilk	1 c
NIGHT SNACK		
Bread	Graham crackers	2
Juice	Pineapple	4 oz

(With exception of meat and fat, no measures are needed. Use only unhydro-
genated fats. All types of fat may be restricted by physician).

*Slightly sweetened and seasoned with vanilla and a bit of cinnamon; nutmeg
may be used in place of cinnamon.

Adapted from the *Diet Manual,* Board for Texas State Hospitals and Special
Schools, courtesy Cynthia Bishop, R. D.

Low Sodium Planning

Residents with cardiac or arteriosclerosis problems, such as congestive heart failure, hypertension, hardening of the arteries, edema, will be on a low sodium diet. Sometimes renal problems call for the diet also. For residents on these diets, the quantity of sodium in the diet is critical. Read labels carefully. Many foods contain sodium that do not have salt in them. For instance, dried potatoes, dehydrated or dried fruit can be processed using sodium sulfite.

Mildly restricted sodium diets allow about 2500 milligrams (mg) of sodium per day or about 3 (gm) of salt per day maximum. Light salting is allowed in cooking. No salt shaker is allowed on the tray or table. Seasonings can be used to reduce the expectancy of a salt flavor. High-salt foods are eliminated, such as commercial broth soups, chili sauce, catsup, mustard, cured meats, cheddar cheese (unless used as a milk substitute in the more liberal sodium restricted diets), pickles, olives, soy sauce, Worcestershire sauce, sauerkraut, seasoned salts, monosodium glutamate, salted crackers, potato chips, Fritos, etc. Chewing tobacco may be eliminated.

With a restriction of 1000 mg or less, some foods that contain even moderate amounts of sodium will be restricted. In very low sodium diets, dialyzed milk may have to be served. This is low in sodium but because of cost or unavailability is seldom served to residents.

For cardiac patients, avoid stimulants, strong spices or seasonings; decaffeinated coffee may have to be given; sometimes no tea is permitted. Broths may be restricted. Iced fluids and ice cream may be restricted and also such gas-forming foods as cabbage, cucumber, corn, dried legumes, melons, onions, radishes, rutabagas, turnips, mustard greens, turnip greens or collard greens. Tables 5-21 and 5-22 are for a 200-mg low sodium diet. It is seldom used in the small health facility because the resident usually cannot receive the medical or nursing care needed. However, it is presented to exemplify the restrictions needed in extremely low sodium diets. Doctors oftentimes are hesitant to use low sodium levels on some geriatrics that deprive them of some food enjoyment. Instead, they may resort to mercurial diuretics. On days when these drugs are administered, plan to serve orange juice, bananas and other high potassium foods.

Again, good menu planning can reduce special preparation for a low sodium diet. Removing food portions for these diets before salting saves special preparation. Use Tables 5-21, 5-22, 5-23 and 5-24 for planning extremely low salt diets.

Table 5-21 – 200 MG LOW SODIUM DIET

Allowed	Avoid	Allowed	Avoid
BEVERAGES Milk, low-sodium Coffee* Tea	Regular milk and carbonated beverages	**DESSERTS** Unflavored gelatin combined with allowed fruits or juices; cobblers and pies with allowed fruit and no salt in crust Cookies with no leavening or made from baking powder and low sodium milk Puddings made from low-sodium milk and no salt	All desserts containing salt, conventional leavening agents or flavored gelatins; do not exceed egg allowance
BREADS AND CEREALS Breads, low-sodium, leavened with yeast or low-sodium baking powder and low-sodium milk Crackers, salt free Farina, grits, oatmeal, rolled wheat, cornmeal, puffed cereals, shredded wheat biscuits, etc.	Egg not to exceed daily allowance; avoid all others; no salt in cooked cereals; read labels on dry cereals		
CHEESE Unsalted dry curd cottage	Use as substitute for meats or eggs	**EGGS** One per day prepared any style; no salted fat; more eggs can be used, an egg per meat allowance, if desired	Milk in omelets, etc. must be low-sodium type

NOTE: For a 500 mg low-sodium diet, use this list and the menu plan that follows, allowing 2 c regular milk and 1 oz more of meat per day; do the same for an 800 mg diet but allow 2½ c regular milk, 3 oz of meat and 3 t salted butter.

---

*In hard water areas, use distilled water, unless sodium content of the water is less than 20 mg per qt.
Use no salt; there will be about a half gram per day in the foods allowed.

Adapted from the *Diet Manual*, Board for Texas State Hospitals and Schools, courtesy Cynthia Bishop, R. D.

Allowed	Avoid	Allowed	Avoid
FATS Unsalted butter or margarine, mayonnaise or French dressings, oil or fats; half-and-half or light cream or whipping cream, limit 1 oz per day	Limit butter or margarine to 2 T per day; no bacon or other salted fats	**MEAT, FISH AND FOWL** Fresh or frozen: Beef, lamb, pork Chicken, turkey or chicken livers **Beef liver** or calves, limit to twice a month Fish	Limit to 3 oz per day (4 oz raw); all salted or canned meats, processed or cured meats; use only fish allowed in Table 5-22; some fish from the sea may be high in salt and some frozen or fresh fish may be lightly salted
FRUIT JUICES Any	Any juices diluted with water must be with distilled in hard water areas		
FRUITS Any fresh, frozen canned or dried, if not salted or dried with sulfites	None, if tolerated, but some raw fruits such as apples, pineapple and melons may cause distress	**POTATO OR STARCHY FOODS** White or sweet potatoes* Rice or macaroni products* if salt-free	All canned, dry or those processed with added salt, sodium sulfite or sodium products

(cont.)

Table 5-21 — 200 MG LOW SODIUM DIET (cont.)

Allowed	Avoid	Allowed	Avoid
SOUPS From allowed vegetables using fresh chicken broth, unsalted tomatoes or tomato juice or low-sodium milk; use distilled water*	Prepared or commercial preparations or beef or other meat broths	VEGETABLE JUICES Only unsalted ones	Juices from carrots or other vegetables to be avoided
VEGETABLES See Tables 5-22 and 5-23 for those allowed or to be avoided; cook in distilled water*		SUGARS AND SWEETS Sugars, any types Jams, jellies and marmalades Honey or sirups	No preserves or other items containing sodium benzoate
		CONDIMENTS AND SPICES See Tables 5-22 and 5-23 for those allowed or to be avoided; watch those that might contain sodium benzoate	

NOTE: For a 500 mg low-sodium diet, use this list and the menu plan that follows, allowing 2 c regular milk and 1 oz more of meat per day; do the same for an 800 mg diet but allow 2½ c regular milk, 3 oz of meat and 3 t salted butter.

---

*In hard water areas, use distilled water, unless sodium content of the water is less than 20 mg per qt.

Use no salt; there will be about a half gram per day naturally in the foods allowed.

Adapted from the *Diet Manual,* Board for Texas State Hospitals and Schools, courtesy Cynthia Bishop, R. D.

Table 5-22–200 MG LOW SODIUM MEAL PLAN AND MENU

Meal Plan	**Sample Menu**	
BREAKFAST		
Fruit	Sliced orange	1
Cereal	Farina, SF	1/2 c
Egg	Poached egg, SF	1
Bread, sliced, SF	Toast	2
Margarine, SF	Margarine, SF	2 t
Jelly	Apple jelly	1 T
Beverage	Coffee, decaffeinated	1 c
Sugar	Sugar	3 t
Milk, low-sodium	Milk, low-sodium	1 c
MID-MORNING NOURISHMENT		
Fruit juice	Grapefruit juice	1 c
LUNCH		
Meat or substitute	Macaroni, ground beef and	
Potato or starch	tomatoes, Italian style, SF	10 oz
Vegetable	Buttered zucchini, SF	1/2 c
Bread, SF	Hard roll	1
Salad	Greens with lemon juice	1 c
Dessert	Cherry cobbler	3/4 c
Margarine, SF	Margarine, SF	2 t
Milk, low-sodium	Milk, low-sodium	1 c

(cont.)

Table 5-22—200 MG LOW SODIUM MEAL PLAN AND MENU (cont.)

Meal Plan	Sample Menu	
MID-AFTERNOON NOURISHMENT		
Fruit juice	Pineapple juice	6 oz
DINNER		
Soup, SF	Cream of tomato, SF	1 c
Crackers, SF	Saltines, SF	5
Meat or substitute	Creamed mushrooms, SF	1/2 c
Potato or starch	Rice, SF	1/2 c
Vegetable SF	Green beans, SF	1/2 c
Salad	Mixed fruit	1/2 c
Bread, SF	Sliced	2
Margarine, SF	Margarine, SF	2 t
Dessert, SF	Baked banana	1
Milk, low-sodium	Milk, low-sodium	1 c
EVENING NOURISHMENT		
Crackers, SF	Saltines, SF	5
Milk or juice	Tomato juice, SF	6 oz

In areas where the water has more than 20 mg of sodium per qt, use distilled water for cooking, drinking, ice cubes, etc. Prepare all foods without salt, baking powder or other substances containing sodium. With the exception of meats, eggs, margarine and low-sodium (dialyzed) milk, measures are not necessary.

Adapted from the *Diet Manual,* Board for Texas State Hospitals and Schools, courtesy Cynthia Bishop, R. D.

Table 5-23—FOODS TO AVOID IN LOW SODIUM DIETS

Food Chemicals with Sodium
Salt (sodium chloride)*
Baking soda
Baking powder
Monosodium glutamate*
Brine (salt and water)*
Sweeteners
 Sodium cyclamate*
 Sodium saccharin*
Bread softener
 Sodium propionate*
Thickeners
 Sodium alginate*
 Disodium phosphate*
 (agent used to make
 legumes and cereals
 quick cooking)
Preservatives
 Sodium benzoate*
Whiteners (for dried
 potato flakes or
 granules)
 Sodium sulfite*
 Sodium hydroxide*
Drugs apt to contain
 sodium; (check labels)
 Alkalizers*
 Headache remedies*
 Cough medicines*
 Laxatives*
 Antibiotics*
 Sedatives*

Vegetables
Canned** unless low sodium
Frozen, if processed with salt**
Artichokes; beets or beet greens;
 carrots; celery; chard; dandelion
 greens; whole hominy*; kale;
 mustard greens; sauerkraut*;
 spinach; white turnips; dried
 peas and beans

Meats
Brains; kidneys**; canned, smoked,
 salted or cured meats (smoked
 tongue, bacon, salt pork, ham,
 etc.*); cured sausage meats such
 as bologna, wieners (unless salt
 free), liverwurst*; frozen fish fillets; canned salted*, smoked* fish
 (anchovies, caviar, dried or salt
 cod*, herring, sardines, canned
 tuna or salmon unless low sodium;
 shellfish** such as clams, crabs,
 lobsters, oysters, scallops, shrimp,
 etc.)

Milk Products
Ice cream sherbet, malted milk,
 milk shakes, instant cocoa mixes**;
 Dutch process cocoa**; milk products except 2 glasses of milk per
 day on severely restricted diets;
 some dairies salt buttermilk; cheddar or other cheeses* except unsalted cottage cheese; products
 made with rennet; allow low sodium cheddar cheese

(cont.)

Table 5-23—FOODS TO AVOID IN LOW SODIUM DIETS (cont.)

Seasonings and Condiments
Vegetable salts* (garlic, onion,
  celery, etc.)
Catsup or chili sauce*
Prepared mustard*
Horseradish (if salted)*
Meat or vegetable extracts*
Soup bases*
Gravy mixes*
Meat tenderizers*
Soy sauce*
Worcestershire sauce*

Cereal or Starchy Foods
Breads**, crackers**, etc.,
  unless low sodium
Bakery or pudding mixes
Cooking cereals unless
  salt free
Dry cereals** unless
  listed as having less than
  6 mg of sodium per 100
  gm of cereal
Self-rising flours*
Potato chips*
Pretzels*
Popcorn, if salted*

Fatty Foods
Salted butter or margarine*
Salad dressings* unless low sodium
Bacon or sausage or ham drippings

Miscellaneous
Beverage mixes
Fruit-flavored beverage powders
Bouillon cubes, powders or liquids*
Commercial candies
Gelatin desserts
Rennet tablets
Molasses
Canned puddings or prepared
  dry mixes

---

*Avoid these in a 2500 gm sodium diet but allow unstarred or ** foods; avoid both * and ** foods for a 1000 mg diet but allow unstarred foods; avoid all foods in this table for a diet less than 1000 mg of sodium.

Adapted from materials of the American Heart Association.

Table 5-24—ALLOWANCES FOR A 500 MG
LOW-CALORIE-LOW-SODIUM DIET*

Milk: 2 c of regular milk or its equivalent gives 240 mg sodium

Whole milk, buttermilk or equivalent such as 2 c non-fat milk, 2/3 c (1-3/4 oz) instant dry or scant 1/2 c (1-3/4 oz) non-fat powdered dry milk, 1 c low-sodium cottage cheese, 7 oz evaporated milk; count milk used in cooking as a part of this allowance. Under medical advice, substitute per 8 oz whole milk: 2 oz meat, eggs, poultry or fish, 6 oz yoghurt; if these are used, the diet is apt to be low in calcium and phosphorus.

Meat: 5oz/day; each oz gives 25 mg of sodium

SF fresh, frozen or canned meat, fish or poultry; only some frozen fish. Kinds: beef, pork, lamb, veal, fresh tongue, chicken, duck, turkey, rabbit or some game meats; liver not more than once every 2 weeks. No shellfish; use most fresh fish but watch those that might be lightly salted or that come from the sea. Substitute for each oz of meat, poultry or fish: 1 egg (only 1 a day), 1/4 c unsalted cottage cheese, 1 oz low-sodium cheese or 2 T low-sodium peanut butter.

Vegetables: 3½ c, 3 oz/½ c; each ½ c gives 5 mg sodium

Allow fresh, frozen or canned vegetables if SF, except those listed in Table 5-23. Frozen and canned peas and lima beans, etc. are tested for maturity by a brine test; avoid these unless sure of the processing.

Fruit: 4 portions; each portion gives 2 mg sodium

All fresh, frozen, canned or dried fruit or fruit juices; no dry fruit should be processed with sodium sulfite; if calories are restricted, sugar-free fruit may have to be used.

Cereal: 7 portions; each portion gives 5 mg sodium

Low-sodium bread, rolls or crackers; unsalted cooked cereals; dry cereals having only 6 mg of sodium per oz or cup; plain, unsalted matzo; unsalted Melba toast; SF macaroni, noodles, spaghetti, rice or barley; SF popcorn; flour or starchy vegetables ad lib.

*Use this for a 250 mg low-sodium diet using low-sodium (dialyzed) dairy products.

(cont.)

Table 5-24–ALLOWANCES FOR A 500 MG
LOW-CALORIE-LOW-SODIUM DIET* (cont.)

Fats: 2 portions; no salt will be in these

Unsalted margarines or butter, etc., unsalted French dressing or mayonnaise; creams in moderation, unsalted nuts. If low-fat dairy products are served in the milk allowance, allow 2 more portions of fat.

Other Foods: 2 portions; almost no sodium

If desired, fruit, bread, cereal, starchy vegetables, sugar (4 t), sirup, honey, jelly, jam, marmalade or 75 calories of candy made without salt or other sodium compounds.

Miscellaneous: allow all desired; no sodium content

Coffee or decaffeinated coffee, if prescribed, tea or coffee substitutes; sweetening substitutes, if allowed, containing only calcium; plain unflavored gelatin, vinegar, cream of tartar, potassium bicarbonate or sodium free baking powder, yeast.

Use any seasoning except those limited in Table 5-23. For instance, try with beef: bay leaf, dry mustard, green pepper, grape jelly, sage, marjoram, mushrooms, nutmeg, onion, pepper, thyme or tomato; with chicken: cranberries, mushrooms, paprika, parsley, poultry seasoning, thyme or sage; with lamb: curry, currant jelly, garlic, mint, pineapple or rosemary; with pork: apples, applesauce, garlic, onion, sage or poultry seasoning; with veal: apricots, bay leaf, curry, currant jelly, garlic, ginger, marjoram, mushrooms, oregano or paprika; with fish: bay leaf, curry, dill, dry mustard, green pepper, lemon juice, marjoram, mushrooms, paprika, tomato or oregano; with eggs: curry, dry mustard, green pepper, jelly, mushrooms, onion, paprika, parsley or tomato.

*Use this for a 250 mg low-sodium diet using low-sodium (dialyzed) dairy products.

Adapted from materials from the American Heart Association.

Mechanically Soft, Soft and Bland Diets

A group of closely related diets, called mechanically soft, soft or bland, can usually be planned together. Many residents will have difficulty in chewing because of poorly fitting dentures, poor teeth or muscular problems. A mechanically soft diet is needed for them. On such a diet the foods are all normal except that they are coarsely chopped or pureed to make mastication and swallowing more simple. Few hard foods are served.*

A soft diet is one that is mechanically soft and further modified for those who have impaired digestion or need foods which are mechanically non-stimulating and contain little fiber. Few rich or highly seasoned foods are allowed. All foods are quite soft. A bland diet is a soft diet without spices, condiments; quite tart foods and juices and sometimes very hot or very cold foods will not be allowed. This diet is used to reduce irritation to the stomach or intestinal area.

Some of these three diets may be deficient in iron, thiamine, niacin and ascorbic acid. Watch protein and increase it by using whole or non-fat milk enriched by adding 1 c of non-fat dry milk per qt. This drink also has a buffering action against irritating substances. Watch calories because they may have to be increased for some. Sometimes these diets must be spoonable for residents with poor eyesight or who have muscular or motor skill problems.

Tables 5-25 and 5-26 and Tables 5-27 and 5-28 cover these diets. In some cases, modification may have to be made for the more severely restricted bland diets. The diet manual should indicate these modifications and the special factors to be considered.

Sometimes progressive soft diets may be prescribed for post-surgery, ulcer patients or other critical cases where more than a soft diet is needed. The first diet is 1/3 c of equal parts milk and cream (half-and-half) given every hour. Sometimes 1 c of non-fat dry milk is added per qt of half-and-half used. Besides increased buffering action, this fortified liquid gives added calcium, phosphorus and B-complex vitamins plus about 300 calories and 30 gm more

---

*NOTE: Mrs. Iris Lochner in her critique of this chapter stressed: "Know the resident's and which ones cannot chew. Some can gum foods quite well. Never puree, if ground will do; never grind, if chopping will do and never chop, if whole will do—and besides the gums need stimulation."

protein. The doctor should indicate this addition and the night feedings.

The second progressive soft diet—it follows the first one as soon as possible—is ¾ c of half-and-half or half-and-half fortified with dry milk at 6:00 am; repeat every 4 hours. The doctor should indicate these and night feedings he desires. Three small meals, not over ¾ c total for each, are served, using foods such as soft eggs, refined cereals (usually strained), strained cream soups, milk toast, rice, white potatoes with butter, saltines or crackers, baked or soft custard, plain gelatin desserts, plain cornstarch puddings, butter or margarine and a small amount of sugar and salt needed for palatability. Both of these soft diets will not be adequate nutritionally and so residents must be taken from these as soon as possible.

The third progressive soft diet continues the ¾ c half-and-half feedings or this can be regular milk. Three meals are given of a volume of 1¼ to 1½ c each. The above-named foods are used plus low fat or creamed cottage cheese, plain cooked macaroni, spaghetti or noodles and 1 strained fruit per day—either apples, apricots, pears, peaches, plums or prunes, and 1 serving daily of strained orange or grapefruit juice. Other strained fruit or vegetable juices may be allowed by the physician. All other foods, especially coffee, tea, carbonated beverages, meat soups and hard foods will be avoided. Only cinnamon and no other spice may be allowed. Eggnogs are allowed, flavored only with vanilla. For some, tender lettuce may be given.

The fourth stage slightly increases the amount of total food allowed and allows such items as strained oatmeal or other cereals, dry cereals, soft cooked vegetables, tender meats, poultry or fish, peeled peaches, apples, pears or bananas, tomato juice, soft cooked fruits, sherbet or ice cream, cream cheese, cakes such as sponge, angel or plain butter. If an order for tea or decaffeinated or other coffee is given by the physician, this is served. Fried foods, most fats, nuts, fruits with seeds, fibrous fruit desserts, meat soups, highly spiced foods, jam or marmalade, pickles, alcohol, iced drinks, vinegar or other similar foods must be avoided.

Table 5-25–MECHANICALLY SOFT MEAL PLAN AND MENU

Meal Plan	Sample Menu	
BREAKFAST		
Fruit	Orange juice	6 oz
Cereal, refined	Farina	1/2 c
Egg	Poached egg	1
Bread, sliced	Toast	2 .
Margarine	Margarine	2 t
Jelly	Apple jelly	1 T
Milk	Milk	1 c
Beverage	Coffee, decaffeinated	1 c
Sugar	Sugar	ad lib
LUNCH		
Meat or substitute	Creamed chicken	6 oz
Potato or starch	Mashed potatoes	6 oz
Vegetable	Buttered carrots	1/2 c
Bread, sliced	Bread	2
Margarine	Margarine	2 t
Dessert	Grenadine pears	2
Beverage	Milk	1 c
DINNER		
Soup	Cream of Tomato	1 c
Crackers	Saltines	5
Meat	Turkey and rice	1 c
Vegetable	Chopped green beans	1/2 c
Salad	Fruit in gelatin	1/2 c
Dressing	Mayonnaise	1 T
Bread, sliced	Bread	2
Margarine	Margarine	2 t
Dessert	Chocolate pudding, whipped cream	1/2 c
Beverage	Tea	ad lib
EVENING SNACK		
Milk and crackers		ad lib

NOTE: If a diet higher in calories is required, add mid-morning and mid-afternoon snacks.

———

Adapted from the *Diet Manual,* Board for Texas State Hospitals and Schools, courtesy Cynthia Bishop, R. D.

Table 5-26—MECHANICALLY SOFT DIET

Allow	Avoid	Allow	Avoid
BEVERAGES Any, as desired	None	**EGGS** Any style	None
BREADS AND CEREALS Refined breads, biscuits, corn-bread, crackers, graham crackers, griddle cakes, muffins, yeast rolls, bread or cornbread dressings, farina, grits, oat-meal, Pettijohns, Malt-O-Meal, cornflakes, bran-flakes, or Special K, etc.	None	**FATS** Any	None
CHEESE Cottage or cheddar	All others; serve cheddar in sauces, etc.	**FRUITS** Fresh, frozen, canned or dry apples, apple-sauce, cante-loupe, prunes, watermelon, fruit cocktail, cooked or soft peaches, pears, etc.	Peelings, ber-ries, raisins, pineapple or hard fruits
DESSERTS Frozen desserts; gelatin (plain, whipped or fruited); fruit whips; snows; creams, baked or boiled cus-tards; starch, bread, rice or tapioca pud-dings, plain cookies; frosted cakes; shortcakes; pies or cobblers	None with nuts, coconut, rai-sins or seeds	**MEAT, FISH OR FOWL** Chopped or ground beef, lamb, pork, chicken, turkey, liver or chicken livers Baked or poached fish Canned fish Any pureed meat Pot pies, loaves, balls, casserole dishes that are soft, preferably in cream sauce	

Allow	Avoid
POTATO OR STARCHY FOODS	
White or sweet potatoes	None
Macaroni products	
Rice	
SOUPS	
All canned or soups made in the facility; strain, if necessary	None
SUGARS OR SWEETS	
Sugars, jams, jellies	No seeds, nuts, coconut, etc.
Honey or sirups	No hard candy
VEGETABLES	
Asparagus, beets, carrots, cabbage (chopped), celery (chopped) dried beans or peas, green beans, pumpkin, chopped spinach, broccoli, green lima beans, squash (winter or summer), turnips, tomatoes	Corn, hominy, collards, turnip or mustard greens; fried vegetables; any with tough skin or seeds; remove seeds in some summer squash
Serve baked, boiled, steamed, creamed, mashed or sauteed	
Any vegetable puree may be used	

Allow	Avoid
SPICES AND CONDIMENTS	
Allow any except those that may be highly spiced; watch items that also may be hard such as pickles, olives, etc.	
FRUIT OR VEGETABLE JUICES	
Allow any except perhaps some that are highly spiced.	

Adapted from the *Diet Manual,* Board for Texas State Hospitals and Schools, courtesy Cynthia Bishop, R. D.

Table 5-27–SOFT AND BLAND DIETS

Allow	Avoid	Allow	Avoid
BEVERAGES Any type milk or buttermilk Carbonated beverages Coffee Tea	Some may need decaffeinated coffee and can have no carbonated beverages or tea	**FATS** Margarine or butter, cooking oil, hydrogenated fats, cream, crisp bacon for some, mayonnaise, French dressing if not too tart, etc.	Fried foods, gravies
BREADS AND CEREALS White bread, day old or Soda or graham crackers Refined cereals Dry cereals that soften well with milk	Whole grain bread, coarse cereals, hot breads, cornbread, bran flakes, all bran	**FRUIT OR VEGETABLE JUICES** All allowed except highly spiced	
CHEESE Cottage, milk yellow (use in cooking)	Sharp or strongly flavored	**FRUIT** Ripe banana or orange sections Cooked or canned applesauce, peaches, pears Dried and cooked apples, peaches, pears, prunes	Fruit with seeds, cherries, figs, pineapple and some raw fruits if they cannot be tolerated
DESSERTS Soft puddings, custards and frozen desserts Gelatin desserts, whips, plain cakes with soft frostings, cookies	Pastries, pies, desserts containing nuts, coconut, dates, raisins, seeds or fruits with tough skins	**MEAT, FISH OR FOWL** Beef, lamb, liver, fowl, or fresh, frozen or canned fish if baked, poached, broiled, roasted, creamed or ground	Fatty pork or ham; luncheon meats, franks, corned beef, spiced products
EGGS Any style except fried	Attempt to soft cook		

(cont.)

Table 5-27—SOFT AND BLAND DIETS

Allow	Avoid	Allow	Avoid
POTATO OR STARCHY FOODS White or sweet potatoes Macaroni products Rice	All others	VEGETABLES Well cooked or canned: Beets, carrots, asparagus tips, green or wax beans, green peas, squash, spinach or others that are tender and are chopped or pureed	Raw vegetables that are hard or others that would be difficult to eat
SOUPS Canned or those made at the facility; strain or puree those needing it	Spicy soups or those containing much fat or substances that are difficult to chew	MISCELLANEOUS Salt, lemon juice, vanilla, cocoa	Spiced condiments, nuts, coconut, gravies, pungent spices
SUGARS AND SWEETS Sugar, sirup, jellies Honey	Jams, preserves with seeds or tough skins; nuts		

Adapted from the *Diet Manual,* Board for Texas State Hospitals and Schools, courtesy Cynthia Bishop, R. D.

Table 5-28 – SOFT AND BLAND DIET MEAL PLAN AND MENU

Meal Plan	Sample Menu	
BREAKFAST		
Fruit	Orange juice	6 oz
Cereal, refined	Farina	1/2 c
Egg	Poached egg	1
Bread, sliced	Toast, white	2
Margarine	Margarine	2 t
Milk	Milk	1 c
Sugar	Sugar	ad lib
Jelly	Apple jelly	1 T
Beverage	Coffee*	ad lib
LUNCH		
Soup	Cream of celery	1 c
Crackers	Saltines	5
Meat	Roast beef	3 oz
Potato, medium	Steamed potato	5 oz
Vegetable	Buttered carrots	3 oz
Bread, sliced	White bread	1
Margarine	Margarine	2 t
Dessert	Applesauce	1/2 c
Milk	Milk	1 c
DINNER		
Soup	Cream of tomato	1 c
Crackers	Saltines	5
Meat	Sliced turkey	3 oz
Potato or starch	Rice	1/2 c
Vegetable	Chopped green beans	1/2 c
Salad	Fruit in gelatin	1/2 c
Dressing	Mayonnaise	1 T
Bread, sliced	White bread	1
Margarine	Margarine	2 t
Dessert	Peaches, halves	2
Milk	Milk	1 c
EVENING NOURISHMENT		
Milk	Milk	1 c
Graham crackers	Graham crackers	2

*If allowed by physician.

Adapted from the *Diet Manual,* Board for Texas State Hospitals and Schools, courtesy Cynthia Bishop, R. D.

Low Residue Diets

A diet low in residue or fiber may be needed when the handling of vegetable or fruit fibers is difficult or when as few irritants as possible are needed as in the case of a resident who has colitis; restriction may be needed on fruits, especially those with skins and a strong structure, vegetables, especially leafy greens, whole grain cereals or breads and even some fibrous or fatty meats. If these are chopped or pureed, they may be allowed. Some doctors allow cooked fruits and vegetables low in fiber to be served whole, such as tender carrots, beets and asparagus tips or canned tender items such as string beans, whole tender meats, canned peeled fruits such as peaches, peeled apricots, pears, etc. depending upon the resident's problem. On the other hand, some doctors may insist on *strained* rather than items processed into a slurry in a blender. Generally, allow lean tender meats, fish or poultry if chopped or minced, fats, milk, cheese and eggs. Allow potatoes and fruit or vegetable juices. Some may have milk and most should. Further restriction on some diets may eliminate fats, especially those that are difficult to emulsify in the intestinal area. For more information see Tables 5-29 and 5-30.

Table 5-29—LOW RESIDUE DIET

Allow	Avoid	Allow	Avoid
BEVERAGES Milk, 2 c/day, coffee, tea, carbonated beverages	An excess of 2 c milk/day; for some de- caffeinated coffee	**EGGS** Cooked in shell, poached or scrambled	Fried
		FAT Butter, mar- garine, cream	All others
BREADS AND CEREALS Enriched white bread or toast, saltine crackers cooked cereal such as farina, cream of wheat, strained oatmeal or dry cereal such as cornflakes	Whole wheat or graham bread, whole-grain cereals	**FRUIT JUICE** Orange, grape- fruit, grapefruit and pineapple, grape, prune for some	None
CHEESE Cottage cheese, mild cheddar cheese in sauces	Sharp cheese	**FRUITS** Canned peaches, pears, applesauce or any strained bland fruit	Raw fruits and all others
DESSERTS* Flavored gelatin, custard, vanilla or chocolate ice cream, plain cake, plain cook- ies, puddings (no nuts, seeds or coconut) made from corn- starch, rice or tapioca, fruit whips from allowed fruit	No desserts with non-allowed fruits or those with nuts; no pies or pastries	**MEAT, FISH AND FOWL** Tender beef, lamb, fowl, boneless fish, liver; broil, boil or roast these items	Tough meat, gristle, con- nective tissue, fried food or fatty meat or fish
		POTATO OR STARCHY FOODS Potato baked, boiled, mashed; rice, noodles, spaghetti, maca- roni	No potato skins, no hominy, no fried foods

Allow	Avoid	Allow	Avoid
SOUPS*		VEGETABLES	
Broths, soups from meat stock, strained cream soups made from allowed vegetables	Spicy soups	Cooked and blendered: asparagus tips, beets, carrots, green beans, green peas, spinach, squash; tomato juice	All others
SUGARS AND SWEETS			
White or brown sugar, jelly, honey, sirup, hard candy	Jams or preserves with skins or seeds		

*Do not exceed 2 c milk allowance including ice cream, cream soups or other milk in foods.

Allow salt and flavorings but no spices, parsley, garlic, onions, etc.

Adapted from the *Diet Manual,* Board for Texas State Hospitals and Schools, courtesy Cynthia Bishop, R. D.

Table 5-30–LOW RESIDUE MEAL PLAN AND MENU

Meal Plan	Sample Menu	
BREAKFAST		
Fruit juice, strained	Orange juice	6 oz
Cereal, cooked, strained	Oatmeal	1/2 c
Egg	Poached egg	1
Bread, sliced	Toast, white	1
Margarine	Margarine	2 t
Jelly	Apple jelly	1 T
Milk	Milk, whole	1 c
Sugar	Sugar	3 t
Beverage	Coffee or tea	1 c
MID-MORNING NOURISHMENT		
Juice	Tomato juice	6 oz
Crackers or bread	White roll	1
LUNCH		
Soup, strained	Chicken broth	1 c
Meat or substitute	Roast beef	2 oz
Potato or starch	Mashed potato	2/3 c
Vegetable, pureed	Carrots	1/2 c
Margarine	Margarine	2 t
Bread, sliced, white	Toast	1
Dessert	Applesauce	1/2 c
Beverage	Tea, iced	8 oz
MID-AFTERNOON NOURISHMENT		
Fruit or dessert	Pureed peaches	1/2 c
Crackers	Saltines	5

Meal Plan	**Sample Menu**	
DINNER		
Meat or substitute	Turkey	3 oz
Potato or starch	Rice	1/2 c
Vegetable, pureed	Green beans	1/2 c
Bread, white	Toast	1
Margarine	Margarine	2 t
Salad	Tomato aspic	1/2 c
Dressing	Mayonnaise	1 T
Dessert	Apricot whip, cream	1/2 c
Milk	Milk, whole	1 c
EVENING NOURISHMENT		
Fruit juice	Pineapple	6 oz
Cereal product	Vanilla wafers	5

NOTE: Sometimes with these diets it may be necessary to reduce irritating substances in the digestive tract. This requires that pungent spices or even meats that develop a high amount of gastric solutions might be limited.

Adapted from the *Diet Manual,* Board for Texas State Hospitals and Schools, courtesy Cynthia Bishop, R. D.

Liquid Diets

For long term care facilities not giving intensive care, liquid diets will usually not be needed because it is generally the critically ill, surgical or others who need such a diet. In some cases, they may be used when individuals get the "flu bug." One diet, called a full liquid, and another, called a clear liquid, are most frequently used; both are usually lacking in essential nutrients and should be continued for as short a time as possible.

When solid foods cannot be tolerated or non-irritating foods are needed, these will be given. The benefit of the diet is that at least something can be taken and some small amount of energy and nutrition given but the diet is usually lacking in nutrients. It is largely psychological and insures that the resident gets fluids. (See Tables 5-31 and 5-32 for a full liquid diet and Tables 5-33 and 5-34 for clear liquid diets.)

Table 5-31—THE FULL LIQUID DIET

Allow	Avoid	Allow	Avoid
BEVERAGES Coffee, tea, milk, milk beverages, carbonated beverages	All others, for some de-caffeinated coffee may be needed	**MEAT, FISH OR FOWL** Strained, served as soup, etc.	All others
BREADS AND CEREALS Cereal gruel (strained highly re-fined cereals)	All others	**POTATO** Strained cream of potato soup	All others
DESSERT Custard, plain puddings, flavored gel-atin, vanilla ice cream, sherbet with-out pulp	All others	**SOUP** Broth Strained soups	Meat broths may be restricted for some
EGGS Custards, milk drinks	All others	**SWEETS** Sugar, honey, sirup	All others
FATS Butter, margarine, cream	All others	**VEGETABLES** Strained or strained served in cream or broth soups: asparagus, carrots, green beans, peas, spinach, tomatoes	All others

Adapted from the *Diet Manual*, Board for Texas State Hospitals and Schools, courtesy Cynthia Bishop, R. D.

Table 5-32—MEAL PLAN AND SAMPLE MENU FOR FULL LIQUID DIET

Meal Plan	Sample Menu	
BREAKFAST		
Fruit juice	Orange juice, strained	6 oz
Cereal	Farina gruel	3/4 c
Sugar	Sugar	
Milk	Milk	1 c
Coffee or tea	Coffee or tea	
10:00 AM NOURISHMENT		
Milk	Milk	1 c
LUNCH		
Fruit juice	Grapefruit juice, strained	6 oz
Soup, strained	Cream of potato	
Dessert	Raspberry gelatin	
Milk	Milk	1 c
Coffee or tea	Coffee or tea	
Sugar	Sugar	
2:00 PM NOURISHMENT		
Fruit juice	Blended pineapple and grapefruit	
DINNER		
Soup	Beef broth	3/4 c
Dessert	Ice cream	
Milk	Milk	1 c
Coffee or tea	Coffee or tea	
Sugar	Sugar	

Adapted from the *Diet Manual,* Board for Texas State Hospitals and Schools, courtesy Cynthia Bishop, R. D.

Table 5-33—THE CLEAR LIQUID DIET

Allow	Avoid	Allow	Avoid
BEVERAGES		**SOUPS**	
Coffee, tea, carbonated beverages	All others, some may have to have de-caffeinated coffee	Fat-free clear broths	All others
		SUGARS	
		Plain sugar candy	All others
DESSERTS		Sugar	
Flavored gelatins	All others		
FRUITS			
Strained fruit juices	All others		

Adapted from the *Diet Manual,* Board for Texas State Hospitals and Schools, courtesy Cynthia Bishop, R. D.

Table 5-34—MEAL PLAN AND SAMPLE MENU
FOR CLEAR LIQUID DIET

Meal Plan	Sample Menu
BREAKFAST	
Fruit juice, strained	Orange juice
Coffee or tea	Coffee or tea
Sugar	Sugar
10:00 AM NOURISHMENT	
Fruit juice, strained	Grapefruit juice
LUNCH	
Broth, strained	Chicken broth
Fruit juice, strained	Orange juice
Flavored gelatin	Cherry gelatin
Tea or coffee	Tea or coffee
Sugar	Sugar
2:30 PM NOURISHMENT	
Broth	Beef broth
DINNER	
Broth, strained	Tomato beef broth
Fruit juice, strained	Orange juice
Flavored gelatin	Strawberry gelatin
Tea or coffee	Tea or coffee
Sugar	Sugar
8:30 PM NOURISHMENT	
Flavored gelatin	Apple gelatin

Adapted from the *Diet Manual,* Board for Texas State Hospitals and Schools, courtesy Cynthia Bishop, R. D.

Miscellaneous Diets

If children or young people are in the facility, different modified diets will be needed by them than those that have been discussed here; diet manuals should list these requirements. Many diets such as tube feedings, high or low protein, high calorie, high calcium, high iron, low purine, acid-ash, dry or others are not covered since they will be seldom used. If the diet manual does not cover them, the physician prescribing the diet should list requirements.

SUMMARY ON DIET PLANNING

After all the modified diets needed are planned, the planner should check to see that all dietary requirements have been met as nearly as possible. The list of those on diets should be checked, also review new admittances to be sure that someone has not been missed. Someone who knows about dietary management should oversee dietary management procedures. Clearly identify diets on the menu and on other materials. Impress upon helpers and diet aides the importance of seeing that the diet program goes as planned. If substitutions are made, substitute with like items. For instance, if you plan a substitution for winter squash, substitute a yellow vegetable such as carrots. This type of substitution is very important and should be stressed in making changes.

TYPES OF MENUS

This text presents a limited number of menus. There are excellent sources for menus and it would only be a repetition to include them here. A recent publication written by Brother Zaccarelli and Mrs. Maggiore entitled *Nursing Home Menu Planning, Food Purchasing and Management* is available and will cover almost any need in menu planning. Others may be secured from government agencies, the American Hospital Association, the American Dietetic Association, etc.

The most common menu is one that is planned for a specific period and then replaced by a new menu for the next period. This is the type of menu described previously in this chapter. Using such a menu, means that the planning task must be repeated each time a new menu is needed. The job is never done.

A much simpler method is being used increasingly. This is the cycle plan method. For this, menus are planned to repeat themselves within a specified period. For long-term care facilities, a menu should not be repeated more frequently than every 18 days. In short-term care institutions, the menu cycle can be 5 to 8 days. In the long-term facility, with an 18-day cycle, plan four Friday and four Sunday menus to prevent detection of repetition on these days since fish may be served on Fridays and Sundays may call for special foods. It is best not to have a cycle menu repeat itself on the same day of the week. Thus, a 21-day menu will repeat each day's meal on the same day when the cycle repeats. Using a 21-day cycle but introducing eight different Sunday meals may hide the fact that the menu is being repeated this often. One could plan a cycle using this pattern so that not until the eighth week would a menu be repeated on the same day; for example:

Week		21-day Cycle					
	Sun	Mon	Tues	Wed	Thur	Fri	Sat
1	1	1	2	3	4	5	6
2	2	7	8	9	10	11	12
3	3	13	14	15	16	17	18
4	4	19	20	21	1	2	3
5	5	4	5	6	7	8	9
6	6	10	11	12	13	14	15
7	7	16	17	18	19	20	21
8	8	1	2	3	4	5	6
9	9	7	8	9	etc.		

This gives no repetition of the same menu on the same day of the week. Normally cycle menus are changed for each of the four seasons of the year. This provides variety and makes it possible to use seasonal foods. Each cycle usually runs for 13 weeks. Special occasions and holidays may require special menus. When this occurs, the cycle meal is dropped and the special meal used. In setting up a cycle, plan the most commonly modified diets with the cycle.

There are advantages in using the cycle menu; more time can be taken in planning and costing because the total overall planning time is reduced. Furthermore, with repetition, experience gained in a previous run of the cycle can be put to use. Refinements can be made; quality improved; costs studied and controlled. Purchasing and requisition may be simplified. Table 35 lists three weeks of a summer/spring general diet cycle planned for the Rice Council by Gilbert-Knotts Dietary Consultants of Houston, Texas under the supervision of the Institutional Department and Mrs. Dorothy F. Hutcheson, Institutional and Consumer Director for the Rice Council. Table 36 shows how 3 days from these 3 week general diet menus are expanded into the most commonly used modified diets in small health facilities. Table 37 provides a menu that can be used when a dietitian is on the staff to indicate selections allowed for each modified menu. This simplifies planning as each dish no longer has to be planned for a specific diet. By using this menu, diet decisions can be made as foods are dished for each particular resident.

Table 5-35–SPRING/SUMMER CYCLE MENU

Spring/Summer		GENERAL	
	MORNING	*NOON*	*EVENING*
SUNDAY	Orange Juice	Roast Beef au jus	Cream of Tomato Soup
	Oatmeal or Ready-to-eat Cereal	Escalloped Potatoes	Egg-Ripe Olive Salad on
	Pancakes with Syrup	Buttered Green Peas	Whole Wheat Bread
	Oven Browned Sausage	with Pearl Onions	Pear-Lime Gelatin Salad
	Butter[1]	Fresh Spinach with Bacon Salad	Oatmeal Cookies
	Coffee–Milk	Hot Roll	Milk
		Butter[1]	
		Cherry Pie	
		Milk, Coffee, or Tea	
MONDAY	Apricot Nectar	Beef and Cheese Patty	Chicken Rice Medley*
	Cream of Wheat or	Hashed Brown Potatoes	Grapefruit and Avocado Salad
	Ready-to-eat Cereal	Seasoned Green Beans	with Dressing
	Poached Egg	Confetti Cole Slaw	Bread
	Cinnamon Raisin Toast	Hot Roll	Butter[1]
	Jelly	Butter[1]	Baked Custard
	Butter[1]	Chocolate Malt Cake	Milk
	Coffee–Milk	with Chocolate Frosting	
		Milk, Coffee, or Tea	
TUESDAY	Stewed Prunes with Lemon	Baked Pork Chop	Hot Creme Vichyssoise
	Cream of Rice or	Candied Sweet Potatoes	Crackers
	Ready-to-eat Cereal	Seasoned Greens	Meat Salad Sandwich
	Fried Egg	Peach Half with Cottage Cheese	Carrot and Celery Sticks
	Crisp Bacon	Cornbread	Butter[1]
	Sweet Roll	Butter[1]	Fruit Bars
	Butter[1]	Lemon Pudding	Milk
	Coffee–Milk	Milk, Coffee, or Tea	

*Rice Council recipe
[1] or margarine

(cont.)

Table 5-35—SPRING/SUMMER CYCLE MENU (cont.)   Week 1

	MORNING	GENERAL NOON	EVENING
WEDNESDAY	Apple Juice Malt-O-Meal or Ready-to-eat Cereal Soft-cooked Egg Toast—Jelly Butter[1] Coffee—Milk	Southern Fried Chicken Whipped Potatoes Buttered Broccoli Tomato Wedges with Mayonnaise Hot Roll Butter[1] Fruited Rice Dessert* Milk, Coffee, or Tea	Neapolitan Spaghetti Tossed Green Salad with Dressing French Bread Butter[1] Orange Sherbet Milk
THURSDAY	Orange Juice Ralston or Ready-to-eat Cereal Scrambled Eggs Crisp Bacon Banana Bread Butter[1] Coffee—Milk	Beef Stew Marinated Cucumbers Cornbread Butter[1] Fresh Berry Cobbler Milk, Coffee, or Tea	Corn Chowder Crackers Ham Salad Sandwich Fruited Raspberry Gelatin Salad Butter[1] Pound Cake Milk
FRIDAY	Grapefruit Juice Grits or Ready-to-eat Cereal Poached Egg Toast—Jelly Butter[1] Coffee—Milk	Swiss Steak Mashed Potatoes Seasoned Yellow Squash Caesar Salad Hot Roll Butter[1] Orange Chiffon Cake Milk, Coffee, or Tea	Soup-er Salmon Bake* Spicy Apricot Mold Bread Butter[1] Peanut Butter Cookies Milk
SATURDAY	Grape Juice Oatmeal or Ready-to-eat Cereal Fried Egg Sausage Patty English Muffin—Jelly Butter[1] Coffee—Milk	Hamburger Casserole with Mashed Potato Topping Buttered Green Peas Perfection Salad Cornbread Butter[1] Chocolate Meringue Pie Milk, Coffee, or Tea	Ham and Asparagus au Gratin Corn O'Brien Bread Butter[1] Fresh Fruit Cup Milk

Week 2

	Breakfast	Dinner	Supper
SUNDAY	Melon Wedge Cream of Wheat or Ready-to-eat Cereal Scrambled Eggs Crisp Bacon Cinnamon Toast Butter[1] Coffee—Milk	Roast Turkey Sage Dressing and Gravy Cranberry Sauce Buttered Cauliflower Assorted Relish Plate Parkerhouse Rolls, Butter[1] Fresh Strawberry Shortcake with Whipped Topping Milk, Coffee, or Tea	Cold Plate: Tomato Stuffed with Seasoned Cottage Cheese Deviled Eggs Bread Butter[1] Apple Crisp Milk
MONDAY	Grapefruit Juice Cream of Rice or Ready-to-eat Cereal Hard-cooked Egg Honey Bran Muffins Butter[1] Coffee—Milk	Marengo Meat Balls with Rice* Baked Summer Squash Tossed Green Salad with Dressing Bread Butter[1] Cherry Cake Pudding Milk, Coffee, or Tea	Beef Noodle Soup Crackers Pimiento Cheese Sandwich Fruited Strawberry Gelatin Salad Butter[1] Frosted Lemon Cupcake Milk
TUESDAY	Apricot Nectar Malt-O-Meal or Ready-to-eat Cereal Fried Egg Crisp Bacon Toast—Jelly Butter[1] Coffee—Milk	Breaded Pork Cutlet with Cream Gravy Whole Kernel Corn Steamed Cabbage Cinnamon Applesauce Hot Roll Butter[1] Ice Cream Milk, Coffee, or Tea	Beef Tips on Mashed Potatoes Grated Carrot and Pineapple Salad Bread Butter[1] Baked Custard with Spring Fruit Sauce Milk
WEDNESDAY	Orange Juice Oatmeal or Ready-to-eat Cereal Creamed Eggs Hot Biscuits—Jelly Butter[1] Coffee—Milk	Savory Liver and Rice* Seasoned Green Beans Marinated Vegetable Salad Cornbread Butter[1] Butterscotch Pudding Milk, Coffee, or Tea	Tomato Bouillon Crackers Hot Open-face Chicken Sandwish Pear-Cottage Cheese Salad Butter[1] Spice Cake with Mocha Frosting Milk

*Rice Council Recipe   [1]Or margarine

(cont.)

Week 2

Table 5-35—SPRING/SUMMER CYCLE MENU (cont.)

	MORNING	NOON	EVENING
THURSDAY	Pineapple Juice Ralston or Ready-to-eat Cereal French Toast with Sirup Sausage Butter[1] Coffee—Milk	Stuffed Cabbage Roll Seasoned Fordhook Limas Congealed Waldorf Salad Cornbread Butter[1] Fudge Brownie Milk, Coffee, or Tea	Ham and Cheese Pudding Buttered Green Peas Tossed Green Salad with Dressing Bread Butter[1] Lime Chiffon Pie Milk
FRIDAY	Grapefruit Sections Oatmeal or Ready-to-eat Cereal Scrambled Eggs with Bacon Chips Raisin Toast Butter[1] Coffee—Milk	Savory Baked Chicken Fluffy Whipped Potatoes Buttered Okra Spiced Peach Salad Bread Butter[1] Burnt Sugar Cake with Caramel Frosting Milk, Coffee, or Tea	Homemade Vegetable Soup Crackers Tuna Salad Sandwich Dill Pickle Chips Butter[1] Tropical Dessert Mold* Milk
SATURDAY	Apple Juice Cream of Rice or Ready-to-eat Cereal Omelet Toast—Jelly Butter[1] Coffee—Milk	Beef Tip Stroganoff on Parsleyed Noodles Buttered Brussels Sprouts Congealed Bing Cherry Salad Bread Butter[1] Sunshine Cake with Fudge Frosting Milk, Coffee, or Tea	Salisbury Steak with Tomato Sauce New Potatoes and Green Beans Bread Butter[1] Bread Pudding with Custard Sauce Milk

Week 3

	Breakfast		
SUNDAY	Blended Fruit Juice Malt-O-Meal or Ready-to-eat Cereal Fried Egg Blueberry Muffin Butter[1] Coffee—Milk	Grilled Ham Steak with Mustard Sauce Au Gratin Potatoes Baked Eggplant with Tomatoes Ribbon Molded Salad Hot Roll Butter[1] Coconut Cream Pie Milk, Coffee, or Tea	Cream of Asparagus Soup Cottage Cheese Fruit Plate Graham Crackers Butter[1] Lime Sherbet Milk
MONDAY	V-8 Vegetable Juice Oatmeal or Ready-to-eat Cereal Poached Egg Crisp Bacon Toast—Jelly Butter[1] Coffe—Milk	Smothered Steak Buttered Crumb Potatoes Buttered Mixed Vegetables Sliced Banana-Orange Section Salad Cornbread Butter[1] Jelly Roll Milk, Coffee, or Tea	Italian Chicken Spaghetti Buttered Green Beans Tossed Green Salad with Dressing French Bread Butter[1] Pineapple-Rhubarb Pie Milk
TUESDAY	Grapefruit Juice Grits or Ready-to-eat Cereal Soft-cooked Egg Cinnamon Coffeecake Butter[1] Coffee—Milk	Meat Loaf with Jardiniere Sauce Mashed Potatoes Buttered Broccoli Sliced Tomatoes Hot Roll Butter[1] Blueberry Cake with Lemon Sauce Milk, Coffee, or Tea	Neptune Casserole* Green Peas with Mushrooms Apricots in Cherry Gelatin Bread Butter[1] Ribbon Pudding Parfait Milk

*Rice Council Recipe   [1]Or margarine

(cont.)

Week 3

Table 5-35—SPRING/SUMMER CYCLE MENU (cont.)

GENERAL

	MORNING	NOON	EVENING
WEDNESDAY	Stewed Prunes Cream of Wheat or Ready-to-eat Cereal Pancakes with Maple Sirup Crisp Bacon Butter[1] Coffee—Milk	Pork Tips Cantonese Parsleyed Buttered Rice Buttered Julienne Zucchini Hot Roll Butter[1] Almond Cookies Milk, Coffee, or Tea	Canadian Cheese Soup Crackers Roast Beef Sandwich Lettuce Wedge with Thousand Island Dressing Butter[1] Strawberry Whip Milk
THURSDAY	Orange Juice Oatmeal or Ready-to-eat Cereal Fried Egg Toast—Jelly Butter[1] Coffee—Milk	Herbed Baked Chicken Escalloped Potatoes Creole Green Beans Grapefruit-Apple Salad Hot Roll Butter[1] Fresh Peach Pie Milk, Coffee, or Tea	Hot German Rice Salad* Buttered Spinach Bread Butter[1] Chocolate Drop Cookies Milk
FRIDAY	Sliced Bananas Malt-O-Meal or Ready-to-eat Cereal Poached Egg Sausage Patty Toast—Jelly Butter[1] Coffee—Milk	Fried Fish Tartar Sauce Hashed Potato Patty Mexican Coleslaw Bread Butter[1] Angel Cake with Raspberry Sauce Milk, Coffee, or Tea	Beef Pot Pie with Pastry Sliced Tomato, Asparagus and Hard-cooked Egg Salad Bread Butter[1] Fresh Melon Balls Milk
SATURDAY	Grape Juice Cream of Rice or Ready-to-eat Cereal Scrambled Eggs with Bacon Bits Toast—Jelly Butter[1] Coffee—Milk	Roast Lamb Buttered New Potatoes Seasoned Turnip Greens Cornbread Muffin Butter[1] Pineapple Upside Down Cake Milk, Coffee, or Tea	Cold Salad Plate: Ham and Cheese Sandwich Potato Salad Jellied Cranberry Sauce Banana Pudding Milk

*Rice Council Recipe   [1]Or margarine   Reproduced through the courtesy of the Rice Council, Houston, Texas, P. O. Box 22802, 77027

Table 5-36—MODIFIED DIETS FROM SPRING/SUMMER CYCLE MENU

TUESDAY
Week 1
Spring/Summer

	GENERAL	SOFT-BLAND	ADA MEAL PLAN NO. 2 (1500 Calories) DIABETIC	RESTRICTED SODIUM (1 gram Sodium)
MORNING	Stewed Prunes with Lemon	Prune Juice	Unsweetened Stewed Prunes (2)	Stewed Prunes with Lemon
	Cream of Rice or	Cream of Rice or	Cream of Rice (½ c) or	SF Cream of Rice or
	Ready-to-eat Cereal	Ready-to-eat Cereal	Ready-to-eat Cereal	Shredded Wheat
	Fried Egg	Scrambled Eggs	Scrambled Egg (1)	SF Scrambled Egg (1)
	Crisp Bacon	Crisp Bacon	Toast (1 slice)	SF Toast—Jelly
	Sweet Roll	Toast—Jelly	Butter[1] (1 pat)	SF Butter[1]
	Butter[1]	Butter[1]	Coffee—Tea	Coffee—Milk
	Coffee—Milk	Coffee—Milk		
		(Decaffeinated for bland)		
NOON	Baked Pork Chop	Baked Pork Chop	Baked Pork Chop (3 oz)	SF Pork Chop
	Candied Sweet Potatoes	Buttered Noodles	Buttered Noodles (½ c)	SF Candied Sweet Potatoes
	Seasoned Greens	Buttered Spinach	Seasoned Greens	SF Turnip Greens
	Peach Half with	Peach Half with	Lettuce Salad with	Peach Half Salad
	Cottage Cheese	Cottage Cheese	Low Calorie Dressing	SF Bread
	Cornbread	Bread	Bread (½ slice)	SF Butter[1]
	Butter[1]	Butter[1]	Butter[1] (1 pat)	Lemon Pudding
	Lemon Pudding	Lemon Pudding	Diet Peach Halves (2)	Coffee—Tea
	Milk, Coffee, or Tea	Milk	Milk[2] (1 c)	
EVENING	Hot Creme Vichyssoise	Hot Creme Vichyssoise	Tomato Juice (½ c)	SF Hot Creme Vichyssoise
	Crackers	Crackers	Meat Salad Sandwich (2 oz meat, 2 slices bread, and 1 t mayonnaise)	SF Crackers
	Meat Salad Sandwich	Meat Salad Sandwich		SF Meat Salad Sandwich
	Carrot and Celery Sticks	Applesauce	Carrot and Celery Sticks (⅛ c)	Applesauce
	Butter[1]	Butter[1]	Diet Applesauce (⅛ c)	SF Butter[1]
	Fruit Bars	Sugar Cookies	Coffee—Tea	SF Sugar Cookies
	Milk	Milk	**BEDTIME:**	Milk
			Milk[2] (1 c)	
			Crackers (4)	
			Butter[1] (1 pat)	

[1] Or margarine
[2] Part of milk may be used for coffee, tea, or cereal

(cont.)

Table 5-36—MODIFIED DIETS FROM SPRING/SUMMER CYCLE MENU (cont.)
SUNDAY
Week II
Spring/Summer

	GENERAL	SOFT-BLAND	ADA MEAL PLAN NO. 2 (1500 Calories) DIABETIC	RESTRICTED SODIUM (1 gram Sodium)
MORNING	Melon Wedge Cream of Wheat or Ready-to-eat Cereal Scrambled Eggs Crisp Bacon Cinnamon Toast Butter[1] Coffee—Milk	Pineapple Juice Cream of Wheat or Ready-to-eat Cereal Scrambled Eggs Crisp Bacon Cinnamon Toast Butter[1] Coffee—Milk (Decaffeinated for bland)	Melon Wedge (1/6) Cream of Wheat (1/2 c) or Ready-to-eat Cereal Scrambled Egg (1) Toast (1 slice) Butter[1] (1 pat) Coffee—Tea	Melon Wedge SF Cream of Wheat or Shredded Wheat SF Scrambled Egg (1) SF Cinnamon Toast SF Butter[1] Coffee—Milk
NOON	Roast Turkey Sage Dressing and Gravy Cranberry Sauce Buttered Cauliflower Assorted Relish Plate Parkerhouse Rolls Butter[1] Fresh Strawberry Shortcake with Whipped Topping Milk, Coffee, or Tea	Roast Turkey Mashed Potatoes Buttered Carrots Cranberry Sauce Salad Bread Butter[1] Peach Shortcake with Whipped Topping Milk	Roast Turkey (3 oz) Sage Dressing (1/2 c) Buttered Cauliflower Radish Roses and Celery Sticks Bread (1 slice) Fresh Strawberries (1 c) Milk[2] (1 c)	SF Roast Turkey SF Sage Dressing Cranberry Sauce SF Bu Cauliflower Radish Roses SF Bread SF Butter[1] SF Strawberry Short- cake, Whip. Topping Coffee—Tea
EVENING	Cold Plate: Tomato Stuffed with Seasoned Cottage Cheese Deviled Eggs Bread Butter[1] Apple Crisp Milk	Cold Plate: Apricot Halves Stuffed with Cottage Cheese Deviled Eggs Bread Butter[1] Apple Crisp Milk	Cold Plate: Tomato Stuffed with Sea- soned Cottage Cheese (1/4 c) Deviled Egg Bread (1 slice) Butter[1] (1 pat) Diet Baked Apple Coffee—Tea BEDTIME: Milk[2] (1 c) Bread (1 slice) Butter[1] (1 pat)	Cold Plate: Tomato Stuffed with SF Seasoned Cot- tage Cheese SF Potato Salad SF Bread SF Butter[1] SF Apple Crisp Tea

[1] Or margarine
[2] Part of milk may be used for coffe, tea, or cereal

WEDNESDAY
Week III
Spring/Summer

	GENERAL	SOFT-BLAND	ADA MEAL PLAN NO. 2 (1500 Calories) DIABETIC	RESTRICTED SODIUM (1 gram Sodium)
MORNING	Stewed Prunes Cream of Wheat or Ready-to-eat Cereal Pancakes with Maple Sirup Crisp Bacon Butter[1] Coffee–Milk	Prune Juice Cream of Wheat or Ready-to-eat Cereal Scrambled Eggs Crisp Bacon Toast–Jelly Butter[1] Coffee–Milk (Decaffeinated for bland)	Stewed Prunes (2) Cream of Wheat (½ c) or Ready-to-eat Cereal Scrambled Egg (1) Crisp Bacon (1 strip) Toast (1 slice) Coffee–Tea	Stewed Prunes SF Cream of Wheat or Puffed Wheat SF Pancakes with Maple Sirup or SF Scrambled Egg (1) SF Butter[1] Coffee–Milk
NOON	Pork Tips Cantonese Parsleyed Buttered Rice Buttered Julienne Zucchini Hot Roll Butter[1] Almond Cookies Milk, Coffee, or Tea	Roast Pork Buttered Rice Buttered Julienne Zucchini Bread Butter[1] Sugar Cookies Milk	Roast Pork (3 oz) Parsleyed Buttered Rice (½ c) Buttered Julienne Zucchini Bread (½ slice) Butter[1] Diet Baked Apple (1) Milk[2] (½ c)	SF Roast Pork SF Parsleyed Bu Rice SF Bu Julienne Zucchini SF Bread SF Butter[1] SF Sugar Cookies Coffee–Tea
EVENING	Canadian Cheese Soup Crackers Roast Beef Sandwich Lettuce Wedge with Thousand Island Dressing Butter[1] Strawberry Whip Milk	Cream of Cheddar Soup Crackers Roast Beef Sandwich Butter[1] Strawberry Whip (no seeds) Milk	Cream of Cheddar Soup (½ c) Roast Beef Sandwich (2 oz beef, 1 slice bread and 1 t mayonnaise) Lettuce Wedge with Low Calorie Dressing Fresh Strawberries (1 c) Coffee–Tea **BEDTIME:** Milk[2] (1 c) Bread (1 slice) Butter[1] (1 pat)	SF Cream of Potato Soup SF Crackers SF Roast Beef Sandwich Lettuce Wedge with Oil and Vinegar SF Butter[1] Strawberry Whip Milk

[1] Or margarine
[2] Part of milk may be used for coffee, tea, or cereal
Reproduced through the courtesy of the Rice Council, Houston, Texas,
P. O. Box 22802, 77027

Table 5-37–GENERAL AND MODIFIED DIETS FOR A LARGE FACILITY WITH A DIETITIAN ON THE STAFF

PRIVATE FLOOR MENU
Grapefruit Jce
Cream of Wheat
Eggs to order
Tiny Sausages
W W Toast–Bu
Coffee–Milk–Tea

WARD MENU
Grapefruit Jce
Cream of Wheat
Eggs to order
W W Toast–Bu
Coffee–Milk–Tea

PRIVATE FLOOR MENU
Gumbalaya–Crackers
Veal Fricassee on Bu Home-
  made Noodles–Parsley
Hearts of Romaine with
  Grapefruit Sections (3)
  and Avocado Slivers (2)–
  French Dressing
Crusty Roll–Bu
Tiny Hermits (2)
Coffee–Milk–Tea

WARD MENU
Gumbalaya–Crackers
Veal Fricassee on Bu Home-
  made Noodles–Parsley
Peach Half with Cottage
  Cheese on Lettuce Leaf
  with Celery Seed Drsg
Crusty Roll–Bu
Tiny Hermits (2)
Coffee–Milk–Tea

PRIVATE FLOOR MENU
Scotch Broth–Crackers
Braised Pork Chop
Cream New Potatoes and Peas
Garden Salad with Chiffonade
  Dressing
Butterfluff Roll–Bu
Warm Rhubarb Crisp
Coffee–Milk–Tea

WARD MENU
Braised Pork Chop–Gravy–Parsley
Whipped Potatoes
Garden Salad with Chiffonade Drsg
Butterfluff Roll–Bu
Warm Rhubarb Crisp
Coffee–Milk–Tea

SOFT MENU
Grapefruit Jce
Cream of Wheat
Eggs to order
Crispy Bacon
White Toast–Bu
Coffee–Milk–Tea

MODIFIED MENU
SF Cream of Wheat
Shredded Wheat
SF Bread

SOFT MENU
Str Gumbalaya–Crackers
Braised Sirloin Tips on Bu Home-
made Noodles–Parsley
Molded Soft Fruit in
Cherry Jello
White Toast–Bu
Snickerdoodle Cookie (2)
Coffee–Milk–Tea

MODIFIED MENU
Str Cr of Spinach Soup
Bouillon
SF Braised Sirloin Tips
(no flour)
SF Veal Fricassee
SF Cubed Veal
SF Ground Veal
Cream Grd Veal
Noodles
SF Noodles
Fluffy Potatoes
SF Fluffy Potatoes
SF Spinach
SF Hot Spiced Beets
(no sugar)
SF Sv Spinach
Oil and Vinegar
SF Bread
SF Crusty Roll
Grapefruit Sections
Tapioca Cream
SF Oatmeal Cookies (2)

SOFT MENU
Str Scotch Broth–Crackers
Plain Salisbury Steak–Parsley
Cream New Potatoes
Bu Sv Peas
White Toast–Bu
Warm Rhubarb Crisp
Coffee–Milk–Tea

MODIFIED MENU
Str Cream of Pea Soup
Broth
Braised Pork Chops
(no flour)
SF Br Pork Chop
(no flour)
SF Gravy
SF Pl Salisbury Steak
Ground Beef in Broth
SF Ground Beef
SF Steam New Potatoes
SF Cream New Potatoes
SF Whipped Potatoes
SF Cauliflower
SF Peas
SF Sv Peas
SF Zero Dressing
SF Bread
SF Butterfluff Roll
Apricot Halves
Banana Slices in D
Pineapple Juice
Baked Custard
SF Warm Rhubarb Crisp

Computers can plan menus. Those who have utilized the computer for menu planning report that a menu lower in costs with a better balance of nutrients can be achieved when it is used.

IBM has a programmed unit called Computer Automated Menu Planning (CAMP) used for planning hospital menus. Trans Tech also has a unique computer controlled program. Using either one, one can set up restraints on cost, nutrients and repetition of menu items. This assures a desired cost, nutritional balance and variety. The programmed unit contains recipes for every menu item in the computer and so it is possible to get, additionally, a recipe print-out which gives the exact recipe needed to produce the quantities required. Orders and requisitions can also be a part of the print-out. The program has been carefully planned, reviewed and tested by experience and it can usually give a better menu of higher acceptability, less cost and increased management control than manual planning. Few small health facilities have a computer or access to one and, therefore, the discussion of the use of a computer program at this time may be somewhat academic. Trans Tech of Kansas City also has an excellent computer program for dietary use.

This small diet card identifies the patient and diet. It can be posted at bedside, kept in a file or accompany meals. Courtesy Physician's Record Co., Berwyn, Illinois.

DIET CARD

Date _____ Room No. _____

Patient _____

Doctor _____

Liquid _____

Soft _____

Light _____

General _____

Drinks _____

Preference _____

Objections _____

FORM N-30.1
P.R.CO.,BERWYN,ILLINOIS   PRINTED IN U.S.A.

DIET ORDER

WARD No._____   _____19___

PATIENTS' CENSUS	
_____Regular_____	_____Ward Nurse, Day
_____Light _____	_____ " " Night
_____Soft _____	_____Special Nurse, Day
_____Fluid _____	_____ " " Night
_____Special _____	_____Orderlies, Day
	_____ " Night
_____Total _____	_____Total _____

GENERAL WARDS

Milk_____   Lemons _____
Eggs_____   Oranges _____

_____   _____
_____   _____
_____   _____
_____   _____
_____   _____

- -

WARD No._____   DIET KITCHEN

Custards _____   Gelatine _____
Baked Apple_____   Junket_____
Beef Juice_____   Cocoa _____

_____   _____
_____   _____
_____   _____
_____   _____
                            _____Head Nurse

FORM N-401   PHYSICIANS' RECORD CO., BERWYN, ILLINOI   PRINTED IN U.S.A.

Fig. 5-5. *Above is a diet order sheet which can be sent to the kitchen f₍ diet foods for a floor. If foods are to be prepared in the diet kitchen, the bc tom part of the sheet can be torn off and sent there for filing.*
Courtesy Physician's Record Co., Berwyn, Illinois.

DIET LIST

Date _____

NAMES	DIET			
	Reg.	Soft	Liq.	Special
1				
2				
3				
4				
5				
6				
7				
8				
9				
10				
11				
12				
13				
14				
15				
16				
17				
18				
19				
20				
21				
22				
23				
24				
25				
26				
27				
28				
29				
30				

FORM N-651   PHYSICIANS RECORD CO., BERWYN, ILLINOIS   PRINTED IN U S A.

Fig. 5-6. *A diet list indicating the type of diets and the names of residents to receive them. Such a record may be kept on the floor and also maintained in the kitchen to indicate diets required. Courtesy Physician's Record Co., Berwyn, Illinois.*

Personnel	Officers	Doctors	Nurses	Special Nurses	Employees	Night Attaches	Total
Breakfast							
Dinner							
Supper							
Nursing Units							
Regular							
Light							
Soft							
Liquid							
Special							
Guests							
Doctor's Rx							
Total							

Dietary   Report   Date

FORM N-652

PHYSICIANS' RECORD CO., BERWYN, ILLINOIS

PRINTED IN U.S.A.

Fig. 5-7. A report on foods served from the food-service department for a day including regular and modified diets as well as foods for staff. Courtesy Physician's Record Co., Berwyn, Illinois.

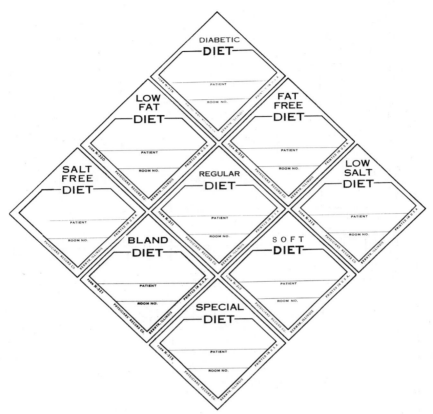

Fig. 5-8. *Modified and regular diet cards in a variety of colors are used on trays or foods to identify the type diet. In addition to color differences, bold letters also identify the diet. The name of the resident and the room number also helps in the identification. Courtesy Physician's Record Co., Berwyn, Illinois.*

Salad dressings are frequently high in calories and high in fat and few references give others that can meet the needs of many modified diets. The following are two salad dressings that can be used for such diets:

NO-CAL SALAD DRESSING

YIELD: 2¼ qt or 96 portions   EACH PORTION: 2 T

INGREDIENTS	WT.	MEAS.	METHOD
Tomato juice	4 lb	2 qt	1. Blend all ingredients together.
Lemon juice or			Stir well before using.
vinegar	1 lb	1 pt	
Onion, minced	½ lb	1 c	
Salt	½ oz	1 T	Note: Omit salt for low-sodium
Pepper, white		1 t	diets and pepper for bland
			diets

SALT-FREE LOW-FAT COOKED SALAD DRESSING

YIELD: 2 qt or 100 portions   EACH PORTION: 1½ T

INGREDIENTS	WT.	MEAS.	METHOD
Cornstarch	4 oz	¾ c	1. Mix dry ingredients together.
Mustard, dry	¼ oz	1 T	
Milk, dry, non-fat	8 oz	2 c	
Pepper, white		2 t	
Water, cool	1¼ lb	4½ c	2. Blend water and vinegar or
Lemon juice or			lemon juice together and mix
vinegar	12 oz	1½ c	into the dry ingredients to a
			smooth paste. Cook until thickened in a double boiler, stirring constantly.
Egg whites	5 oz	6	3. Whip egg whites to a soft foam,
Sugar	4 oz	½ c	adding sugar to make a soft meringue. Pour <u>hot</u> mixture into meringue, folding carefully.
Salt	½ oz	1 T	4. Remove salt-free portions and add salt in the proportion of ¼ t per c of mixture remaining. ½ oz of salt would be used with the total recipe.

Bibliography

American Dietetic Assn. *Guidelines for Developing Diet Manuals for Nursing Homes and Related Facilities.* Chicago: American Dietetic Assn.,610 N. Michigan, 1967.

American Dietetic Assn. *Handbook of Diet Therapy,* 4th ed. Chicago: American Dietetic Assn., 610 N. Michigan, 1965.

American Dietetic Assn. *Meal Planning with Exchange Lists.* Chicago: American Dietetic Assn., 610 N. Michigan, 1964.

American Heart Assn. *Sodium Restricted Diets.* New York: American Heart Assn., 44 E. 23rd St.

American Hospital Assn. *Diet and Menu Guide for Extended Care Facilities.* Chicago: American Hospital Assn., 840 Lake Shore Drive, 1967.

American Hospital Assn. *Cycle Menus for Small Hospitals and Nursing Homes.* Chicago: American Hospital Assn., 840 Lake Shore Drive, 1964.

Federation of Protestant Welfare Agencies, Inc. *Manual for Homes for the Aged.* New York: Federation of Protestant Welfare Agencies, 281 Park Ave., So.

Federation of Protestant Welfare Agencies, Inc. *Menu Maker for Homes for the Aged.* New York: Federation of Protestant Welfare Agencies, Inc., 281 Park Avenue, So.

Howell, Sandra C. and Loeb, Martin B. "Nutrition and Aging," *The Gerontologist.* Washington, D. C.: 1969.

Iowa State Dept. of Health. *Simplified Diet Manual,* 3rd ed. Ames, Iowa: Iowa State University Press, 1969.

New York State Dept. of Social Welfare. *Diets for Use in Homes for the Aged,* 2nd ed. Albany, N. Y.: 112 State St., 1966.

U. S. Dept. of Agriculture. *Food Guides for Older Folks,* Home and Garden Bulletin, No. 17. Washington, D. C.: Government Printing Office, 1969.

U. S. Dept. of Health, Education and Welfare, Public Health Service. *A Guide to Nutrition and Food Service.* Washington, D. C.: Government Printing Office, 1965.

University of Massachusetts. *The Cyclical Menu,* Food Management Program Leaflet, No. 6. Amherst, Mass.: Co-operative Extension Service, 1962.

Zaccarelli, Herman E. and Maggiore, Josephine, R. D. *Nursing Home Menu Planning, Food Purchasing and Management.* Boston: Cahners/Institutions Books, 1972.

VI: FOOD PRODUCTION PRINCIPLES

We can live without poetry, music or art,
We can live without conscience or live without heart,
We can live without friends or live without books,
But civilized man cannot live without cooks.

AUTHOR ANONYMOUS.

QUANTITY FOOD PRODUCTION Producing food in quantity is a highly specialized task. It requires a well planned foodservice department with good equipment, good organization and planning, a skilled staff, well planned menus, accurate recipes, good purchasing and cost control and good cooks. The cook is one of the most important factors and must be an individual who possesses knowledge and skill plus a real interest in doing a good job.

Unfortunately, the knowledge and skill needed to produce good foods in quantity cannot be acquired by reading one chapter. It takes a book and, in addition, perhaps a number of separate articles plus a lot of experience to acquire enough knowledge to know how to cook in quantity. The references given at the back of this chapter will be helpful to those who would seek to learn more. But, even if one reads all these, the job will not be done. It is a lifetime job of learning. It never ends.

Many foods are highly perishable products. Their quality lasts for only a short time. For this reason, production and service must be timed to occur close together. Foods are made up of chemical substances that can react with other food substances and we must control these reactions, allowing them to occur when we want them to but stopping them from occurring when we don't want them to happen.

Cooking an egg, making a cake, broiling meat or even making coffee requires some knowledge of the physical and chemical reactions that go on. If one understands these reactions, he has a better chance of producing a higher quality product. While few cooks would think of themselves as skilled chemists, they really are. Many of our finest chefs are not only skilled in the physical manipulation needed to produce foods but they are also highly trained in the technological problems involved in quantity food production.

Quantity cooking methods should not be confused with cooking small quantities at home even in those cases where only a single egg is cooked at a time. The planning, organization, service and other techniques used are much different than for home cooking. If home methods are used, we frequently get a poor quality product because such a method is not suited to the production of foods in quantity. Professional methods are required and, to gain proficiency, one must learn these methods.

THE STANDARDIZED RECIPE   A standardized recipe is a control used to produce a specific quantity of food of known quality. It should be set up to give, in an organized manner, all the information needed to produce the item. Ingredients should be listed in order of use. They should also be listed by weight and by measure. The method of handling these ingredients must be precisely stated. (See page 235 for an example of a good recipe form.)

There are many acceptable forms for quantity recipes, but usually the form shown at the end of the preceding chapter on Menu Planning is used. Some of the major rules in establishing the format for this type of presentation are:

1) Place title in the center of the top line and the code letters or numbers on the same line, top right.

2) In the line below, on the left, indicate the total yield and portions and opposite, on the right, indicate the portion size.

3) On the next line, list as headings: Ingredients, Weights, Measures and Methods. Leave space for columns below these.

4) List the ingredients in order of use in the first column on the left. Separate ingredients into groups as used and leave a space between groups. In the proper columns, indicate the weights and measures of the ingredients. In the Methods column, list by number the various procedures that must be used to prepare these ingredients.

5) At the bottom of the card note the pan or baking container size, panning or baking instructions, temperatures, times, special notes or substitutions. Sometimes special portioning instructions must be given.

6) Use only one side of a recipe card. The back of the card can be used for information on quality of product or observations noted in preparation, etc. Use two cards if more space is needed.

7) Recipes for certain categories of menu items are frequently put on colored cards with the color indicating the kind of food. Thus, meat and entree recipes may be on pink cards; cakes, on white, etc.

8) It is desirable to indicate total time needed to produce the recipe and not only the time needed for a worker to put the ingredients together.

Ingredients should be precisely identified. The word "flour" is not enough; there could be confusion between cake, pastry, rye, bread, potato or another kind of flour. For the same reason, do not put the word "sugar" down without describing the type required; it may be "granulated," "brown" or "powdered" or whatever is needed to assure use of the right ingredient.

List all ingredients by weight and measure. Some thick liquids and a few other ingredients may be listed by measure only. The best cooks and bakers weigh rather than measure.

Use precise terms; there is a big difference in the action taken in a recipe depending on whether the words "whip," "beat," "stir" and "fold" are used. Using one technique for another can ruin a product. Give exact quantities needed. Use spaces or capitals to emphasize. Seldom italicize or underline. Do not say "season to taste." Give exact quantities.

Write out abbreviations for weight or measure in the singular even though there are more than one—for instance, write "4 qt" not "4 qts." The following abbreviations are considered standard in recipe work:

t	teaspoon	in.	inch
T	tablespoon (3 t)	lb	pound
c	cup (8 oz. or 16 T)	oz	ounce
gal	gallon (16 c)	gm	gram
pt	pint (2 c)	mg	milligram (1/1000 of a gram)
sec	second	AP	as purchased
min	minute	EP	edible portion
hr	hour	AS	as served

Note that no periods are used after these abbreviations except for inch; a period is used after in. to prevent confusion with the word "in."

Recipe cards are usually put into stiff plastic covers to protect them from soil. Some facilities provide recipe card holders at work spaces so workers do not have to keep picking up the recipe to read it while producing the item. Instead, the recipe is right in front of them where they can see it.

Recipe Development

Every facility will need to develop its own recipes. New recipes need changing to suit special needs and old ones need constant revision. Set up a standard procedure for testing and standardizing recipes.

To check a recipe, note the ingredients and their ratio to each other. There are standard proportions needed in food preparation; for instance, a medium thick sauce or gravy takes from 10 to 12 oz of pastry flour per gal of product. If there is a high sugar or acid content, more will be needed. Some other ingredients may also thicken, however, and so the amount of flour may have to be reduced.

A high ratio butter cake has about 45% shortening, 100% flour, 70% eggs, 100% liquid, 125% sugar—all ingredients are stated in percentages to flour—and if a recipe varies too much from these ratios, the product will not be a good one. The memorization of the most frequently used ratios is recommended so one can quickly spot problems. While the rules may not always hold—a German Chocolate Cake recipe doesn't—usually they do.

Next, check total yield. Add up the weights of all ingredients and, after allowing for baking loss, preparation loss, etc., see if the yield is logical. Some quantity recipes can actually claim a greater yield than the total weight of the ingredients used!

The portion size divided into the total yield gives the number of portions obtained. Check this. Thus, if the yield for salad dressing is a gallon and the recipe says the number of portions obtained is 100 and the portion is 1¼ T, this is not correct. A gallon has 256 tablespoons in it and so a gallon would give 200 1¼ T portions rather than 100.

Then, break the recipe down to a small batch and prepare it. Check quality, yield and set up what might be considered to be a desirable portion. Note flavor, appearance, color, texture, etc. and write down your observations.

It is wise to have the reactions of others also. If necessary, retest the recipe incorporating changes. When satisfied, bring the recipe up to the amount needed to give the desired number of portions. Test. Revise. Constant checking of recipes should also occur after they go into production. Train the staff to jot down suggestions on the back of the recipe card when they use a recipe.

QUANTITY COOKING

MEATS Meat is usually the most expensive item in a meal. Frequently, it is also the item around which the other foods served are planned. Equally important, the meat served has a great deal to do with the satisfaction offered by the meal.

The method of cooking used must suit the meat. Some meats are quite tender and require very little cooking while others are tough and take a long time to cook and need special methods that will tenderize them. Even though a flesh item might be tender, it still may not be possible to treat it by a method considered suitable for very tender products. For instance, most veal is very tender but is so low in fat that it cannot be broiled, although the method of broiling is used frequently for quite tender meats. Some quite tender meats may best be cooked by the moist heat method usually used for tougher meats. For instance, tender pork chops are often braised.

Two things must be remembered in cooking meat: 1) it is about three-fourths water and 2) its solids are largely protein and these coagulate in cooking. Incorrect cooking can cause a sizable moisture loss with a consequent loss of moistness, tenderness, texture, flavor and portions in the finished product. It can also toughen the protein, making it unpalatable.

Gentle heat causes meat to lose less moisture and also results in a less solidly coagulated product. The flesh of animals, fish and fowl is composed of very long, tiny, slender fibers or tubes filled with a liquid. The finer the fibers, the more delicate and tender the meat; young animals have fine fibers, the size increases with age. A soft, smooth, silky sheen on the cut surface of meat usually indicates tenderness and fine quality.

Heat makes a change in meat fibers. The change starts at around 145°F, when the fibers lose moisture. Then, around 165°F, much of the moisture remaining within the fiber sheath firms up and the color changes; this process is called "coagulation." We can see coagulation when an egg cooks—it becomes solid and changes color.

If the heat is intense or lasts too long, the moisture loss is increased and the coagulated protein becomes more solid and, thus, tougher. Of the two, intense heat is worse than extended heat, especially if the cooking is gentle. Fish, crab, oysters or other shellfish become extremely tough and shrunken if cooked too long or cooked by too high a heat. If cooked gently for only a short time, they will be plump and tender. Animal flesh, cheese or other products high in protein behave somewhat similarly.

Meat fibers are bound together by connective tissue and the amount and kind varies in different flesh foods. Young animal flesh has less connective tissue than that from older animals. The muscles on the animal receiving the most exercise have the most connective tissue. Different breeds or kinds of animals have different amounts of connective tissue in the msucles. Dairy cattle will have more than beef cattle. The amount of connective tissue in meat has much to do with its tenderness; if there is a lot, the meat will usually be tough.

There are two kinds of connective tissue; one is called collagen and is the white connective tissue, the other is called elastin and is the yellow connective tissue. Collagen can be dissolved by gentle moist heat into water and gelatin; acid speeds this reaction. Elastin cannot be tenderized by cooking. It must be broken up in the meat by pounding, grinding, cubing or by other mechanical means.

An enzyme, usually papain from papaya, can be used to dissolve connective tissues; we call such substances "tenderizers." Some animals may have a tenderizer injected into them just before slaughter so their flesh has a tenderizer in it when we buy it. Other meats are dipped into a liquid tenderizer or the tenderizer may be a powder sprinkled onto the meat. The enzyme works slowly, or not at all, at low temperatures but works fast as the meat warms up. At around 130°F, it will be quite active and at 150°F it will be destroyed. If we cook tenderized meat to the rare stage (140°F) and hold it for a long time, it becomes pulpy and soft.

Tender meat—meat from young animals or fowl—is usually cooked by dry heat cooking methods and tough meat is cooked by moist heat cooking methods. Dry heat methods do little tenderizing of meat. Too much dry heat will cook meat to a well done stage and make the meat slightly tough because so much moisture is lost and the protein is so thoroughly coagulated. It is possible to have a very tender sirloin steak, cook it under a broiler under high, intense heat and wind up with a rather tough product.

Moist heat methods cook to complete doneness while at the same time they tenderize, the moisture slowly dissolving the collagen. Meat cooked by moist heat is usually well done; meat cooked by dry heat can be either rare, medium or well done.

The moisture loss we get in cooking meat is called *shrink*. The longer the cooking time, the greater the shrink. Also, the higher the cooking temperature, the greater the shrink. The greater the shrink, the more moisture loss. This means less portions as well as a loss in palatability. Meat from young animals is higher in moisture and, therefore, shrinks more than meat from older animals. Meat that is aged shrinks less than unaged meat but, since meat loses some moisture in aging, the final yield is about the same.

The following definitions are usually applied to dry and moist heat cooking methods:

Dry Heat

Broil   To subject to radiant (glowing) heat.

Panbroil   Cooking in a pan or griddle with no fat; accumulated fat is removed.

Saute   To fry in 1/8- to 1/4-in. of fat.

Deepfry   To immerse and cook in hot fat.

Barbecue   To subject to radiant heat while basting with a special sauce or to bake in a sealed enclosure heated previously with glowing coals.

Roast or bake   To cook in an oven with no moisture and in an uncovered pan.

Ovenizing   Placing in shallow pans and baking in an oven; a small quantity of fat may be put on the pan bottom, or oil or melted fat may be drizzled over the items; they end up much like sauteed foods.

Moist Heat

Stew   To cook in a small quantity of water but in more water than is used in braising.

Simmer or poach   To cook immersed in water without boiling; poaching is gentle cooking in only enough water to cover.

Braise   To cook in natural meat juices or in a very small quantity of water with the cover on; may also be called Swissing, casseroling, pot roasting, jugging, etc.

Steam   To cook in steam either under pressure or free-venting.

Blanch   To steam or dip into very hot water for a short time; usually used to pre-prepare meat for other cooking, such as preparing liver so sinews and membranes can be removed.

Meat is not usually boiled because this toughens it; simmering is a preferred way of cooking meat that must be cooked in water.

Fatty meat tissues may contain from 20 to 50% moisture; fat meat is apt to be more moist after cooking than lean meat. Some fat must be present in meat if it is to broil or bake properly. This fat can be on the outside or can be the fat flecks between the meat tissues called *marbling.*

The moisture in the fat bastes the meat as it cooks and keeps it moist. For this reason, when we put a rib roast in the oven, we turn it with the fat side up; or we roast a fowl with the back up so the fat from the back melts and drips down over the breast, keeping it moist.

Lean meat needs some fat if it is to be cooked by dry heat and this is why we may *lard* meat (pull strips of fat through it) or *bard* meat (lay fatty meats such as bacon or salt pork over it). The flesh of young animals contains less fat than that of older ones but very old animals have a very lean flesh. Desexing a male bird or animal puts more fat on and in the flesh. A recipe for roasting veal may say to cover the roasting pan although this ordinarily should not be done when roasting. With veal, it is desirable because it helps keep some of the moisture around the meat, thus preventing it from drying out.

Each type of flesh has its own flavor. Sardines have a different flavor than veal. The most distinctive flavor in flesh is in the fatty tissues, although the flesh will also have a distinctive and definite flavor.

Fat is an organic substance that can absorb other organic substances. (Alcohol is an organic compound used to absorb flower essences and thus make perfume.) The fat in the flesh is more able, therefore, to absorb organic aromatic compounds (in chemistry called *esters*) than is the moisture in the flesh. When corn, seaweed, fermented mash or peanuts, for instance, are eaten, the fat of the animal easily picks up the aromatic esters in this feed and builds up a flavor from these in the flesh. This is why cornfed beef or pork, wild ducks feeding on wild rice, or Smithfield hams from hogs fed on peanuts have such distinctive flavors. Beef cattle fattened on beer in Japan are considered a superior product.

Meat can be aged under the proper temperature and humidity to become more tender, more moist and more flavorful. This occurs because natural enzymes in the flesh create desirable changes in the meat during such storage. Aged meat is more expensive because it costs money to age meat since money is tied up during the aging process. Aged meat must also be trimmed and this loss must be made up by charging more for the meat when it is sold.

Meat, to age well, must have a good fat cover on the outside to protect it from bacteria, molds and tarnish. Meat that does not have such a covering can be put into moisture-vapor proof bags. This is called Cryovacing. The meat will be more moist than that aged by conventional methods but it shrinks more in cooking, so the end result is about the same. Aged meats may brown a little more easily. Aged meat, because it is more acid, turns to a done color at a lower temperature than unaged meat. Salt delays the browning of meat and so we usually do not salt meat until browning is complete.

The color of the meat usually indicates doneness. Meat that is still red is called *rare*; if pink, *medium* and, if a completely done color, *well done*. Temperatures can also be used to indicate doneness. Temperatures that indicate specific degrees of doneness are:

Beef	Rare 140°F, medium 160°F and well done 170°F.
Lamb or mutton	Medium 160°F, well done 170°F.
Pork, fresh	Well done 165°F—pork is always cooked well done.
Pork, cured	Well done 160°F to 170°F.
Veal	Well done 165°F.
Poultry	Well done 175°F in breast or thigh; 160°F in dressing center.

In quantity cookery, we cook meats to a lower temperature than in small quantity cooking. This is because we have larger pieces of meat which build up heat inside them and continue to rise in temperature for a time after we remove them from the oven heat. Thus, if we want a sirloin roast or a rib roast rare, we take it from the oven when the temperature is about 115° to 125°F because it will rise in temperature after it is removed from the oven and, if we take it out at 140°F, by the time we use it, it will no longer be rare.

In quantity cooking, we also frequently heat meat again before serving it. Thus, we might cook a pot roast, slice it, put it in pans, put a bit of the meat juices over it, cover it and put it into a steam table or oven to hold it for service. This cooks the meat more. Remember, aged meats cook to doneness at a lower temperature than the temperatures listed above, but since health facilities usually will not be using aged meat, this problem will rarely be encountered.

It takes longer to cook frozen meat than meat that is not frozen. If frozen meat is allowed to *nearly* thaw, the time difference is not too great. Hard frozen meat takes two to three times as long to roast as thawed meat.

When meat thaws, it loses a lot of the B-vitamins in the drip. This drip is usually lost. Therefore, meats should be almost thawed by holding in a refrigerator and then cooked. Covering a frozen beef patty on a grill helps to speed thawing. After the patty is thawed, it can be uncovered and cooked the same as one that is thawed would be. Cooking in hot fat speeds thawing. After the meat treated this way is almost thawed, it can be removed from the fat and cooked normally.

Do not thaw meats at room temperature; thaw them under refrigeration. Gentle thawing, like gentle cooking, is best for meat. Learn how to preplan the thawing time so meats are removed long enough before cooking to come to the proper temperature. Products that have been frozen and thawed and then refrozen lose quality. There is also a danger that the product may have become contaminated in the long process and be a food that could make individuals ill.

VEGETABLES AND FRUITS

The preparation and cooking of vegetables and fruits are very important because quality and nutritional yield are closely associated with the methods used. Most of the important minerals and vitamins in these items are water soluble. If left in contact with water too long, especially after paring or cutting up, a large loss of these nutrients can occur. Therefore, observe the rule, "Soak for as short a time as possible and divide up fruits and vegetables as little as possible during soaking."

Deep paring can also increase the loss of nutrients because they may be concentrated under the peel. Ascorbic acid oxidizes easily and so chopped fruits or vegetables allowed to stand a long time may lose a lot of this nutrient. Aerating juices helps to encourage this loss, especially if the juice stands; aerating just before serving reduces the loss and may help palatability enough to make this desirable.

Heat can destroy nutrients, especially thiamine or ascorbic acid. If these are in an alkaline medium, the rate of destruction is increased. This is why we do not recommend adding soda (an alkaline medium) to the cooking water for green vegetables, to keep them green, or to dry beans, peas, etc., to make them become tender more quickly.

We recommend that fruits and vegetables be cooked for as short a time as possible and just before they are to be served. Batch cooking is recommended so fresh-cooked items can be served. No fruit or vegetable should be kept in the steam table or held for service longer than 20 to 30 minutes. Not only nutrients but quality is also lost by a long holding time. Normally, the best flavored, best appearing, best textured product is also the most nutritious. We should guard against nutrient loss; nutrients are badly needed by those who eat the food. We may not always know when we are losing nutrients; riboflavin can even be destroyed by sunlight.

The vitamin and mineral content of fruits and vegetables will be found to be greatest at the peak of their maturity. Buying them at this stage, holding them for as short a time as possible and preparing and cooking them correctly can do much to assure that products of top nutritional value are served.

Vegetables and fruits depend for best acceptability upon their color, flavor and texture. The preparation and cooking methods used can be influential in giving these qualities.

Color in Vegetables

Some color pigments in fruits and vegetables are easily destroyed or changed. They are chemicals and react chemically. Red items such as beets or plums are red because they contain a substance called *anthocyanins.* It is water soluble and turns red in an acid solution and a dirty blue or purple in an alkaline one. This is why we usually see beets treated with vinegar and why red cabbage is cooked with tart apples. For the same reason, we do not use soda when we want a nice looking blueberry or cranberry muffin.

Anthocyanins are stable to heat but if we cook beets too long, sometimes there is a color change. These pigments can react with metals and produce a muddy, murky liquid. We see this in punch sometimes, especially if we add tea to the punch and the tannins from it join with the iron salts in the juice.

Some other red vegetables or fruits contain a red pigment called *lycopenes.* This is not soluble in water and is very stable to heat, acids or alkalies. These pigments are related to the *carotenes,* pigments found in carrots, peaches, squash and other yellow or orange fruits and vegetables. The carotenes are very stable and are not destroyed by heat, acids or alkalies. They are also not very water soluble. Carotenes can be used by the body to produce vitamin A.

Flavones are the white pigments found in many fruits and vegetables. They are very soluble and turn white in an acid medium and yellow in an alkaline one. This is why onions may turn yellow when cooked in hard water. A bit of cream of tartar can give an acid reaction and the onions will turn white again. Some white vegetables of the cabbage family may turn red with long cooking. This is not because of the flavones but because sulfur compounds in the vegetable turn red.

Green vegetables contain *chlorophyll,* a green pigment; it is destroyed by heat and the destruction is speeded if acid is present. It is not water soluble. Quick cooking and quick serving will keep green vegetables green.

Many flavors in fruits and vegetables are easily lost or changed in cooking. They can be leached out or can boil off in cooking. Delicately flavored items should be cooked for as short a time as possible in as little water as possible. A bit of salad oil, about 2 t per qt of water, helps to absorb these flavors and keep them from boiling away.

To shorten cooking time, have the water salted and boiling when the vegetables are added—unless the vegetables are for a low-salt diet; then omit the salt. Bring back to a boil as quickly as possible. Cook uncovered. If you wish to speed the heating-to-boiling stage, cover, but remove the cover when boiling starts. Vegetables have an acid in them that is quite volatile and, if we leave the cover off, this escapes in the steam and does not fall back into the vegetables.

Members of the onion and cabbage families have a lot of flavor and we don't mind losing some of it. Therefore, we cook these in a lot of water. If vegetables of this group are young, they have milder flavors. They develop strong flavors if they are stored a long time.

Sometimes shortening the cooking time helps to stop flavor development in members of the cabbage family. Because acids help to develop strong flavors in these vegetables, we usually cook them with the cover off. Members of the onion family, however, lose some of their pungent flavor with long cooking. This is why we may fry them a bit before putting them into dressing, or we may add them to a stew sooner than we add the other vegetables. Dividing members of the onion family into small bits also helps to get rid of some of the strong flavor.

Cellulose, a carbohydrate, is the item giving much of the texture to fruits and vegetables. It is this product that we say gives bulk in the diet. The amount of cellulose in an item determines whether it is tough or tender.*

---

*The tenderness or softness in fruits also depends upon the softening effect of enzymes or pectins and other products.

Old beets, asparagus or other old vegetables have more cellulose than young ones. Different parts may also vary in the amount of cellulose they contain. The stems of asparagus, broccoli or kale are tougher than the tips. We may peel these tougher parts or cut them up to remove a part of the cellulose. Or, we may cook them longer than the more tender parts. This is why we may tie asparagus into bundles, cook the bundles standing up for a short time and then tip them over, cut the strings and cook stems and tips together. Most fruits will have less cellulose in them than vegetables so there may not be the problem in cooking them tender that vegetables present.

Cooking softens cellulose and the amount of cellulose present will decide how long an item must be cooked. Tender spinach or new peas cook quickly but carrots, turnip greens and potatoes take longer because they contain more cellulose. An alkaline medium softens cellulose more than an acid one. Tender vegetables get mushy and slimy when cooked in alkaline water. If we add an acid medium such as molasses, catsup or vinegar to dried beans or other legumes, it may take them a long, long time to cook tender.

Sugar strengthens cellulose. If we want a fruit to be broken up, we cook it in water and then sweeten it after cooking. If we want it to stay in whole pieces, we add sugar to the water, dissolve it and then cook the fruit in this.

Vegetables high in starch need special cooking so they have enough moisture to swell the starch. Thus, potatoes, squash and others should be steamed or boiled. If boiled, the boiling should be gentle so as not to break up the product. These vegetables can also be baked since they have enough moisture in them to soften the cellulose.

Canned vegetables and fruits require limited preparation for cooking, but the practice of just warming vegetables and serving them is sometimes the reason why they are not well received. Attention should be given to adding flavor or other desirable attributes to vegetables to help gain acceptance.

Frozen vegetables (except corn-on-the-cob and perhaps some greens, such as spinach) should be cooked from the frozen state. Have the water boiling and drop the vegetables into this in pieces, if possible. Cover and bring to a boil as rapidly as possible. Thaw frozen vegetables before trying to steam them because the mass is usually so great that the outside is cooked long before the inside and an unevenness in doneness occurs. Most frozen vegetables are preblanched which partially cooks them. They require less cooking for this reason. Presoak most dried, dehydrated or freeze-dried vegetables. This gives a plumper product and a better yield. Cooking time is also shortened.

Pasta, Rice, Grains, Cereal

Macaroni, spaghetti and other similar products, rice and grains must be boiled in a considerable amount of water, a gal of water to a lb of product. We cook these to tenderness and no more. The Italian chef says "al dente" which means "to the tooth." Thin, shell macaroni products can be brought to a boil, covered and allowed to stand in a warm place for about 20 minutes to become adequately cooked. Blanch in cold water and then use. Rice can be moistened with a bit of oil, about 1 T per c of rice, and then, using 2 parts water to each part of rice, be brought gently to a boil. Stir only once before the mixture boils. Then cover and cook gently. The rice will absorb all of the moisture and come out with separate grains. If there is excess moisture, uncover and allow the rice to steam for a short time and dry out.

To cook breakfast cereals, use a gal of water per lb of fine cereal and 3 qt of water per lb of coarse cereal, such as oatmeal. Have the water boiling and drop the cereal in slowly, stirring constantly. Stir slowly until boiling starts and then stop. Stirring after this makes a more pasty, sticky product. Salt may be added after the salt-free portions of the cereal are removed. The amount of salt to be added is a scant T of salt per gal of cereal.

Make a dry dressing or stuffing by using an oz of moisture (2 T) per cup of soft bread cubes or double this for a more soft, moist dressing. Remember to bake dressing immediately after making it or, if it is to be held for a period, cool all items separately before mixing. This safeguards against bacterial growth. Refrigerate also, if you must hold it before baking. Do not stuff dressing into poultry or meats. Bake separately in shallow quantities not more than 2 to 3 in. deep and bake *thoroughly*. Cool any dressing remaining after a meal is served and then spread it thinly in pans, cover and place under refrigeration.

Deep Frying

Deepfrying may nave limited use in a health facility because of the restriction on fried foods for many. However, some may be able to have them and, if they can, should. Just because some residents cannot have certain food items, all should not be denied. Deepfrying gives high palatability to some fruits and vegetables.

Because hot fat can be dangerous and cause fires or give dangerous burns, good frying techniques should be used. A good, heavy duty gas or electric deepfryer with thermostatic control is needed. Use a good frying oil or a fat made especially for deepfrying. If special fats for deepfrying are not used, use refined salad oils such as cottonseed, soy or peanut oil. Do not use fats that are hydrogenated or emulsified for use in the bakeshop. Fats containing emulsifier break down very rapidly when subjected to heat above 360°F.

Keep the fryer and oil clean. Smoking oil indicates a breakdown of the oil. Acrolein, a white smoke, is a substance that irritates the eyes, nose and throat and is produced when oil or fat smokes. Most good frying fats, the first time they are used, should reach 440°F before smoking and after considerable use should not smoke at 375°F. If they smoke below this, they should be discarded. A fat that foams instead of bubbles when foods are added to it should be discarded.

If about 20% of the oil or fat in the kettle is used each time deepfrying occurs and is then replaced with new oil or fat, there will be little need at any time to throw away any fat, especially if the oil is strained each time it is used. Crumbs and sediment cause a fat to break down. Store frying oils under refrigeration when not in use, except those that have not yet been used. These can be stored in regular cool storage. Melt solid fats at a temperature below 200°F to prevent charring the fat around the heating coils in the fryer.

The knowledge that hot fat is combustible should always be kept in mind. A grease fire is a terrible thing and a great danger to residents. (See the chapter on Safety for a discussion of grease fires.) An accurately calibrated thermostat and precision in following correct frying temperatures is needed. Any time a fat smokes, there is danger present. The flash point of old frying fats is lower than that of good ones. The following are smoke and flash points for good frying fat or oil:

	SMOKE POINT	FLASH POINT*
General purpose shortening, hydrogenated, solid	400°F	600°F
Emulsified shortening, baking type, solid	360°F	550°F
Deepfrying fat, liquid	440°F	616°F
Salad oil, vegetable	400°-430°F	600°-620°F

*Flash point means the temperature at which fat bursts into flame.

In deepfrying, do not try to cook too much at one time. Use a ratio of 1 part of potatoes to 6 of fat for deepfrying potatoes and 1:5 to 1:8 for other foods. A fryer holding 15 lb of fat should not be loaded with more than 2½ lb of potatoes at one time and not more than 2 to 3 lb of other foods. Use recommended temperatures. If the fat is colder than recommended, the product will soak up grease. When at the proper temperature, the food cooks properly and when done reaches the proper color.

Metals, such as copper, brass or nickel, cause fat to break down more quickly; stainless steel does not. Salt or curing salts from cured meat also break down fat. Salt foods after frying and do it away from the kettle. Do not deepfry bacon or other cured meats. This puts unsaturated fatty acids into the fat which lower its smoking temperature. Water can speed the breakdown of frying fats and so foods should be as dry as possible. Keeping foods dry also helps to reduce spattering and bubbling.

Sauteing

Sauteing is frying in shallow fat. Many factors to be observed in deepfrying should be observed in sauteing also. Lower frying temperatures for sauteing in butter, bacon fat, olive oil, etc. may be needed. As fat spreads into a shallower area, therefore covering a greater surface area, it smokes more easily.

Keep pans and griddles used for sauteing clean. Once a griddle or pan is fixed so foods do not stick on it, it should not be washed or allowed to contact water. Cleaning can be done with a clean, soft cloth. Use the griddle or pan only for sauteing. This is especially important for pans that eggs are cooked in. To condition a griddle or pan for eggs, put some oil into the pan with some coarse salt. Heat the pan and rub with a cork, piece of paper or cloth as the fat comes up to a hot temperature. Remove and continue to scrub. Then, discard the fat and salt and clean the surface with a soft, clean cloth. If this surface is washed, it usually must be reconditioned.

About 1/8-to 1/4-in. of fat is needed on the frying surface for sauteing. This is different from panbroiling where no fat is put into the pan and what does accumulate is poured off. Fit the size of the pan to the amount to be sauteed so burning does not occur in the free areas of the pan.

Sauteing may be a preliminary method used before another type of cooking occurs. Vegetables and fruits may be sauteed. American fried, hash brown or cottage fried potatoes are sauteed. Apples are excellent sauteed and served with pork. Tender green, or other, vegetables can be quickly sauteed by tossing them in a pan. At the last stage, a bit of water can be added to help in cooking them. Vegetables are frequently prepared this way by the Chinese and are served before they are completely cooked which gives them unique yet appealing texture, color and flavor.

EGG COOKERY

Eggs are high in protein; consequently, high heat and long cooking can toughen them just the same as they do meats. Those cooking methods also develop strong sulfur flavors and dark colors in eggs. A fresh egg develops these undesirable conditions less easily than an old one. If a small bit of cream of tartar, lemon juice, vinegar or other acid is added to the eggs used for scrambled eggs, souffles or other mixtures, the change is delayed. Holding scrambled eggs or other eggs at too high a temperature can cause them to toughen, develop a strong flavor and become a greenish-black. If the eggs are slightly acid, this will not happen as easily.

Boiling eggs too long causes a greenish-black ring to form around the yolk and a strong flavor to develop. Cooking for a short time or cooking at a lower temperature helps to avoid this. Also, if the egg is immediately plunged into cold water to stop cooking, this undesirable reaction may be avoided.

If an egg is to be sliced or cut in half, some toughness is desirable. Therefore, for eggs to be handled in this manner, boiling at a higher temperature than simmering may be recommended. If the egg is cooked at a low temperature, as is the case when an egg is coddled, the egg may be so tender it cannot be cut even though it is hard cooked. Use the freshest possible eggs for breakfast eggs.

Scrambled eggs are made from a whole egg mixture cooked on a griddle, in a pan or in a bain marie or double boiler. In cooking, they should be lifted up and away from the cooking surface to allow the uncooked portions to come in contact with the heat. Do not overstir but leave the eggs in fairly large segments. Cook only to a soft stage. The eggs should still be moist since, while being held for service, they will cook more. Serve as soon as possible.

Poach eggs in a 4-in. deep shallow pan in water which has 1 T of salt and 2 T of vinegar per gal of water. The salt and the vinegar give a whiter, better bunched-up egg. No more than 16 eggs should be poached at one time per gal of water. Slide the eggs gently, one at a time, from a saucer or put a larger number onto a platter and slide these, all at one time, into the water which is boiling gently. After the eggs are added, they should just simmer. Dropping an egg flat onto the water spreads it out. Sliding it in helps to cushion the entrance and keeps the egg together. Simmer 3 to 5 min. Remove, place in quite warm salted water, never over 160°F, to hold for service.

An egg should be fried or sauteed in a suitably sized pan. There are 1-egg and 2-egg pans. Larger quantities of eggs can be fried in a larger frying pan. Teflon pans help to reduce the amount of fat needed for frying. If not frying in a Teflon pan, have 1/8- to 1/4-in. of quite hot oil, butter or bacon fat in the pan. Add the egg or eggs and drop the heat so overcooking does not occur, since it produces a crusty, strongly flavored egg.

Having the oil hot when the egg is added helps to keep it from spreading out, but as soon as the egg is added the temperature should be dropped. Cover tightly for country-style eggs or add a bit of water and cover so the steam coats the eggs over the top. An over-easy egg is fried until it is almost done and then turned over and cooked until the white is cooked. Sometimes, we baste eggs with hot fat to cook them "country-style." Good, well-conditioned pans are needed to fry eggs.

Omelets may be made singly or, for larger quantities, can be baked in a large pan. They may be plain or foamy. A plain omelet is made from a well blended whole egg mixture. Usually no liquid is added. At first, the egg mixture is lifted as one does scrambled eggs but enough flowing eggs must be left to make a solid continuous mass.

When the pan omelet has set, it can be filled in the center with creamed meat, fish, poultry, mushrooms or other mixture such as marmalade. It is then folded. Press the folded top down around the edges, turn the omelet over and cook until done. Cook at a slightly higher temperature than is used for scrambled or fried eggs.

If the plain omelet is baked, it cannot be filled or manipulated as a pan omelet can be. Items are usually added to the egg mixture for baked omelets. Baked omelets are cut into squares and served with an appropriate sauce. A foamy or puffy omelet is made of well beaten egg yolks and whipped whites which have been carefully folded together and baked in a pan. It is much like a souffle. Souffles are usually easier to make.

The base of a souffle is a fairly heavy, starch-thickened mixture with uncooked egg yolks blended into it. Whipped whites are then carefully folded into this mixture and the product is baked. Chopped or minced ham, melted cheese, chicken, mushrooms or other items can be added to the starch-yolk mixture before folding in the egg whites. It is advisable to serve a sauce over a souffle. A cheese souffle is excellent served with slightly sweetened crushed strawberries.

A baked or shirred egg is baked or steamed. The heat should be gentle so as not to toughen the egg. Place an egg or eggs into a well buttered, small baking dish and place this on a heated surface until the bottom shows a trace of white. Then, put the dish into the oven and bake until the white is done but the yolk is still slightly soft. Chicken livers, strips of bacon, creamed chicken or other items can be placed over the eggs.

Shirred eggs and hash are good. The hash should be *very* hot and about 2-in. deep in a pan. Make indentations in the hash and put an egg into each indentation. Place in an oven and bake. The hash should be hot enough to bake the lower part of the egg. Eggs can be put into a steamer and shirred, but it is difficult to do this and not overcook the yolk.

Boiled eggs for breakfast should be simmered, not boiled. Extend the time a bit to get the same degree of doneness reached by the usual boiling process. The time must also be adjusted to the altitude because water boils at a lower temperature at higher altitudes. At sea level, a soft-cooked egg will be ready at from 4 to 5 min in simmering water, medium-cooked at 5 to 8 min and hard-cooked at 15 min or more. It is difficult to cook breakfast eggs under steam pressure but, if the eggs are the same size and the same temperature each time this is done, experience can finally bring about satisfactory results. Plunge the eggs into warm water to stop their cooking.

Hard-cooked eggs are most easily peeled if they have been hard-cooked at *boiling* temperature for about 15 minutes or more. They should then be plunged into cold water. To peel them, crush the shell well and then, starting at the broad end where the air sac is, begin to peel the shell down. It may be helpful to allow a stream of cold water to run on the egg while peeling it. The water's force loosens the shell and makes it easier to peel away.

Eggs cooked and immediately peeled are usually easier to process than those which have been left in water before peeling. Extremely fresh eggs are difficult to peel. If eggs are to be chopped for egg salad, sandwiches, creamed eggs, and similar uses, break eggs into a greased pan to make a layer about 1 in. deep and bake or steam gently until the eggs are hard cooked. Then, chop.

A fondue or timbale is an egg-thickened mixture that is baked or steamed. The mixture is the same as that used for custard except that it is unsweetened. The baking techniques are the same.

Dessert custards are an egg and milk mixture, sweetened and flavored, and then baked in a low to moderate oven. A soft or stirred custard is not baked but is cooked in a double boiler and stirred until a smooth mixture, much like heavy cream, is obtained. For both types of custards, an egg is used

Table 6-1 –DRY EGG EQUIVALENTS TO FRESH EGGS

	Quantity Fresh			Equivalent in Dry Eggs*	
	Wt (lb)	Measure	Number Large Eggs	Wt (oz)	Measure
Fresh whole eggs	1	2 c	9 to 11	4-1/2	2 c. 2 T
Whites	1-1/8	2-1/4 c	17 to 19	2-1/4	1/2 c
Yolks	7/8	1-3/4 c	20 to 24	7-1/4	1 c

*Add water to make equal to fresh measure

for every cup of milk. The milk and sugar mixture should be about 160°F and blended well into the eggs. Yolks make a stronger custard than whole eggs. Dry whole eggs make a weak custard. Frozen eggs are much the same as fresh eggs but a high quality frozen egg should be used. Dry milk makes a weaker custard than whole or diluted evaporated milk.

To make a custard, use 1½ lb of whole eggs mixed with about 2 c of sugar to 1 gal of hot milk. (Put the milk mixture into the eggs, stirring well.) Flavor. Bake in a pan or in cups in a 325° to 350°F oven. Usually we put the pan or cups into a pan of water so the water bath surrounding the product buffers against the oven heat and lessens the danger of breakdown which is called *syneresis*.

A stirred custard must be stirred constantly in a double boiler over hot water. Overheating must not occur at any point and all areas must be reached frequently in the stirring process. A stirred custard is done when it coats the spoon. It thickens a bit more when it cools. A stirred custard is also close to being done when the foam disappears.

A stirred custard will rise in temperature until it reaches about 175°F and then the temperature will stop rising for a brief period. During this period, coagulation of the egg is occurring. When the temperature starts to rise again, coagulation is completed and there is danger of the eggs separating out from the mixture (syneresis). The product should be removed from the heat and stirred awhile until it cools slightly.

Eggs will form a foam when beaten. A whole egg or yolk can be beaten to a stable foam, especially if sugar is an added ingredient. Egg whites can be beaten more easily into a stable foam. There are commercial stabilizers available which help to make egg foams more stable. These are added to commercial pie meringues, etc. A small quantity of cornstarch also helps to make a meringue more stable.

Eggs beat best to a foam if they are slightly acid and warm. The acid added can be lemon juice, vinegar, cream of tartar, etc. Salt helps to make eggs more extensible and, therefore, to beat up to a better foam.

Egg foams can be separated into four stages of progression from least to most stable foams. These four stages of progression are:

Stage 1: Well blended, still liquid with the foam forming large bubbles; used for scrambled eggs, French toast, cooking or baking.

Stage 2: Soft foam which is shiny, moist and fluid throughout; tips fold over in soft peaks; liquid separates out on standing; this stage is used for sponge or angel cakes, soft meringues, foamy omelets, etc.

Stage 3: Stiff foam; small air cells; lacks fluidity, especially in the whites; still moist, smooth and glossy; points stand when peaked. Used for frostings, divinity, hard meringues, tortes, etc.

Stage 4: Dry foam, dull, dry, brittle, flakes off and can be cut into rigid pieces; some coagulation may appear as curds; it is difficult to beat whole eggs and yolks to this stage; has little use in food preparation because such eggs are so overbeaten they are not extensible in baking or cooking.

To make a stable meringue use 3/4 t of cream of tartar per lb of egg whites. Whites should be at a temperature of about 110°F. Whip and when a fairly good foam is obtained, start to add sugar while continuing to whip. Whip until all the sugar has been added. You should obtain a strong foam that peaks and is quite glossy and smooth. If hard meringue shells are being made, some moisture may have to be added to dissolve all the sugar and not have grainy shells.

For soft meringues for pies and desserts, use about 14 oz of sugar (1-7/8 c) for every unwhipped pt of egg whites. To make hard meringues, use 1-3/4 to 2-1/2 lb of sugar to each pt of egg whites. Bake soft meringues at 350°F for 12 to 18 min; do not bake at lower temperatures because if the whites contain salmonella bacteria, the bacteria will not be destroyed and can be the cause of food poisoning. Bake hard meringues for 1-1/2 hr at 275°F or 50 min at 375°F. Do not overbake because the meringues become too fragile to handle.

MILK PRODUCTS

Milk is a liquid in which are suspended milk fat globules and proteins, milk sugar (lactose) and minerals in solution. One of the big problems in using milk in cooking is its tendency to curdle. This can easily happen with escalloped potatoes, cream soups, milk sauces, etc. Milk is very unstable in the presence of acids such as lemon juice, vinegar, fruits, molasses, brown sugar, calcium chloride used to make canned tomatoes more firm, curing salts, etc. Heat and/or table salt make milk more susceptible to curdling. To prevent curdling, we can do the following:

1. Bind the milk with starch, thickening it somewhat as we do to make a thin white sauce for cream soups.

2. Keep the acid from the milk as long as possible; mix just before service.

3. Salt only before serving.

4. Cook and hold at as low a temperature as possible.

5. Avoid blending milk with items that curdle it.

6. Introduce the product that may curdle the milk to the milk, slowly, giving good agitation; *do not pour the milk into the curdling agent.*
It is not recommended that soda be used to retard curdling since this destroys vitamins. Evaporated milk is the most stable in terms of curdling, fresh milk, next and dry milk solutions, the least.

A considerable quantity of non-fat dry milk should be used in small health facilities for nutritional reasons and because of the cost of fresh milk. It should be used extensively in cream soups, cocoa, puddings, etc. If the concentration of milk solids in non-fat dry milk solutions is greater than that of regular milk, improved nutrition may occur. One can increase the milk solids in puddings, breads and pastries without a loss of quality. About 13 oz of non-fat dry milk per gal of water will give the amount of non-fat solids found in regular liquid non-fat milk, but we usually use 1 lb of dry milk to the gal to get the solid content up.*

Dry or evaporated milk can be whipped to a foam. While these foams are not as stable as foams from whipped cream or the non-dairy type whips, they are adequate. Dry milk foam is not stable over 4-hr; evaporated milk

---

*The Public Health Service and the public health divisions in many states do not always allow the use of dry milk solids in a mixed, unpasteurized solution to be used as a beverage, yet they do allow the use of dry mixes for eggnogs, etc. If the dry milk has been properly pasteurized, the water is potable, and the utensils and container clean, a safe drink *can* be prepared, especially if the product is promptly refrigerated. We frequently recommend for some diets that whole milk be fortified with non-fat dry milk solids, but this is usually done under a doctor's orders. If a doctor will order a patient to have non-fat dry milk mixed as a beverage, the procedure is not questioned.

holds for a longer time. Dry and evaporated milk foams can also increase the intake of milk solids while giving a low yield in calories.

To whip evaporated milk, scald 14½ oz (a No. 1 can) of the milk 5 to 10 minutes in a double boiler. Dissolve into this ½ t of gelatin which has been soaked in 2 T of cool water. Chill and whip. During the beating, add 3 T of lemon juice and flavoring. Sweeten and hold chilled at 50°F.

To whip dry milk, use 1½ c dry regular non-fat milk or 2 c of instant to 1 pt of water. Blend into this ½ t of gelatin which has been soaked in 2 T of cool water and dissolved by heating. Chill. Beat to a soft foam and while beating, add ¼ c of chilled lemon juice. When stiff, fold in 1 c powdered sugar and hold below 50°F. The yield on either of these formulas is about 2 qt. of foam.

Cheese is made from milk. It is a high protein food that reacts much like other proteins to heat. It is also high in fat. Intense heat toughens cheese and drives the fat from it. We try, therefore, to blend cheese into sauces at around 125 to 150°F. We also do not overbake or overcook items containing large quantities of cheese.

If eggs and cheese are to be added to a hot sauce, add the eggs first and then the cheese. The cheese blends in better this way. Processed cheese is pasteurized and then emulsified. It is, therefore, easier to handle in cooking than regular cheese. Aged regular cheese is easier to melt into a sauce than medium cured or unaged cheese. A cheese and egg mixture will curdle easily, so high heat on a mixture such as rarebit should be avoided.

SOUPS, SAUCES AND GRAVIES

Stocks are the basic ingredient used in soups, sauces and gravies. A good stock can be made by using, for each 1 gal of stock desired, 5 to 6 qt of water to 4 lb of bones or meat and 1 lb of mixed chopped vegetables, such as carrots, onions, leeks, parsley, turnips, etc. A teaspoon of salt helps to increase the solubility of the liquid for extracting flavors but if the stock is to be used for low-sodium diets, omit it. Spices or seasonings such as whole cloves, peppercorns, bay leaf, marjoram, etc. can be tied into a small cloth and left in the stock until the seasoning is as desired.

Knuckle, shin or other bones with a lot of white gelatinous particles make good stock. Veal bones or pork bones are good for adding gelatin which gives body to a stock. Beef bones give good flavor strength. Chicken bones produce a delicate stock and turkey bones a more pungent one. Bones and meat from cured meats make a stock good for use in chowders, split pea soup or other legume soups. Lamb and mutton give a strongly flavored stock that is good for soups such as Scotch Mutton Broth or sauces or gravies for these meats. Fish stock is good for fish chowders, stews or fish sauces or gravies.

If the stock is started in hot water, a clearer stock results, but slightly more flavor is extracted if the start is in cold water. Beef bones can be simmered up to 12 hr without clouding; veal, lamb and mutton, less than this and chicken or other poultry, even less; fish can be simmered for only 4 to 5 hr before a stock clouds. Hard boiling encourages clouding.

Stock should be allowed to flow freely from the simmered materials. Use several thicknesses of cheesecloth to catch flocculant materials. Cool by placing in a good draft with the bottom of the container placed on a rack or similar object that raises it up slightly, so circulation of air occurs underneath the pot. Cover. Or place the container in a bath of running cold water. Cover it. Raising the bottom of the container from the bottom of the sink helps to cool the bottom of the container faster. When stock reaches room temperature, put the stock into a refrigerator.

If the stock contains 2% or more gelatin, it will solidify. To use a stock, remove the congealed fat, then use the fat-free stock for soups, sauces or gravies. A stock pot can be kept going continuously in large operations where enough meat, bones, vegetable scraps and other usable items accumulate. French chefs and others have long used this method to extract edible flavor components and valuable nutrients from foods. Canned vegetable juices or suitable products from the steam table, stems from parsley, cut-away ends of tomatoes, celery tops and other items can be saved for such stock.

Today we can use food bases instead of stocks. One of the problems is that many are high in salt, containing 25% or more—in fact, if one looks at the list of ingredients on the label, he will see salt as the first in a line of ingredients, indicating it is greatest in quantity among the ingredients listed. Such a base cannot be used for low-sodium diets or where a rather low level of salt is desired in all the foods served.*

While a quantity food production center will have a fair amount of stock accumulating if proper care is taken to save and use edible products, concentrated food bases can be valuable supplements to increase the flavor of such stocks or in the making of soups, sauces or gravies. Many prepared soups,

---

*The Minor Corp. bases are about the lowest in salt available on the market.

sauces and gravies are also available which can be used to reduce labor and give acceptable products. For instance, an operation purchasing cooked frozen chicken meat could use these bases for gravies for chicken pies, fricassee, chopped chicken cacciatore, chicken sandwiches, chicken turnovers, chicken and noodles, etc.

There are basically two stocks: a white and a brown. A brown stock is made from well browned vegetables, meat and bones. A white stock is made from similar unbrowned products. A meat stock is used for a meat base sauce. A brown stock is used for brown sauce and gravies and a white stock is used for fricassee, veal gravy, fish sauces, etc. A neutral stock is made from a non-meat base, such as cream or cheese sauce, tomato sauce, raisin sauce, etc.

A stock may be thickened by using a roux which is a cooked mixture of equal parts, by weight, of flour and fat. We may have a white or a blond roux for white sauces and a browned roux (the flour is browned well) for brown sauces. When flour or other starches are browned, some of the thickening power of the starch is destroyed and, therefore, more will be required to give thickening equal to that provided by the same amount of unbrowned flour. Be sure to cook rouxs slowly for about 10 min before using them. Rouxs can be made and put into jars and used as needed. A slurry, i.e. a mixture of liquid and starch, such as flour, can be used to thicken sauces and gravies but the texture and flavor is not as good as when roux is used. Other foods can be used as thickeners such as eggs, bread crumbs, tapioca, etc.

If a gravy or sauce is acid, it takes more starch to thicken it. If arrowroot, potato or cornstarch is used, only about three-fourths as much is required as when flour is used. More thickener is required per gal of liquid when large batches are made. Flour gives a more opaque, stringy, thickened product than cornstarch or other starches. The following is a rough guide for use of pastry flour per gal of liquid in thickening food products:

	Soups				**Sauces and Gravies**			
	Fat		Pastry Flour			Fat		Pastry Flour
	oz	c	oz	c		oz	c	oz	c
Thin	6	¾	4	1	Very thin	6	¾	4	1
Medium	8	1	6	1½	Thin	8	1	8	2
Heavy	12	1½	10	2½	Medium	12	1½	12	3
					Very heavy	20	2½	20	5

NOTE: These quantities are for a gallon of product.

Starch thickens by a process called gelatinization. There are about 770 billion tiny starch particles in a pound of cornstarch. Each one can absorb moisture and swell when heated in moisture. If there are enough, they will crowd one another and thicken the solution. Some starches, such as those in flour, contain other substances such as proteins and these too thicken, and they may also join together to give some stringiness, especially those in bread flour which has a high protein content.

Lumping occurs if the starch grains are not well separated before the mixture is heated. We use liquids, sugar or fat to achieve this separation and then we stir the starch well when we add it to the hot solution, or until the product comes up to a temperature at which gelatinization occurs.

All starches do not behave in exactly the same way. Most cereal starches begin to thicken at around 144° to 162°F and complete the process around 203°F. These starches thicken more as the mixture cools. Cornstarch breaks down into a straight break when a thick mass of it cools. Some other starches used for pie fillings make a sticky, soft paste. They give a weaker paste.

Flour starches and some other starches are much more opaque when they thicken. Other starches, such as cornstarch, arrowroot, waxy maize starch or converted starches, give a more clear paste. The last two starches thicken around 155° to 167°F and will be no thicker when they are cool. They are frequently used for fruit pies because they give a soft paste that clings around the fruit. Cornstarch is commonly used for cream pies. Thus, when such a pie is cut, the edge is more firm and straight.

Products thickened with waxy maize and converted (modified) starches do not break down when frozen as they do if cornstarch, flour or some other cereal starches are used. The product and its processing dictates the type of starch needed. Consult a good bakery supply house to find out what is available on the market and how these products might be used in a small health facility.

Gourmet foods as a steady diet would not be desirable in an extended care facility because, among other reasons, many of the residents would not like them. However, the use of some gourmet foods may do much to "pep-up" a menu. Sauces can do this.

For instance, a good fricassee gravy thinned with a bit of cream becomes a Supreme Sauce and if we add a few chopped almonds to this, we get a

Reine or King Sauce which is superb over boiled veal. Boiled veal shoulder is not expensive, neither is Reine Sauce which utilizes some of the rich stock from the veal and for this low cost, a rather good product can be made which many residents can eat.

For another gourmet touch, take a brown stock and add a bit of tomato sauce and a bit of crushed garlic or garlic powder and you have a Provencale Sauce which is excellent over spaghetti, especially if topped with a bit of grated Parmesan cheese. Turkey meat diced and served with a Brandy Peach Sauce could be offered on a general menu and might gain much favor with the residents. The sauce is made from peach preserves or crushed peaches with just a bit of brandy added. This served with tiny noodles, delicately seasoned with poppyseeds or marjoram, makes a "different dish." Perhaps one might not want to serve these dishes too often, but occasionally they might be welcomed.

A French chef makes about 13 basic sauces and from these he gets literally hundreds of secondary or what he calls "petite" (small) sauces. While opportunities to use the techniques of the French chef may be limited in extended care facilities, some knowledge of the techniques that have produced some of the best food in the world might be helpful in improving foods in the small health facility.

A gravy is a thickened mixture in which the flavor of a particular meat predominates. It is not a blend of flavors in which no flavor predominates such as one obtains in a sauce. Some gravies, such as *au jus* (a serving of the meat drippings), are just unthickened meat juices.

Soups are nutritious, well-liked food items. They are usually low in cost. Broths, consomme and bouillons are light, clear soups that contain very few nutrients but stimulate the appetite and prepare one for a meal. Broths are stocks rich in meat flavor and served as a light soup. Broths, consommes or bouillons can be used frequently for residents who eat little but whose appetites are whetted by such a food. Usually an extended care facility will make its own broth but will use canned or other products for consommes or bouillons.

Cream soups are very nutritious and are very well tolerated by residents. They are made by preparing a lightly thickened flavor base such as thickened tomato puree, asparagus puree, celery puree, etc. This hot mixture is then blended into milk, rich milk or a lightly thickened milk mixture. Use a minimum amount of salt and do not hold too long or it may curdle. A bisque is a cream soup made from shellfish.

We have many other soups. Some of medium consistency made with stock—chicken noodle, beef vegetable or Scotch mutton broth. Besides being nutritious, they stimulate the appetite. Legumes, potatoes or other vegetables can be pureed and made into soups. They usually have a sufficient amount of thickening to make a soup of medium thickness but if they do not, the soup is thickened slightly with a roux. Mashed potatoes can also be used as a thickener. Usually these soups are counted as a B-vegetable in the diabetic exchange lists. If they are rich in fat, they may also have to be counted as 1 or 2 fat exchanges.

Chowders, heavy purees or broths thickened with vegetables or rice or other products are used to make a rather substantial item in a meal. If served with a sandwich, they can provide a complete meal with perhaps a bit of salad and a light fruit dessert added.

SANDWICHES AND SALADS

Salads and sandwiches are usually made in a section of the foodservice called the pantry. These foods are high in labor costs because of the number of manipulations needed to make them and because they are usually made up as individual products. Sandwiches may be greatly appreciated by residents. Salads are also popular and can add good nutrients, color and texture to a meal. Some type of salad should be served daily on every type of diet, except perhaps liquid diets.

Because of the labor required, watch to see that salads are made in a work center that makes the work easy and promotes productivity. Freshness is an all important factor also. Vegetables and fruits have texture when their tiny cells are filled with moisture. When moisture loss occurs, the item wilts.

To prevent this, dip salad greens in water. Shake off the excess water, put greens into a moist cloth, or in a container that does not permit them to dry out, and place in a refrigerated area with plenty of air circulating around the packet or container. This allows the tiny cells to pull in moisture until they are plump and swelled. Soaking in water does not give as much crispness as letting air circulate around a moistened product.

Plan salads that will have form, texture, color and flavor. They should not appear messy or overworked. Too much garnish detracts from the appearance of a salad. Mix fruit and cooked vegetable salads as little as possible. Make salads as close to the time of service as possible. A good recipe service should indicate exact quantities required for salads. About 3/4 of a c of salad greens makes a portion, whereas it takes only about 1/2 c of a molded, meat salad, potato salad or other rather dense type of filling to make a portion. If the salad is used as the main entree item, the quantity should be doubled or even tripled.

Molded salads should be made using 2-2/3 oz of plain gelatin per gal or 1-1/2 lb of gelatin dessert. In using plain gelatin, soak it first in cold water and then dissolve it by heating the solution or add the gelatin to a hot solution to dissolve it. (Gelatin desserts do not have to be presoaked.) Have the liquid over 170°F to dissolve the gelatin product.

All the liquid need not be added at this point when either product is used. The water not used to dissolve the product can be added cold or as finely chopped ice to decrease the setting time—a bit more gelatin or gelatin dessert may have to be added if this is done because this method reduces the thickening power of gelatin. If a gelatin mixture cools slowly, it gives a more firm gel. Sugar makes gelatin mixtures more firm while acids such as vinegar or lemon juice make them more tender. If one whips a gelatin mixture or adds a lot of chopped vegetables or fruits to it, the quantity of gelatin may have to be increased since these ingredients weaken a gelatin mixture.

A French dressing is made by blending 1/3 part of vinegar or lemon juice with 2/3 part of oil and adding desired seasonings. If gum tragacanth, Irish moss or some other emulsifier is added, it becomes a permanent emulsion.

Mayonnaise is a permanent emulsion made by beating oil slowly into eggs, seasonings and vinegar or lemon juice. As the oil being added becomes a greater part of the mixture, larger amounts of oil can be poured in when making each addition.

Another salad dressing used frequently—and one that perhaps should be used even more—is a boiled dressing. This is thickened with flour, or other starch, and eggs. It is excellent for cole slaw, potato salad or, when blended with honey and whipped cream, makes an excellent dressing for fruit salads. Normally, the dressing for a salad should be tart and give a good flavor contrast.

Sometimes, to heighten flavor, we soak fruits or vegetables and meats in a *marinade*. V⌣iy frequently this is a mixture much like French dressing.

BEVERAGES   There is no in-between in beverage tem-
                                      peratures. They either should be quite
hot or quite cold, except for those individuals who cannot handle either extreme. There will be many kinds of beverages that can be used in an extended
care facility, but fruit-based beverages, tea and milk will usually be most popular. Coffee will also be a favorite of those who are allowed to have it. A good
beverage can do much to improve the quality of a meal. Knowing how to
make and serve beverages properly requires some technical knowledge.

A pound of coffee to 3 gal of water is a normal ratio for coffee. If this
is too strong, make it this way and then dilute the brew with very hot water.
Having over 3 gal of water contact the grounds brings out too much bitterness
and this overwhelms the sweet, robust, full flavor of the coffee that comes
off during the first part of the brewing.

The equipment should be kept scrupulously clean. Coffee contains an
oil that is part of the coffee flavor but this oxidizes easily and gives a soapy
flavor to the coffee. Coffee oils can cling to the equipment and quickly oxidize. This is why good cleaning is needed.

The right grind of coffee should be used for the equipment. Fine grinds
are needed for vacuum units, coarser grinds for urns or percolators. Use water that has been freshly boiled. About 20% of the coffee should be extracted.
The amount of water, its temperature, the grind and the time the water is in
contact with the grounds will determine how much flavor is extracted.

Urn or drip coffee should be extracted in 4 to 6 min; vacuum coffee in
2 to 4 min and percolated or boiled coffee in about 10 min. Coffee is best
not boiled but steeped. The water poured over coffee grounds for drip or urn
coffee should be boiling. This makes it about 205°F when it strikes the coffee, a good extracting temperature. Hold coffee for service at from 185° to
190°F. It should be at 160°F when the residents get it.

Freshly boiled water should be poured over tea and allowed to steep
from 3 to 5 min. Use 1 t of tea per cup; use 4 oz (2 c) of tea per 5 gal of boiling water to make 100 6-oz cups of tea.

Green tea is an unfermented tea; oolong is partially fermented and black tea is fully fermented. In fermenting, tannins and other flavor compounds are oxidized, giving a tea different in flavor as well as color. Black tea has less tannin in it than oolong or green tea and, for this reason, is milder in flavor. Tannin is the substance that clouds tea; putting tea into a refrigerator encourages clouding. Leave it at room temperature.

Make 50 portions of iced tea by pouring 1 qt of water over 2 oz of tea and steeping for 6 min. Remove the tea and pour the brew into 3 qt cold tap water. This method is called the 1-2-3 method because of the ratio of ingredients used. This brew can be held up to 4 hr without loss of quality. Pour this brew over ice and serve.

Tea is less apt to cloud if it is slightly acid. Tea made from hard water has a dark, dull color but a bit of lemon juice brings about the right color. Never make tea by serving hot water to the resident with a tea bag on the side. The water is too cool by the time it is served to make good tea. Tea water should be boiling when tea is made. Water not at the right temperature extracts too many bitter flavors and not enough of the right ones.

For 50 portions of cocoa, mix ½ lb of cocoa (2 c) with 1 lb of sugar (2¼ c) and stir this into 2½ gal hot milk. One can use 2½ lb of non-fat dry milk and 2½ gal of water. If added richness is desired, whip into the mixture 12 to 16 oz of margarine or butter. Chocolate can be substituted by using 5 oz (squares) for every 8 oz of cocoa. Sirups, pastes or prepared mixes can also be used. Whip cocoa with a wire whip to create a foam which prevents a scum from forming over it. "Breakfast" cocoa contains 22% or more of cacao fat but cocoas with less than 8% cacao fat can be obtained and these may be desirable in an extended care facility for those on low-fat diets.

BAKING

A small health facility is apt to buy most of its breads and pastries. The bakeshop itself may be limited and baking may even be done in the cook's section. Only simple desserts will be prepared.

BREADS   Commercial breads have become so poor in recent years that it may be necessary to make one's own. The use of bread softeners and mold inhibitors and the method of processing and baking has produced a product which is extremely soft, high in moisture and is gummy to chew.

People with poorly fitting dentures have difficulty eating a hot sandwich because such bread sticks to their dentures. Toast made from this bread is sticky inside and sandwiches soak quickly. Good bread should be firm, solid and have some chew. Today, in this country, the amount of bread eaten is constantly decreasing and this is because bread lacks quality. As a result, many in our population are not getting the nutrients they should because the nutrients they should get largely from bread are not consumed.

The ratio of ingredients in bread, with flour as 100%, should be:

Flour, bread	100%	Milk, non-fat	0-8%
Liquid, water	60%	Salt	1-2½%
Sugar, granulated	2-3%	Yeast, compressed	2-3%
Shortening	1-12%	Yeast conditioner	¼ to ½%

A dough richer than this in sugar and shortening is called a sweet dough. It is used for breakfast rolls, coffee cakes, etc. A rolled-in or Danish dough is a sweet dough with shortening spread between layers. This is folded and rolled a number of times so there are many layers of dough and shortening alternating. When baked, a light, flaky, rich product is obtained.

Large facilities may use sponges rather than regular doughs for making bread. In the sponge method, a part of the flour is withheld until the second fermentation. However, the regular method is simpler and more adapted to smaller quantity methods. Bread should be made with a bread flour, a product high in gluten. This gives a strong, firm bread and a dough sufficiently strong to withstand the strong pressures developed during fermentation.

To produce a regular dough, crumble compressed yeast into a small amount of warm water (keep water below 100°F in temperature); if active dry yeast is used, use 40% as much of it, i. e. slightly less than a half ounce for every ounce of compressed yeast. With active dry yeast, water at temperatures up to 110°F can be used. (Freezing yeast for a short time does not harm it.) Never add salt to a yeast mixture since salt is antagonistic to yeast. Put the salt into water to be mixed into the dough later. If the eggs—if eggs are used—and flour are cold, add warm water to the eggs to prevent them from chilling the yeast; also warm the flour slightly. Blend the water containing the salt, the eggs, sugar, flour, yeast solution and fat together.

Knead well until the dough is smooth and can be stretched paper thin. There should be no dense areas in the dough. It is extremely difficult to overmix the dough. The dough should be from 74° to 84°F. When kneading is finished, coat the top of the dough lightly with shortening to prevent drying out and place it in a warm place away from drafts. Cover. Let rise for 4 hr. If more than a normal amount of yeast is added and the temperature of the dough is about 90°F upon completion of kneading, the bread can be fermented more rapidly. This is sometimes called a *no-time* dough because the time is shortened. The quality is not as good, however.

When the fermented dough has doubled in volume, or puckers away. when 3 fingers are inserted into it, it is fully fermented. If the area is warm or if a lot of make-up work is required, it may be desirable to use the dough before it is fully fermented. Rye, whole wheat or rich, sweet doughs should also be used early. If the bread is to be made up into specified shapes and then refrigerated (called a *retarded* dough), the dough also should not be fully fermented. (A retarded dough should also be prepared by using a bit more sugar and yeast than is used for a normal dough.)

When the dough is fermented to the desired stage, it is punched. This is a process of lifting up the dough from the sides and folding it over repeatedly until dough is back to its original volume. It is then flipped upside down. After resting 10 to 20 min, the dough can be made up into loaves, rolls or other shapes.

Since baking loss is about 12%, use nearly 2 oz of dough to get a 1½ oz finished roll or slightly over 20 oz for every 1 lb of bread desired. Place on greased pans and proof in a moist area at from 90° to 100°F for 15 to 25 min for rolls and small breads and 20 to 45 min for loaf products. Bake loaves for 1 hr at 375° to 400°F and rolls and small breads at slightly higher temperatures for shorter times. Remove from the pans when baked and set on racks to cool. After cooling, put the products into polyethylene bags and freeze to hold quality. Do not refrigerate. This speeds staling. For immediate use, store in a cool, dry place.

Baking powder, soda or some other leavening agent is used in place of yeast to leaven quick breads. They should be made with pastry flour or a blend of pastry and bread flour. Pastry flour gives a delicate, tender texture.

Keep the batter cool by using cold water. This helps to retard gluten formation. Overmixing also develops gluten, giving a tough product. (Baking powder biscuits and some other quick breads are kneaded to develop gluten so they have a firmer texture.) Thin batters such as popovers or hotcakes can be manipulated more than thicker batters. Items high in shortening and sugar can also receive more manipulation. If a quick bread is overmixed, it will be tough, rubbery, have tunnels (tiny hollows in the product) and will not color well in baking. A muffin mix should be given only a maximum of 6 stirs to blend it into the liquid.

Muffins, cornbread, gingerbread and many other products belong to a group that should have little mixing. Sift the dry ingredients into a mixing bowl, dump in the liquid ingredients which have been blended together and stir only enough to blend, about 15 to 20 sec with the mixer on slow. Bake at once since if the batter stands, tenderness decreases.

When dipping, dip from the outside to the mixing bowl side. Dipping from the center works the dough. Bake at 375°F. Unpan muffins before they cool, if not used at once. This prevents them from becoming moist and soggy.

Baking powder biscuits have less liquid than muffins. The shortening is cut or worked into the dry ingredients until the mixture looks like coarse cornmeal. The liquid is added and mixed until a soft dough forms. This is turned onto a lightly floured board and kneaded lightly 1 min. It should then be rolled out to about 3/4- to 1-in. thick and cut into desired shapes. Put onto greased pans. Bake at 425°F.

Dropped biscuits are not kneaded and are spooned from the mixing bowl, dropped onto greased pans and baked. Scones are made from a rich baking powder biscuit dough. Shortcakes contain more sugar than the regular baking powder biscuit dough and also may have more shortening added to them. Eggs may also be added. Butter or margarine may be spread between the uncooked layers to give a richer product. A dumpling is a variation of a baking powder biscuit.

Hotcakes or waffles are made much like muffins, but the ratio of liquid to flour is higher. In fact, one can take a muffin recipe and about double or triple the amount of liquid and have a fairly good hotcake. A waffle is usually richer than a hotcake since it has more sugar and shortening. Swedish hotcakes, crepes (French), blinis (Russian) or other thin hotcakes are unleavened. They usually contain more eggs.

Bake hotcakes on a lightly greased griddle at 350° to 375°F. If the ratio, by weight, of shortening to liquid is 1 to 4, the griddle need not be greased except lightly at the start of baking. This is also true for waffles. Pour the hotcake batter onto the griddle and allow it to bake until it bubbles on the top and a slight drying appears at the edge. Turn lightly and bake the same length of time. Hotcakes are better if they are not turned too often. Have a waffle griddle hot and fill it about 2/3 full. Put the cover down and bake until steaming stops. The longer a waffle is baked, the crisper it gets.

Popovers are made from a thin milk, egg and flour batter. This is poured into muffin pans and baked in a 450°F oven until steam inside raises the popover. The heat is then reduced to 350° to 375°F. Baking continues for another 30 to 40 minutes. Better popovers result if special heavy metal popover pans are preheated and used. Yorkshire pudding is a popover batter.

CAKES   Cakes are classified by the way they are leavened: 1) by air in egg foam as in angel; 2) by air incorporated in creamed eggs, sugar and shortening as in pound; 3) by gas generated by a chemical leavener as in butter cakes.

1) Angel, sponge and chiffon cakes are light, delicately textured products. To make good ones takes knowledge of how to produce a good egg foam plus skill in blending the foam with the other ingredients. Baking is another important step.

The angel mix available today has the whites so well stabilized that it is best and safest to make cakes of this type from a mix rather than from scratch. They can be baked in angel or loaf pans. Since the sides of the pan are needed to help support this cake in baking, it is difficult to bake them in shallow pans.

A sponge cake is leavened by whole eggs or yolks. Hot liquid may be added; some have baking powder added and some may even have a melted shortening added at the last minute. Since oil or fat tends to break down egg foam, this addition of shortening is a very critical step.

To make sponge cakes, the warm eggs (120°F) are beaten with a bit of cream of tartar until they are creamy in color. Sugar is added and beating continues until the eggs are lemon-colored and fairly stiff. The flour and baking powder—if used—are folded into the egg mixture. This can be done by operating the mixer carefully at low speed. Delicate sponges may have hot milk (140°F) carefully folded in at this point or melted shortening may be folded in. The batter should not be below 110°F. Pan it in loaf, tube or cake pans. It can be baked in a sheet pan and frosted or rolled into a damp cloth while still warm and filled later with jelly or other fillings. Baking should be done at around 360°F. A chiffon cake is much like a sponge cake. It has oil, liquid and baking powder added to it. It has a bit more compact grain than an angel or sponge cake.

2) Before chemical leavening agents were invented, bakers had to depend upon the air incorporated in egg foams or creamed eggs, sugar and shortening to give the necessary leavening. Thus, pound cakes and other cakes made by creaming eggs, shortening and sugar have been produced for a long time.

Pound cake gets its name, "pound," from the fact that a pound of flour, a pound of sugar, a pound of eggs and a pound of shortening can be used to make it. The best temperature for creaming the ingredients is 75°F. Cream the shortening first; then add the sugar; cream the mixture again and finally add the eggs and cream until the mixture appears much like stiff whipped cream. The more air incorporated, the better the texture of the cake. If there is a tendency for the mixture to curdle when all the eggs are added, a bit of the flour called for in the recipe can be added to absorb excess moisture. The flour is folded in last.

Some pound cake recipes may require up to 50% bread flour blended with cake flour to give a more solid product. Bread flour also has a high moisture absorption power. Since shortening and sugar are tenderizing agents, the extra strength of the bread flour is somewhat modified by the high content of these two ingredients. These cakes are baked in a greased and floured bread pan, or a paper-lined pan, in a 325° to 355°F oven.

3) The most common cake produced is the butter cake. There are many good mixes available today and much bakery production of these cakes is now from mixes. Because we have improved flour and shortenings, we can make richer butter cakes than we formerly could and our recipes should be revised to produce these higher quality products. Normally, the ratio of ingredients to flour, with flour as 100%, is 45% shortening, 70% eggs, 100% liquid and 125% sugar. In these cakes, the shortening is usually creamed first, sugar is added and creamed and the eggs are added and creamed. Dry sifted ingredients are then added alternately with the milk. Baking is in a 375°F oven.

With some new shortenings, the shortening, flour and baking powder can be mixed first and then blended dry milk and sugar can be added with a part of the liquid. After a smooth paste is formed, the last of the liquid is added. This gives a high quality product with a fine, soft grain that is tighter than that obtained by the conventional method of mixing. The cakes stay moist longer.

This method of mixing is called the high ratio or blending method.

A quick cake can be made using the method described for muffins where all dry ingredients are put into a bowl and the liquids, including melted shortening or oil, are dumped in. This cake is good fresh but stales rapidly. It is good for cottage pudding, etc.

COOKIES Cookie recipes should be selected taking into consideration the time needed to make them. Some are high in labor requirements. There are many types popular with residents that are suitable for them and can be easily eaten. A dump method of mixing is simplest. This is where all ingredients are added at one time and the mixture mixed into a batter or dough. Doughs can be rolled into cylinders, chilled and then sliced and panned; or, the dough can be dropped in chunks or scooped onto greased pans. Batters can be poured onto greased pans, the product baked and then cut into portions. Many cookies should be removed from their pans while warm as they will break up if left until cool.

PIES Three types of crust are used for pies: mealy, semi-flaky and flaky. Mealy crusts are used for custard, pumpkin or other pies in which the filling is baked in a single crust. A semi-flaky dough is an all-purpose dough, useful for double crust pies, although when production of pies is high, a mealy dough is sometimes used for the under crust of fruit pies with a flaky or semi-flaky crust put on top. Flaky crusts are most often used for single crust pies where the crust is baked and filled.

A mealy crust has a flour-shortening ratio of 100% to 60% by weight. The shortening is worked well into the pastry flour and this mixture is dampened with water and lightly mixed until a dough forms. Too much mixing toughens the product. Cool ingredients discourage gluten formation. In rolling crusts, do not stretch the dough. Crusts tend to pull back in baking if this has been done. Let the roller press the dough out and this will not happen.

A semi-flaky dough has about 75% shortening to 100% flour by weight. The shortening is divided into the pastry flour in particles the size of peas. This mixture is moistened with water and bunched together to make a dough. Many bakers put the salt into the water and dissolve it. They feel this makes a better product.

A flaky dough is made by using 100% shortening to 100% flour by weight. The shortening is divided into the flour in pieces about the size of walnuts. After moistening and forming into a dough, the dough is usually rolled into a rectangle and folded 4 times by folding the left side into the center and the right side into the center and then folding these 2 together. Next it is put into a refrigerator to rest for about 15 to 20 min. Then, it is rolled out and folded 4 times again. It is allowed to rest and at this point can be used for pie crust. This folding and rolling out spreads the shortening into thin sheets between layers of dough which form flaky sheets when the crust is baked. Such a crust is a little tough but quite flaky. About 5 to 6 oz of dough is needed for each crust. Frequently, we form the pie dough into cylinders and slice them into the proper size rounds. A good baker can roll a crust so there is very little trim. Reworking dough makes it tougher.

A graham cracker crust is made by using 100% graham cracker crumbs, 30% sugar and 55% margarine. Vanilla wafers, chocolate wafers or other crumbs may be used in place of graham crackers. About 2 oz is needed for the bottom crust of a 9-in. pie.

A 9-in. pie takes from 1½ to 2 pt (3½ to 4 c) of filling. A gal of filling makes between 4 and 5 pies. For a plain custard pie, use 2½ lb of whole eggs to each gal of milk. Have the milk quite warm as for regular custards. Pumpkin pies require fewer eggs but pecan pies take more because the high sugar and sirup content interferes with the thickening of the eggs.

Test custard pies for doneness by putting a knife about half way from the center to the edge of the pie. If it comes out clean, the pie is ready to come from the oven. The center will not be completely baked but there is enough heat to finish baking after removal from the oven.

Fruit fillings are best thickened with waxy maize or modified starches. The ratio of fruit to liquid should be 2:1 to 3:1. The starch is most often blended with the sugar and this is added to the hot juice and cooked until thickened. Pies made from frozen fruits can have the juice drained, thickened with a cold-setting (instant) starch and can then be topped and baked. This avoids a double baking and gives a fresher tasting pie.

Cream fillings are usually nothing but cream puddings. Cream pies are frequently not filled until just before service. This avoids soaking the crust. A lemon pie filling is best made by thickening the water and sugar with cornstarch, blending some of this hot mixture into the egg yolks using good agitation and then adding this yolk-mixture to the rest of the hot filling and cooking gently for about 5 min to set the eggs. After removing the filling from the heat, the lemon juice is added. This prevents the acid in the lemon juice from breaking down the starch and thinning the paste.

DESSERTS

Many simple desserts will be better for residents than cakes, pies or cookies. They also will be popular and lower in cost.

Fruit is an excellent dessert served plain, with sugar, or as a sauce or in a cobbler, betty, crisp, shortcake or other product. If served fresh, it is best served chilled. Frozen fruits have a better texture if still slightly frozen when served.

Baked fruits such as apples or pears or a broiled grapefruit, baked banana or other fruit served slightly warm are also well received. Dried fruits should be checked carefully for extraneous matter, washed, soaked at least 4 hr and then gently boiled or simmered until tender. Rapid cooking may toughen these products slightly. About 3 to 4 oz (½ c) of berries, sauce or sliced fruit make a portion.

Some cooked fruit desserts are best served warm. Some of these are:

Crisp
Fruit topped with a mixture of flour, sugar and fat and baked. It has a crisp top and fruit under this.

Betty
Baked layers of bread crumbs, butter or margarine and sugar alternated with fruit.

Cobbler
A rich biscuit topping baked over fruit.

Shortcake
Rich baking powder biscuit served with fruit over it; cream or whipped cream may be served with it.

Roly-Poly
Fruit rolled in biscuit dough and baked; sliced after baking; usually served with some type of hot sweet sauce.

Fruit Roll
Fruit rolled in biscuit dough, sliced and baked; usually served with some hot, dessert sauce.

Dutch cake
Fruit pressed into a rich biscuit dough and baked; also served with a hot, dessert sauce.

Dumpling
Fruit wrapped in biscuit dough or non-rich pie dough and baked partially immersed in a sweet liquid; this liquid thickens and is served over the dumpling.

Most steamed puddings are popular and inexpensive; there are a variety of fruit and nut puddings, but carrot, plain vanilla, chocolate or other steamed puddings can also be served. It is usually best to steam the batter in a well greased and floured pan or tin and serve with a hot dessert sauce. Cover when steaming to prevent condensate from making an overly moist product.

Old-fashioned steamed puddings are steamed in a cloth that has been dipped into cold water, wrung dry and then the inside part of the cloth that will come in contact with the batter is dipped into flour. The batter is next placed on the floured part of the cloth, and the bag, tied loosely to permit expansion, is either suspended over steam or put into water and gently boiled. When cooked, the pudding is dipped into cold water to help free the cloth which is then removed. It is wise to wrap a warm pudding in a moist cloth to prevent its drying out and forming a tough skin on the surface. Steamed puddings can be refrigerated for long periods of time, reheated and served.

A blanc mange or cornstarch pudding is made with milk, sugar, flavoring and perhaps margarine. It is thickened with cornstarch or another cereal thickener. A cream pudding is a blanc mange with eggs as part of the thickener. The method for adding the eggs is first to allow the starch to thicken thoroughly, then to remove a small quantity of this cooked filling and add it to the eggs, blending well. Next, blend this mixture back into the hot mixture using good agitation. Allow to cook for 5 min or more so the eggs cook thoroughly.

For a chiffon cream pudding, we reserve all or some of the egg whites and sugar from the recipe and make a meringue of them. The yolks are incorporated into the hot cornstarch mixture, using the technique described here, and allowed to cook for about 5 min to cook the yolks. This hot mixture is carefully folded *into* the meringue. The hotter the mixture, the thicker the product. If the folding is carefully done and the mixture is not mixed too much, a light, aerated pudding results. This is the reason for the name "chiffon." This is delicious served over berries that have been lightly sweetened. A tapioca cream can be made this way and served combined with fruit.

Sago or arrowroot are two thickeners that make very delicate puddings which may be better for residents that have some digestive problems. Farina or cornmeal can also be used to make acceptable puddings. It takes about 1½ gal of pudding to serve 50; the portion is usually ½ c.

Gelatin desserts are popular, refreshing and low in cost.* They may be

---

*Also see material on gelatins previously discussed under salads.

served in various colors, plain or in assorted cubes; riced, as a parfait combined with blanc mange or a cream pudding; with fruit; whipped to a foam to make a snow; combined with cake cubes or crumbs and in many other ways.

Whipped cream combined with a sweetened gelatin mixture makes a *bavarian*; sometimes, instead of whipped cream, we can use a blanc mange or cream pudding or even melted ice cream. A *Spanish cream* is made by blending a stirred custard with another flavored, sweetened gelatin and letting it set until it is rather sirupy. Whipped cream is then folded into this and the mixture is allowed to set until solid.

Fried desserts may be well liked. Crepes or hotcakes filled with fruit and served hot may be a nice variation, especially if a nice hot sauce is served over them. Fritters are not difficult to make; the batter is closely related to a muffin. Doughnuts are also popular and are well known to most residents. A cake doughnut, frosted and decked with nuts, can take the place of a standard dessert. Rich waffles can be made and these can be served hot with fruit and whipped cream, or ice cream can be put onto a hot waffle square and topped with fruit or a fruit sauce.

Most frozen desserts will be purchased. These are well liked and, because the labor cost is low, can be quite low in cost. Dish these products when they are from 8° to 15°F. Temperatures either lower or higher than this give a packed, dense product that has less flavor. Also, the packing gives fewer portions per quart of product. Ice creams are usually 8 to 10% milk fat; iced milks are usually around 4% and sherbets may be the same.

Bibliography

Amendola, Joseph. *The Bakers' Manual for Quantity Baking and Pastry Making.* New York: Ahrens, 1966.

Amendola, Joseph and Lundberg, Donald. *Understanding Baking.* Chicago: Cahners Books, 1970.

American Home Economics Association. *Handbook of Food Preparation.* Washington, D. C.: By the Association, 1964.

American Institute of Baking. *Modern Sandwich Methods.* Chicago: By the Institute, 1952.

Fowler, S. F.; West, B. B.; and Shugart, G. S. *Food for Fifty.* New York: John Wiley and Sons, 1961.

Kotschevar, Lendal H., and Margaret McWilliams. *Understanding Food.* New York: John Wiley and Sons, 1969.

Kotschevar, Lendal H. *Quantity Food Production.* New York: John Wiley and Sons, 1961.

Kotschevar, Lendal H., and Lundberg, D. *Understanding Cooking.* Amherst, Mass.: University of Massachusetts Bookstore, 1965.

McWilliams, Margaret. *Food Fundamentals.* New York: John Wiley and Sons, 1966.

U. S. Navy. Bureau of Supplies and Accounts, Subsistence Division. *FORM.* Washington, D. C.: Government Printing Office, 1968.

West, Bessie B.; Wood, LeVelle; and Harger, V. *Food Service in Institutions.* New York: John Wiley and Sons, 1966.

Wheat Flour Institute. *Baking Basics.* Chicago: Wheat Flour Institute, 1966.

VII: PURCHASING

It's unwise to pay too much, but it's worse to pay too little. When you pay too much, you lose a little money, that is all. When you pay too little, you sometimes lose everything, because the thing you bought was incapable of doing the thing that it was bought to do. The common law of business balance prohibits paying a little and getting a lot. It can't be done. If you deal with the lowest bidder, it is well to add something for the risk you run; and, if you do that, you will have enough to pay for something better.

—John Ruskin

INTRODUCTION

A quantity kitchen is a factory. It processes raw materials into finished products. Perhaps, a better term for "kitchen" should be "production center" because this term would agree more with what actually goes on there.

A factory's production order is the input that starts manufacturing action. A menu is a foodservice's production order, telling it what to manufacture and how much. Likewise, a recipe is a production specification, telling what raw materials to use and how to process them. The number of portions needed, as listed on the menu, times the portion size on the recipe gives the quantities to manufacture.

THE PURCHASING TASK

Quantity purchasing differs from home purchasing. Foodservices are industrial consumers buying materials to manufacture for ultimate consumers. Ultimate consumers, such as homemakers, buy to satisfy their own needs. Industrial buyers buy to satisfy the needs of ultimate consumers. Buying to satisfy someone else is much more difficult than buying to satisfy yourself.

Industrial buyers also buy on different markets and in larger quantities. They are seeking products that best meet a manufacturing need and rational motives predominate, not the emotional ones that frequently motivate an ultimate consumer's choice. An apple's red skin may compel an ultimate consumer's choice but the industrial buyer wants to know what's inside because he knows the apple will be peeled before it is used.

Purchasing is a supporting function of the manufacturing task. It is a management function, too important to quality and cost not to be. If purchasing is to be delegated, management should stay close to it at all times. A foodservice food buyer must be highly competent, knowing both the market and the products needed.

Indiscriminate ordering by untrained kitchen personnel can lead to low quality and high costs. Buying must be co-ordinated with food production schedules. The buyer must know a lot about food production and how foods perform in the kitchen and during service.

The ability to obtain the right product at the right time in the right quantity at the right cost is needed. A good buyer is constantly learning because the market in which he deals is a dynamic thing, constantly changing. He must keep abreast of change.

An individual outside the foodservice department can buy, providing there is a proper division of responsibility. The foodservice should decide what is needed in grade, size, quantity and quality. It should write the specification but the buyer can assist by 1) suggesting ways to cut costs; 2) making a tighter specification; 3) increasing the list of potential vendors; or 4) indicating ways in which procurement can be facilitated. The buyer can search the market, negotiate, keep abreast of market conditions but must always keep in touch with the foodservice and never make decisions as to grade, size, quantity and quality. He should keep the foodservice advised of the status of purchase orders.

A foodservice buyer's main goal in searching the market and selecting items for purchase should be *to best suit the production need.* This need may not be for the highest grade or the highest priced item. Solid pack tomatoes are high in quality but a lower, cheaper grade is more suitable for stews, soups and sauces. Ground beef from Choice beef makes a fatty meat loaf and ground meat from Good or Standard grades a leaner one. Why purchase fancy half walnut meats when they are chopped up for baking? Lower cost broken nut meats would do as well.

Price as the primary purchase criteria is wrong. Value, instead, should be the primary consideration. Buyers today operate on information gained through *value analysis,* which can be defined as "selecting the most suitable material at the least cost for a manufacturing need, designing in it, if necessary, special features to make the material have greater value." Values can quickly change in dynamic markets and buyers should constantly be seeking out new products or changing old ones to improve quality or lower costs. Many times, products have characteristics that do little or nothing for the manufactured product. Such characteristics are superfluous and if eliminated, lower cost and do no harm to the final product.

To do value analysis, follow materials through production and evaluate their performance. Yields on foods purchased should be constantly checked to see if they are giving the yields and quality expected. Ask constantly, "Can a different product do a better job or lower the cost?"

Value is the balance between what we get and what we pay. We can equate value to price and quality as follows: Value = $\frac{Quality}{Price}$. If Q equals 1 and P equals 1, then V equals 1 (V = $\frac{Q}{P}$ or $1 = \frac{1}{1}$). Now, double Q but keep P the same. We get a V of 2 (V (2) = $\frac{Q(2)}{P(1)}$). If we reduce price in half but keep quality the same, we again double value (1/2 = 2). If we double quality but also double price, we have not increased value ($\frac{2}{2} = 1$). Doubling price, but leaving quality the same, reduces value in half (1/2 = $\frac{1}{2}$).

A buyer's goal is to constantly improve value by getting a more suitable item for the same price. When value analysis is practiced, the performance of purchases improves because value is stressed and stands out. A buyer interested in value analysis might ask the following questions on a material:

QUESTION	EXAMPLE
1. Does its use contribute value?	An electric Teflon pan will reduce fat in many fried foods so they can be served to residents on low-fat or some other types of diets. For a small increase in cost, value for some residents is increased. The Teflon pan makes it possible to reduce the use of expensive substitutes such as broiled meats.
2. Is cost proportional to usefulness?	Prepared mixes were made by the facility rather than being purchased, reducing cost without reducing quality.
3. Are all features useful?	Using a bakery shortening containing emulsifiers for ordinary cooking fat increases cost and also is not as good since such a sho₁tening performs poorly in many cooking processes because it contains an emulsifier. Eliminating this shortening for ordinary cooking and using less expensive plain shortenings improves quality and lowers cost.

QUESTION	*EXAMPLE*
4. Can a better quality be used?	Aged cheddar cheese is substituted for a medium cheddar cheese in a macaroni and cheese recipe, improving quality and, because less of the aged cheddar had to be used than of the milder medium cheddar, cost was reduced.
5. Can price be lowered but quality maintained?	A year's supply of canned goods is contracted after checking quality. Price is guaranteed with a stipulation that should prices drop during the contract, the lower price would go into effect. Quality was maintained but price lowered.
6. Will standardization help?	A facility had its own meat specifications but changed to the *Federal Institutional Meat Specifications* achieving a more standard product.
7. Is it overvalued?	A list of ingredients on a soup base label reads: "Monosodium glutamate, salt, beef fat, seasonings, etc. . . ." A different base's label reads: "Beef extract, beef fat, monosodium glutamate, salt. . ." The government requires ingredients in non-common foods to be listed in order of greatest to least amount. On the basis of ingredients, the second product is of higher quality.
8. Can another dependable vendor provide it for less?	A better search of the market frequently shows this to be true.
9. Do others buy it for less?	A group of institutions decided to buy co-operatively. When they compared milk prices, they found that from the same dairy, for the same products, for the same quantities members of the group paid different prices.
10. Can a new material be found?	An operation changed from the purchase of bones for stocks to a soup base. Cost

was reduced through a reduction in labor.

11. Can a different procedure be used?

A liquid shortening, new on the market, was used in cake making. Now, all ingredients could be dumped together and a high quality product obtained. Although the new shortening cost more, the saving, in labor more than made up for it. An additional favorable factor was that quality in the cakes was improved.

SEASON AND PRICE

There is a time to buy and a time to stay out of the market. Certain foods are more plentiful at some times and lower in price than at others. Usually a food is best in quality and lowest in price at the peak of its season. The U. S. Dept. of Agriculture publishes lists of plentiful foods for certain periods. These usually are at their lowest in cost. Meat, fish and fowl are high or low in price at different seasons. Pork, for instance, is usually most plentiful and lowest in price in the fall and early winter. Fish is most plentiful and lowest in price in the spring and summer.

Salesmen can be very helpful in indicating market trends. Keeping records also can help. Good records may indicate that one doesn't buy ham, fresh asparagus or eggs just before Easter because everyone is in the market buying them.

Market supply or price should not always be the major considerations in buying. Poor menus frequently result from such a practice. Normally, prices do not change on a number of items once the season's production is in. Thus, flour, canned goods, beans and other staple items will not change much during a year. Perishable and seasonal items, however, do change price and sometimes very rapidly. Staple items, including apples, pears, cabbage, potatoes, etc., will vary in price from 3 to 9%; moderately perishable, 10 to 15% and highly perishable, 16 to 25%. Items with a steady even supply, even though perishable, will not vary much in price. This could be an item such as bananas.

WHERE TO PURCHASE

Moving things from the original producer to the consumer takes money. About 38¢ of every dollar spent for food goes to the farmer or grower and 62¢ goes to those who process the food or move it through the market.

Finding ways to reduce this cost is of concern to many buyers because, instead of decreasing, this processing-marketing percentage is increasing.

Delivery costs and small orders are said to be one of the reasons why vendors must have such a high mark-up. As a result, some vendors are trying to sell a wider range of items to include more in orders. They are also encouraging buyers to consolidate orders and order less frequently, if possible. In addition, buyers are trying to by-pass middlemen who tack on a mark-up and on more occasions are going direct to producers. Normally, commission men charge about 5%, wholesalers 25% and retailers 35%.

Supermarkets, because of direct buying, large volume and cost-of-business reductions, can charge less than the 35%. They have little risk also because they sell for cash. Many times a supermarket can sell items for less than wholesalers can purchase them.

Co-operative buying groups can sometimes reduce costs. If a foodservice group joins together and has only one delivery truck make all deliveries in the area, instead of getting the items individually from a number of trucks from different vendors—even though all purchases come from a very few—costs can be reduced and some of the savings passed on to the group.

Most foodservices purchase from wholesalers or brokers. The sale is usually on credit which costs the sellers money. Sometimes, it is 60 days or more before they get their money.

Foodservices should not overbuy to save. The involvement of the money, the chance for deterioration of quality, or loss, can frequently wipe out any savings. Health facilities are not in business to speculate on the market, but are in business to render service to their residents. In comparing prices, be sure that the comparison covers the same factors and that the value of the service rendered, quality and volume purchased are considered.

CONSUMER PROTECTION   Our government has laws
                                           which protect consumers
from unethical practices and false claims and also require proper sanitary controls to insure that foods and supplies are safe to use. Our Pure Food and other laws regulate the sanitary aspects in manufacturing and marketing plants, fill of the container, labeling and identification of items.

Reading labels and getting information about products are important activities. A label must list the net contents on cans and packages plus the name and address of the supplier or some individual or company concerned with marketing the product. The name of the item must be given and imitation substances, dietary properties (if claimed) must be indicated.

On non-common foods, a list of ingredients in their greatest to least proportion in the food must be given. Pictures or other illustrative materials on labels must be characteristic of the product. The net weight of contents may not mean much on vegetables in brine or fruit in sirup since one cannot tell how much of fruit or vegetables is in the can in relation to the liquid. Stating drained weight is a better safeguard. The government forbids false bottoms or other deceptive practices in packaging. Cans and packages must be filled to certain levels; if not, the label must read "Below Standard in Fill."

A standard of identity for a food establishes a standard by stating what a food item is. Butter, to carry its name, must be more than 80% milk fat, contain only a restricted percentage of salt and moisture. Ice cream, to be called that, must contain a certain quantity of milk solids; if it is vanilla ice cream, it must be 10% or more of milk fat; if flavored ice cream, 8% or more of milk fat.

Freestone is one species of peach and clingstone another. If a label uses one term for the other, it is mislabeling under standards of identity. "Semolina" means that the macaroni product must come from a special type of durum wheat. If a label states "Mission olive," it must come from that variety. Cheddar cheese must contain 50% milk fat on a dry basis and not be over approx 40% moisture to be called "cheese." A "cheese food" is not cheese under the standards of identity. To use the word "egg" with noodles, standards of identity require that 5½% egg solids must be incorporated in the noodles.

There are quality standards (grades) for food also. These vary, depending upon the food. Many foods must be graded to move through the market. Frequently, government graders inspect foods and give them a grade indicating their quality. Quality can change, however, after such grading, especially in fresh items, eggs, butter, apples, etc., but the grade given it by the federal grader usually does not change. Buyers should be aware of this. Quality can also be assured through the use of brand but buyers should know that a brand is only as good as the vendor who sells that brand wants it to be.

If a buyer has his own specifications that name the quality of the item desired, among other things, he can ask that government graders check the items he is to get and certify they meet his specification. This is called "acceptance buying." The graders will stamp the invoice and the sealed tapes on the package, marking it "Officially Sampled." There will be a date also in this stamp.

Government graders may also inspect items and issue a certificate indicating their grade. Buyers can ask for the certificate number or even a copy of the certificate that certifies the grade.

Before an item will be graded by a government grader, it must be inspected and passed as a wholesome product. This is done to assure the item is safe to consume and use. A federal grade stamp is in the form of a shield, while a federal inspected and passed for wholesomeness stamp is in the shape of a circle. Inside the circle will be the following: "Insp't'd and Pass'd, USDA." The number in the circle indicates the number of the plant in which the inspection occurred. All meat, poultry as well as some other foods must be inspected and passed, even if the item does not pass over state lines during marketing.

ORDERING Quantities needed should be written up as orders or requisitions. An order will be placed with a vendor while a requisition is usually a request for foods or supplies from stores in the facility. The name of the item, the quality, the size of the item or package and other pertinent information should be given, as well as amounts wanted, in either the order or requisition.

Many operations require that all orders carry an order number and requisitions may have to be numbered also. High or low levels of stock or inventory may trigger an order. Or, the items needed for production may be determined for order from the menu. It is wise to keep an order book in which items needed or low in stock are noted. Items should not be tallied from memory or from scraps of paper. Some facilities keep an "order pending" file and when orders are received, transfer the orders out into an "order received" file.

Price negotiation may have to occur before awarding an order. For this, a sheet listing items needed can be set up in a left-hand column. Then, allowing a column for each vendor contacted, prices and other information from a particular vendor can be written in the column reserved for him. After contacting the vendors, the list can be studied and the items circled in the column of a vendor to indicate that those items are to be ordered from him. A clerk or secretary can then place the orders with the respective vendors. Such a sheet is called a *call* sheet or *price quotation* sheet or *quotation and order* sheet.

When the quantity ordered is large, this technique is very desirable but when the facility is small, it is too cumbersome to use. Furthermore, a sufficient number of vendors may not be available to use for comparison of prices, quality, etc. Also if they are small, orders cannot be spread among too many vendors.

Price should not always be the basis for making a decision in *call* buying. Service, average quality delivered by a vendor, reliability, etc. also should enter into making market decisions. Fig. 7-1 shows an order sheet which also gives some receiving information.

SPECIFICATIONS A specification is used to state the quality, size and other factors needed to secure the right item for the manufacturing need. In addition, the purchase order written from this specification should state how much is wanted. Specifications can be entered on cards or filed in a loose-leaf book so reference to them can be made quickly. If an operation awards purchases on bids, then the call for bids must also give the specification for the items wanted.

Well-written specifications lower bid prices because vendors know the buyer *knows* what he wants and, also, they know what they are bidding on. Well-written specifications favor the best vendors.

Specifications are of two types: general and specific. General specifications cover factors wanted for all foods and supplies in dealing with vendors, such as the method of payment, billing procedures, submission of samples for inspection, failure to perform, etc.

Specific specifications, the second type, cover one product or a group of very similar products. They give the exact characteristics wanted in these. They should leave no doubt as to what is wanted. Every health facility should have its *own* specifications and not those written for another facility. Each facility has its own specific needs in production and its specifications should reflect these.

Keep specifications brief and as simple as possible. Eliminate detail. For instance, a buyer can eliminate a considerable amount of wordage if he

Fig. 7-1—ORDER AND

DATE	FOOD ITEM	AMT NEEDED	AMT ON HAND	AMOUNT TO PURCHASE	PURCHASE INFORMATION (QUALITY, ETC.)
7/8	Lettuce, Iceberg	10 hds	4 hds	1 ctn, 24 hds	US No 1, min wt 45 lb well trimmed
7/8	Onions, dry	—	0	50 lb sk	US No 1, Globe
7/8	Eggplant	30 lb	0	1 bu (33 lb)	US No 1, 24 to 30 size, 1½ lb
7/8	Tomatoes	12 lb	4 lb	1 lug (32 lb)	US No 1, full ripe, 5×5 size (32 lb min wt)
7/8	Cantaloupe	1 crate	0	crate	US No 1, full slip, hand ripe 45 count, 65 lb min wt
7/9	Chicken, broiler	50 lb	0	50 lb	Grade A (2¼ to 2½ lb) ready to cook
7/9	Hamburger	30 lb	10 lb	20 lb	⅛ grind, 18% fat US Good Beef, 3 oz patties
7/9	Tuna, cnd	1 cs	0	1 cs	12/5's/cs, flakes, 38 oz min drained wt
7/9	Beans, green cnd	5/10's	4/10's	2 cs 6/10's	B grade, cut, Blue Lake, Mission brand
7/9	Dried prunes	½ cs	0	1 cs, 30 lb	Grade B, French 40/50 size
7/9	Flour, pastry	100 lb	—	1 sk	Pillsbury or Gen Mills or N.D. maid brands
7/9	Broccoli, frz	40 lb	20 lb	30 lb	Grade A, chopped 2½ lb pack, 12/cs
7/9	Cherries, frz	1 can	0	1 can, 30 lb	pitted, RSP, 1:5 fruit/ sugar ratio
7/9	Cod, frz	42 lb	0	42 lb	Cod or haddock fillets 1½ to 2 lb each
7/9	Eggs, shell	1 cs	8 doz	1 cs, 30 doz	Grade A large
7/9	Ice cream	4 gal	0	4 gal 16 bricks	Brick cut 8/qt Crown brand

Fig. 7-1. *An order and requisition sheet used by one health facility for contacting vendors and obtaining quotations from vendors. Note orders are bunched as much as possible for individual purveyors. Circles indicate purveyors selected. Note comments.*

REQUISITION SHEET

PRICE QUOTATIONS PURVEYOR					DATE REC'D.	QUAN-TITY	PRICE	COMMENTS
ad	be	co						
$4.00	$4.10	(4.05)			7/9	1 ctn	$4.05	good quality
5.50	5.65	(5.50)			7/9	1 sk	5.50	
4.80	(5.00)	5.00			7/9	1 bu	5.00	good
6.10	(6.10)	6.10			7/9	1 lug	6.10	
8.25	8.60	(8.40)			7/9	1 crt	8.40	sent 46 count
			Le	Str				
			30¢	(29¢)	7/9	53 lb	15.37	20 chickens
			65¢	(65¢)	7/9	20 lb	13.00	Frozen
Re	We	Gr						
$13.40	$13.30	(13.30)			7/12	1 cs	13.30	
4.20	4.20	(4.20)			7/12	2 cs	4.25	Price change accepted
6.30	6.20	(6.30)			7/12	1 cs	6.30	
6.50	6.50	(6.50)			7/12	100 lb	6.50	no maid sent
Je	Sa	Pr						
$8.42	(8.20)	$8.30			7/12	1 cs	8.20	slightly melted
7.50	(7.50)	7.50			7/15	1 can	7.50	Royal Brand delivered
Tr	ab	Ro						
(6.59)	6.44	7.14			7/10	41½ lb	27.30	charged for 42 lb
Bu	Co							
(16.30)	16.30				7/9	1 cs	16.30	
(2.10)	2.15				7/9	4 gal	8.40	

will specify a shoulder clod of beef for pot roasting as 1114R under the Federal Institutional Meat Specifications rather than writing up all the details needed to get this product. Also, by specifying *U. S. Grade A* for a canned product, one avoids a long detailed description of the quality factors desired.

Use terms known to the market. These save time and usually are precise in their meaning. For instance, the word "young," when used in a turkey specification, means it has to be of the current crop, under 1 year old. If clarity is needed, it is better to write too much rather than too little in a specification. If, by law, certain factors are required in a product, there is no need to repeat these: For instance, since canned tomatoes to meet a grade must be of a certain drained weight, there is no need to write in the drained weight, if the grade is specified.

Usually a specification should contain:

1. The name of the item (trade, common, standard of identity or other).

2. The quantity wanted (usually stated in cases, pounds, pieces, cartons, etc.).

3. The quality (government or other grade, brand, etc.).

4. The size of the item (such as weight range, number of units per carton or case or sometimes minimum or maximum weight).

5. The unit on which a price shall be quoted (100 lb sack, 24/No. 2 cans).

6. Miscellaneous factors needing statement to obtain the exact item required, such as Blue Lake green beans, Hawaiian pineapple, a particular blend of coffee or tea, cornfed beef, Beltsville turkeys, etc.

FOOD SELECTION

MEAT   Meat grades or brand qualities for meat are based largely on *conformation,* which covers the shape of the animal and its ability to yield good meat cuts; *finish,* which indicates the amount of fat—but not too much—on the outside and inside of an animal and, to a lesser extent, the quality of this fat, and *quality*, which covers the color of the flesh, its appearance, marbling (flecks of fat within a muscle) and other factors. Grades for meat purchased by foodservices usually are:

Class	Market Grades Normally Used by Institutions
Beef, steer or heifer	Prime, Choice, Good, Standard and Commercial
Beef, cow	Choice, Good, Standard and Commercial
*Beef, bulls or stag**	Choice, Good and Commercial
Calf or veal	Prime, Choice, Good or Standard
Lamb or yearling mutton	Prime, Choice and Good
Mutton	Choice or Good
Pork (barrows and gilts)	Selection No. 1 and Selection No. 2**

*Stags are mature bulls that have been castrated.
**These are new grades for pork.

Grades based on expected yield also can be specified. Yield No. 1 indicates that meat shall come from a carcass giving a maximum quantity of flesh to fat and bone. From this Yield No. 1, yield grades go down to Yield No. 5.

To utilize both grading factors, a buyer would have to specify both for meats, i.e., for a beef cut "U. S. Grade Choice, U. S. Yield No. 2." All meats should be specified as "Inspected and Passed" also. This is because, although almost all meats must be inspected and passed, many states have not yet complied with federal regulations.

Federal Institutional Meat Purchase Specifications can be used to specify meats. When these are used, all one needs to do is to specify the number of the cut and the range plus other information as to whether the meat shall be aged or unaged, frozen or unfrozen, etc. The use of these FIMP specifications simplifies purchasing meats and also standardizes the product.

Health facilities usually operate on limited budgets and will want maximum value for their money, often even being willing to take a less tender cut to stay within a price restraint. Tender cuts, such as steaks, chops, roasts for cooking in dry heat, and some variety and specialty meats will cost more. Specify these in the Choice grade and, if beef, either in the *Top* or *Bottom* grades because beef is usually graded either as *top* or *bottom* within the grade.

Meats cooked by moist cooking methods will usually be used by small health facilities unless they cater to a clientele of rather good income. These cuts are as nutritious as those costing more. Because the higher grades have more fat, they may not be as desirable dietwise for some residents as lower grades.

Small facilities will usually purchase meats in a ready-to-cook state.

Cutting one's own meat from wholesale or carcass meats is usually wasteful and costly. It also does not give good management control. Waste or trim products must be considered in cost calculations—difficult to do—and utilizable products must be worked into the menu which may also be difficult to do. If wholesale cuts or carcass meats are used, butchers must be on the staff to process these into ready-to-use cuts. Good butchers today are hard to find.

POULTRY   Few facilities will purchase other than U. S. Grade A fowl. These should bear the circle stamp which may be attached as a tag indicating that poultry has been inspected and passed. Grade is decided by the quantity of fleshing or meat yield, the type and amount of fat and the absence of defects. Grade A poultry should be full and plump, fat should be evident in the crotch and on the back and the color of the bird should not be blue, but rather a yellowish color indicating fat beneath the skin. There should be few, if any, broken bones and few pinfeathers or hairs showing. Broken skin, bruises and other defects should be limited.

Today, most poultry can be purchased ready-to-cook or in parts. Only a few facilities, such as those catering to a Kosher group, will purchase poultry alive or have them butchered by required methods. Many facilities purchase their poultry by specifying poultry parts, turkey rolls or other items that do not need further division or processing to be ready for production.

FISH   Unless a fish or shellfish is a processed item, it is apt not to be graded or inspected and passed for wholesomeness. Shellfish must come from ocean beds certified as producing wholesome items, but the U. S. Public Health Service itself has admitted it frequently has difficulty in making "sure-fire" certifications.

Purchase fresh fish in season. Fresh, whole fish should have bright eyes, bright red gills, only a small quantity of slickness on the outside and the odor should be sweet and not one with an ammonia smell. The flesh should be firm and when pressed by the finger, the indentation should not remain. Scales should come out with difficulty and the flesh should not come freely from the bones.

Fresh fish on many markets comes whole (as it comes from the water), dressed (eviscerated with the head either on or off, sometimes called pan-dressed), as steaks, as fillets or as pieces. Wastes may be large on whole or even dressed products. Upon delivery, all fresh fish should be from 32° to

40°F inside and out and should be well iced. Weigh after draining all moisture and removing all ice. Do not weigh in wet containers or papers.

Whole or dressed fish may be stored with a coating of ice on the outside and when delivered this coating may still be on the fish. Good delivery procedures insure that it is.

Fish may be purchased frozen but the quality is usually lower than fresh fish, especially in seafood. Frozen fish comes in the same market forms as fresh fish: whole, dressed, etc. Frozen fish should not have brown edges or other evidences of having been thawed and then refrozen. The color should be good. Some frozen, packaged fish bear government grades. If so, purchase Grade A.

Canned tuna is available in light or white meat in styles called grated, flaked, chunk or solid pack, either packed in brine, oil or water. Light meat should usually be specified. Solid pack means the tuna is in one or in several large pieces. The form of the other types is self-explanatory.

The best canned salmon comes in large body pieces; lower quality is indicated when tail pieces, cheeks and other cuts of lesser value are included. The price of salmon is guided more by color than any other factor. Deep red salmon is highest in price and pale pink or white or yellow, the lowest. While the reddest salmon has the most fat and perhaps a superior flavor, the other grades are as nutritious and are suitable for small facility use.

Maine sardines are government graded; the quality is good and competes well with the famous Silt or Norwegian products. Pilchard sardines are really mackerel caught in the Pacific and packed in water, oil, tomato sauce or mustard sauce in 15-oz cans. Small sardines usually come in 3¼-oz cans, 100 per case.

Oysters and clams are canned in 51-oz cans; smaller sizes are available. Purchase by brand. Oysters are usually whole, but clams can be obtained whole, minced or chopped. Watch for tender, flavorful clams and oysters, creamy white in color, not dark or gray. There should be little evidence of silt, dirt or shells.

The odor of canned crab, shrimp or lobster should be pleasant and sweet. The color of the interior flesh should be a good white with a redness on the outside. Watch texture.

The drained weight of oysters and clams should be 59% of the total can's capacity. Wet pack shrimp should be 64%. Tuna, salmon and other similarly packed canned fish should have very little liquid on them.

Fresh oysters, clams, soft shell crabs and lobsters in the shell should be alive when purchased. Some of these may sometimes be cooked in the shell. Watch that these do not come from stocks that were about to perish. A strong odor will be evident, if they were. Shucked raw oysters, scallops or clams may be purchased fresh or frozen. Purchase oysters, crabs or scallops sized to meet your portion needs. Scallops will be sea or bay, the former being larger and less expensive.

Cooked crab, lobster or shrimp meat may be available in 1-lb or 5-lb cans, either fresh or frozen. The quality deteriorates rapidly when held frozen. Frozen cooked or green (uncooked) shrimp in the shell with heads on or off may be obtained. With the heads off, large sizes run 18 or under per lb; mediums 18 to 35 per lb and small over 35 per lb. Breaded fish should be about 1/3 breading and 2/3 meat; government standards allow almost 50% breading. A good specification states from 33% to 40%.

BUTTER

The grade of butter is determined by scoring quality factors. The following summarizes butter grades:

Score	U. S. Grade	
93 or better	AA	Clean; highly pleasing flavor; fresh sweet cream base; low salt.
92	A	Desirable flavor; clean; lacking somewhat in creamy flavor; used usually by institutions.
90	B	Cooking grade; fairly pleasing flavor but may have slight off-flavor or sour taste.

LIQUID MILK PRODUCTS

All milk products, except aged cheese, should come from pasteurized milk. Occasionally, unpasteurized milk may be required for a special diet. If so, purchase *certified* Grade A raw milk; it has a 10,000 bacterial count per cu centimeter or less. Grade A pasteurized milk normally has a count of 30,000 or less per cubic centimeter. Whole milk should contain not less than 8¼% non-fat milk solids and not less than 3¼% milk fat. Without the milk fat, it is skim milk. Fat-free or defatted milk must have no more than 0.1% milkfat. Buttermilk is usually non-fat milk clabbered by using lactic acid bacteria. Some claim buttermilk soured with *L. Acidolphilus* has therapeutic value.

Fortified milk contains nutrients approved by the government. Flavorings have been added to flavored milk; if the product has less than 8¼% milk solids, it must be called a milk drink. Reconstituted or recombined milk is made from dry milk and water. Frequently, non-fat milk, buttermilk or cottage cheese is made from dry milk.

Cream must be pasteurized. Coffee cream is 18% milk fat; when soured by lactic acid-producing bacteria, it is sour cream. Half-and-half (half 18% cream and half 3¼% milk) is about 11% milk fat; it cannot be called cream because the standards for identity state "cream is a product containing 18% or more of milk fat." Light whipping cream may contain from 30 to 35% milk fat; heavy whipping cream has over 35% milk fat.

There are a number of products today used as substitutes for cream and even some for milk. Some are made with a dried milk base but many have no milk in them. Check labels to ascertain contents for modified diets.

Evaporated milk is a fluid milk product concentrated so a 14¼-oz can plus enough water to make 1 qt is the equivalent of 1 qt of whole milk, the ratio being 1:2.2 of evaporated milk to whole milk. If a cup of evaporated milk is used, 2¼ cups of water is added to get about the equivalent of whole milk. Non-fat evaporated milk is also available. Condensed milk is evaporated milk containing 45% sugar. Purchase processed milk products fortified with vitamin D.

Dried milk may be whole, non-fat or buttermilk. Some dried creams are available; do not confuse these with the artificial cream products. Purchase dried dairy products that are fortified with vitamin D. A pound of instant non-fat dry milk is about 6½ c; regular, about 3¼ c and whole regular, about 3½ c. Normally, in quantity work, we weigh and do not measure, so this variation is not a problem.

Buy dried milk products pasteurized in U. S. Extra grade. Reconstitute in clean, cold water in a very clean container and store immediately under 40°F. Because lactose or milk sugar goes into solution slowly, reconstituted milks are better stored under refrigeration for 24 hr before use. Malted milk contains from 55 to 60% dried malt.

FROZEN DESSERTS   Ice cream should contain 1.6 lb of
milk solids per gal. If vanilla ice
cream is not 10% or more milk fat, and flavored varieties not 8% or more milk
fat on a liquid basis, they cannot be called "ice cream."

Frozen desserts foam as they are being made and this increase in volume
is called *overrun*. Ice cream should have an overrun of 80 to 100%; that is, 1
gal of liquid mix could make as much as 2 gal of frozen ice cream. Sherbet
swells about 35% and ices 25%.

Sherbets should have a milk solid content of 4% or more on a liquid basis. Ices do not have to have milk in them. A gallon of ice cream should weigh
4½ lb or more if it contains the right amount of ingredients and the proper
amount of overrun. A 5-gal can, therefore, should contain 22½ lb of ice
cream plus the weight of the container. A quart of ice cream should weigh 1
lb 2 oz plus the container. Quality scoring for frozen desserts is: flavor 35,
texture 20, body 20, appearance 15 and packaging 10; these are maximum
values.

CHEESE   Soft cheeses will be cottage, cream, Neufchatel,
Philadelphia and a few others. Cottage cheese
may be non-fat or creamed, the latter being 4% milk fat. The size curd should
be specified. A dry cottage cheese contains around 70% moisture. It is used
for salads or for cheese cakes, etc. The regular cottage cheese is about 80%
moisture. Cream cheese contains 35% milk fat and Neufchatel is about 22%.
All should come from pasteurized milk. Cottage cheese should not contain
gelatin. Specify that it should be made by souring milk with lactic acid, although some acceptable products may be made by setting the cheese with
rennin.

Cheddar cheese is usually thought of as our yellow or white American
cheese, but there are many other Cheddars. Cheddaring is a process in which
a clabbered, drained solid mass of curd is cut into strips and these strips are
piled alternately on top of one another to press out additional whey. The
arrangement of the strips is changed from time to time so all are subjected to
the same pressures. The curd is then cut into cubes, put into hoops and
pressed into the desired shape and sent in to cure. Swiss cheese is a cheddared
cheese. So are Roquefort, Provolone, etc. Many cheeses get their special flavor and texture because they are processed differently or are inoculated with
special bacteria.

Purchase U. S. Grade A cheeses. Specify age; the term *current* means aging up to 30 days for American and up to 60 days for Swiss; *medium* means aging from 30 days to 3 months for American or 60 days to 6 months for Swiss, and *aged* or *cured*, over 3 months for American or over 6 months for Swiss. Foreign imports are usually aged a longer time than domestic cheeses. If cheese is held over 60 days in cure, it need not be made from pasteurized milk, this cure being sufficient to destroy harmful bacteria. It takes 100 lb of whole milk to make from 7½ to 9½ lb of cheese.

Processed cheese is regular cheese that is cut up, emulsifiers added to it and then pasteurized. It is then molded, usually in a brick form. Pasteurization stops aging. Processed cheese goes into solution more easily in sauces because of the emulsifiers in it.

FRESH FRUITS AND VEGETABLES

The purchase of fresh fruits and vegetables varies considerably in different localities. This is because local crops are frequently used and both the product and its marketing may vary from those in other areas. Georgia peaches are different from California peaches; Georgia frequently markets its peaches in bushel baskets and California, in lugs. Thus, grading standards must provide a rather wide range so as to cover all conditions in the many producing areas.

Fruits and vegetables may be purchased by brand or by federal grade. Brand buying is practiced quite frequently and if buyers get to know the quality represented by the brand of a reliable firm, this can be one way of assuring consistency in quality. The federal grade, U. S. No. 1, is a standard wholesale grade used for products of *good* quality. U. S. No. 2 is the remainder of the crop that is marketable but this grade is usually not suitable for institutional use.

A U. S. Extra No. 1, U. S. Fancy or U. S. Extra Standard, etc. are grades indicating a product higher in quality than U. S. No. 1. These grades exist so that during years when the crop is above a *good* level or above U. S. No. 1, grades will exist for marketing such a crop. Besides these wholesale grades, there are consumer grades such as U. S. Grade A or AA or B. During out-of-season periods, a higher grade may have to be specified than would be purchased during times when the crop is good and the price is low.

Factors determining grade are color, size, shape, maturity, character and freedom from defects. In most cases, size is not a grade factor. Special grade factors may be used for some items. Florida and Texas citrus that develop a russeting, because of a tiny mite that bites into the oil sacs of the fruit, are graded under federal grades but also according to the amount of tarnish on the fruit. Thus, we can have a number of U. S. No. 1 grades such as Fancy, Bright, Golden, Bronze and Russet depending upon the amount of tarnish on the Florida or Texas fruit.

In apples, color is an important factor in determining grade and since the apples from Washington State take on a high color, this fruit usually moves in the grades above U. S. No. 1. Buyers should realize that items may deteriorate after grading so the specification should state that the grade indicated in the specification should be the grade *upon delivery*.

Watch packs and fills. Many items packed in bushel baskets or hampers should be in bulging pack which keeps the items tight in shipment. "Struck full" in a specification means the container is level full. A specification should also require that "fill shall be equal to facing" which means the items below the nicely arranged top must be equal to the top in size and quality.

Overly large or small fruits and vegetables may lack quality. In specifications, state the minimum weight of a container. For instance, a bu of 45 count cantaloupes should weigh between 60 and 65 lb, a bu of spinach or other greens not less than 18 lb, and a crate of celery 60 to 65 lb. A Florida pepper crate normally holds about 34 lb of peppers but if loosely packed can hold only 24. Knowing standard container weights can save a lot of money. Table 7-3 indicates many of the minimum weights recommended for containers of fresh fruits and vegetables.

Check quality upon arrival. Quality in cucumbers, celery, apples, potatoes, etc. will be reflected in a fresh, appealing appearance with a crispness indicated by a snap when bent or juiciness when the thumb is pressed through the skin. Greens or other products that appear wilted, damaged, deteriorated or are otherwise poor in appearance are apt to be poor in quality. Items such as grapefruit, onions or peaches should be "heavy in the hand" when lifted.

Some items should be inspected for quality based on special characteristics they should possess. For instance, good quality cranberries bounce; a sack of dry onions should rustle when shaken; a beet cut through with a knife should not give a grating sound; berries should not have wet or stained box bottoms; eggplant should have a good bloom, and mature seeds inside cucumbers and summer squash indicate over-maturity. Table 7-1 also suggests the best sizes to purchase for institutional use.

Table 7-1 – SUGGESTED FOOD PURCHASE STANDARDS

Key to abbreviations: sq cut = square cut; reg = regular; bnls = boneless; rst = roast

Item	Grade	Purchase Data	Desired Weight or Count
BEEF			
Brisket, fresh	Good	Deckle off, No. 120*	10-13 lb**
Corned Brisket	Choice or Good	Deckle off	10-13 lb
Chucks, sq cut	Choice or Good	No. 113, bone-in or bnls	34-45 lb
Cube steaks, reg	Good[a]	No. 1100	4 per lb
Swiss steaks	Choice or Good	No. 1102	4 per lb
Rib steaks	Choice[a]	No. 1103	6 to 8 oz each
Rib steaks, bnls	Choice[a]	No. 1103A	4 to 6 oz each
Ribeye roll steaks	Choice[a]	No. 1112	4 to 6 oz each
Ground patties, reg	Good[a]	No. 1136	3 to 4 oz each
Inside round steaks	Choice or Good	No. 1168	4 to 6 oz each
Outside round steaks	Choice or Good	No. 1169	4 to 6 oz each
Porterhouse steaks	Choice[a]	No. 1173	12 oz each
T-bone steaks	Choice[a]	No. 1173A	8 oz each
Strip loin steaks	Choice[a]	No. 1180, bnls, short cut	4 to 6 oz each
Top sirloin butt steaks	Choice[a]	No. 1184, bnls	4 to 6 oz each
Tenderloin steaks	Choice[a]	No. 1189, close trim	4 to 6 oz each

*The numbers in this column indicate Federal Institutional Meat Purchase Specification Items. By specifying this number, most details for purchase are stated. **The weights in this column are for animals in weight range No. 2 as listed in the Federal Institutional Meat Purchase Specifications.

(cont.)

Table 7-1—SUGGESTED FOOD PURCHASE STANDARDS (cont.)

Key to abbreviations: sq cut = square cut; reg = regular; bnls = boneless; rst = roast

Item	Grade	Purchase Data	Desired Weight or Count
BEEF (cont.)			
Rib roast, tied	Choice[a]	No. 1108R, short cut, bnls*	17-19 lb**
Rib roast, rst ready	Choice[a]	No. 1110R, bnls	14-16 lb
Beef ribeye roll	Choice[a] or Good	No. 1112R	7-8 lb
Shoulder clod	Good	No. 1114R, rst ready	16-18 lb
Chuck roll, bnls, tied	Good	No. 1116R	15-17 lb
Knuckle, bnls	Good	No. 1167R	10-12 lb
Inside round	Choice or Good	No. 1168R	18-20 lb
Outside round	Good	No. 1169R	11-13 lb
Strip loin, bnls	Choice[a]	No. 1180R, short cut	8-10 lb
Top sirloin butt	Choice[a]	No. 1184R, bnls	8-10 lb
Bottom sirloin butt	Choice[a]	No. 1186R, bnls, trimmed	4-6 lb
Tenderloin, reg	Choice[a] or Good[a]	No. 1189R	5-7 lb
Beef stew	Good	No. 1195	specify amount
Tongue, fresh or smoked	No. 1 quality	Shortcut	3-5 lb
Oxtails	Good	Fresh	1½ lb each
Rounds, bnls	Good	No. 159	50-69 lb
Ground beef, reg	Good	No. 133	specify amount
Flank steak	Good	No. 186	2-3 lb
Spencer roll	Choice[a] or Good	No. 111	18-20 lb
Short ribs	Good	No. 123	specify amount
Diced chili beef	Good	No. 127	specify amount

Item	Grade	Purchase Data	Desired Weight or Count
LAMB			
Rib chops	Choice[a]	No. 1204*	3 to 5 oz each**
Shoulder chops	Choice[a] or Good	No. 1207	4 to 5 oz each
Loin chops	Choice[a]	No. 1232	4 to 5 oz each
Shoulder rst, bnls	Choice[a] or Good	No. 1208R, tied	4-6 lb
Leg, bnls, tied	Choice[a] or Good	No. 1234AR	6-8 lb
Stew	Good	No. 1295	specify amount
Ground	Good	Not over 20% fat	specify amount
VEAL AND CALF			
Shoulder clod, rst, bnls	Choice[a] or Good	No. 1310R	6-8 lb
Chuck, rst, sq-cut, clod out, bnls, tied	Choice[a] or Good	No. 1311R	6-8 lb
Cubed steaks (cutlets), reg	Good[a]	No. 1300	3 to 5 oz.
Rib chops, bone-in	Choice[a]	No. 1306	4 to 6 oz
Shoulder chops, bone-in	Choice[a] or Good	No. 1309	4 to 6 oz
Shoulder clod steaks, bnls	Good	No. 1310	4 to 5 oz
Loin chops, bone-in	Choice[a]	No. 1332	4 to 6 oz
Cutlets, reg, cubed	Good[a]	No. 1336	3 to 5 oz
Chuck, rst, sq-cut, bnls, tied	Choice[a] or Good	No. 1309R	10-15 lb
Leg, bnls, tied, rst ready	Choice[a] or Good	No. 1335R	15-22 lb
Stew	Good	No. 1395	specify amount
Breast	Good	No. 314	6-9 lb
Ground	Good[a]		specify amount

*and **see page 299 for explanation.

(cont.)

Table 7-1—SUGGESTED FOOD PURCHASE STANDARDS (cont.)

Key to abbreviations: sq cut = square cut; reg = regular; bnls = boneless; rst = roast

Item	Grade	Purchase Data	Desired Weight or Count
PORK, FRESH *(for frozen add "F" after the number)*			
Filets, cubed or uncubed	Sel. No. 1***	No. 1400*	3 to 5 oz.**
Boston butt steaks, bone-in	Sel. No. 1ᵃ or 2	No. 1406	4 to 6 oz.
Shoulder butt steaks, bnls	Sel. No. 1ᵃ or 2	No. 1407	3 to 5 oz
Pork chops, reg	Sel. No. 1 or 2	No. 1410	4 to 6 oz
Pork chops, with pocket	Sel. No. 1ᵃ or 2	No. 1410A	5 to 7 oz
Rib chops, with pocket	Sel. No. 1ᵃ or 2	No. 1410B	5 to 7 oz
Pork chops, center cut	Sel. No. 1ᵃ	No. 1412	4 to 6 oz
Pork chops, center cut, bnls	Sel. No. 1ᵃ	No. 1412B	4 to 6 oz
Pork chops, bnls	Sel. No. 1ᵃ or 2	No. 1413	4 to 6 oz
Ham (leg) rst, bnls, tied	Sel. No. 1ᵃ or 2	No. 1402R	6 to 8 lb
Boston butt rst, bnls, tied	Sel. No. 1ᵃ or 2	No. 1406R	6 to 8 lb
Pork loin rst, bnls, tied	Sel. No. 1ᵃ or 2	No. 1413R	8 to 10 lb
Spareribs	Sel. No. 1ᵃ or 2	No. 416	3 to 5 lb
Pork loin, reg, bnls	Sel. No. 1ᵃ or 2	No. 413	6-8 lb
Pork loin, reg	Sel. No. 2ᵃ or 2	No. 409	10-12 lb.
Hocks, shoulder	Sel. No. 1ᵃ or 2	No. 417	1-1½ lb
Feet, (front)	Sel. No. 1ᵃ or 2	No. 420	¾-1½ lb
Neck bones	Sel. No. 1 or 2	No. 421*	¾ to 2 lb**
Trimmings (90%)	From clear meat-	No. 418	specify amount
Sausage, country, bulk or links	Maximum fat 40%		specify amount

*and **see page 299 for explanation.

Item	Grade	Purchase Data	Desired Weight or Count
CURED PORK			
Hams, reg, skinned			12-14 lb
Ham, reg, bnls			
Ham, canned	Maximum 4% jelly		10-12 lb
Bacon, slabs, rind on or off	8 to 10 in. wide		8-10 lb
Bacon, sliced, rind off	18-22 slices/lb		
Frankfurters, all meat****	6/ lb		specify amount
Weiners, all meat****	10/lb		specify amount
			specify amount
POULTRY (specify whether fresh killed or frozen)			
Broiler fryers	Grade A	ready-to-cook	2¼-3½ lb
Roasters	Grade A	ready-to-cook	3½-4½ lb
Capon	Grade A	ready-to-cook	5-6 lb
Stewing hens	Grade A or B	ready-to-cook	3-5 lb
Duck, young	Grade A	ready-to-cook	3-5 lb
Goose, young	Grade A	ready-to-cook	10-14 lb
Turkey, young roaster	Grade A	ready-to-cook	20-30 lb
Turkey roll, uncooked	from Grade A	ready-to-cook	12-16 lb
Turkey, roll, cooked	from Grade A	4% max juice	8-12 lb

Chicken parts should come from 2½ lb Grade A poultry; specify chicken breasts in half, 5 oz each: drumsticks, 3 oz; thighs, 3½ oz; drumsticks and thighs, 6¼ oz; wings, 2½ oz; backs, 5 oz; specify turkey breasts, whole, 14-20 lb; legs, 3-4 lb.

***Pork is graded for highest quality U. S. Selection No. 1 and for second quality U. S. Selection No. 2. While Selection No. 1 is indicated as suitable for dry heat cookery, most of the Selection No. 2 items in this column might also be suitable. ****Extenders such as cereal, bean flour, dry milk up to 4% can be added to other than all meat frankfurters and weiners. *(cont.)*

Table 7-1—SUGGESTED FOOD PURCHASE STANDARDS (cont.)

Key to abbreviations: sq cut = square cut; reg = regular; bnls = boneless; rst = roast

Item	Grade	Purchase Data	Desired Weight or Count
FISH (specify if frozen is acceptable)			
Fresh water:			
Blue pike	Fresh	Whole, dressed	3-6 lb
Brook trout	Fresh	Whole, dressed	½-¾ lb
Lake trout	Fresh	Dressed, head on	¾-3 lb
Whitefish	Fresh	Dressed	2-4 lb
Perch	Fresh	Dressed or fillets	3 lb
Smelts	Fresh	Dressed, heads off	6 to 10/lb
Salt water:			
Bluefish	Fresh	Dressed, heads on	5-6 lb
Butterfish	Fresh	Whole, dressed	¾ lb
Cod	Fresh	Whole, dressed	2½-9 lb
Flounder	Fresh	Dressed	¾-1 lb
Flounder, sole	Chilled	Fillets	4-6 oz
Haddock	Fresh	Dressed	4-6 lb
Haddock, fillets	Chilled	Fillets	1-2 lb
Halibut, chicken	Fresh	Dressed	7-12 lb
Halibut steaks	Chilled	Steaks	4-5 oz
Mackerel	Fresh	Dressed	1½-2 lb
Pollock	Fresh	Dressed	6-8 lb
Pollock, fillets	Chilled	Fillets	2-3 lb

Item	Grade	Purchase Data	Desired Weight or Count
FISH- Saltwater (cont.)			
Salmon	Fresh	Dressed, heads off	6-8 lb
Salmon fillets	Chilled	Fillets	2-3 lb
Salmon steaks	Chilled	Slices	4-5 oz
Sea Bass	Fresh	Dressed	¾-1 lb
Smelts, silver	Fresh	Whole	6-8/lb
Striped Bass	Fresh	Dressed	4-5 lb
Swordfish, steaks	Chilled	Slices from center	4-5 oz pcs
White (Rose) Perch	Fresh	Whole or fillets	6-8 oz ea
SEAFOOD			
Oysters, shucked	Chilled	200 count	per gal
Clams, shucked	Chilled	350-500 count	per gal
Crabs, whole, Blue	Chilled, cooked	¼ to 1 lb	individually
Crabmeat, Blue	Chilled, cooked	Lump or mixed	5 lb cans
Crabs, Dungeness	Chilled, cooked		¾ to 3 lb
Crabmeat, Dungenese	Chilled, cooked	Mixed in natural portion	5 lb cans
Crabs, Alaska	Chilled	Legs in shell	specify by lb
Lobster tails	Frozen	4-6 oz each	in 5 lb boxes
Lobster, Eastern	Chilled, cooked or (ray) alive	chicken size	¾ to 1 lb
Scallops	Chilled	med size, sea grade	110-170/gal
Shrimp, small, Pacific	Frozen or chilled	Cooked and shelled or per lb raw (green) unshelled	Large-Medium 26-30 lb

(cont.)

Table 7-1—SUGGESTED FOOD PURCHASE STANDARDS (cont.)

Key to abbreviations: sq cut = square cut; reg = regular; bnls = boneless; rst = roast

Item	Grade	Purchase Data	Desired Weight or Count
SEAFOOD (cont.)			
Shrimp, Gulf	Frozen	Cooked and shelled or raw (green) unshelled	
Softshell crabs	Eastern Blue	per doz	2½-4 in. diam ea
DAIRY PRODUCTS			
Butter	92 or 93 score (AA) or (A)	in lb or pats 72 to 80/lb	in single lb or 5 lb boxes in pat
Milk, non-fat	Grade A	½ pt, qt, gal	These milks may be specified fortified with Vitamin D, etc.,
Milk, whole 4%	Grade A	½ pt, qt, gal	pasteurized, homogenized
Milk, 2%	Grade A	½ pt, qt, gal	pasteurized
Cream, coffee	Grade A	18-20% milk fat	pasteurized
Cream, light whip	Grade A	36% milk fat	pasteurized
Cream, heavy whip	Grade A	40% milk fat	
Cheese, cottage, low fat	Grade A	60-80% moisture	1 lb or 5-lb packs
Cheese, cottage, dry salad	Grade A	60-70% moisture	1 lb or 5-lb packs
Cheese, cottage, creamed	Grade A	4% milk fat, 60-80% moisture	1 lb or 5-lb packs
Cheese, cheddar	Grade A	specify age as current medium or cured	5-lb bricks or 20-30 lb rounds

(cont.)

Item	Grade	Purchasing Data	Desired Weight or Count
DAIRY PRODUCTS (cont.)			
Cheese, Swiss	Grade A	specify age as current, medium or cured cheddar, Swiss type	best buy by lb as needed; 1 lb to 10 lb bricks
Ice cream, vanilla, 10%	High quality	80 to 100% overrun	by gal
Ice cream, flavored, 8%	High quality	80 to 100% overrun	by gal
EGGS			
Shell	AA or A	specify size as med or large	30 doz/case
Frozen, whole	AA or A	Pasteurized	30 lb cans
Frozen, whites	A or B	Pasteurized	30 lb cans
Frozen, yolks	A or B	Pasteurized	30 lb cans
Dry, whole	A or B	Pasteurized	1 lb to 25 lb packs
Dry, whites	A or B	Pasteurized	1 lb to 5 lb packs
FRUITS AND VEGETABLES			
Fruits, fresh:			
Apples, baking	Fancy or A	R. Beauty, Baldwin, Greenings, Winesap	113 count (2½ in. diam)
Apples, cooking	No. 1 or C	Sauce, Gravenstein, Transparent; Pies: Spy, Cortland, Wealthy	100 or 113 count
Apples, eating	Fancy or A	Jonathan, Delicious, York, Imperial, McIntosh	113 count

Table 7-1–SUGGESTED FOOD PURCHASE STANDARDS (cont.)

Key to abbreviations: sq cut = square cut; reg = regular; bnls = boneless; rst = roast

Item	Grade	Purchase Data	Desired Weight Coung
FRUITS AND VEGETABLES–Fresh (cont.)			
Apricots	U. S. No. 1	Tree picked, ripe	25 lb lug or 5 lb baskets
Avocado	U. S. No. 1	Calif. 16/28/flat	Lug or flat
		Flor. 8 oz to 1½ lb	
Berries	U. S. No. 1	pt or qt	crate of 12
Bananas	Fancy	specify ripeness	by lb or 30 lb box
Cherries, sweet	U. S. No. 1	watch fill	by flat or basket
Grapes, California	U. S. No. 1	specify kind	by flats or lugs
Grapes, Eastern	U. S. No. 1	usually Concord	by flats or lugs
Grapefruit	U. S. No. 1	specify Fla. or Texas	32 or 36 size carton
Lemons	U. S. No. 1	Eureka or Lisbon	by doz, 165 size
Melons, cantaloupe	U. S. No. 1	half or full slip	54 size, about 1 lb ea
Melons, honey dew	U. S. No. 1	per ea or crate	4-6 lb size
Melons, Persian or Cranshaw	U. S. No. 1	per ea or crate	3-6 lb size
Melons, water	U. S. No. 1	per ea	20-25 lb size
Oranges, slicing	U. S. No. 1	Box, Cal. or Fla.	72 or 88 size
Oranges, juicing	U. S. No. 1 or 2	Box, Fla or Texas	113 or sample market
Peaches	U. S. No. 1	Freestone, ¾ lb	20 lb lug or bushel 45-48 lb
Pears	U. S. No. 1	Select by time of year	Box, min wt 45 lb, 120
		for variety	or 135 size
Pineapple	U. S. No. 1	Hawaiian or Philippine for	Doz, 15/half crate
		best; specify ripeness	

Item	Grade	Purchase Data	Desired Weight or Count
FRUITS AND VEGETABLES—Fresh (cont.)			
Plums	U.S. No. 1	Specify ripeness	Lugs or baskets
Prunes	U.S. No. 1	Specify Italian or French	Lugs or baskets
Rhubarb	U.S. No. 1	Strawberry (red or early hothouse)	5 lb or 20 lb packs
Tangerines	U.S. No. 1	Specify type	Box approx. 72 to 80
Fruit, canned, specify kind, grade, type, style, count, sirup density, size of pack (usually No. 10 can)			
Apples, solid	A or Fancy	7½ lb min can wt/No. 10	min dr wt 96 oz
Applesauce	A or Fancy	6 lb 11oz/No. 10	
Apricots, halves	B or Choice	64 oz min dr wt/No. 10	
Berries	A or Fancy	55 to 60 oz dr wt/No. 10	75/85 count No. 10
Cherries, sweet	B or Choice	66 to 70 oz dr wt/No. 10	for pies specify solid pack
Cherries, RSP, pie	A or Fancy	74 oz dr wt/No. 10	290 to 335 count/No. 10
Cranberry sauce	A or Fancy	No. 2 or No. 10 cans	
Figs, Kadota	B or Choice	over 71 oz/No. 10	No. 10's 7 lb 5 oz net wt.
Fruit Cocktail	B or Choice	watch fruit ratios	
Fruits for Salad	A or Fancy		No. 10's min dr wt 71 oz
Grapefruit sections	A or Fancy	46 oz size	Min. dr. wt. 65 oz/No. 10
Grapefruit juice	A or Fancy	46 oz size	Min dr wt 29 oz
Orange sections	A or Fancy	46 oz size	12/cs
Peaches	B or Choice	Clings or Freestone; halves, diced or sliced	Min dr wt 29 oz
			about 66 oz/No. 10, drained wt
			for clings; 35/45 count
Pears	B or Choice	Bartlett, halves or diced	23 to 30/No. 10, 62½ oz dr wt

(cont.)

Table 7-3—SUGGESTED FOOD PURCHASE STANDARDS (Cont.)

Key to abbreviations: sq cut = square cut; reg = regular; bnls = boneless; rst = roast

Item	Grade	Purchase Data	Desired Weight or Count
FRUITS AND VEGETABLES—*Canned Fruit* (cont.)			
Pineapple	B or Choice	whole, half or broken slices, chunks, spears or crushed	No. 10 slices min dr wt 61½ oz; other types heavier; No. 2 size slices run 50/No. 10
Plums or Prunes	B or Choice		No. 10 min dr wt 60 oz
Dried prunes	B or Choice	No. 10 dr wt 110 oz	Sweet: French or Imperial. Tart: Italian
Frozen Fruit (judge quality thawed)			
Apples, slices	A or Fancy	Sugar-fruit ratio 1:7	25 or 30 lb cans
Apricots, halves	B or Choice	Sugar-fruit ratio 1:5	8, 10, 25 and 30 lb pack
Berries	A or Fancy	Sugar-fruit ratio 1:4	1 to 30 lb packs
Blueberries	B or Choice	Sugar-fruit ratio 1:4	some packs frozen without sugar
Cherries, RSP, pie	A or Fancy	Sugar-fruit ratio 1:4 or 1:5	usually packed 30 lb cans
Cherries, sweet	A or Fancy	Sugar-fruit ratio 1:7, pitted or unpitted	Light: Royal Anne or Napoleon, Dark: Bings, Lamberts, Tartar
Peaches, half or slice	B or Choice	Sugar-fruit ratio 1:4; clings or freestone	
Pineapple	B or Choice	Styles same as canned	Sirup density 20 to 25° Brix
Plums	A or Fancy	Red, yellow-green or purple	1:5 sugar-fruit ratio
Rhubarb	A or Fancy	Sugar-fruit ratio 1:3 or 1:4	Specify red(hothouse)or green

Item	Grade	Purchase Data	Desired Weight or Count
Dried Fruit			
Apples	B or Choice	rings, slices or pie pieces	If low moisture, order flakes, wedges or nuggets
Apricots	B or Choice	Available loose or slab	If low moisture, order nuggets or wedges
Currants	A or Fancy	order seeded	
Dates	B or Choice	Whole (pitted), pieces or slab	
Figs	B or Choice	White: Adriatic, Calimyrna, Kadota; black: Mission	
Peaches	B or Choice	Freestone or cling	If low moisture, order nuggets or wedges
Pears	B or Choice	halves, slices or pieces	med size: 67/lb, large 53/lb
Prunes	B or Choice	French are sweet, Italian are tart	
Raisins	B or Choice	seeded, seedless or with seeds	Select grade size, 3/8 in. diam
Fresh Vegetables			
Artichokes, globe	U.S. No. 1	6 doz/box or 3 or 4/lb	20 to 26 lb per ½ box
Asparagus	U.S. No. 1	crate: six 2 to 2½ lb bunches; wt net 26-32 lb	Washington No. 1 equals U. S. No. 1 wt 28
Beans, Lima	U.S. No. 1	Fordhook or Baby varieties	bu basket wt 28-32 lb net
Beans, snap	U.S. No. 1	Wax or Green	bu basket min wt 30 lb net
Beets, topped	U.S. No. 1	50 lb sacks; specify short trim (2 in. or less)	crate of bunches-5 doz bunches approx., net wt 45 lb

(cont.)

Table 7-1–SUGGESTED FOOD PURCHASE STANDARDS (cont.)

Key to abbreviations: sq cut = square cut; reg = regular; bnls = boneless; rst - roast

Item	Grade	Purchase Data	Desired Weight or Count
FRUITS AND VEGETABLES—*Fresh Vegetables* (cont.)			
Broccoli	U.S. No. 1	Bunch 2-2½ lb; crates of 14, 18 or 28 bunches	Wirebound crate, bunches 25 lb 14 bunch crate, 20-23 lb
Brussels sprouts	U.S. No. 1	Fiberboard box or drum 25 lb	1 pt cups should weigh 1 lb
Cabbage, green	U.S. No. 1	Bu-40 lb; 50 lb sack	Varieties: Domestic or Early
Cabbage, white	U.S. No. 1	Bu-40 lb; 50 lb sack	Danish (white) is a good keeper
Cabbage, Chinese	U.S. No. 1	Purchase singly by lb	
Cabbage, red	U.S. No. 1	Purchase singly by lb	25, 50 or 100 lb bag; bu
Carrots, topped	U.S. No. 1	Well-trimmed; not over 1 in.; accept ¾ to 2 in. diam	50 lb; crates 55 to 60 lb
Cauliflower	U.S. No. 1	Pony crate 12-15 heads, 42 lb	
Celery, green	U.S. No. 1	16 in. tall bunch crate 55-70 lb; ½ size carton 30-33 lb	1 to 1¾ stalks best size; celeriac is celery root
Corn, in husks	U.S. No. 1	Bag 45-50 lb; crate 40-60 lb	50 lb equals about 60 ears
Cucumbers	U.S. No. 1	Bu-2 doz, 48 lb; max diam 2-3/8 in.; min length 6 in.	In off season specify U.S. Fancy, min length 5 in.
Eggplant	U.S. No. 1	Bu 30-34 lb, 24 to 30 size	Each should weigh about 1½ lb

Item	Grade	Purchase Data	Desired Weight or Count
Garlic	U. S. No. 1	25 lb bag; Creole strong flavor, easy to peel	Italian mild flavor difficult to peel
Greens, cooking	U. S. No. 1	Bu should weigh 18 to 25 lb	Specify Savoy spinach, Scotch (green) or blue for kale
Greens, salad	U. S. No. 1		
Escarole, endive or chicory		Bu 25, wirebound crate 36 lb	Whitloff (Belgium or French)
Lettuce or romaine		Carton 38-55 lb; leaf or bibb may come in 5 or 10 lb baskets	Iceberg is hard headed; Boston (Butterhead) is soft; romaine may also be called Cos lettuce
Kohlrabi	U. S. No. 1	Specify bulbs about 2 in. in diam	Also called "cabbage turnip"
Leeks	no grades	Bu 24 to 30 lb	Specify bulbs over ¾ in. in diam
Mushrooms	U. S. No. 1	By lb or 2 qt basket	Med 1 to 1-5/8 in. diam
Okra (gumbo)	U. S. No. 1	Specify 2 to 3½ in. pods	35 3-in. pods equal 1 lb
Onions, dry	U. S. No. 1	25, 50 or 100 lb bags	Specify variety
Onions, green	U. S. No. 1	Order by bunches as needed	should have 2 to 3 in. of white showing on each onion
Parsley	U. S. No. 1	Order by single or doz bu	A bunch weighs about 2 oz
Parsnips	U. S. No. 1	Purchase in 25 lb bags	4 med size equals 1 lb
Peas in pod	U. S. No. 1	Bu 28-30 lb	Purchase snow peas frozen
Peppers, green	U. S. No. 1	Bu 28-30 lb; carton 30-34 lb	Should have 2½ in. diam

(cont.)

Table 7-1—SUGGESTED FOOD PURCHASE STANDARDS (cont.)

Key to abbreviations: sq cut = square cut; reg = regular; bnls = boneless; rst = roast

Item	Grade	Purchase Data	Desired Weight or Count
FRUITS AND VEGETABLES—*Fresh Vegetables* (cont.)			
Potatoes, Irish	U. S. No. 1	100 lb sack; bakers may come in crates; specify size of bakers	For baking, deep frying or mashing, select dry or mealy varieties; for salads, hash browns, frying, etc., select moist ones
Potatoes, sweet	U. S. No. 1	sold in bu-50 lb net	yams are considered sweet potatoes but are less expensive but more moist
Radishes	U. S. No. 1	purchase by bunch as needed	best ¾ to 1 in. diam
Squash, summer	U. S. No. 1	bu-48 lb, lug 20-30 lb carton 40 lb	
Squash, winter	U. S. No. 1	Order singles by lb; bu 50 lb	
Tomatoes	U. S. No. 1	Lug 30-32 lb; 3 med/lb	Specify ripeness
Turnips and Rutabagas	U. S. No. 1	50-lb bag; bu-55 lb	Reject turnips over 2½ in. diam
Vegetables, Canned			
Asparagus	A or Fancy	No. 10 dr wt 63-64 oz	Spears, cut spears; green or white should be specified
Beans, snap	B or Ex-S[b]	Specify wax or green (Blue Lake), whole or cut	specify medium-large size; min dr wt 63 oz/No. 10

Item	Grade	Purchase Data	Desired Weight or Count
Beans, Lima	B or Ex-S	Thin-seeded best; green or white can be specified	min dr wt 72 oz/No. 10
Beets	B or Ex-S	Sliced, whole, dried, quartered or julienne (shoestring)	min dr wt 68-72/No. 10
Carrots	A or Fancy	Whole, sliced, quartered, diced, julienne or cut	min dr wt 68-72 oz/No. 10
Chili Sauce	A or Fancy		
Corn, whole kernel	B or Ex-S	White or golden, brine or vacuum pack	min dr wt 72 oz/No. 10
Corn, cream style	B or Ex-S	White or golden	Best bought in No. 2 cans
Hominy	A or Fancy	White or golden (yellow)	min dr wt 72 oz/No.10
Mushrooms	A or Fancy	Med. size (No. 3) 7/8 to 1-1/8 in.; min dr wt 12 oz/ No. 2	Whole, sliced whole, sliced buttons, stems and pieces
Onions, whole	A or Fancy	Med size 80-100/No.10	min dr wt 60 oz/No.10
Okra	A or Fancy	Cut, whole; min dr wt 12 oz/No.2; 60 oz/No. 10	
Peas	B or Ex-S	Early or sweet varieties	
Pimientos	A or Fancy	Whole, whole and pieces, pieces sliced or diced	med sieve No. 4 recommended
Pumpkin	A or Fancy	Fill shall be 90% of can	min dr wt 13½ oz/No. 2
Sauerkraut	A or Fancy	min dr wt 16 oz/No.2, 80 oz No. 10	

(cont.)

Table 7-1—SUGGESTED FOOD PURCHASE STANDARDS (cont.)

Key to abbreviations: sq cut = square cut; reg = regular; bnls = boneless; rst = roast

Item	Grade	Purchase Data	Desired Weight or Count
FRUITS AND VEGETABLES—*Canned Vegetables* (Cont.)			
Spinach	A or Fancy	min dr wt 60 oz No. 10	
Sweet Potatoes	A or Fancy	Liquid, vacuum or solid pack	Liquid pack min dr wt 72 oz/No. 10
Tomatoes	B or Ex-S	Solid; tomatoes with juice tomatoes with puree packs min 33% solids	Must drain 56% or more
Tomato catsup	A or Fancy		
Tomato paste	A or Fancy	Salt-free solids: heavy 33%; medium 29-33%; light 25-29%	Heavy 1.14 specific gravity; med, 1.11: light, 1.09
Tomato puree	A or Fancy	10.7 to 12% salt-free solids is medium thickness; heavy, 12 to 25%	
Tomato sauce	A or Fancy	Contains spices, vinegar, etc.	
Frozen Vegetables (cook and judge)			
Asparagus	A or Fancy	Spears, tips, cut spears or center cuts	Specify med size; green
Beans, snap	B or Ex-S	Use cut wax or green	
Beans, Lima	B or Ex-S	Green or white	Thin or thick seeded
Broccoli	A or Fancy	Spears, short spears, cuts, chopped	

Item	Grade	Purchase Data	Desired Weight or Count
Brussels sprouts	B or Ex-S		
Carrots, diced	A or Fancy		
Cauliflower	A or Fancy		
Corn on the cob	A or Fancy	Yellow or white	
Corn, kernel	B or Ex-S	Yellow or white	
Greens (except spinach)	A or Fancy	Whole, sliced leaves or chopped	Beet, collard, kale, mustard Swiss chard, turnip
Mixed vegetables	B or Ex-S	Watch mixture proportion	
Okra	A or Fancy	Whole or cut	
Onion rings, breaded	A or Fancy		
Peas	B or Ex-S	Early or sweet	Telephone variety freezes best
Peas and carrots	B or Ex-S	Peas not less than 50%, carrots not less than 25%, of wt	
Spinach	A or Fancy	whole, whole leaf, cut or chopped	
Squash, summer	A or Fancy	Sliced (transverse cut) or cut	
Squash, winter	A or Fancy	Should be cooked and mashed	
Succotash	B or Ex-S	Watch mixture proportion	

Vegetables, Dried

Institutions usually specify U. S. No. 1 grade for beans, peas and lentils. There are many varieties of beans; white varieties are pinto, marrow, old-fashioned yellow-eye, navy and great northern. Lima beans are baby (small), medium and large in size. White beans are either small or large. Peas come whole or split, green or yellow.

Low moisture, dry vegetables are used in considerable quantities in some institutions. Onions, green peppers, cabbage, carrots,

(cont.)

Table 7-1–SUGGESTED FOOD PURCHASE STANDARDS (cont.)

FRUITS AND VEGETABLES *Dry Vegetables* (cont.)

celery, potatoes and tomatoes are the most commonly used kinds of this processed vegetable. No grades exist for these and buyers should set up their own specifications but watch quality also upon delivery.

[a]Cook by dry heat methods; all others by moist heat methods. For tenderest cuts specify beef at the top of the grade; moist cooking beef cuts can be specified at the bottom of the grade.

[b]Ex-S stands for Extra-standard, the second grade in vegetables and equivalent to the Choice grade in fruits.

Source: Summarized from *Quantity Food Purchasing*, Kotschevar, L. K. New York: John Wiley and Sons, Inc. 1961.

Learn the areas from which the best quality comes. Hawaiian pineapple will be found to be superior to others in flavor and texture. Citrus fruit from the Rio Grande area in Texas or the Indian River area in Florida is apt to be excellent in quality. The best Brussels sprouts come from Long Island or California. At times, to obtain the necessary quality, a buyer should specify tomatoes from Mexico or from the Salton area of California or to get good leaf lettuce in winter, a hothouse leaf lettuce. Learning how to move from one product to the other and shifting quality factors to meet seasonal differences can save while at the same time maintain quality.

PROCESSED FRUITS AND VEGETABLES

Quality standards for processed fruits and vegetables are:

Item	First Quality	Second Quality	Third Quality
Canned or frozen vegetables	Grade A or Fancy	Grade B or Extra-Standard	Grace C or Standard
Canned or frozen fruits	Grade A or Fancy	Grade B or Choice	Grade C or Standard
Processed juices	Grade A or Fancy	Grade B, Choice or Extra-Standard*	
Dried fruits	Grade A or Fancy	Grade B or Choice	Grade C or Standard

*Processed juices usually have two grades; sometimes the second grade listed here is omitted and a Grade A or Fancy and a Grade C or Standard grade are made for juices.

Some dried vegetables and other processed product grade terms may be different from these but this is not often the case. There are also trade grades which buyers may have to know.

A grade is determined by scoring various quality factors, the total score indicating the grade. When three federal grades exist, C grade is indicated by a score from 70 to 79, B grade by a score of 80 to 89 and A grade by a score of 90 to 100. The factors scored and the total points for a factor vary with different products. For instance, the clarity of the juice is an important factor in scoring pears but not for some other fruits. Usually, the quality factors scored are color, uniformity of size, absence of defects, character or maturity. Size is usually not a factor affecting grade. Drained weight is a part of the grade for canned fruit cocktail, canned citrus fruit, canned tomatoes and canned crushed pineapple. Catsup and some other items have the amount of solids or specific gravity as a quality requirement.

Buyers will find many processed fruits and vegetables have no grade on the label. The market has been reluctant to put grades on products, preferring to sell by brand instead. Buyers must then learn what the grades of various brands are. Usually wholesalers will have three labels for their first, second and third quality products. If a product is labeled "Below Standard in Quality," this does not mean the item is inedible but that it does not meet the minimum standards in *quality* for the product.

Buyers should watch drained weights. Table 7-2 lists recommended drained weights for canned fruits and vegetables. Canned fruits or vegetables will be 1/3 liquid and 2/3 solids, with vegetables running slightly higher than fruits. Frozen vegetables should usually be 100% of the net contents.

Frozen fruit is usually packed with some sugar to retain shape, color and flavor. A label that shows "1:5" means 1 part sugar to 5 parts fruit. Frozen fruits usually are less than 50% of the net weight after draining. In canned items, "solid pack" indicates no liquid; "heavy pack" indicates a little liquid is added and in "sirup or juice pack," the item is about 1/3 liquid

Standards of identity are important. The names or terms used mean precise things and buyers should know what these are. The term "large" used with a ripe olive means that the size is about 6 olives to the oz, not a very big size. If the label shows an olive larger than shown here, the product is mislabeled and is in violation of federal standards for labeling.

Labels used on products must be approved by the federal government. Standards of fill have also been established. No. 10 or No. 3 cylinder cans must be filled to 27/32 in. from the top of the can; No. 2 1/2 cans, 20/32 in. and No. 2 cans, 19/32 in.

Counts or sizes should be specified. Using a 64-count pineapple slice in No. 10 cans permits the giving of 2 slices rather than 1 large slice from a 28-count. Counts best for institutional use are listed in Table 7-2. Canned peas, lima beans and green or wax beans have sieve sizes, No. 1 being smallest and No. 5 being largest. Beets, onions, asparagus and some other products are also sized.

Canned or frozen vegetables are usually 1% salt. Canned fruits are packed in water, juice, light sirup, medium sirup, heavy sirup or extra heavy sirup. Sirup densities vary; a light sirup on cherries is between 16° and 20° Brix (each degree of Brix is about 1% sugar) while a light sirup on peaches is between 14° and 19° Brix. The heavier the sirup, the higher the cost usually. The heavier the sirup, the less chance of the fruit being broken up because sugar strengthens the fruit, but there are also more calories. Fruit sirups or juices should be used for other things if they are not used with the fruit. Check labels to see if an item is salt-free or contains no sugar. The word "dietetic" is not enough. Check also *which* artificial sweetener is used; many contain sodium.

Institutions usually purchase cases of No. 10, or 46-oz, can sizes of fruits and vegetables and 2½ to 5-lb frozen items. Sometimes, it is desirable to have some smaller packs on hand to avoid opening a large size just for a few portions. The following indicates some of the more common can sizes and the amounts they contain:

Table 7-2—DRAINED WEIGHTS, COUNTS AND USES FOR

Can Name	Cups	Ounces
6Z	3/4	5-3/4
No. 1 (picnic) (24 or 48/case)	1-1/4	10-1/2
No. 300 (24 or 48/case)	1-3/4	15-1/2
No. 303 (12, 24, or 48/case)	2	16
No. 2 (24/case)	2-1/2	20
No. 2-1/2 (24/case)	3-1/2	28
46-oz (12/case)	5-3/4	46
No. 10 (6/case)	12	105
Gal (4/case)	16	8 lb

CEREAL PRODUCTS   Wheat flour and other cereal products are seldom graded; they should
be purchased by brand. Watch net weights; some cereal packages look like a
lot but weigh very little.

Wheat flour for bread is called *strong* or *hard* flour. It is high in protein
and usually costs more than other flours, except fine cake flours. Pastry flour
is made from *soft* wheat; it is lower in protein. It is used for pies, biscuits and
some pastries. It is good for use as a dusting flour, thickener for gravies and
sauces and for general cooking. Cake flour comes from carefully selected soft
wheat; it is used for cakes, cookies and delicate pastries.

All-purpose flour is used for both pastries, pies and breads; it can be
used also for general cooking purposes. Specify flour that is bleached and
aged. Graham or whole wheat flour contains some of the bran and inner part
of the kernel not found in white flour. Rye flours come light, medium or
dark (pumpernickel); light rye flour contains very little bran while pumpernickel contains much more. Buckwheat flour may also be purchased light or
dark, depending upon the amount of bran in the product.

CANNED FRUITS AND VEGETABLES

Uses	Approximate Substitutions
Concentrated frozen juice; Individual juice	17 equal a No. 10; 8 equal a 46-oz can
Condensed soup; fruits and vegetables	10 equal a No. 10; 2 equal a No. 2 can
Pork and beans; spaghetti, cranberry sauce	7 equal a No. 10; 2 equal a No. 2-1/2; 3 equal a 46-oz can
Canned fruits and vegetables; juices	7 equal a No. 10; 2 equal a No. 2-1/2; 3 equal a 46-oz can
Vegetables, fruits and juices	5 equal a No. 10; 2-1/2 equal a 46-oz can
Vegetables, fruits and juices	3-1/3 equal a No. 10; 1-1/2 equal a 46-oz can
Juices; canned chicken etc.	2-1/3 equal a No. 10 can
Fruits, vegetables and juices; jams and jellies Mayonnaise, catsup, pickles	Net weight varies; 105 oz in canned fruits or vegetables

Rice may be purchased polished or brown; the latter has some of the bran remaining on it. Long grain rice cooks up more easily into separate grains. Round grain rice, used by the Japanese and by some Chinese, tends to stick together when cooked. Purchase Extra Fancy or Fancy or federal grades No. 1 or No. 2.

Purchase oatmeal, cornmeal, hominy, grits, etc. by brand. Do not purchase too much since these can become infested with weevils. Stoneground means coarsely ground and because they contain the germ of the cereal these may be more perishable than other meals. Bulk or large quantity prepared cereals are more economical than smaller or individual packs, but for sanitary reasons and convenience, the extra cost of the smaller packs may be justified.

Macaroni products are made from the inner part of the wheat kernel. Semolina pastes come from high protein durum wheat; they are yellowish and cook up into a firmer product than pastes made from lower quality wheats. Maximum salt content is 1 to 2%; salt-free pastes are available. If salt-free, they should contain no disodium phosphate added as a dough conditioner. Egg noodles must contain at least 5½% dry egg solids.

GROCERIES   Quality factors should be known for many
                                 of the miscellaneous groceries that must
be purchased. There are factors in pickles, sugars, flavorings, spices, fats and
oils, sirups, nuts, beverages and even yeast and vinegar that make some more
desirable than others for use in quantity preparation. Buyers should learn what
these are and select those best suited for the facility's needs. A list of references at the end of this chapter will give much of the information needed to
perform the purchasing task for these items.

SUPPLIES

As much as 6 to 8% of the foodservice budget may be spent for supplies.
Knowing how to select and purchase these items can not only save money but
can improve performance standards.

SERVICEWARE   The appearance of food is much af-
                                 fected by the dishes, glassware and flat-
ware (eating utensils) used. Color, shape, decoration, sparkle and tone should
be sought. Select also for serviceability, durability and cost. The least expensive items may not save the most in the long run.

China
Ceramic dishes may be made from earthenware, pottery, stoneware or
china (porcelain). China or porcelain is best. It is shaped from refined clay
and fused at very high temperatures giving a strong vitrified base or bisque
that takes considerable shock. It also has beauty. It may be decorated or
colored to make it more attractive and is then covered with a protective glaze
to make it more durable. China should be evenly shaped and possess balance
so it can be handled easily. Misshapen products do not stack or wear well.

A dish possessing proper hardness and resilience should give a bell-like
tone when struck. The fusing process should give a continuous, solid mass
that shows no bubbles, pitting or otherwise uneven appearance on a broken
edge. Glazing should be thick, even and possess no pitting or bubbles. A good
glaze cleans easily and should wear 5 years, even on the edges of items. If a
glaze is cleaned well with alcohol and the item is dipped in lukewarm water,
the water should cover the cleaned area in a thin film. A dish should be able
to be heated to 347°F and then plunged into room temperature water at least
5 times without breaking.

Extra strength is gained by adding weight—doubling weight increases durability 75%; adding an extra rim or bead around the edge or on the bottom or adding extra clay at the well (the center part) will provide needed weight. Compactness also gives strength and also a variation in shape; a scalloped edge is stronger than a plain one.

Plain white china is the least expensive; colored or simply decorated, next, and highly decorated china, the moxt expensive. Silver or gold must be put on over the glaze and this adds to the cost.

Use actual sizes in ordering, not trade sizes. A trade size is actually smaller than the dish, usually the distance from the edge of the well to the opposite edge; an 8-in. trade size will actually measure nearly 10 in. Specify cups, bowls, sauce dishes, etc. by volume.

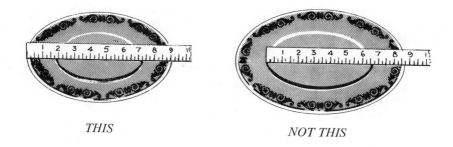

THIS   NOT THIS

Fig. 7-2—*The method which can be used to compare a trade measurement with an actual measurement is shown here.*

The size of a dish has much to do with showing food to good advantage. Limited depth tends to make the portion appear larger but cools the food more quickly. Fill a dish with a standard portion and see how it appears.

Deep cups require one to put the head far back to drain them, but shallow ones cool the contents more quickly. Watch that handles are big enough for the resident's finger to hold the cup well. Check also for balance and handling of a dish when filled. Weighted drinking cups may help residents who have poor co-ordination. Covers with spouts that fit over glasses, cups or bowls may be used. Some merely need flexible straws or plain straws to handle liquids well.

China is priced per place setting of 5 pieces consisting of a cup and saucer, plate, sauce dish and bread and butter plate. Other pieces are purchased separately. Open stock indicates china is available upon reorder in less than 30 days. Special design china takes about 4 to 6 months for the original order to be delivered and about 2 months for delivery upon reorder. But watch; some companies discontinue open stock when they find a line unprofitable. Reputable dealers with a large volume of business tend to keep open stock patterns longer than others.

China is priced per place setting of 5 pieces consisting of a cup and sau-lows: 1) Selects, perfect; 2) Firsts, almost perfect; 3) Seconds, minor defects not observable; 4) Thirds, obvious blemishes but still serviceable; and 5) Culls or Lumps, badly warped, chipped or scarred. *Run of the kiln* is a grade that includes the first two grades and the best of the seconds. Specifications should contain the size, weight, pattern, shape and other factors needed to identify color, decoration or rim style. Use either heavy (banquet) or medium weight china. Light weight is usually not suitable for institutional use.

If one dish size can be used for more than one purpose, the inventory that must be carried can be reduced; thus, if a 5½ in. plate is used for salads, bread and butter, desserts, etc., the inventory of dishes used for these items can be cut by at least 20%. Normally, a facility should carry an additional 50% in inventory for replacement. Some averages in numbers of dishes carried in a small health facility are:

Item	Actual Size	Number/Resident*
Dinner plate	9-1/4 in.	1
Bread and butter	5-1/2 in.	2
Saucer	5-5/8 in.	1
Cup (conic or ovid**)	7-1/4 oz	1-1/4
Bowl	8 oz	1-1/4
Vegetable (fruit) dish	4-7/8 oz	2

*Carry an additional 50% on inventory. **The ovid shape is also called regular.

Glassware

Plain glass is silica (sand) fused at high heat with soda and lime. It scratches and shatters easily. It is low in cost. Pyrex is stronger than glass and withstands sudden changes in temperature better than glass because it contains boric oxide instead of lime. Corning glass contains boro-silicates and some metals to give it extra durability and hardness; it is also heat-hardened to give it strength. This method gives it a defect, however; it has the tendency to shatter when cracked or chipped. Corning glass is slightly less expensive than plain china and will last as long. Pyroceram, used in the cones of rockets, is clay fused with silica and some rare metals. It is harder, more durable and resilient than china but costs about 3 times as much.

Good quality glass is sparkling and clear. Strength is given by putting a bead at the top, by bulging or curving the shape, such as with barrel glasses, or by adding extra glass on the base or at points of wear where shock will occur. Carry a reserve inventory 100% over needs. Normal sizes for glassware used in institutions are:

Fruit or vegetable juice	5 oz	Iced tea	12 oz
Water or milk glass	10 oz	Sherbet glasses	5½ oz
Fruit cocktail dishes	4½ oz		

Plasticware

Plastic dishware is usually made from melamine. It is light in weight, not costly and may be decorated or colored without too much cost. It softens at 300°F. Plastic trays should be laminated for extra strength. Wear should be assured for about 5 years. A cup should stand about 500 fillings but with good handling and destaining should give 800 fillings.

Disposable ware made from plastic or paper is being used more. Disposables increase sanitation and may not increase cost. Some papers withstand high temperatures, so it is possible to bake in them, serve in them or store in them. Purchasing sirups, jams or jellies, cream or other items in plastic containers saves having sugar bowls, small pitchers, etc. on the tray but the containers may be difficult for some residents to handle. A large quantity of paper or plastic may create a disposal problem. Up to this time, incineration with a recapture of polluting vapors has seemed the best method of getting rid of these items.

Flatware

Eating utensils, such as teaspoons, forks, knives, etc., are best made from high grade stainless steel for facility use. Low cost stainless steel flatware has a bluish color; the better steels have a soft, silver color. Low cost items are stamped from stainless steel sheets and have the same thickness throughout. They will show a roughness at the edges and on fork tines, etc.

The better stainless steel units are graded; this is a fashioning or rolling between instruments to give the units a variation in thickness which improves appearance and balance. The better ware is also polished to a soft sheen, except for knife blades which are polished to a mirror finish. Specify stainless knives as solid which means the handle and blade are one piece. A serrated blade gives a better cutting edge than a plain edge. When these become dull, they can be re-serrated at small cost. Specify the serrated edge as not less than 1¾ in. from the tip of the blade.

Silverplated flatware has beauty, is durable but is more costly than stainless steel. Silverplate is blanks of metal other than silver covered with a silver coating. Specify Extra-heavy Hotel Plate which is equal in silver depth to 8 oz of silver per gross of standard teaspoons or Triple Plate equal to 6 oz of silver per gross of standard teaspoons. Require that all pieces be inlaid with extra silver at points of most wear. An inventory of 1¼ of each utensil used per resident should be carried with a reserve of 100% for replacement.

Hospital supply houses usually carry utensils that assist those with special eating problems. A fork with a cutting edge can be obtained. Extra long handles on utensils are available. Some utensils can be fixed so they strap onto the hand.

Cleaning Supplies

In cleaning, two things must be done: remove soil and sanitize. Heat can assist in removing some soils and, if moist, sanitize as well. Ten seconds in 180°F or 30 seconds in 170°F water destroys most bacteria. Chlorine in a concentration of 100 ppm (parts per million) or iodine products (iodophors) in a concentration of 25 ppm will sanitize without heat. Commercial sanitizers containing either chlorine or iodine are available. Many detergents on the market also contain these sanitizing agents. The goal in sanitizing is to try to reduce the bacterial count on utensils below 100 per cubic centimeter, although some municipalities allow 200.

To clean, we must soften soil with heat or moisten it with water, then remove it with some type of friction and finally keep it away so the item remains clean. Most cleaning compounds contain substances that speed moistening and also help to remove soil. Grease can be removed by emulsifying it or by making it into soap by using alkaline agents. Some cleaning compounds contain substances that keep soil away from the clean items once it is removed. These are called *sequestering* or *chelating* agents because they hide the soil away or pick it up. (*Sequester* means to hide and a *chela* is the claw of a crab or lobster that can pick up things and hold them.)

Water over 7 grains in hardness causes problems in cleaning. Spotting and interfering with the work of the soap or detergent are two of the problems. Water containing hard water salts shows spots when it dries on a surface and these easily show up on glassware, flatware and less easily on dishes. Hard water salts can also combine with cleaning agents to form a solid compound or sediment which shows up sometimes as a sediment. Also, when these hard water salts combine with the compound, they prevent it from doing its work. To avoid this, phosphates are added to the compound and the mixture acts to prevent this combining.

Hard water salts precipitate when the water becomes warm and they may then clog pipes and hot water heating coils or deposit on the insides of dishwashers or other equipment. It is almost impossible to remove hard water salts from pipes but we can use special compounds to remove them from the insides of equipment.

Good handling procedures can do much to make dishes, glasses and flatware last longer and maintain a good appearance. Good procedures should be established for clearing tables of these items. In separating items from trays, have cups, glasses and other items stacked separately into racks so they can be washed and stored without rehandling. Keep heavy and light pieces separated. Separate flatware, putting it into water to soak. Avoid rubbing china together, since this friction wears away the protective glaze. Soak dishes and glasses that have heavy soil. Destain with proper compounds when items need it.

Each cleaning job usually requires a different cleaning agent. Salesmen representing good cleaning companies or sanitarians can often be of assistance in solving special problems.

Do not store cleaning agents with food supplies. Provide a separate place for such storage.

RECEIVING

PROCEDURES   If goods are not properly received, all the work in setting up good specifications, purchasing the right product and getting the right price may go for naught. Receiving should see that 1) the right items are delivered; 2) that they are of correct quality; 3) come in the amounts ordered, and 4) are billed at the proper price. Sometimes price is not checked upon receiving but, instead, by the accounting office later.

The purchase order of the facility gives essential information needed in receiving, such as company, date of delivery, pertinent delivery conditions, kind of item, amount, item size, perhaps price, etc. The delivery invoice should be checked against the purchase order. If there are discrepancies, these should be noted on the invoice which is to be sent to the accounting office. The same information should be put on the invoice that is returned to the vendor.

Differences in weights or amounts between what is received and what is shown on the invoice should similarly be noted on both invoices. A receiving report may also be maintained. This lists information contained on the invoice or delivery ticket. In small operations, this may be only a memorandum booklet which is sent to the accounting office and then returned.

"Blind receiving" is a procedure in which the receiver is given an invoice which does not list quantity or weight. The receiver must check either quantity or weight or both and put this on both invoices. This is done to prevent the receiver from automatically taking the count or weight listed on the invoice.

In most facilities, receiving will not be a full-time job. It is important that the individual assigned to receive knows how to count and also to judge quality. If he cannot judge quality, someone else should check this factor for him. For instance, if he cannot tell Good from Standard beef, or medium from large eggs or the difference between a case of 6/10 cans and 24/2 cans, someone must do this who can. It is also important that casual, daily deliveries, such as milk or bread, are not brought in by the delivery man, stored by him in their proper place and then the delivery ticket brought to a busy cook who wipes wet hands impatiently on a soiled apron and scrawls a signature indicating acceptance.

The receiver should check the temperature of frozen goods to see that they have not been thawed and then refrozen. Contents should be inspected at several places and from different containers. They should not be received thawed or thawing. Use an unbreakable, stainless steel dial thermometer, inserting it into the case in a hole made with a sharp instrument; after it has been in the case for about 5 min, read the temperature. Or, open the container flap, lay the thermometer inside, close the flap and after 5 min read the temperature. In doing this, the thermometer stem should have a firm contact with the package or its contents.

Be sure the thermometer is accurate. To check it, fill a glass with chipped ice and water; insert the thermometer and after 10 min, the temperature should be 32°F. When delivered, chilled or refrigerated foods should not have a temperature over 40°F inside or outside. Check deliveries for bulging cans, dents, etc. Note tears or damage to sacks or other packages.

STORAGE

As soon as possible after goods are received, they should be moved to storage; this is especially important for chilled or frozen items. The possibility of theft is always there as well as the chance for deterioration.

Many health facilities have limited storage space and purchasing procedures must suit these limitations. If there are only 1 or 2 reach-in refrigerators and perhaps an old ice cream cabinet for frozen storage, the quantities ordered must be extremely limited and turned over often. The storage facilities must also be adequate to protect the products. Even under the best conditions some deterioration occurs but when storage conditions are poor, the loss is greatly increased.

Fresh fruits and vegetables are living things. They breathe and they have life processes still going on. If these processes stop, the item deteriorates rapidly. Fruits and vegetables need air but not so much that they dry out. If kept cool and sufficiently moist so they do not dry out and some air is allowed to get to them, they will keep for a long time.

If oxygen is not available, the produce cannot respire and it quickly dies. Lettuce or other products frequently become slimy when they cannot breathe. Putting items into polyethylene bags to keep them fresh is all right but not for over 24 hr because air cannot get into the bag. Move foods through storage as quickly as possible.

In general, refrigerated spaces for fruits and vegetables should be from 32° to 45°F. Keep the moisture level high. An 85 to 90% relative humidity is desirable. However, if the moisture is too high, spoilage may be encouraged. Bruising or rough handling encourages deterioration and decay.

Deteriorating or decaying products can start the same process in others. Check through items and remove those that will do this. Remove wilted or damaged portions. Store foods that give off odors away from other foods that will absorb such odors. The following information may be helpful in this respect:

Item	Release Odors	Absorb Odors	Item	Release Odors	Absorb Odors
Apples, fresh	yes	yes	Cheese, cheddar	yes	yes
Butter	no	yes	Cheese, cream	no	yes
Cabbage	yes	no	Fish and seafood	yes	no
Eggs, shell, fresh	no	yes	Onions	yes	no
Milk or cream	no	yes	Peaches, fresh	yes	no
Cheese, cottage	no	yes	Some berries	yes	yes
Potatoes	yes	no	Turnips, rutabagas	yes	no

Soaps, detergents, cleaning solvents, paints, etc. also give off odors.

Canned foods deteriorate rapidly above 100°F. The area where they are stored should not have higher temperatures than 60° to 70°F; should be well ventilated and away from direct sunlight. Most canned foods keep well for six months; maximum storage is a year. Freezing does not harm edibility unless the can breaks, but some quality is lost with freezing and thawing.

Coffee, tea, flour or rice may cake and lose quality under poor storage. Insect infestation is also a danger, especially if temperatures are above normal. Some dried fruits, dried vegetables and cereals may have to be stored under refrigeration to prevent insect damage. Store these foods in containers with tightly fitting tops and purchase limited supplies.

Store frozen foods at -10°F or below. The quality loss is from 2 to 5 times as rapid with each rise of 5 degress above this. At 15°F, the deterioration is twice as rapid as at 0°F; at 25° to 30°F, it is again doubled. Fluctuating frozen temperatures increase ice crystal growth which, in turn, damages the cellular structure of meats, fruits and vegetables. Once such damage occurs, it cannot be corrected.

Tropical fruits such as avocados, pineapples, bananas or vegetables such as cucumbers, eggplant, onions, peppers, potatoes and winter squash may keep best at temperatures around 50° to 60°F. Refrigerate these items only to hold them. Potatoes lose quality if stored below 50°F. If stored for any length of time below this temperature, potatoes must be conditioned at a temperature above 50°F to return cooking quality.

Encourage workers to open and close refrigerators as little as possible to prevent a rise and fall in temperature in the storage area. Plan removals of foods so they are done all at one time. If this is done, operation costs are also decreased.

The best storage management is to use storage as little as possible. Storage is another work motion and if we can eliminate it, we gain. Few foods improve with storage except meat and some cheese. Deterioration usually begins as soon as the food enters the marketing channels. Storage is a device or delay between order and use and creates little or no value.

Watching production schedules and having foods delivered just before use may save using storage. The items can go into production from receiving. If items are frozen, they should be removed and placed in refrigeration in sufficient time to defrost unless they are to be cooked from the frozen state. Several days are needed to defrost turkeys, chickens, roasts, frozen eggs and other large food pieces. Slow thawing is recommended. Fast thawing may cause an increase of drip loss in flesh foods and a texture loss as well. Fast thawing can harm the texture of frozen fruits and vegetables.

It is best not to refreeze once food is thawed. The quality loss is great and also the danger of food poisoning. Many operations have a rule that no food will be frozen after it is thawed. Once frozen foods are brought to a serving temperature, cook them or serve them as soon as possible.

Some recommendations for storing dairy or egg products are:

Food	Storage Requirements
Eggs	32° to 40^OF; do not freeze. Cross-stack crates or individual cartons. Handle as little as possible; watch odor absorption; eggs at room temperature deteriorate very rapidly.
Milk or cream	Keep cold and covered at 40^OF or slightly lower; watch for absorption of odors and flavors; rotate stocks properly.
Cheese	Keep cottage and cream cheeses tightly sealed; watch odor and flavor absorption. Wrap all cheese to retard drying. Store at 38° to 40^OF. Freezing may damage texture but not flavor. Wrap frozen cheese in moisture-vapor proof wraps for storage.
Butter	Watch odor absorption; keep tightly wrapped; 40^OF is recommended; butter can deteriorate in storage and so do not store too much too long.

Tables 7-3, 7-4 and 7-5 present some helpful storage data. Table 7-6 gives approx quantities of foods needed to produce 100 portions.

Table 7-3— STORAGE LIFE OF SOME FROZEN FOODS
(at 0°F, in months)

FRUITS AND VEGETABLES

Fruit with sugar	12
Asparagus, Snap Beans	8-12
Beans, Lima or Broccoli	12
Brussels Sprouts	8-12
Cauliflower, Cut Corn	12
Corn on the Cob	8-12
Carrots, Peas, Spinach	12
Mushrooms	8-12
Squash	12
Potatoes, French fries	4-8
Potatoes, scalloped, etc	1

BAKERY GOODS

Quick breads	2-4
Yeast breads	6-12
Rolls	2-4
Cake	4-6
Fruit Cake	12
Cookies	4-6
Pies, fruit	12
Pies, mince	4-8
Chiffon or Pumpkin	1
Cream	1

COOKED DISHES

Meats, vegetables, etc in a sauce	4-8
Soups	4-6
Chicken, Turkey, Sliced Meats	3-4

MEAT, FISH OR POULTRY

Beef roasts or steaks	12
Ground Beef	8
Cubed Beef	10-12
Veal Roasts or chops	10-12
Cutlets or Cubed Meat	8-10
Lamb roasts or chops	12
Ground Lamb	8
Pork roasts or chops	6-8
Ground Sausage	4
Ham and other cured meats	4
Bacon	
Lean Fish (sole, cod, perch, haddock, etc.)	6
Fat Fish (whitefish, salmon, trout, swordfish, mackerel)	3
Crab or Lobster in shell	2
Shrimp in the shell	6
Crab meat, Lobster meat, etc.	4
Shrimp meat	4
Oysters	3-4
Scallops	3-4
Clams	3-4

MISCELLANEOUS

Sandwiches	2*
Ice Cream and Frozen Desserts	6-8
Frozen Puddings, etc.	4-6

*Not all sandwich fillings freeze well; eggs, for instance, toughen.

Table 7-4— STORAGE REQUIREMENTS OF FRESH FRUITS AND VEGETABLES

Item	Recommended Temperature °F	Relative Humidity %	Storage Life*	Normal Freezing Point °F
FRUITS				
Apples	30-38	85-90	4 mo	28.4
Avocados	45-55	85-90	2-3 wk	27.2
Bananas	58-60	85-90	7 days	**
Grapefruit	32-55	85-90	1 mo	28.4
Lemons	55-58	85-90	1-3 mo	28.1
Oranges	30-37	85-90	1-3 mo	30
Peaches	31-32	85-90	2-4 wk	30
Nectarines	31-32	85-90	2-4 wk	29.4
Pears	30-31	90-95	4 mo	28.5
Pineapples:				
Mature-green	50-60	85-90	2-3 wk	29.1
Ripe	40-45	85-90	2-4 wk	29.9
Strawberries	31-32	85-90	7 days	29.9

*The storage life will depend upon the ripeness of the fruit; for instance, a full ripe banana may store only 1 day; a ripe avocado, several days.
**Bananas begin to darken below 50°F; tropical fruits are best held at 50°F or above and used quickly.

Item	Recommended Temperature °F	Relative Humidity %	Storage Life*	Normal Freezing Point °F
VEGETABLES				
Asparagus	32	85-90	3-4 wk	29.8
Beans, green or wax	45-50	85-90	7-10 days	29.7
Limas, shelled	32-40	85-90	2 wk	30.1
Limas, unshelled	32-40	85-90	2 wk	30.1
Broccoli	32-36	90-95	1-1½ wk	29.2
Brussels Sprouts	32-36	90-95	3-4½ wk	29.2
Cabbage, Early	32-36	90-95	3-6 wk	31.2
Cabbage, Danish	32-36	90-95	3-4 wk	31.2
Carrots, topped	32-36	90-95	4-5 mo	29.6
Carrots, bunched	32-36	90-95	1½-2 wk	29.6
Cauliflower	32-36	85-90	2-3 wk	30.1
Celery	31-32	90-95	2-4 wk	29.7
Cucumbers	45-50	85-90	2-4 wk	30.5
Lettuce	32-36	90-95	1-2 wk	31.2
Onions	40-45	70-75	6-8 mo	30.1

Item	Recommended Temperature °F	Relative Humidity %	Storage Life*	Normal Freezing Point °F
VEGETABLES (cont.)				
Potatoes, new	50-70	85-90	1 mo	28.7
Potatoes, mature	50-60	85-90	4 mo	28.9
Radishes	32-36	90-95	1½-2 wk	29.5
Spinach	32-36	90-95	1½-2 wk	30.3
Tomatoes, ripe	45-50	85-90	8-12 days	30.4
Tomatoes, mature, green	55-70	85-90	2-6 wk	30.4

Adapted from "The Commercial Storage of Fruits, Vegetables and Florist and Nursery Stocks," *Agricultural Handbook No. 66,* USDA, 1954.

Table 7-5—GENERAL STORAGE TEMPERATURES FOR FOODS

Food	Short Term Storage °F	Long Holding Storage °F	Maximum Recommended Relative Humidity %
Meat box	34-36*	30-34*	10 days, 75-85%
Fish	30-34	28-32	5 days, 75-85%
Dairy Box	35-45	35-40	varies, 75-85%
Fruits and vegetables	36-45	32-36	1-2 wk, 85-95%
Frozen foods	0-10	0-10	varies

*Meats darken below 34°F.

Table 7-6— APPROXIMATE QUANTITIES FOR 100 PORTIONS*

Food	Portion Size	Units to Purchase for 100 Portions
BAKERY		
Breads and Crackers		
Biscuits, bak. pow. or soda	2 2-oz	16-2/3 doz
Coffee cake, 12 x 20 in.	2 oz (2 x 2-1/2 in.)	2-1/4 cakes
Cornbread, 12 x 20 in.	2-1/2 oz (3 x 3 in.)	3-3/4 cakes
Crackers, graham	2	4 lb
Bread loaf, quick; 8 in. loaf	1-3/8 in. slice	5 loaves (8 lb)
Muffins	2 oz	8-1/3 doz
Rolls	1 roll	8-1/3 doz
White or whole wheat bread	1-5/8 in. slice	6-1/4 lb
White or whole wheat bread	1-1/2 in. slice	5 lb
White, rye, whole wheat	1-3/8 in. slice	4-1/2 lb
Crackers, soda, 2 x 2 in.	2	2 lb
Cakes		
Angel, plain 10 in.	1 oz	6 cakes
Cup cakes	1-1/2 oz	8-1/3 doz
Fruit cake	2-1/2 oz	16 lb
2 layer, 10 in.	2 to 2-1/2 oz	5 to 6 cakes
Pound or loaf	2 to 3 oz (1/2 in. slice)	6 to 8 loaves
Sheet cake, 18 x 26 in.	2 oz (3 x 3 in.)	2 sheets
Pies		
All types, 9 in.	7 cuts/pie	15 pies
CEREALS		
Cooking		
Cornmeal	4 oz (1/2 c)	4 lb
Farina, Cream of Wheat or Wheat Grits	4 oz (1/2 c)	4 lb
Grits, Hominy	4 oz (1/2 c)	4-1/2 lb
Pettijohns	5 oz (2/3 c)	5 lb
Oats, rolled	5 oz (2/3 c)	5 lb

Food	Portion Size	Units to Purchase for 100 Portions
CEREALS (cont.)		
Prepared		
All-Bran	1/2 oz (1/2 c scant)	6 16-oz pkg
Bran flakes	1 oz (3/4 c)	10 10-oz pkg
Cornflakes	1 oz (3/4 c)	12 8-oz pkg
Grapenuts	1 oz (1/2 c)	9 12-oz pkg
Krumbles	1 oz (3/4 c)	12 8-oz pkg
Puffed Rice or Wheat	1/2 oz (1 c)	10 5-oz pkg
Rice Krispies	1 oz (1 c)	8 13-oz pkg
Shredded Wheat	1 biscuit	7 12-oz pkg
Wheat Krispies	3/4 oz (3/4 c)	7 10-1/2 oz pkg
Whole Wheat Flakes	1 oz (3/4 c)	10 10-oz pkg
Farinaceous Pastes, Etc.		
Macaroni	1/2 to 2/3 c (4 to 5 oz)	8 to 10 lb
Noodles	1/2 to 2/3 c (4 to 5 oz)	7 to 9 lb
Rice	1/2 to 2/3 c (4 to 5 oz)	6 to 8 lb
Spaghetti	1/2 to 2/3 c (4 to 5 oz)	8 to 10 lb
BEVERAGES		
Apple or other fruit juice	4 oz (1/2 c)	9 46-oz cans
Cocoa, dry	6 oz c	1 lb
Cocoa, instant	6 oz c	4-1/2 lb
Coffee, ground	6 oz c	2 lb
Coffee, instant	6 oz c	12 oz
Lemonade	8 oz glass	2-1/2 qt (5 doz lemons)
Orange juice, fresh	4 oz (1/2 c)	14 doz med size
Orange juice, frozen	4 oz (1/2 c)	8 12-oz cans
Tea, hot	6 oz c	4 oz
Tea, iced	8 oz glass	8 oz
DAIRY PRODUCTS AND EGGS		
Milk and its Processed Products		
Cheese, cheddar, cottage, cream	2 oz	12-1/2 lb
Cream, light (coffee)	2T (1 oz)	3-1/4 qt
Cream, heavy (whipping)	1-1/4 T whipped	1 qt
Ice cream, etc., brick	1 slice (8 to a brick)	12-1/2 qt(bricks)
Ice cream, etc., cups	3 oz plain, 2 oz Sundae	8-1/3 doz

(cont.)

Table 7-6— APPROXIMATE QUANTITIES FOR 100 PORTIONS* (cont.)

Food	Portion Size	Units to Purchase for 100 Portions
Milk and Its Processed Products (cont.)		
Ice cream, etc., bulk	1/3 c (No. 12 scoop)**	4 gal
Milk, evap. for coffee	2 T (1 oz)	7 14-1/2-oz cans
Milk, fluid, any type	8 oz glass (1 c or 1/2 pt)	100 1/2 pt; 25-qt or 6-1/4 gal
Milk, dry, non-fat	8 oz (1 c or 1/2 pt)	6-1/4 lb
Milk, dry, whole	8 oz (1 c or 1/2 pt)	7-1/4 lb
Butter or Margarine		
For spread***	1 pat (80 per lb, 2/3 T)	1-1/4 lb
For vegetables		1 lb
Eggs		
Eggs, fresh	1 (approx 1-1/2 oz)	8-1/3 doz
Eggs, frozen, whole	1-1/2 oz	
high quality		10 lb
Eggs, dry, whole	1-1/2 oz	3-1/8 lb

FRUITS AND VEGETABLES

Food	Portion Size	Units to Purchase for 100 Portions
Canned Vegetables		
Canned vegetables, drained	3 oz (1/2 c)	4 No 10 cans
Canned vegetables, un-drained	3 oz (1/2 c)	3 No.10 cans
Dried Vegetables		
Beans, any variety	1/2 c	9 lb
Peas	1/2 c	9 lb
Split peas for soup	1 c soup	8 lb
Fresh Vegetables		
Asparagus	3 oz (1/2 c)	45 lb
Beans, Lima in pods	3 oz (1/2 c)	50 lb
Beans, Snap or Wax	3 oz (1/2 c)	22 lb
Beets, without tops	3 oz (1/2 c)	27 lb
Beet greens	3 oz (1/2 c)	40 lb
Broccoli	3 oz (1/2 c)	40 lb
Brussels Sprouts	3 oz (1/2 c)	24 lb
Cabbage, raw	3 oz (1/2 c)	16 lb
Cabbage, cooked (incl. Chinese or red)	3 oz (1/2 c)	24 lb
Carrots, without tops	3 oz (1/2 c)	24 lb

Food	Portion Size	Units to Purchase for 100 Portions
Cauliflower	3 oz (1/2 c)	25 lb
Celery, raw	3 oz (1/2 c)	20 lb
Chard	3 oz (1/2 c)	29 lb
Collard	3 oz (1/2 c)	25 lb
Corn in husks	1 ear	50 lb
Cucumbers, 9 in., raw	5 slices	18-3/4 lb
Eggplant	3 oz (1/2 c)	
Endive or Chicory, raw	2-1/2 oz (3/4 c)	7 lb
Kale	3 oz (1/2 c)	29 lb
Lettuce, iceberg, wedges	2 oz	12-1/3 heads
Lettuce, underliner, iceberg	2 leaves	15 heads
Lettuce, chopped, iceberg	2 oz (3/4 c)	17 lb (untrimmed)
Lettuce, romaine	2 oz (3/4 c)	12 lb
Mustard greens	3 oz (1/2 c)	34 lb
Onions, mature, dry	3 oz (1/2 c)	29 lb
Parsnips	3 oz (1/2 c)	29 lb
Peas in pod	3 oz (1/2 c)	50 lb
Peppers, green	3 oz (1/2 c)	27 lb
Peppers, green	half pepper for stuffing	50 peppers
Potatoes, baking	1 baked (5 oz)	32 lb
Potatoes, mashed	4 oz	30 lb
Potatoes, brown or scallop	4 oz	30 lb
Potatoes, sweet or scallop	4 to 5 oz	30 lb
Radishes	2 ea	20 bunches
Rutabagas	3 oz (1/2 c)	37 lb
Spinach	3 oz (1/2 c)	37 lb
Spinach, raw for salad	2 oz (3/4 c)	20 lb
Squash, summer	3 oz (1/2 c)	29 lb
Squash, winter acorn	1/2 squash	50 lb
Tomatoes, raw	3 slices (3 oz) or 1 small	20-25 lb
Turnips, no tops	3 oz (1/2 c)	35 lb
Turnip greens	3 oz (1/2 c)	37 lb
Frozen vegetables	3 oz (1/2 c)	19-20 lb
Canned Fruits		
Apple slices in juice or applesauce	4 oz with juice (1/2 c)	4 No. 10
Apricots, 75/85 count/ No. 10	4 oz (1/2 c)	4 No. 10

(cont.)

Table 7-6—APPROXIMATE QUANTITIES FOR 100 PORTIONS* (cont.)

Food	Portion Size	Units to Purchase for 100 Portions
FRUITS AND VEGETABLES *Canned Fruits (cont.)*		
Berries in juice	4 oz with juice (1/2 c)	4 No. 10
Cranberries	2 T	1-1/8 No. 10
Figs	4 oz with juice (1/2 c)	4 No. 10
Fruit cocktail	4 oz with juice (1/2 c)	4 No. 10
Grapefruit sections	4 oz (1/2 c)	9 46-oz
Peaches, 35/45 count/ No. 10	4 oz (2 halves)	5 No. 10
Peaches, sliced	4 oz (1/2 c)	4 No. 10
Pears, 35/45 count/No. 10	4 oz (2 halves)	5 No. 10
Pears, diced	4 oz (1/2 c)	4 No. 10
Pineapple slices, 57/64 count/No. 10	2 slices with juice	4 No. 10
Pineapple chunks	4 oz (1/2 c)	4 No. 10
Pineapple, crushed	4 oz (1/2 c)	4 No. 10
Plums or prunes in juice	4 oz (1/2 c)	4 No. 10
Pie Fruits, solid or heavy pack		
Apples	1 No. 10 makes 8 pies	
Berry fruits	1 No. 10 makes 5-6 pies	
Cherries, RSP	1 No. 10 makes 5 pies	
Peaches, Apricots, etc.	1 No. 10 makes 5-6 pies	
Dried Fruits (Cooked)		
Apples (sliced), Apricots, Peaches, etc.	3 oz (1/2 c)	9 lb
Dates	4 ea	8 lb
Figs, cooked	2	4-1/2 lb
Prunes	3 oz (1/2 c)	11 lb
Raisins	2-1/2 oz	9 lb
Fruits, Fresh		
Apples, 113 count	1 2-1/2 in. diam	1 box or bu
Apples, for sauce	3 oz (1/2 c)	30 lb
Apples, for pies, 8 in.	7 cuts per pie	30 lb
Apricots	2	20 lb
Bananas, small	1	32 lb
Bananas, sliced	2-1/2 oz (1/2 c)	25 lb
Bananas, for pies	7 cuts per pie	10 lb
Berries	2 c, raw	13 qt
Cherries, sweet	1 c, raw	20 lb
Cherries, red sour	7 cuts per pie	18 qt

Food	Portion Size	Units to Purchase for 100 Portions
Fruits, Fresh (cont.)		
Cranberries, raw, chopped	1/2 c	17 lb
Cranberries, sauce	1/2 c	7-1/2 lb
Grapefruit	1/2 c sections	59 lb
Grapefruit	1	50 grapefruit
Peaches	1	100 peaches (25 lb)
Peaches, sliced or diced	1/2 c	29 lb
Pears	1 med	34 lb
Pears, diced	1/2 c	22 lb
Pineapple, raw	1/2 c or med slice	40 lb (10 units)
Plums	3 med or 2 large	25 lb
Rhubarb, sauce	1/2 c	50 lb
Fruits, Frozen		
Apples, Apricots, etc. for pies, 9-in.	7 cuts per pie	20 lb
Apricots, Peaches, Strawberries, etc., dessert	1/2 c with juice	20 lb
Fruit or Vegetable Juices		
Canned	1/2 c (4 oz)	9 46-oz cans
Frozen, concentrated	1/2 c (4 oz)	8 12-oz cans

MEAT, POULTRY AND FISH (for 100 2-oz portions, lean boneless meat)

Beef		*Beef*	
Brisket, corned, bnls	20 lb	Rump or other roasts, bnls	18 lb
Brisket, fresh, bone in	22 lb	Rump or others, bone in	22 lb
Chuck roast, bnls	19 lb	Steaks	
Dried beef, creamed (3 oz)	10 lb	Loin, 6-oz, bnls	38 lb
Ground meat in gravy or		Fried cube steak	20 lb
creamed (3-oz portion)	15 lb	Flank	19 lb
Ground meat patties	17 lb	Swiss	19 lb
Heart	40 lb	Round, bone-in	22 lb
Liver	18 lb	T-Bone (8-oz steak)	50 lb
Rib roast, rib in	40 lb	Tongue	22 lb
Rib roast, boned, rolled	18 lb	Stew, bnls	17 lb
Lamb		*Lamb*	
Chops, 4/lb, 3-oz cooked	25 lb	Roast, shoulder, bone-in	29 lb
Roast, leg, bone-in	29 lb	Roast, bnls	20 lb

(cont.)

Table 7-6—APPROXIMATE QUANTITIES FOR 100 PORTIONS* (cont.)

MEAT, POULTRY AND FISH—LAMB (Cont.)

Lamb (cont.)

Ground	18 lb	Stew, bnls	18 lb
Roast, leg, bnls	20 lb		

Pork — *Pork*

Chops, 4/lb, 3 oz cooked	34 lb	Heart	31 lb
Chop suey or chow mein meat	15 lb	Link Sausage	29 lb
Cutlets, 4/lb, 3 oz cooked	25 lb	Liver	21 lb
Grilled ham, bone in	30 lb	Loin Roast, bnls	21 lb
Ground pork patties	22 lb	Luncheon Meats	12-1/2 lb
Ham, cured, bone-in, baked	31 lb	Shoulder, cured, bone-in	29 lb
Ham, cured, bnls, baked	20 lb	Shoulder, roast, bnls	20 lb
Ham, cured, sliced (1 oz)	6-1/2 lb	Shoulder, roast, bone-in	25 lb
Ham, fresh, bnls, roast	17 lb	Weiners or Franks	12-1/2 lb
Ham loaf, ground (veal, pork, beef 4 lb; ham 16 lb)	20 lb		

Veal — *Veal*

Breaded Cutlets (clear meat)	17 lb	Roast leg, bnls	18 lb
Birds	20 lb	Roast leg, bone-in	30 lb
Chops, 4/lb, 3 oz cooked	27 lb	Roast, loin, bone-in	22 lb
Loaf, 2/3 veal, 1/3 pork	25 lb	Stew, bnls	19 lb

Poultry — *Poultry*

Chicken, ready-to-cook		Duck or Goose	
A la King, 4 oz portion	24 lb	Allow 1 lb per person	
Baked (Roaster or capon)	29 lb	Turkey	
Creamed, 4 oz portion	36 lb	A la King, creamed, etc.	20 lb
Fried, 2 pieces, 5 oz	42 lb	Creamed, etc. from turkey roll	14 lb
Stewed	40 lb	Roast	34 lb
Canned	12-1/2	Roll roast	20 lb

Fish — *Fish*

Canned		Dried, bnls	17-1/2 lb
Salmon, 1 lb cans	16	Dried, bnls, creamed, 4-oz portion	12-1/2 lb
Sardines, 15 oz cans	18	Fresh or Frozen:	
Tuna, fish flakes, etc.		Fillets	20 lb
solid pack, 7-oz cans	34	Whole, dressed	36 lb
or large No. 5 cans	5	Smoked, bone-in	17 lb

MEAT, POULTRY AND FISH (Cont.)

Seafood

Crab, creamed, etc.,		Clams, shucked, chowder	1 gal
clear meat	10 lb	Clams, canned, chowder,	
Crab, in shell, 1/2 lb/person	50 lb	15 oz	8 can
Lobster, creamed, etc.,		Shrimps, small, cooked and	
clear meat	10 lb	shelled for cocktails	10 lb
Oysters, shucked, 200 size	4 gal	unshelled and uncooked	20 lb
Oysters, stew	5 qt	Shrimps, large, cooked and	
		shelled, 4/portion	12 lb
		unshelled and uncooked	25 lb

MISCELLANEOUS

Honey, 3 T	10 lb	Salad dressing, French,	
Nuts, 1 T/portion	2 lb	1-1/3 T/portion	2 qt
Olives, 3 or 4/portion	1 gal	Sirups, 2 T/portion	3/4 gal
Peanut Butter, 1/4 c		Sweets:	
portion	14-1/4 lb	Candy, small	
Pickles, 3 in., 1/2/portion	3 lb	2 T/portion	2 lb
Relishes	4 lb	Sugar, loaf, 1 to 2/portion	2 lb
Salad dressing, 2 T/portion	3 qt	Sugar, gran., 1-1/2 t/portion	1-1/2 lb

*Note: Some portions may be slightly smaller in this table than normal because experience has shown in extended health care facilities that this size portion is more typical of what is actually consumed

**A No. 12 scoop has a 2-2/3 oz volume but will give only about 10 scoops of frozen dessert per qt.

***See requirements for spread for sandwiches, etc. later in this table.

****Cooked unless otherwise stated.

(See also detailed information in cookbooks or texts such as *Food for Fifty*, Fowler, West and Shugart, *Large Quantity Recipes* by Terrell; *Quantity Food Production* and *Quantity Food Purchasing* by Kotschevar also contain much more detailed information on quantities required.)

Additional Bibliography

American Hospital Assn. *Hospital Food Service Manual.* Chicago: The Assn., 1954.

Kotschevar, Lendal H. *Quantity Food Purchasing.* New York: John Wiley & Sons, Inc., 1961.

Kotschevar, Lendal H. *How to Select and Care for Serviceware, Textiles, Cleaning Compounds, Laundry and Dry Cleaning Facilities.* Boston: Cahners Books, 1969.

National Assn. of Meat Purveyors. *Meat Buyers Guide.* Chicago: The Assn. 1967.

Peterkin, Betty, and Evans, Beatrice. *Food Purchasing Guide for Group Feeding,* USDA Agricultural Handbook No. 284. Washington, D. C.: Government Printing Office, 1965.

Proud, D. M. *Buying for Your Nursing Home,* Food Marketing Leaflet 12. Ithaca, New York: Cornell University, 1961.

University of Massachusetts. *Receiving Food,* Food Management Leaflet No. 3, Extension Service. Amherst, Mass.

U. S. Dept. of Agriculture. *Institutional Meat Purchase Specifications.* Washington, D. C.: Government Printing Office, 1961.

VIII: SANITATION

Cleanliness is a way of life. It is the quality of living that is expressed in the clean home, the clean farm, the clean business and industry, the clean neighborhood, the clean community. Being a way of life it must come from within the people; it is nourished by knowledge and grows as an obligation and an ideal in human relations.

The National Sanitation Foundation.

INTRODUCTION

A well defined sanitation program is needed to assure safe and clean food. To have a satisfactory sanitation program, everyone who works in the foodservice must be well informed about sanitary principles and how to put them into practice. Failure to do this may endanger the well-being not only of residents but of those who work in the facility. Sanitation is so important that *all* employees are charged by law to see that good sanitary practices are followed.

It is impossible for us to live in a completely sanitary and safe world but, by observing good sanitary practices, we can do much to reduce the chances of danger. We live always on an "armed truce" or "cold war" level with the harmful factors about us. If we drop our guard, we may find ourselves, or others for whom we are responsible, under attack. A good sanitation program helps to set up safeguards against harmful elements so we can remain healthy. Further, the residents of a health facility usually have enough health problems and should be spared any failure by workers that may add to their problems.

THE PROGRAM In addition to the employees of the health facility, local, state and federal governments are also charged with responsibility for seeing that sanitation codes and regulations are observed. Usually, the model for local and state codes is the federal Public Health Service regulations, and, in general, this chapter is based on those regulations. It is necessary for the individual foodservice to determine what the regulations are for the local and state areas in which it operates and to follow these as well as the federal statutes.*

---

*See the Food Service Sanitation Manual, Pub. No. 934, U. S. Dept. of HEW, Public Health Service, Washington, D. C., 20025 and National Sanitation Foundation Standards No. 3 and No. 5, Ann Arbor, Michigan. These outline sanitary principles which are followed nationally.

Most states require that a foodservice operation have a permit to operate. This is granted after an inspection of the facility by sanitation authorities. After the permit is granted, the operation is usually inspected twice a year. An inspection report, made out after such visits, notes deficiencies, listing them as demerits. Usually Form 4006 of the Public Health Service is used and a copy given either to the foodservice department or the administrator of the facility. Failure to correct major deficiencies within a specified period may lead to cancellation of the permit or to the closing of the facility.

A grading system is frequently used to indicate how well a facility meets sanitation standards. Usually a grade of "A" indicates a facility with 10 or less demerits, "B" from 10 to 19 and "C" from 20 to 40. Grades can be raised or lowered depending upon subsequent findings on other inspections. If the facility protests a finding, a hearing will be granted.

Normally, the Public Health Service or other authorized agency must approve all plans for construction or remodeling of foodservice spaces. They can also require that employees be removed from their jobs if they are suspected of being disease carriers or of willfully violating good health standards in any way.

WHAT ARE CLEAN AND SAFE?   Clean and safe food is
                                         the concern of a sanitation program. *Clean* means the absence of dirt or soil or undesirable substances. *Safe* means nothing harmful is present. Some things can appear clean but not be safe while an item that may not be clean still can be safe. For instance, a glass may appear clean but have dangerous unseen bacteria on it or it may appear soiled but still be safe to use because there is nothing harmful on it. We clean to remove soil because soil can harbor and feed harmful things such as bacteria. Then, we sanitize to make sure the item is safe to use. We usually clean and sanitize in one process.

FOOD DETERIORATION

Food can deteriorate either because of spoilage or contamination. *Spoiled* means food that has deteriorated to a point that is not edible or is almost inedible. *Contaminated* means food that is dangerous because of some substance in it although it may appear edible. Some spoiled foods can be consumed and do no harm. What might be spoiled food to some may not be to

---

*See Form 4006, pp. 392-396; for suggested self-inspection form, see pp. 397-399.

others, such as a piece of well ripened cheese. Spoilage and contamination may be caused by the same agent; however, there are some agents that pave the way for invasion of contaminating agents by first starting spoilage.

SPOILAGE

Spoilage in food should be avoided not only because it is responsible for economic loss but also because it leads to a loss of nutrients, prime appearance, flavor or texture in the food. It may also cause illness.

Spoilage Agents

Spoilage is caused by a variety of factors or conditions. Physical or chemical changes in food that lead to spoilage are activated by substances called enzymes. Enzymes are non-living compounds but are much like living compounds in their actions. A fruit or vegetable can be softened by enzymatic action to a point where it is considered spoiled.

Another spoilage agent is a mold. It can invade foods and grow in them, causing undesirable changes. Molds are living plants that are always floating in the air as spores or seeds. They start to grow when they contact food and, as they grow, they become visible.

Bacteria or germs cause food spoilage. Some can sour milk or soups. Others may putrefy meat. Yeasts spoil foods by a process called fermentation. They are plants that cause fermentation by converting carbohydrates into carbon dioxide gas, water and alcohol. Fermentation changes the flavor, texture and appearance of the food.

Chemicals can spoil food, as happens when sulfur and iron combine in an egg to make it rotten. Weevils, rats, mice or other living things can attack food and spoil it. Physical damage from bruising, heat, freezing, crushing or other causes may also render food inedible.

The same agents that spoil food may also be used to improve it. Bacteria that sour milk or soup can be used to make sauerkraut or pickles. Bacteria similar to those that putrefy meat may be used to make Swiss or Limburger cheese. The English eat game birds that have been allowed to age to a point where many would claim they have become putrefied. Some individuals claim they get ptomaine poisoning from such foods, but this is not true. We no longer think ptomaines cause food poisoning. Ptomaines are broken down proteins and the illness they cause may be more from a dislike of the changes they cause in food than from any harmful substance developed by them.

Yeasts are helpful in making wine or bread or foods like sour dough hotcakes. Roquefort or bleu cheeses are developed through the use of molds. Penicillin, a helpful drug, is made from mold growth.

Enzymes can be used to improve food. If we encourage a pear's enzymes to go to work, a hard pear becomes ripe and luscious through their action. Papain is an enzyme taken from papaya fruit which is used to tenderize meat.

CONTROLLING SPOILAGE. We can control or retard spoilage. Enzymes, bacteria, molds or yeasts work best with moisture present and when temperatures are between 45° and $110^\circ F$. Enzymes act with increasing speed as the temperature rises and, frequently, act fastest at just below the point where they are destroyed by heat. That is why meat treated with papain undergoes the greatest tenderizing action at around $120^\circ F$ or slightly higher.

If we heat a food to $140^\circ F$ or higher, we usually destroy spoilage agents. A higher temperature can sterilize the food; then, if we seal the food so no spoilage agents can get to it, we can hold it for a very long time. This is called *preservation,* a process used in canning.

We can *pasteurize* food by destroying spoilage or contaminating agents at $146^\circ F$ for 30 min or at $161^\circ F$ for 15 sec. Quick chilling of a pasteurized food and then sealing it off from the air may make it possible to keep the food for a much longer time.

Freezing preserves foods by inactivating spoilage agents. Bacteria, yeasts and some molds gradually die when frozen foods are held for a long time.

Drying stops the action of spoilage agents by withholding from them the moisture they need to grow. A food containing 8% or more of table salt spoils with difficulty. Other salts such as nitrates or nitrites can be used to preserve foods.

Some chemicals such as salicylic acid (aspirin) or sodium benzoate preserve foods. Molds are controlled in bread through the use of sodium or calcium pantothentate. Phenols, creosote and other compounds in smoke help preserve foods. Food with more than 55% sugar in it is usually preserved. Ultra-violet rays can destroy spoilage agents and are used in refrigerators or other areas to retard the action of spoilage agents. Wines and other items with

14% or more alcohol will keep well if kept from the air since the alcohol is antagonistic to spoilage agents. Irradiation from a cathode tube or from cobalt-60 also can be used to destroy spoilage agents.

Of course, if foods are kept clean and spoilage agents are kept away from them, they will keep longer. This is why foods are thoroughly washed and cleaned, put into clean containers, and then stored in clean spaces. Ordering just the right amount of food and using it as soon as possible is another good way to avoid spoilage.

Harvesting does not kill many fresh foods; they still breathe oxygen and expel carbon dioxide. Unpasteurized cheese, meats, poultry and fish are also biologically active. Enzymes in meat and unpasteurized cheese continue to work even though the item does not appear to be living. If fresh fruits and vegetables cannot get air, they spoil more quickly.

Lowering temperatures also slows down deteriorative actions. Therefore, fruits and vegetables held loosely packed in a cool area, with about 90% relative humidity, keep well. Spoilage bacteria grow well on meat that is neutral or slightly alkaline. We can retard spoilage on the surface of meat by wiping it daily with a cloth moistened with vinegar or by soaking the meat in an acid marinade. The high amount of acid in salad dressings, pickling solutions, tomatoes and many other foods helps to preserve them.

CONTAMINATION

The elimination of contamination is more important than the elimination of spoilage because contamination causes illness and even death. There are many ways we can control contamination and prevent it from harming others; one is to avoid purchasing contaminated food and another is to control chances for contamination in the facility through good layout, equipment or work procedures.

Purchasing

The chapter on PURCHASING tells how to buy foods from approved sources. Buy only meats, poultry, pasteurized dairy products and eggs that have been inspected and approved. All processed foods should come from manufacturers who comply with desirable sanitary standards.

Shellfish should come from beds approved by the Public Health Service and a tag on the container or other information on the label should indicate such approval. Bakery products should come from bakeries having high standards of sanitation and cleanliness that deliver products wrapped or protected from contamination.

Frozen foods should not have been thawed and refrozen. Chilled foods should not be above 40°F either in the interior portions or surface areas. Ground or sliced meats should come from pure carcasses and contain only authorized additives.

Fruit and vegetable purveyors should handle only clean, fresh items and should operate clean, sanitary establishments. Delivery trucks should be clean and the deliverymen should be clean and use sanitary handling procedures. It is advisable to visit the establishments of purveyors to note whether they hold to good sanitary standards.

We can buy food that is dangerous because it is poisonous, as some mushrooms are. Cows give a poisonous milk if they eat snakeroot. Solanine, the green on potatoes, is poisonous but it takes 17 lb to cause death. Ergot, a poisonous fungus, develops in moist rye and rye flour.

Some other poisonous plants are: the Jimson weed, a plant with large coarse leaves and large tubular white flowers; all parts of the leander; larkspur foliage; raw poke salad greens; rhododendron and the azalea; the vine and flowers of the Carolina Jessamine vine; all parts of the Yew; the berries of the common Privet hedge; the leaves of the common houseplant, Diffenbachia; and all parts of the castor bean, especially the seeds.

Some fish are poisonous but normally these are kept off the market, although the Japanese take a chance with some! A red plankton can make shellfish poisonous. When it appears at sea, the Public Health Service seals off the contaminated area and forbids the taking of shellfish from that area until the plankton have disappeared.

It is recommended that no canned foods be held longer than a year and some that are high in acid, such as sauerkraut or plums, should probably not be held longer than six months. We no longer depend on tin to prevent foods from reacting with the metal of cans as we have developed lacquers that are sprayed inside the cans to prevent reactions. This makes it possible to leave foods in cans after opening them, but usually it is preferable to empty the contents from cans, putting them into a non-metal or stainless steel container. Meats or shellfish may develop a dark substance at a point where they touch the can. This is not harmful but should be trimmed away because it may have a pungent sulfur flavor.

A can that is swelled or puffed should be carefully inspected. This may occur from denting but if the can is not dented, discard it. Look for evidence of leakage on containers; if noted, discard the item. It is not recommended that you taste foods that lack good appearance, color or texture since such foods may be poisonous.

Physical Facilities

The physical plant and equipment should be designed to promote sanitation. Walls should be smooth, painted plaster or tile. A floor that is smooth and impervious to soil and moisture is desirable. Ease of cleaning, with coving at wall junctures or where equipment touches the floor and floors properly sloped to drains, promotes cleanliness. Good sewage and plumbing facilities are needed.

Proper storage facilities that keep foods, dishes and utensils from the floor and sealed from dust or other contaminants should be installed. The right kind of containers for trash, rubbish or garbage are needed. These should be made of non-absorbent material, be equipped with covers and be leakproof.

Dishwashing and other sanitizing equipment should meet National Sanitation Foundation (NSF) standards and proper water temperatures and sanitizing agents must be provided. Frequent air changes should remove stale and humid air in the facility. Good light is needed.

The facility should be protected against the entry of insects, vermin, rodents or other agents carrying contaminants. The Public Health Service requires that all equipment, working surfaces and utensils be designed to be smooth, durable, easily cleaned, non-toxic, corrosion resistant and relatively non-absorbent. If approved, cutting boards, meat blocks and bakers' tables may be of plastic, hard maple or other equivalent material which is non-toxic, smooth and free of cracks, crevices or open seams. They should be easy to wash and sanitize after each use. Chapter X which covers Layout, Design and Equipment Selection will give more information in this area.

The Work Program

Sanitation problems are caused 10% of the time by equipment failure and 90% by human failure. Food is most frequently contaminated because people come in contact with it. People are always potential germ carriers.

Bacteria will be found in the nose, mouth, ears, on the hands, in the digestive tract and in cuts, acne or boils. The hands or a cough or sneeze easily spread the bacteria. Individuals ill with a cold or otherwise not well should not be permitted to work around foods. Some individuals are disease carriers but are not ill from the disease. Such a carrier cannot work around food.

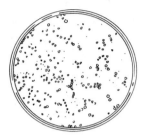 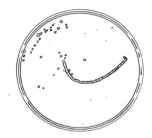

Fig. 8-1. *A sneeze and a human hair in a short time produced these cultures. Courtesy Dr. J. Rakosky, Jr.,* Sanitation Simplified, *Central Soya, Chicago.*

A foodservice should provide good locker facilities so workers can keep themselves and their clothes clean. Adequate washing and toilet facilities are needed. Provide satisfactory paper supplies and soap.

Good personal hygiene is most important because it keeps a worker healthy and prevents spreading disease to others. A thorough physical examination should be given once or twice a year. This should include a tuberculin test and a stool examination. Blood tests do not tell the whole story.

A daily bath is needed for proper cleanliness. Clean inner and outer garments should be worn. Aprons should be clean and wiping cloths should be used for the hands. Well groomed, clean hair is essential and caps or hairnets should be worn. Fingernails should be trimmed and clean.

Thorough washing of the hands is essential before starting work, after visiting the toilet or when handling foods that might be contaminated. For instance, the intestinal area of poultry is frequently contaminated with *Salmonella* which causes food poisoning. Therefore, hands should be washed after handling it. Be sure also that work surfaces and the utensils it has touched are thoroughly cleaned. The use of tobacco should be prohibited because its use may contaminate the fingers and hands with saliva or may promote spitting which can spread contaminants.

Cosmetics and perfumes should be used in moderation. Jewelry can also be a hazard. Dangling bracelets may get into food or a broken string of beads may ruin a mixer of food. Many operations allow only the wearing of a watch and a wedding band.

Workers should develop work habits that assure clean, safe food. While such a list of "no-nos" is long, they need mentioning even though briefly.

It is essential that workers know what they are supposed to do in the sanitation program and a schedule should be made up outlining the proper procedures to follow. Supervisors and management should check to see that the work is done. To assure that workers are aware of proper sanitation procedures, training sessions should include such basic instructions as:

It is a mark of professionalism in food work to use a "clean-as-you-go" technique. Dispose of waste and wipe up spillage immediately. Keep doors, drawers and bins closed. Clean work surfaces as you go. Ovens, griddles and other cooking units should be tidied after each use and cleaned each day. It is a requirement of the Public Health Service that food contact surfaces, dishes, glasses and other utensils be thoroughly cleaned and sanitized after use.

Disassemble and wash can openers frequently. Use tongs, a fork or a knife to open can lids; bend them back, thus avoiding touching the food.

Improperly cleaned brushes, mops and other cleaning equipment can spread soil. Minimize the use of bare hands in handling food. Use tongs, picks, spatulas, scoops or plastic gloves. Do not use glasses or cups as scoops. Do not cover one utensil with another; never cover a milk bottle with a glass or stack one pot on top of another.

Pick up utensils by their handles. Avoid handling dishes so the lip or inside is contaminated by your fingers. Single-service articles should not be handled but should be dispensed so that surfaces coming in contact with the food or the user's mouth have not been contaminated. Use care in handling soiled items so that soil is not spread to clean items.

Use two spoons in tasting, one to take a sample which is then poured into a second spoon that is used for tasting. Do not take and taste samples with the same spoon. Check refrigerators to see that foods are not held too long. Keep refrigerated foods covered and clean refrigerators frequently.

Use individually portioned foods as much as possible such as individual butters, jams, sirups and sugars. The safest sugar bowl is the closed, pouring type. Individual units, once served, cannot be used again unless they are in a plastic or other wrap and the wrapping has not been disturbed.

Chill potentially dangerous foods before mixing them with other foods which also are cold. Do not mix hot foods into cold ones or vice versa. For instance, do not mix hot sauteed vegetables into a cold bread dressing or a hot cream sauce into a cold meat mixture to be used for croquettes unless you use the mixture *immediately*. Cook all dressings to an internal temperature of 160°F.

Watch foods that are not cooked to a high temperature or are held at moderate temperatures. A hollandaise sauce should be prepared only from high quality eggs or pasteurized processed eggs and preferably the latter. Hold the sauce only 3 hr and then discard it as waste. A mock hollandaise sauce is preferable to a true one because it is not potentially as dangerous a food. See that foods transported to residents and others are carried in closed carts unless the distance is relatively short.

Store perishable foods under 40°F or hold for service above 145°F, if served hot. Keep cold foods under refrigeration until served. Thaw frozen foods under 45°F. It is preferable to cook frozen foods from the unthawed state.

Process foods through mechanical equipment as much as possible to avoid contaminating food with the hands. For instance, use a mixer to make mixtures such as meat loaves or croquettes and a slicer for slicing meats, using wax paper or plastic gloves to catch the food or arrange it in pans. Refrigerate custard-filled or other potentially dangerous food.

Watch the handling of ice. Employees should not store carbonated beverages, lunches or other foods in ice chests. Ice should be taken from bins with appropriate dippers. The dippers should not be handled carelessly or put down where they can be contaminated. Ice chests should be closed. Require that ice be carried in clean containers. If a canvas container is used, it should have a waterproof lining. Clean dippers frequently and the ice machine once a month. Purchase clean block or ground ice, being sure it comes from clean sources and is handled correctly by the deliverymen and then afterwards in your facility.

A good training program should be a part of every sanitation program. As a part of this program, see that workers are trained to report potential hazards or violations of the sanitation program to supervisors or management. No live animals should be permitted in foodservice areas except for seeing-eye dogs that may come into dining areas.

Contaminating Agents

Items that contaminate foods may be classified as poisons, bacteria (germs), viruses or parasites. Knowing what these are and how they act will help a lot to control them. Therefore, they will be discussed in the order given.

POISONS. Sprays or fertilizers may be harmful; therefore, all fresh vegetables and fruits should be carefully washed before they are used. Poisons used to destroy insects, rats or mice may contain arsenic, fluorides, lead or other harmful substances and should not be left around food. Store toxic substances away from food and keep cleaning supplies in locked storage; be sure they are clearly labeled since mistakes can easily happen.

Tri-sodium phosphate, an efficient washing compound, looks much like cornmeal while sodium fluoride, used in roach poison, looks like dried milk. Oxalic acid is a good bleach but should not be kept around food for it is poisonous. Lead, antimony, cadmium, zinc and some other heavy metals are poisonous. Cadmium and antimony may be found in enameled (granite) ware and enameled shelving or equipment as well as in some plated ware. There may be cadmium in paint. Acids or acid foods can react with copper to create a poison.

Galvanized iron (galvaneal) can be used for shelving, work surfaces or equipment, if its zinc covering will not touch food. Avoid lead piping; use plastic or copper instead. Also be sure that lead-plated equipment, lead soldering or other lead surfaces do not contact food. While tin could be harmful, it is safe unless attacked by strong acids and they are not usually found in sufficient concentration in foods to be dangerous.

BACTERIA. There are two ways in which germs poison food. One is by infection and the other is by intoxication. Bacteria may get into food that we eat and then we get an infectious disease that makes us ill. Cooking food can destroy infectious germs making the food safe to eat. Although some toxins from toxic agents are destroyed by long time cooking, others may not be, so long time cooking does not always make food safe.

Some of the most dangerous infectious bacteria people can get through food are: typhoid or paratyphoid, scarlet fever, diphtheria, tuberculosis, bacillic dysentery, undulant fever or brucellosis, tularemia, septic sore throat and some food poisoning bacteria. Most bacteria are extremely hardy and live for a long time in milk, protein foods, raw shellfish, food mixtures, eggs or undercooked foods. Tularemia may be found in undercooked rabbit or bear.

Raw milk or its products may carry many harmful bacteria. Tuberculosis germs are always in the air, especially around infected individuals who may cough or sneeze. People can also get tuberculosis from cattle or through their milk. Water can be contaminated with many harmful bacteria; sources should be checked to be sure supply is safe.

Normally, after an individual comes in contact with these dangerous bacteria, he becomes ill within 1 to 3 weeks after his contact. The illness is usually severe and death can result, although we can immunize against most of these diseases.

Some food poisoning bacteria are infectious. Three of these are much alike in some respects: *Salmonella, Streptococci and Clostridium Perfringens.* They are frequently found in meat or poultry dressing, croquettes, meat pies, poultry or meat salads, custard-filled desserts or reheated meats, cold meats, poultry or meat left in its drippings overnight, reheated soup or stews and some sausages.

Salmonella are found in raw eggs and in the intestinal tract of poultry. All three are found in the intestinal tracts of birds, animals or insects and in soil or fecal matter. Water or other liquids can become infected with them. They like to grow in non-acid or low acid foods at room temperature.

Salmonella and *Streptococci* need oxygen to grow, but *Clostridium Perfringens* do not. Illness from the infection of any of these three usually occurs from about 4 to 24 hr after eating the contaminated food. Symptoms will be gastric or abdominal discomfort, vomiting and diarrhea.

Shigella bacteria are also infectious. They can cause food poisoning, mainly evidenced by dysentery (diarrhea) but not vomiting. Food can become contaminated with them through the excreta of animals, birds or insects. They are common in the soil and in unsanitary areas, therefore, cleanliness is an important factor in controlling them. Moist prepared foods, milk and its products and protein-carbohydrate food mixtures are foods they like.

Illness usually occurs from 1 to 4 days after infection.

One of our most common intoxicating agents in food poisoning is *Staphylococci,* usually referred to as "staph." It is everywhere in the air, in water, milk, sewage, dust, in the pus of sores or boils and in the mucous membranes of men, birds, insects and animals. Unlike infectious bacteria, which first enter the host and then develop a toxin, staph and other intoxicants develop their toxin in the food so that illness is caused when the food is consumed. It is difficult to destroy this toxin with heat so, even though food containing the toxin is cooked and the bacteria destroyed, the toxin remains to make one ill. Staphs like to grow in mixtures of food such as macaroni and cheese, cream pies, custard fillings, ham and some other meats, as well as poultry, fish and meat mixtures.

One of the most dangerous food poisons known is the toxin from *Clostridium Botulinum.* Even tasting and spitting out food contaminated with this toxin has been known to cause death. The germs are found in the soil and air. They cannot grow in the presence of oxygen or in acid foods. They have been found in commercially canned tuna, soups, smoked fish packaged in an air-tight wrap, sausage and some other foods. The most common cause of this poisoning used to be home-canned, non-acid foods. The toxin is destroyed by 20 min of boiling.

One may wonder why some get sick on a food while others who eat the same food do not. This can happen because one individual has higher resistance to the toxin or infectious agent than another, or it may be because the food is infected or contains toxin only in one area and the infecting agent has not spread throughout the food, thus, when the food is dished up, only some patrons get it.

Time is an important factor in the development of food poisoning. It normally takes about 4 hr at room temperature after contamination for infectious germs to develop or for toxin-developing germs to develop enough toxin to make one ill. This is why at one time we had the rule, "Never leave food standing at room temperature for over 4 hr." We no longer use this rule because many workers turned out to be poor time keepers. They would forget how long they'd had a food out of refrigeration and put it back into the refrigerator, later take it out again, so that often, before the food was eaten, it had been at unsafe temperatures well over 4 hr. It is also possible to put a warm food into a refrigerator and have the center remain warm enough to continue developing bacteria for more than 4 hr. This happens with dressings, thick puddings, gravies and some other foods unless they are put into shallow containers so they cool quickly. Stirring thick foods helps to cool them down below temperatures where bacteria thrive.

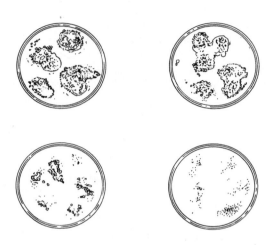

Fig. 8-2. *The top left plate shows bacteria from unwashed fingers and the one on the top right from these same fingers after rinsing with water. The lower left plate shows how contamination is reduced with a good handwashing with soap and water and how it is reduced even more after two washings with soap and water. Courtesy Dr. J. Rakosky, Jr.,* Sanitation Simplified, *Central Soya, Chicago.*

Food cools almost as rapidly at room temperature as in a refrigerator so it is possible to cover a hot food, cool it at room temperature until around 120°F and then refrigerate it. A knife or small object placed under the bottom of the container facilitates cooling. Containers can also be put into a cold running water bath for more rapid cooling.

With today's modern refrigeration equipment, hot or warm foods can be put into most refrigeration units without raising the temperature and thus spoiling the other foods already in the unit. In the old days when we used ice boxes, this was not true. Putting hot or warm food into a box would raise the temperature so all the food inside quickly spoiled. Covering cooling food

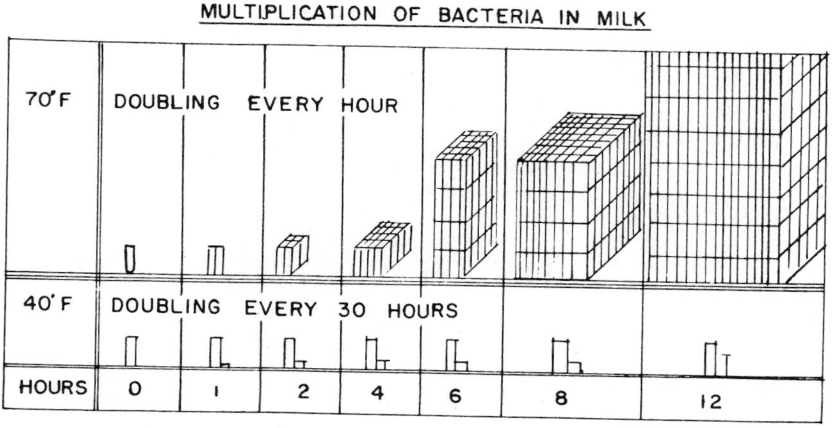

MULTIPLICATION OF BACTERIA IN MILK

Fig. 8-3. *The comparison of growth of bacteria in milk at temperatures of 70° and 40°F. (Each unit represents 100 bacteria).—from* Preventing Food Borne Diseases, *Texas State Department of Health.*

keeps dust particles and other items from falling into the food.

Some germs are highly resistant to moist heat and may not be destroyed in cooking. Such bacteria might be in what we call spore form. This means the bacteria are enclosed in a tough, hard outer coating that protects them from heat, drying or other destructive agents. In this shell, they can exist a long time and then, when conditions are favorable, they break out of it and go on their merry way, setting up house-keeping and multiplying. Canned food may spoil from such action. Such food can be identified by a rancid, sharp odor, gas formation, oversoft appearance and an untrue color. Never taste such food. Or, if you want to taste, boil it hard 20 min and then do so. But, why take a chance? It may contain *Botulinum.*

VIRUSES. An infectious disease can be caused by a virus. There are somewhat like bacteria in that they can increase, need food and moisture and are inactivated by low temperatures and destroyed by high ones. They are extremely small; some can pass through the finest filter. Hepatitis, poliomyelitis, New Castle disease and ornithosis are some diseases we can get from viruses in food.

Hepatitis, an extremely dangerous infection of the liver, comes from fecal matter or other soil or filth. The urine of infected rats can be a carrying agent. It can spread easily and a person who has hepatitis should be isolated from others. Dishes and other items used by the person who has hepatitis must be handled and sanitized with extreme care. Poliomyelitis may be transferred in unpasteurized milk or other dairy products, by other human beings or animals, by the air or in foods. Ornithosis may be transferred by birds as well as some of the other carriers mentioned in this chapter.

PARASITES. Various parasites can infect food and cause illness. One, a protozoa or tiny plant, may cause amoebic dysentery. It is found in soil, sewage, the fecal matter of rodents, insects, human beings or other manures. It is frequently transferred in water. Either iodine or chlorine in water destroys it. Heat does also.

Another parasite is *Trichinae* which enters the body as a tiny larvae or round worm and gets into the blood stream by burrowing through the intestinal walls. The females mate, lay eggs in the body tissues and die. In a short time, the eggs hatch into tiny larvae and these now infect the body causing illness. We can get trichinosis from undercooked pork but we may get it from undercooked bear or rabbit. It is destroyed at 137°F but, to be sure, the federal government requires cured pork products to be processed to an interior temperature of 155°F. We usually cook pork to about 170°F interior temperature in our kitchens.

Trichinae are destroyed by holding meat frozen for 20 to 30 days at 5°F or below. Hogs get the disease from the soil or from garbage infected by rats or mice having the disease. It is possible for infected pork to contaminate tables, meat blocks and other surfaces, leaving *Trichinae* to be picked up by other foods and thus infect individuals. In post-mortem examinations in 1930, 1 out of every 6 individuals showed he had had an infection from *Trichinae* at one time or another but today the number has dropped to 1:20.

Tape worms are parasites that come from the eggs of tape worms deposited in raw beef, fish or other raw foods.

Germ or Bacterial Life

Germs or bacteria are probably best described as tiny plants invisible to the eye. They are so small about 10 million will go on the head of a pin and they are everywhere. The various germ families can be identified by their shapes which are different for each family. Some are round, others are shaped like rods, while others are oblong and others come in long chains.

Some germs like to grow in a cold environment. These are the ones that break down organic substances in the soil so plants can absorb them and grow. Other germs like very hot or warm conditions. We find them in hot springs or hot pools of water. However, the germs that we must deal with most are those that like moderate or lukewarm temperatures. These, if harmful to man, are called pathogens. The cold or heat loving germs don't like us too well. Our bodies do not provide a favorable environment.

Freezing will usually stop the growth of bacteria—as a matter of fact, they slowly die if held in a frozen state a long time. Pathogenic bacteria multiply rapidly at body temperatures. At 40°F a germ will multiply once in about 30 hr but it multiplies 90 times or faster at body temperatures. It has no sex and grows or multiplies by dividing itself in two. Then, these 2 become 4 and the 4 become 16 and then become 256. If we have 1 germ, in 4 hours we can have 4096; in 24 hr, we can't even think of the number—4,720,000,000,000,000,000,000!! Actually, this does not happen because some die and do not multiply. Dormant germs, such as those in refrigerated food, live a long time. Typhoid germs in refrigerated oysters have been known to live 5 weeks.

Pathogens grow better in a food mixture where there is some protein with carbohydrate and other nutrients. They love meats in gravy, soups, stocks, cream pies, meat salads and other items. Some need oxygen to grow; others don't. Most like a neutral or slightly acid or an alkaline medium. Few bacteria can grow in acid foods such as tomatoes, lemon juice or mayonnaise. However, when mayonnaise is diluted by other foods, it can be an excellent culture.

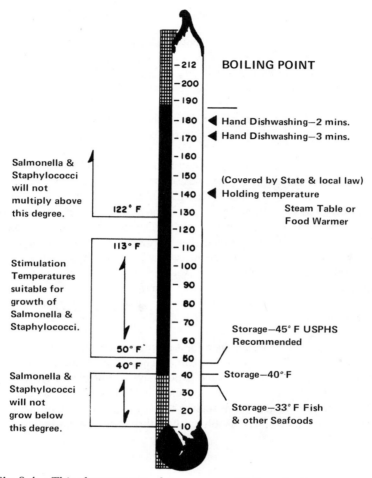

Fig. 8-4. *This thermometer shows some critical sanitation temperatures that all foodservice workers should know.—from the Texas State Department of Health.*

Hitch-Hiking on Carriers

Germs can't travel very far on their own. They have to hitch-hike on dust, the air, on droplets of spittle, on people, insects or animals. The things bacteria and viruses ride on are called *vectors*. People are one of the most frequently used vectors. Germs like to live in the moist, mucous areas of the human body, so, when we touch our lips or our nose, we pick germs up and transfer them to food or to other objects.

Germs are present in fecal matter and hands that are not washed after a visit to the toilet may spread them about. Some thrive in boils and cuts. Milk and water can contain them. Germs love sewage and garbage. They will be in drains and places where we leave or deposit garbage. Some health authorities specify that drains connected to sewer lines cannot be connected to equipment. This is done to break the germ's travel line from the sewer up to the equipment. We put traps in drains to prevent vermin and insects from crawling up through them. Flies, roaches, silverfish, weevils and other hitch-hikers carry harmful germs; for instance, fleas on rats can carry bacteria that cause typhus fever or bubonic plague.

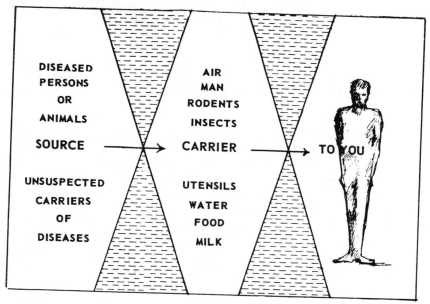

Fig. 8-5. *How diseases are carried to man the host.—from* Preventing Food Borne Diseases, *Texas State Department of Health.*

FLIES. Flies are one of the worst bacteria spreaders. These friendly little pests hatch in excrement, rotting or fermenting wastes, putrefying tissues or manures. The fly is first a maggot, a small white worm feeding on filth; it becomes a pupa and later an adult fly. The whole cycle may take as little as 7 to 10 days from egg to adult fly. Flies can travel up to 15 miles from where they are born but usually they are found within 500 yards of where they hatch. If there are flies, look for a breeding place nearby.

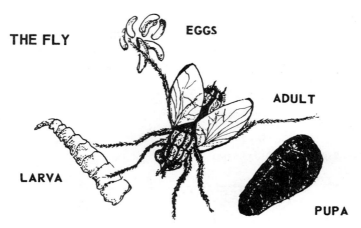

Fig. 8-6. *A fly starts as an egg, develops into a larva or worm, next goes into a dormant or pupa stage and then develops into an adult fly.—from* Preventing Food Borne Diseases, *Texas State Department of Health.*

Tiny hairs cover a fly's body, all heavily infected with germs and filthy material. Its feet have sticky material on them, helping the fly to walk upside down. The feet leave filth and germs wherever the fly walks. A fly may have 5 million germs on the body and feet and 25 million more in the alimentary tract. Its excreta is always contaminated; its toilet habits are atrocious, leaving "fly specks" freely on our food, etc. A fly absorbs food only as a liquid; when he feeds, he regurgitates or vomits a liquid—of course, filled with germs —which moistens the food. He then sucks this all up but not completely, so he always leaves some germs for us. A fly lives from 3 to 4 weeks but during a lifetime a female can lay nearly 30,000 eggs.

To control flies, search out their breeding places, usually found in damp areas. Destroy these. Be sure not to create other areas with garbage, rubbish or other trash where eggs can be laid. Screen all doors and windows and close off any other places where flies can enter. Air currents can suck flies up or force them from places. In outside areas away from foods, use fly sprays, poisons or traps approved by health authorities, such as residual spray that contains 5% malathion and 12½% sugar. Kill flies whenever seen. Keep food covered and in places where flies cannot get at it since flies have a tremendous sense of smell and when they get an aroma beam on food or garbage, they zero in.

Fig. 8-7. *A fly walked across this culture plate. It leaves the same path of bacteria when it walks over our food. Courtesy Dr. J. Rakosky, Jr.,* Sanitation Simplified, *Central Soya, Chicago.*

Cockroaches

Cockroaches are one of the world's oldest inhabitants, having been in existence over 300 million years. One may not know they are present since they move at night and feed. They are also adept at hiding in dark corners, under equipment, in cracks and crevices and behind baseboards, etc.

Cockroaches like damp areas and lay their eggs there. The eggs hatch into nymphs. These later metamorphize into adult roaches that can live up to 2½ years. Roaches are always thirsty and will be found in wet or damp areas. They have many germs on their bodies and their excreta is also filled with them. Some roaches spit up a brown, foul-smelling liquid which contaminates anything it touches. If many roaches are around, an odor indicates their presence. They like warmth. Once in a building they are difficult to eradicate.

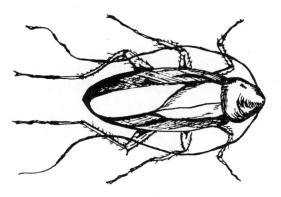

Fig. 8-8. *The cockroach is one of the most difficult of insects to eradicate and one of our worst disease spreaders.—from* Preventing Food Borne Diseases, *Texas State Department of Health.*

Roaches are controlled by eliminating their breeding places and by keeping equipment clean and free from grease and soil. Keeping food, especially if it's greasy, from them starves them out. Eradication by chlordane or other substances is effective. All incoming foods should be inspected to see that roaches are not present.

Silverfish are insects that frequently live where roaches live. They are much like roaches both in their habits and in the harm they can do. They can be eliminated by similar methods.

Insects

Ants and other insects carry contaminants on their bodies which they spread around. Ants live in colonies in nests where fertile queens lay eggs. These hatch into pupas and then into ants. The nests will be found in protected open spaces, under foundations, buildings, in building timbers, under floors or protected surfaces. Keep wastes and foods away from such areas and, what is even more effective, close such areas up, blocking even the tiniest crevices which ants will otherwise come through to get into food areas. Approved chemical substances can be used to destroy them.

Beetles, weevils and other insects can infest a foodservice. Some of these live on dried legumes, dried fruits, flours or other cereals. Store and hold such foods so insects can't get to them. It may be necessary in some climates to store foods that these insects infest in refrigerated areas.*

Rats and Mice

Rats and mice carry many diseases. They destroy as well as contaminate food. Their droppings or urine carry *Salmonella* and other dangerous bacteria or virus. The hair on their bodies is loaded with disease organisms. They are good swimmers, especially rats. Rats also like to live in dumps and in sewage areas. A female rat has from 3 to 5 litters a year averaging 7 or 8 young per lit-

---

*See U. S. Public Health Service, Communicable Disease Center, Atlanta, Ga., publications:

772 P I, *Introduction to Orthopods of Public Health Importance,* 1960,

772 P II, *Insecticides for the Control of Insects of Public Health Importance,* 1962,

772 P V, *Flies of Public Health Importance and Their Control,* 1964.

772 P XII, *Household and Stored Food Insects of Public Health Importance and Their Control,* 1965.

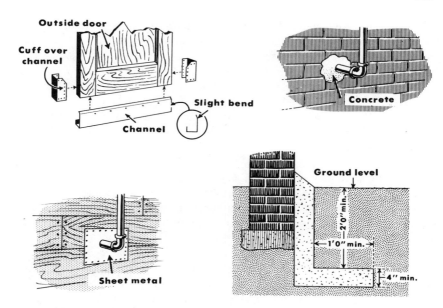

Fig. 8-9. *Some approved methods for blocking out rodents and insects. Courtesy of Texas State Department of Health.*

ter. Females live for about 2 to 3 years. Mice are similar to rats except they are shorter lived. The best control for these rodents is to eradicate their breeding places and remove food sources from them. Mice are more easily trapped than rats who are smarter and more wily.

ERADICATION   Cleanliness is the best control for bacteria or other contaminants. It is also one of the best ways to eliminate pests that carry them. As noted previously, either refrigeration or freezing and heating foods will control bacteria, viruses and parasites. Good air, sunlight, detergents and sanitizers also are effective.

Insects, rodents and other pests are not as easily dispensed with. Operations should retain the services of a reliable pest control company to get rid of these unwanted intruders. This should be a continuing service, done periodically. Also, as suggested, get rid of places where they can breed and keep food away from them.

Insects may be eradicated by using a dust or spray containing chlordane, malathion, lindane, dieldrin, heptachlor or by using sodium fluorid or barium carbonate bait. Remember some of these are dangerous poisons. Bait is a less effective and slower method of control than spraying or dusting. Never use insecticidal vaporizers around food.

One of the most effective residual sprays that can be used in nesting places is 2½% chlordane (chlorinated hydrocarbons), 1% lindane, 2% malathion or ½% of a diazonon emulsion. This can also be used as a pin-stream spray directed into cracks, crevices in walls, baseboards, furniture, fixtures, cabinets and other hiding places.

Where spray may do damage, and in dead spaces, dusting or blowing a 5% chlordane dust or a 3% malathion dust or finely powdered silica gel will be effective. Do not apply chlordane in rooms in which a person will spend more than 8 hours and also do .1ot cover more than 10% of any floor area with chlordane.

On occasion, Public Health officials will assist municipalities and businesses in eradicating mice and rats. Frequently the poison used is an anticoagulant, such as warfarin, fumarine, pival, PMP or diphacin added in proportions of 1 part to 19 parts of cereal such as cornmeal or oatmeal. It is left in place for 5 to 14 days. It should not be placed where chickens or other poultry would have a chance to get at it. Red squill is much more effective and faster than anticoagulants but not as simple to use. Trapping is good for both rats and mice.

Cracks in walls and improper door, window or other openings that permit the entrance of insects, vermin or rodents should be sealed off. Ventilating and air-conditioning ducts and grills can be places of entrance. Rat stoppage devices that prevent gnawing through can be used. These are usually hardware cloth, galvanized sheet metal, kick plates or similar devices.

CLEANING AND SANITIZING
INSTRUCTIONS FOR WORKERS

Knowing what cleaning is, what must be cleaned, how to do it, and the proper tools and procedures to use is essential if good cleaning is to be done.

WHAT IS CLEANING? Removing soil from where it is not wanted and putting it somewhere else is the process called cleaning. Soil may be misplaced grease, bits of

TWO-WEEK CLEANING SCHEDULE

FOR WEEKS OF _____

INITIAL ☐ WHEN YOU HAVE COMPLETED YOUR ASSIGNED DUTY

SHIFT ASSIGNED TO	CLEANING TO BE DONE ACCORDING TO CLEANING PROCEDURES:	S	M	T	W	T	F	S	S	M	T	W	T	F	S
	RANGE, FOOD GRINDER														
	CONVECTION OVEN & MIXER														
	STEAMERS														
	WORK TABLES, BLENDER														
	SINKS, CLEAN DISH AREA														
	TRAY SERVING EQUIPMENT														
	CAFETERIA EQUIP-MENT														
	REFRIGERATORS/ DEEP FREEZERS	X	X	X	X	X	X		X	X	X	X	X	X	X
	ICE BINS														
	TRASH CAN LIDS														
	DISHMACHINE & SOILED DISH ROOM														
	COFFEE POTS	X		X	X	X	X	X	X		X	X	X	X	X
	TEA POTS, TEA KETTLES	X	X	X		X	X	X	X	X		X	X	X	X
	CLEAN ALL DINING ROOM TABLES WITH PLEDGE MORNING, NOON & NIGHT														
	CLEAN TRAY CARTS & DISINFECT PROPERLY														

Fig. 8-10. *A two-week cleaning schedule used for long term care facilities making assignments to various shifts. Assignment by shift rather than person assures that if the job is filled by a relief, the work will be done.*

food, dirt or other undesirable compounds. Wetting soil or softening it with heat or chemicals, using friction to remove the soil and then keeping the soil away from the object are the steps in cleaning.

Heat can harden soils as well as soften them as is true with uncooked egg. If an alkali is present, grease can be saponified or made into a soap. Some substances in cleaning compounds emulsify and/or peptize soil and the use of such substances makes soil easier to remove. Alkalies can hydrolyze proteins and help to dissolve them. Water dissolves many substances, especially sugars. Enzymes are not too effective in removing stains or soil.

The friction used in soil removal is usually mechanical. A goodly amount of "elbow grease" is frequently essential in cleaning. As a matter of fact, 30% of cleaning occurs in the wetting of the soil and in softening it and 70% in the friction used.

Once soil is removed, we don't want it back. Rinsing is the most effective way to keep soil away. Some detergents contain compounds that grab onto soil and hold it in suspension. Clean washing water is helpful in keeping soil from items. Some rinses contain a rinsing agent that helps make soil slip away more easily.

SANITIZING   Sanitizing is a process in which we destroy harmful bacteria and is the last step in the cleaning process. We sanitize by immersing the cleaned item into 170°F water for 30 sec, by spraying it for 10 sec with 180°F water or by using a sanitizing compound such as chlorine, iodine or other approved substance. Some dishwashing compounds may contain enough chlorine to yield about 2% in the washing solution—it usually takes from 5 to 10% in the compound to do this. This sanitizing compound is usually sodium hypochlorite. While soaps and detergents do not sanitize, they help by removing bacteria in washing and they also reduce the surface tension on places bacteria cling to, making them easier to kill. Some strong soaps or detergents can actually dissolve bacteria.

DETERGENTS AND SOAPS   The cleaning agent most often used will be a soap or detergent. Soap is a detergent but not every detergent is a soap. Soaps are made chemically by joining a fat and an alkali. If we have just enough fat to neutralize the alkali, we get a neutral soap. Most soaps and detergents are fairly alkaline which helps to saponify grease and peptize proteins. Soaps to be used in the hand washing of utensils should not be over 10 to 10.5 pH.* Many dishmachine compounds are 11 to 12 in pH. Soaps for washing the hands should not have a higher pH than 9.

A detergent is usually a blend of cleaning agents. Frequently, the base is tri-sodium phosphate to which different compounds are added so the detergent will perform the best job. Some may be added to hold soil in suspension or sanitize or create a heavy alkaline reaction for rugged cleaning action.

Special detergents have been developed to do specific cleaning jobs. Neutral ones are used for cleaning floors or for cleaning work surfaces. Where metal corrosion is a problem, a neutral detergent is recommended. As we noted, alkaline detergents are used for heavy duty cleaning. Some may be so strong they corrode metals. Acid detergents are used less often. They are helpful in removing lime scale, milkstone (a combination of milk protein and hard water salts that shows as a film on glassware) and other soils that an alkaline or neutral detergent will not attack.

Soap combined with hard water creates a precipitate. If only a small quantity is used, the hard water salts use the soap up so none is left for cleaning. We have to use a lot of soap in hard water if enough is to be left for cleaning. Detergents perform better in hard water because they can have substances in them that keep the hard water salts from reacting with the cleaning agents. Usually these are metasilicates or phosphates. ABS or alkyl-benzene-sulfonate also is a good substance to use for this purpose.

If soap is to be used with hard water, use a good water softener with it. Water is hard if it exceeds 65 parts per million of calcium carbonate, or seven grains, of hard water salts. Below this, it is considered soft. Some hard water salts and soft water can corrode metals.

Sanitizers can be used separately from the cleaning agent. Calcium hypochlorite with 70% available chlorine is good for general disinfecting and deodorizing. We can also use the bleaches used for washing clothes for sanitizing providing they are chlorine substances. A solution of 5 to 10% sodium hypochlorite is the equivalent of these bleaching solutions used for washing clothes.

---

*In pH, 7 is neutral; numbers lower than this indicate acidity and higher numbers, alkalinity. A pH1 is an extremely strong acid and a pH 14 is a very strong alkali.

To sanitize, we should have a standard plate count of 100 or less of bacteria per centimeter. Or, a plate count of 10 or less of *E. coli* bacteria may be a standard. *E. coli* are harmless bacteria that live in the intestinal tract. They are easily identifiable and, if present, indicate that perhaps other dangerous bacteria may also be.

HANDLING CONTAGIOUS ITEMS   A long term care facility will usually not have individuals in residence with infections, but should there be any, special care must be taken with items they contact. Single service, disposable dishes and eating utensils should be used and nursing services should take care of these and all wastes without returning them to the kitchen.

If permanent ware is used, nursing services should sterilize all items in an autoclave and dispose of wastes.   If nursing services cannot take care of items, have the utensils, dishes and left-over solid food, including the tray, placed into a polyethylene bag or other suitable container. Nursing services should dispose of all liquid foods. The bag should be tightly tied. This bag is a signal that contaminated items are inside. To be more sure, tagging can be used. *Only the nursing staff should go into infectious areas.*

When the sealed bag arrives at the kitchen, set it aside in a safe place. When *all* cleaning tasks are over, take the bag and place it upon clean papers spread on a hard, impervious surface. Put on rubber or disposable gloves and remove all contents with metal tongs. Set the utensils and dishes into a clean washing basket. Leave uneaten food in the bag. When these jobs are done, fold the paper carefully and place, with the disposable gloves, in the bag and seal it. Send the sealed bag to the incinerator, or if an incinerator is not available, obtain instructions from health authorities as to the method for disposing of it. If rubber gloves are used, remove these. Put them into a marked container to be sent for sanitizing. Put on fresh rubber or disposable gloves.

After the bag arrives in the kitchen and is spread on clean papers, an alternate method of handling—especially if the items must be handwashed— might be to place the dishes and utensils into a metal pot containing a sanitizing solution, using gloves and tongs as instructed above. (Table 8-4 will indicate the amount of sanitizing solution to use.) Soak the items 15 min including the tongs. Then, boil vigorously for 10 min or more. Cool in the hot water bath until the items can be handled. Pour off the water; remove the items using fresh gloves and fresh tongs. Wash the items, using good sanitizing tech-

Table 8-1–APPROXIMATE DOSAGE REQUIRED FOR
100 P. P. M. TREATMENT

Gallons Treated	5.25% Sodium Hypochlorite			12% Sodium Hypochlorite		
	Teaspoon	Tablespoon	Ounces	Teaspoon	Tablespoon	Ounces
1	1¼			½		
2	2½			1		
3	4	1¼		1½		
4	5¼	1¾	1	1¾		
5	6½	2¼	1¼	2¼		
6	7¾	2½	1½	2¾	1	
7	9	3	1¾	3¼	1	
8		3½	1¾	3¾	1¼	
9		4	2	4¼	1½	
10		4¼	2¼	4¾	1½	
11		4¾	2½	5¼	1¾	
12		5¼	2¾	5¾	2	1
13		5½	3	6	2	1
14		6	3¼	6½	2¼	1¼
15		6½	3½	7	2¼	1¼
16		7	3¾	7½	2½	1¼
17		7¼	4	8	2¾	1½
18		7¾	4¼	8½	2¾	1½
19		8¼	4½	9	3	1½
20		8¾	4¾		3¼	1¾
21		9	5		3¼	1¾
22		5¼	5¼		3½	2
23			5½		3½	2
24			5½		3¾	2
25			5¾		4	2

Weight of 5.25% Sodium Hypochlorite assumed to be 8.7 pounds per gal.

Weight of 12% Sodium Hypochlorite assumed to be 10.5 pounds per gal.

One (1) Tablespoon . . . = 3 tsp.
One oz . . . . = 2 tbsp. (approx.)
One cup . . . . = 8 oz. (approx.)

From Texas State Dept. of Health.

niques. Dispose of disposable gloves and paper as instructed above. Also, follow the above directions for disposal of the sealed bag.

CLEANING AND   It is wise to consult a reliable
SANITIZING AGENTS   manufacturer of detergents, soaps
                                    and sanitizers on any problems
one may have in cleaning or sanitizing. Good assistance can sometimes be given by health inspectors or by municipal water authorities. You will want other cleaning agents besides detergents and soaps for general cleaning, pot and pan washing and the dish washing tasks. Perhaps a dip may be advisable for flatware (knives, forks, spoons, etc.). Silver polish should remove tarnish quickly without scratching and should not contain cyanides (poisons). It should not be flammable.

Metal polishes should polish and not scratch. To see if they do, rub some on a piece of glass. You can test scouring powders and other cleaners this way. Scouring powders should have a pH of 5 to 11.5 to minimize corrosive action. They should rinse quickly.

Thorough understanding of cleaning products and what they can do is required, if you are to have good cleaning results. For instance, one should know that composition floors require special cleaners. The product used should clean well, dilute easily, mix readily with water and rinse without leaving film or residue. It should not have high foaming characteristics and should contain no substances harmful to the flooring. Some floor cleaners for health facilities have sanitizers in them to reduce the number of *staph* bacteria and, if this is desired, the cleaner should have such an ingredient in it.

Table 8-2—MISCELLANEOUS CLEANING COMPOUNDS FOR A FOODSERVICE

Name	*Description*	*Recommended Use*
Soap, scouring	Cake type, ground quartz grit	Rough scouring, pots and pans, etc.
Brick, scouring	Oblong pumice block with holder	Scouring and cleaning griddles and grills
Tableware destainer	Powder or liquid	Dip for flatware or for removing stains on plastic ware or destaining coffee urns, etc.
Ammonia, household	Liquid	Cleaning solution for tile, windows
Isopropanol alcohol	Rubbing alcohol	Cleaning windows or glass surfaces
Sweeping compound	1. Sand, sawdust and wax 2. Sawdust and wax	Use 1 where oil is undesirable; 2 on composition floors.

CLEANING AND SANITIZING JOBS

It is wise to have instructional materials for workers so they can do cleaning tasks properly. (See Fig. 8-10, p. 371, for suggested cleaning schedule.) The following cover most of the major cleaning tasks done in an extended care facility:

Floors

Step	*Procedure*
1. Prepare cleaning solution	Fill scrub bucket two-thirds full with warm, not hot, water; add 2 T detergent per gal water
2. Scrub	Pre-sweep floor. Then, use scrubbing machine or stiff bristle tampico hand brush; apply minimum of solution and remove soil. If soil is not great, do this with the heel of the mop. When needed, remove grease and spots with special solvents or friction cleaners.
3. Rinse with clean water	Use scrubbing water and clean mop to pick up soil. Wring out mop. Dry until surface is only damp.

The dining room floors should be kept free of food and trash. Clean when the room is empty. Use motions in sweeping that minimize raising dust.

If chairs are placed on tables, wipe and sanitize the tables after removing the chairs. Mop as instructed above.

Dust furniture and equipment. Wipe tables and chairs daily with a clean, moistened sponge or cloth dipped into a water-detergent solution—a water-detergent solution means an oz (2 T) of detergent to each gal of water.

Empty, wash, sanitize and refill vinegar cruets, salts and peppers, sugar dispensers, etc. frequently. Wipe condiment bottles and refrigerate those having perishable contents. No food in open containers should be in the room when cleaning is being done.

Serving Counter and Steam Table

Turn off the heat and allow the unit to cool. Remove insert pans and removable parts of the top. Take these to the sink or dishmachine for cleaning and sanitizing. Drain water by removing overflow pipe, if water is used. Scrub interior using a brush and hot water with detergent. Use only the moistness needed on electric units. Wipe dry. Wash off exterior. Air dry and replace parts.

To remove scale, periodically fill unit to point that covers deposits with water and descaling compound in proportions recommended by the manufacturer. Bring to a boil, turn off the heat and leave overnight. In the morning brush, drain, rinse and refill for use.

Wash counter top and wipe dry. Periodically clean shelves, removing all objects from them. Wash outside and sweep well under the counter if an open space exists.

Ventilating Units

Once a week remove filters from units. Soak filters in a sink for 10 min in a good mixture of detergent and water or send the filters through the dishmachine for cleaning. If cleaned in the sink, scrub filters with a stiff bristle brush, rinse and dry them and then replace filters.

Once a month, brush the top and underside of the hood, globes and the wire jacket protectors for the lights. Then, clean free of grease using 120°F water with a detergent in it and wipe dry. Send globes and wire jackets through the dishmachine with a weight on the globes to prevent water pressure from lifting them up. *Dry thoroughly* before replacing globes and wire jackets.

Twice a year clean air ducts. Clean from the top as well as the bottom, getting into the ducts as far as possible with cleaning implements.

Windows

A solution of 1 qt isopropanol alcohol, 1 fluid oz (2 T) nonionic detergent or wetting agent with 2 qt water can be sprayed onto the glass and then wiped off with soft paper toweling or a non-linting, soft cloth.

Stainless Steel

Prepare a solution with mild (not abrasive) cleanser, ammonia and warm water. Wash well and rinse. Wipe dry in a horizontal direction with the "grain" or polishing line. Do not allow food spatters to dry on stainless steel; they may tarnish it.

Tile or Porcelain Surfaces

Use an all-purpose detergent for washing and scrubbing cleaning surfaces free of soil. Rinse and wipe dry. For stubborn greasy or mineral films, use a destaining compound and then rinse and wipe dry. If water spots, finger prints or streaks.are not wiped off daily, dulling deposits will accumulate.

Can Opener

Clean the shaft daily by lifting it out of its base. Soak it in hot detergent-water, then scrub it with a stiff-bristled brush. Rinse with hot water and air dry.

Check cutting edge and can-holding mechanism. Replace if nicked or worn. Occasionally remove base by unscrewing it, then soak, clean, rinse and dry it. Clean under the base, using a brush or scraper if necessary. Apply a thin film of rust preventative to shank and bottom of the base before assembling.

Coffee Urns

Coffee is a highly perishable food and to be a quality product must be made in *absolutely* clean equipment. One of the problems is that coffee oils are easily oxidized and give off a disagreeable flavor. *Cleanliness is essential.* Coffee equipment must be cleaned after each use and a more thorough cleaning should be scheduled bi-weekly. If this is done, the coffee made in it will be of higher quality. The steps to follow for daily and for bi-weekly cleaning are:

DAILY. After use, flush the equipment with cold water. Fill outer tank of urn to about 2 in. from the top. Add 1 to 2 oz (2 to 4 T) of cleaning compound per gal of water. With a stiff brush, scrub the inside of the tank or the equipment.

Use small brushes to clean small apertures, glass tubes, etc. Disassemble all units and thoroughly wash all parts. Remember that rims, etc. will have coffee oils on them and these oils must be removed.

Be sure to soak all filters or cloth parts thoroughly in cold water. In urn cleaning, draw off a bit of the cleaning solution and return it. Next, drain thoroughly. Rinse *very* well; be sure to allow sufficient time for all liquid to drain away. Reassemble the unit.

BI-WEEKLY. Twice a week fill the urn with, or put the coffeemaking equipment into, a destaining compound, using about 2 T per 5 gal of water or other proportions as directed by the manufacturer. Rotate the water; with an urn, draw off a gal and return it. Tag equipment to indicate destaining is going on. Rotate occasionally for an hour maintaining water at a 170° to 180°F.

Disassemble and clean all parts. Soak filters or cloth parts in cold water after a thorough cleaning. Reassemble and rinse with several cold rinses. Air dry.

Vacuum-type units should be allowed to go through a coffee-making cycle with the destaining compound and then rinsed and dried. For non-cycle units such as coffee pots, etc.,clean thoroughly, using brushes and detergents; rinse and air dry.

Miscellaneous Mechanical Equipment

Always disconnect electrical equipment before cleaning it. After using a meat chopper, disassemble it and clean out all foods. Scrub, using a proper mixture of detergent and water and a stiff brush. Air dry. Store.

After using a food slicer, disassemble it, removing knife, guard and other items that need cleaning. Clean and rinse each part. Air dry. Wipe the machine, freeing it of all food and soil accumulation. Reassemble. Periodically oil those parts needing it.

Disconnect a slicer and remove the guard and blade. Soak both but not in a sink where other workers might put their hands and come in contact with the blade. Remove the guiding mechanism and soak. Clean away all food particles and all food particles from the area underneath the slicer. Wipe the machine clean with a cloth moistened with water-detergent. Wipe dry. Wash, rinse and sanitize soaked parts. Air dry. Reassemble.

After using a food mixer, soak bowls and mixer beaters. Wash in water containing sufficient detergent, rinse and air dry. Wipe the machine down, cleaning off all accumulated grease, food or other soil. Reassemble. Periodically drop 5 to 6 drops of oil on the shaft or auxiliary drive. After most of the basic soil has been removed and they have been rinsed, small bowls and beaters may be put through the dishmachine.

A vegetable peeler should be cleaned after each use. First, flush it with cold water. Disassemble and remove the lid and disc. Wash the interior, flushing preferably with hot water. Scrub the interior thoroughly. Wash the outside similarly. Scrub the disc, strainer and stopper and leave these to air dry. Empty and clean the peel trap by raising the lid, strainer and stopper. Flush. Reassemble after air drying. Wipe outside with wet cloth.

A rotary toaster should be disconnected. Then, the crumb tray and baskets should be removed, emptied and cleaned. Brush out crumbs. Wipe the machine on the outside with a damp cloth. If greasy, use a water-detergent solution or a non-abrasive cleaning agent. Avoid getting water into elements or the conveyor chain. Air dry and reassemble.

Mobile Equipment

After each use, wipe equipment with a cloth or sponge dipped into a water-detergent solution. Once a week take the units to the receiving dock or other area for a thorough cleaning. Vacuum insides first, if possible. Scrub, rinse and sanitize. Steam cleaning or sanitizing with one of the solutions mentioned in Table 8-4 is desirable. Do not moisten electrical units.

Self-leveling equipment should be completely emptied and the tubes removed. Disassemble the spring equipment by releasing the locking pin and slide the tube through the top. Wash, rinse and sanitize the tubes. Clean the mobile unit; air dry and reassemble.

Cooking Equipment

Cool equipment. Then, clean the body with a cloth moistened with a warm water-detergent solution; include the back apron and warming oven or shelf. Remove hardened substances with a spatula. Clean and dry. Clean burned material from plates or burners using a stiff bristle brush. Do not use metal sponges or metal brushes.

Gas burners may be removed and soaked, or else boiled in a water-detergent solution, then brushed free of soil. Invert to air dry. Ring-top electric burners should be lifted up and the lower part cleaned thoroughly. Remember to remove drip pan from under burners and soak and clean.

Clean frying plates and griddles with oil and salt and a pumice stone. Some slight heat helps. Scrape and clean all oil troughs. Empty and clean grease receptacle. Wipe dry. Stubborn grease and food soil on ranges and griddles can be more easily removed by first covering the area with a cloth dampened with household ammonia. Steam cleaning is very effective in removing soil.

Cool an oven before attempting to clean it. Scrape burned food from oven decks using a spatula, stiff bristle brush or scraper. Begin with the top deck and work down. Wash doors, using hot water-detergent solution. Rinse and wipe dry. If the oven is gas, clean the combustion chamber with a small broom or brush. Wipe controls and dry them. Polish stainless steel. Stubborn grease or burned soil may be removed by moistening with household ammonia or covering for a short time with a cloth dampened with the ammonia. Sometimes baking soda or cleaning soda is placed on soil to help remove it.

A fry kettle should be cool when cleaned but the frying fat should still be liquid. Remove the baskets and take them to the sink for soaking. In newer electric models, you can lift up heating elements and wipe off excess fat. Open drain valve and drain fat from container, filtering fat as it drains. Close drain.

If the frying kettle can be removed, take it to the sink. Scrape the bottom clean of crumbs and collected foods. If not movable, clean on location. Wash with a hot water-detergent solution of 2 oz (4 T) detergent to each gal of water, scrubbing inside with a stiff brush. Do not use steel wool or any abrasive on electrical heating elements. Scrape off hardened fat and food particles on baskets. Scrub vigorously with a stiff bristle brush. Rinse and sanitize all items and leave them to air dry. Return kettle to fryer. Fill with fat, adding enough new fat to fill. Heat to 200°F if solid fat is used. Replace baskets but do not put in fat; store them free standing on the holding rack.

Stack steamers should be cleaned daily, if used. Cool first, then clean the interior chambers by removing shelves and scrubbing interior with a brush. Wipe out the water pan and flush the drain line. Wash shelves and return.

Examine gaskets and safety mechanism for steam. Wash the doors and dry. Check wheel screws and oil them, if necessary. When the unit is clean, close the doors and turn the steam on for a minute to sanitize. Shut off and open door to air dry. Do not obstruct or tamper with safety valves in cleaning.

If food overflows in chamber during cooking, wipe up the food and liquid. Remove shelving and clean. If a steamer must be descaled, use a descaling solution, allowing the unit to stand overnight. Then, removing descaling solution, flush with 2 qt clean water and clean using method outlined in preceding paragraphs.

High-speed steamers should be cooled, disassembled and the drain siphon and drain pan removed. Use a water-detergent solution and stiff brush to clean the interior. Check drain to see that it is not plugged. Wash door and spray nozzle. Soak cooking chamber parts for 15 min. Clean, rinse and sanitize. Air dry.

Steam-jacketed kettles should be soaked as soon as food is removed from them, especially if the food is one that might bake onto the metal. To clean, work the rough soil into the soaking water and drain this away. Fill with clean, hot water. Add a detergent and scrub with a long-handle fiber brush. If there is considerable soil, drain and refill. Add detergent and clean again. Wash the outside, top, sides, hinges, draw-off valve, etc. Use a bottle brush for the valve. Drain the kettle and rinse it out. Rinse outside. Wipe dry. Fill one-third full with clean water; heat to sanitize. Drain and leave valve open. Put the cover down.

Refrigeration and Freezing Equipment

Food under refrigeration and in the freezer should be inspected daily. Then make plans to utilize those items that should not be held any longer. Discard perishable foods that cannot be used or are beginning to deteriorate. Do not store medicines with foods. Put the foods that are used most in front. Arrange foods so the freshest items are in back. Cover. Watch to see that no drip falls into foods.

Once a week remove foods, shelving and loose equipment and scrub the interior. Dry it thoroughly. Wash doors, openings, hinges and latches. Do not use ammonia or scouring pads. Then, clean the shelving and removable parts by sending them through the dishmachine, if desired. Check gaskets on doors to see that they are tight-fitting.

If not self-defrosting, defrost when about ¼ in. of frost appears on the coils. Clean under the refrigerator, making sure that floor drains are open. Periodically vacuum the compressor, condenser coils, motor and related areas. Try to organize use of the refrigerator so it is opened and closed as little as possible.

Freezer cabinets should be emptied periodically and the freezer cleaned. Shelving and other removable parts should be soaked, washed, rinsed and sanitized. The doors, outsides, hinges and other parts should be washed, rinsed and dried periodically. Check defrosting units.

Foods removed for cleaning can be stored temporarily in another refrigerator or held in a cool place if they do not stand too long. Check gaskets and clean motors, condensers, etc. as indicated above for refrigerators. Chipping of ice may endanger walls or refrigeration parts so, instead, wet ice with warm water or put a pan of warm water into the unit and close it. Loosen ice as it starts to melt and free itself. Do not use ammonia or metal cleaning compounds.

An ice machine should be cleaned about once a month or, if needed, more frequently. To clean, turn the motor off, empty the bins and allow the machine to defrost. The drain should be clean and free to carry off defrosting moisture. Scrub all parts including ice buckets, scoops, bin and so forth with a plastic fiber brush using a water-detergent solution. Check the freezing board; it may need descaling or the inside evaporator shell may need cleaning to remove mineral deposits. Rinse all cleaned surfaces and equipment and sanitize. Clean outside and wipe dry. Vacuum the compressor and motor units. Reassemble. Turn motor on. Check water flow valve. Is the unit freezing properly? To be sure, return in about an hour and make another check. Then, later make another.

Storage Units

A garbage storage area should have a pipe-, or other type of stand, upon which the cans rest. Remove stand; scrub the interior floors and doors in area with a long handled brush using a warm water-detergent solution of the heavy duty type. Hose out. Wipe doors dry. Spray with sanitizer. Clean floor drain and pour a gal of sanitizer down the drain. Clean outside. Clean pipe-stand, rinse and sanitize and place back into the chamber.

Clean trash or garbage cans with equipment having water pressure and steam-injection units. If not available, scrape cans out, soak. Pour enough hot, heavy-duty water-detergent solution (2 oz or 4 T/gal water) to permit scrubbing with a long handled brush. Scrub vigorously. Empty by inverting can over drain. Scrub lids and outside. Hose inside and outside with hot water. If steam is available, sanitize. If not, sanitize with sanitizing solution.

Dry food storage containers, vegetable bins, other bins, condiment lockers, drawers and other storage units should be cleaned frequently. Set up a periodic schedule for this. Empty and remove items from the unit, if possible. Vacuum or brush the unit out. Wipe the surfaces clean with a wet cloth and wipe dry. Allow surfaces to dry before replacing food on them. See that larger storage areas are clean and trash is picked up. Check vegetable areas for deteriorating foods. These areas should have good ventilation.

Pots and Pans

Care in using a pot or pan can give it a longer life and maximum utility and can also make it easier to clean. Pots and pans should not be abused or become dented and out of shape. Dented bottoms mean uneven heating since the heat flows only through the dent that touches the heating surface. Misshapen baking units give misshapen products.

Stainless steel and aluminum are antagonistic to each other so keep them apart during washing as much as possible. Rinse pots and pans immediately after use and soak those needing it. Warm water softens grease and cold water softens dried-on spots of potatoes, thickened sauces, puddings, eggs, rice and cereals. Sugar is soluble in water but more soluble in hot than in cold water.

To wash pots and pans, scrape them as free of soil as possible. Rinse. Then wash in water, 110° to $120^\circ F$, treated with the right amount and right kind of detergent. Fill the wash sink 2/3 to 3/4 full. Add detergent in an amount sufficient for the approximate gallons of water in the sink. A 24-in. by 30-in. sink, 14 in. deep, filled to the 10 in. line holds 26 gal of water. There are 231 sq in. in a gal. Thus, a 20- by 30-in. sink 16 in. deep would hold about 40 gal of water and if 3/4 full would hold 30 gal (20 x 30 x 16 = 9600 cu in. ÷ 231 = 41 gal).

Some pot and pan detergents maintain a certain color until their effectiveness is used up; then, the color changes. When this happens, start over with fresh water and detergent. Fill the second tank with rinsing (120° to 140°) water. If only two tanks are available, fill with $170^\circ F$ water for both rinsing and sanitizing. If there is a third tank, fill with $170^\circ F$ water. If the water is below this temperature, add a sanitizing solution.

The tools and materials needed to do a good pot and pan washing job are:

1. Metal scraper
2. Stiff plastic fiber scrub brush
3. Wire brush for burned food
4. Corrosion-resistant metal or plastic scouring pad

5. Scouring powder
6. Washing sponge
7. Washcloths
8. Baskets for sanitizing tank

Do not use steel wool; it breaks up and gets into food; it also rusts.

Wash small tools and equipment and lightly soiled units first. Wash outsides as well as insides. Put these into the rinsing sink, keeping your hands out of the rinsing water as much as possible. If a spray is available, spray first, especially if the second tank is also used for sanitizing. (A deep pan can be used for rinsing small items, if a third tank is not available.) Use tongs to remove items, if necessary.

Slide items carefully into the sanitizing bath. Hold for at least 30 sec in 170°F water and 1 min in chlorine or iodine sanitizer baths. (Counting slowly to 43 gives about 30 sec.) Remove the items from the sanitizing bath with the basket or with tongs. Invert and air dry. Next, start washing larger items or those having more soil.

Remember to empty all units of soaking water before starting to wash, unless there is a drain or sink convenient where this can be done during the washing process. If a floor drain is used, a can without a bottom placed over the drain helps to reduce splash. Scrapings should be put into a designated can, garbage can or scraping sink. If large pots cannot be immersed in the sanitizing solution, spray or swab the sanitizing solution on.

Place cleaned items on carts; deliver them to the storage areas and place them inverted on clean shelves. Then, clean the brushes and other tools and put these away. Clean carts. Empty garbage cans and clean these or take them to the garbage collection area. Return with clean cans.

Wash shelving and wipe dry. Clean sinks using a stiff brush. Clean drain boards. Wring out wet cloths, wipe sinks dry and put cloths in laundry bag or hang them up to dry. Sweep and mop the floor. Put garbage cans into place.

Dishwashing

If units are washed as soon as they are returned from service, they will be easier to clean. Items are best separated when they are placed into tote baskets or trays are assembled at the carts providing this is done where the mess is not observed. When separating glassware and cups for machine washing, it is recommended they be inverted in their washing baskets. If not, separate these inverted into baskets at the soiled dish table. Put flatware into a soaking bin but do not soak over 15 min because a longer soaking period encourages pitting. Put garbage, paper and other wastes into the proper collection units. Separate and stack heavier flat china to prevent the heavier pieces from breaking the lighter ones. During this separation, spray rinse to remove soft food and light soil. Pre-soak those items needing it, such as egg dishes or others with encrusted food on them. Use a deep pan or soak pan for these hard to clean items.

Machine washing procedures will differ according to the type of machine used. In a single tank machine, the opening and closing of doors takes time and, if the rinse in such a machine has to be manually operated, this will take additional time. A single tank machine should have a 40 sec wash and a 10 sec rinse. Wash temperatures should be between 120° to 140^oF and rinses at 180^oF, although longer rinses and lower temperatures may be found on some machines. Machines should be operated without dishes for a few minutes at first until water comes up to the proper temperature.

With a conveyor machine, do not allow employees to reach in and drag baskets out. This shortens the rinse time and the full time is needed to give proper rinsing and sanitizing.

Semi-automatic or automatic detergent dispensers may be installed on a machine. The automatic ones show the degree of detergent concentration in the wash tank. If not enough detergent is present, a red light goes on indicating the supply valve must be opened more. A green light indicates enough detergent is present. The semi-automatic units lack these warning lights. In these dispensers the action usually is: water comes up from the machine through tubing into the detergent container with the flow controlled by a valve; the water dissolves the detergent and runs back through another tube into the tank. Rinse units may also have a rinse facilitator or wetting agent injected into the rinse water. This is usually a liquid that promotes water run-off and, in addition, may help to sanitize.

Dishwashing instructions to employees should cover points such as the following: To start washing, fill the wash tank and, if there is no detergent dispenser on the machine, add the proper amount of detergent. (See Table 8-3 for the proper amount to add or consult the label on the detergent package.) Glassware may be given a preliminary brushing to free it of soil. An acid base

Table 8-3—INITIAL LOAD OF DETERGENT FOR DISHMACHINE*

Type Water	Gal Wash Water in Tank	1 Tank Machine oz	or c	2 Tank Machine oz	or c
Soft (0 to 7 grains	10	3-1/2	1/2	3-1/2	1/2
or 0 to 120 ppm)	15	5	2/3	5	2/3
	20	7	1	7	1
	25			9	1-3/4
Medium (7 to 14 grains	10	5	2/3	5	2/3
or 120 to 240 ppm)	15	7-1/2	1	7-1/2	1
	20	10	1-1/3	10	1-1/3
	25			12	1-1/2
Hard (14 to 20 grains	10	7	1	7	1
or 240 to 342 ppm)	15	10	1-1/3	10	1-1/3
	20	14	1-3/4	14	1-3/4
	25			16-1/2	2-1/4

*after every 10 min of operation, add 1/4 again as much as in the initial load.

NOTE: These concentrations are about double those recommended by the Public Health Service but should be followed to be sure the concentration continues to be adequate as the efficiency of the detergent declines.

Table 8-4—COLD WATER SANITIZER-WATER RATIOS

Gal Water	Calcium Hypochlorite (70% Tech.)* t	fl oz	Iodine-type Disinfectant** c	fl oz
5	3/4	1/8	1/4	2
10	1-1/2	1/4	1/2	4
15	2-1/4	3/8	3/4	6
20	3	1/2	1	8
25	4	5/8	1-1/4	10

*Approx 100 ppm; immerse not less than 1 min in water not less than 75°F.

**Approximately 50 ppm; immerse not less than 1 min in water not less than 75°F; adding 1/2 c of vinegar for every 5 gal of water, especially if the water is hard, helps to make the iodine more effective as a sanitizer.

NOTE: One of the problems of using temperatures as low as 75° is that items do not dry well at those temperatures. If these solutions are to be sprayed on rather than having the item immersed in them, it is best to double the strength of the solution.

detergent might be used during this prewash to remove milkstone film. The glass is then washed.

Next, flatware may be put into washing baskets in shallow layers or into washing cups with the eating ends up and unseparated—if silverware is separated and put into cups, pieces tend to stack together making cleaning more difficult. Load dishes next. Place in baskets and do not allow them to cover one another since that will prevent some from receiving a full washing, rinsing and sanitizing treatment. *Never work between the soiled and clean dish section without washing hands.* Also dry hands with a clean paper towel before handling clean dishes.

As the baskets come from the machine, give them a quick shake to remove any free flowing water. If the rinse is at the proper temperature, the dishes will air dry quickly. Never towel; this spreads soil around. If desired, cup and glass racks can be stacked on clean dollies. Flatware can be given a vigorous shake in the basket and then separated, placing the pieces on clean towels or placing them directly into dispensing cups with the eating end down. This makes it necessary for individuals to remove them by their handles.

If a dip is used, plunge the handles into the hot dip; repeat, plunging the eating ends into it. Put these items into clean cups, eating end down, or onto a clean surface to air dry. In separating clean silverware, pick units up by the handles.

Lift dry dishes from their baskets and stack. As stacks accumulate, place the dishes into the mobile units, carts or self-leveling equipment designated to take them to enclosed storage. Keep stacks away from your body. Store mobile units under tables or shelving to protect dishes or cover with clean toweling.

Shut off the steam on the dishmachines. (It is desirable to clean machines at the end of the day.) After draining the machine, remove scrapping trays. Remove the tank strainers and doors, if they are removable. Remove curtains. Flush out the tanks to remove any collected soil. Check the drain for obstructions. Clean tanks with a stiff brush dipped into a detergent-water solution. Flush out well. Check the wash arms and demount; remove inside soil. Wash, rinse and sanitize. Check pumps for leakage. Wash, rinse and sanitize trays, doors and strainers. Scrub curtains with a good detergent-water solution. Dip them into a sanitizing solution and hang them up to dry. Air dry and replace all these items. Clean the outside of the machine. Shut off the water. Leave the machine open to air dry. Clean tables and shelves. Sweep and mop.

To descale a dishmachine:

1. Fill tank or tanks to half their capacity.

2. Add a descaling solution in the ratio recommended by the manufacturer, or add 7 fluid oz (scant cup) of phosphoric acid, or the same amount of a 2% vinegar solution, per gal of water using, in addition, 1 fluid oz of wetting agent per gal of water.

3. Complete filling the tanks with hot water.

4. Operate the machine at the highest temperature possible (full steam) for 1 hr.

It is advisable to descale frequently since once scale builds up in a fairly thick coat, it is extremely difficult to remove.

If you hand wash dishes, separate as instructed above. Presoak silverware and heavily soiled dishes. Brush glasses, if necessary. Fill the wash sink ¾ full with 110° to 120°F water and add the proper amount of the right kind of detergent. Fill the rinse and sanitizing sinks also. Have the rinse water at 120° to 140°F and the sanitizing water at 170°F. If only two sinks are available, follow the procedures outlined for pots and pans.

Start washing glassware first; then wash silverware. Place glasses carefully into baskets in the rinse water and, when the basket is full, lift up and immerse in the sanitizing solution—instead of 170°F water, a chlorine or iodine solution can be used. Leave the items 30 sec in the hot water or 1 min in the other solutions. Remove the baskets from the sanitizing solution. Invert the glasses to drain. Do not put hands inside glasses. Be sure hands are clean. Gloves may be recommended.

Next, wash flatware. Be sure to wash every unit, working quickly and rapidly. Pieces can be dropped into clean cups in the baskets in the rinse water. When washing is completed, lift the baskets from the rinse water and immerse them into the sanitizing solution for the proper length of time. If a dip is used, follow the directions above for machine washing. Separate, also, as instructed above.

Dishes are washed next, usually starting with the cups and saucers, sauce dishes and other dishes that are lightly soiled. Of these small items, wash the bread and butter plates last. Change water when the soil begins to build up. Remember to check temperatures occasionally. Next wash the larger and heavier pieces. As these are washed, deftly drop them into the rinse sink into baskets. Do not have the rinse sink over half full. Lift the baskets and place them in the sanitizing solution for the proper time. Lift out to air dry. Stack with clean hands, placing the dishes into their proper storage units.

Finally, clean the area. Follow directions for cleaning the pot and pan section, finishing with a clean area with everything in its proper place. See that wash baskets are properly stacked and put into their storage places.

Additional Bibliography*

Economic Laboratories. *Food Equipment Sanitation Cleaning Procedures.* New York: By the Laboratories, 1965.

Iowa State Department of Health. *Sanitation of Food Service Establishments.* New York: Economic Laboratories, 1962.

Longree, Karla. *Quantity Food Sanitation.* New York: John Wiley and Sons, 1967.

Rakosky, Joseph Jr. *Sanitation Simplified.* Chicago: By Central Soya, Chemurgy Division.

Richardson, Treva M. *Sanitation for Foodservice Workers.* Boston: By Institutions/VFM, 1969.

Texas State Department of Health. *Preventing Food-Borne Diseases,* 2nd Rev. Austin, Texas: Texas State Department, 1966.

U. S. Department of Health, Education and Welfare. *"You Can Prevent Foodborne Illness."* Washington, D. C.: Government Printing Office, 1963.

U. S. Department of Health, Education and Welfare. *Environmental Aspects of the Hospital, Vol. I, "Infection Control"* and X, *"Food Services."* Washington, D. C.: Government Printing Office, 1967.

U. S. Department of Health, Education and Welfare. *Selection and Use of Disinfectants in Health Facilities.* Washington, D. C.: Government Printing Office, 1967.

University of Massachusetts. *Bacterial Food Poisoning.* Amherst, Mass.: Food Management Leaflet No. 1, 1959.

---

*In addition to those included in this chapter.

PHS-4006
4-62

FOODSERVICE INSPECTION REPORT

INSPECTION REPORT
FOOD SERVICE ESTABLISHMENTS

Permit No._____
Type____ NSD____

CITY, COUNTY OR DISTRICT	NAME OF ESTABLISHMENT	ADDRESS	OWNER OR OPERATOR

Sir: Based on an inspection this day, the items marked below identify the violation in operation or facilities which must be corrected by the next routine inspection or such shorter period of time as may be specified in writing by the health authority. Failure to comply with this notice may result in immediate suspension of your permit (or downgrading of the establishment).* An opportunity for an appeal will be provided if a written request for a hearing is filed with the health authority within the period of time established in this notice for the correction of violations.

SECTION B. FOOD
1. FOOD SUPPLIES

Item		Specify:	Bakery products	Poultry and poultry products	Meat and meat products	Frozen desserts	Shellfish	Milk and milk products	Demerit Points
1	Approved source								6
2	Wholesome - not adulterated								6
3	Not misbranded								2
4	Original container; properly identified								2
5	Approved dispenser								2
6	Fluid milk and fluid milk products pasteurized								6
7	Low-acid and non-acid foods commercially canned								6

SECTION C. PERSONNEL
1. HEALTH AND DISEASE CONTROL

Item		Demerit Points
26	Persons with boils, infected wounds, respiratory infections or other communicable disease properly restricted	6
27	Known or suspected communicable disease cases reported to health authority	6

2. CLEANLINESS

28	Hands washed and clean	6
29	Clean outer garments; proper hair restraints used	2
30	Good hygienic practices	4

(cont.)

SECTION D. FOOD EQUIPMENT AND UTENSILS

1. SANITARY DESIGN, CONSTRUCTION AND INSTALLATION OF EQUIPMENT AND UTENSILS

		Good repair; no cracks	No chips, pits or open seams	Cleanable; smooth	Approved material	No corrosion	Proper construction	Accessible for cleaning and inspection
31	Food-contact surfaces of equipment							2
32	Utensils							2
33	Non-food-contact surfaces of equipment							2
34	Single-service articles of non-toxic materials							2
35	Equipment properly installed							2
36	Existing equipment capable of being cleaned, non-toxic, properly installed and in good repair							2

2. CLEANLINESS OF EQUIPMENT AND UTENSILS

37	Tableware clean to sight and touch							
38	Kitchenware and food-contact surfaces of equipment clean to sight and touch							4
39	Grills and similar cooking devices cleaned daily							
40	Non-food-contact surfaces of equipment kept clean							2
41	Detergents and abrasives rinsed off food-contact surfaces							2
42	Clean wiping cloths used; use properly restricted							2
43	Utensils and equipment pre-flushed, scraped or soaked							2
44	Tableware sanitized							
45	Kitchenware and food-contact surfaces of equipment used for potentially hazardous food sanitized							4

2. FOOD PROTECTION

		Preparation	Storage	Display	Service	Transportation
8	Protected from contamination					4
9	Adequate facilities for maintaining food at hot or cold temperatures					2
10	Suitable thermometers properly located					2
11	Perishable food at proper temperature					2
12	Potentially hazardous food at 45°F. or below, or 140°F. or above as required					6
13	Frozen food kept frozen; properly thawed					2
14	Handling of food minimized by use of suitable utensils					4
15	Hollandaise sauce of fresh ingredients; discarded after three hours					6
16	Food cooked to proper temperature					6
17	Fruits and vegetables washed thoroughly					2
18	Containers of food stored off floor on clean surfaces					2
19	No wet storage of packaged food					2
20	Display cases, counter protector devices or cabinets of approved type					2
21	Frozen dessert dippers properly stored					2
22	Sugar in closed dispensers or individual packages					2
23	Unwrapped and potentially hazardous food not re-served					4
24	Poisonous and toxic materials properly identified, colored, stored and used; poisonous polishes not present					
25	Bactericides, cleaning and other compounds properly stored and non-toxic in use dilutions					6

*Applicable only where grading form of ordinance is in effect.

FOODSERVICE INSPECTION REPORT (cont.)

SECTION D. FOOD EQUIPMENT AND UTENSILS (cont.)

Item		Demerit Points
46	Facilities for washing and sanitizing equipment and utensils approved, adequate, properly constructed, maintained, operated	4
47	Wash and sanitizing water clean	2
48	Wash water at proper temperature	
49	Dish tables and drain boards provided, properly located and constructed	2
50	Adquate and suitable detergents used	2
51	Approved thermometers provided and used	
52	Suitable dish baskets provided	
53	Proper gauge cocks provided	2
54	Cleaned and sanitized utensils and equipment properly stored and handled; utensils air-dried	2
55	Suitable facilities and areas provided for storing utensils and equipment	
56	Single-service articles properly stored, dispensed and handled	2
57	Single-service articles used only once	
58	Single-service articles used when approved washing and sanitizing facilities are not provided	6

SECTION E. SANITARY FACILITIES AND CONTROLS (cont.)

Item		Demerit Points
	4. TOILET FACILITIES	
72	Adequate, conveniently located, and accessible; properly designed and installed	6
73	Toilet rooms completely enclosed, and equipped with self-closing, tight-fitting doors; doors kept closed	2
74	Toilet rooms, fixtures and vestibules kept clean, in good repair, and free from odors	2
75	Toilet tissue and proper waste receptacles provided; waste receptacles emptied as necessary	2
	5. HAND-WASHING FACILITIES	
76	Lavatories provided, adequate, properly located and installed	6
77	Provided with hot and cold or tempered running water through proper fixtures	4
78	Suitable hand cleanser and sanitary towels or approved hand-drying devices provided	2
79	Waste receptacles provided for disposable towels	2
80	Lavatory facilities clean and in good repair	2

SECTION E. SANITARY FACILITIES AND CONTROLS

1. WATER SUPPLY

No.	Pts	Item
59	6	From approved source; adequate; safe quality
60	4	Hot and cold running water provided
61	6	Transported water handled, stored; dispensed in a sanitary manner
62	6	Ice from approved source; made from potable water
63	2	Ice machines and facilities properly located, installed and maintained
64	2	Ice and ice handling utensils properly handled and stored; block ice rinsed
65	2	Ice-contact surfaces approved; proper material and construction

2. SEWAGE DISPOSAL

No.	Pts	Item
66	6	Into public sewer, or approved private facilities

3. PLUMBING

No.	Pts	Item
67	2	Properly sized, installed and maintained
68	1	Non-potable water piping identified
69		No cross connections
70	6	No back siphonage possible
71	2	Equipment properly drained

6. GARBAGE AND RUBBISH DISPOSAL

No.	Pts	Item
81	2	Stored in approved containers; adequate in number
82	2	Containers cleaned when empty; brushes provided
83	2	When not in continuous use, covered with tight fitting lids, or in protective storage inaccessible to vermin
84	2	Storage areas adequate; clean; no nuisances; proper facilities provided
85	2	Disposed of in an approved manner, at an approved frequency
86	2	Garbage rooms or enclosures properly constructed; outside storage at proper height above ground or on concrete slab
87	2	Food waste grinders and incinerators properly installed, constructed and operated; incinerator areas clean

7. VERMIN CONTROL

No.	Pts	Item
88	4	Presence of rodents, flies, roaches and vermin minimized
89	2	Outer openings protected against flying insects as required; rodent-proofed
90	2	Harborage and feeding of vermin prevented

SECTION F. OTHER FACILITIES

1. FLOORS, WALLS and CEILINGS

No.	Pts	Item
91	2	Floors kept clean; no sawdust used
92	1	Floors easily cleanable construction, in good repair, smooth, non-absorbent; carpeting in good repair
93	2	Floor graded and floor drains, as required

(cont.)

FOODSERVICE INSPECTION REPORT (cont.)

SECTION F. OTHER FACILITIES (cont.)

1. FLOORS, WALLS, CEILINGS (cont.)

Item		Demerit Points
94	Exterior walking and driving surfaces clean; drained	2
95	Exterior walking and driving surfaces properly surfaced	1
96	Mats and duck boards cleanable, removable and clean	2
97	Floors and wall junctures properly constructed	2
98	Walls, ceilings and attached equipment clean	2
99	Walls and ceilings properly constructed and in good repair; coverings properly attached	1
100	Walls of light color; washable to level of splash	2

2. LIGHTING

Item		Demerit Points
101	20 foot-candles of light on working surfaces	
102	10 foot-candles of light on food equipment, utensil washing, hand-washing areas and toilet rooms	2
103	5 foot-candles of light 30 in. from floor in all other areas	
104	Artificial light sources as required	2

3. VENTILATION

Item		Demerit Points
105	Rooms reasonably free from steam, condensation, smoke, etc.	2
106	Rooms and equipment vented to outside as required	2

VENTILATING (cont.)

Item		Demerit Points
107	Hoods properly designed; filters removable	2
108	Intake air ducts properly designed and maintained	1
109	Systems comply with fire prevention requirements; no nuisance created	2

4. DRESSING ROOMS AND LOCKERS

Item		Demerit Points
110	Dressing rooms or areas as required; properly located	1
111	Adequate lockers or other suitable facilities	1
112	Dressing rooms, areas and lockers kept clean	2

5. HOUSEKEEPING

Item		Demerit Points
113	Establishment and property clean, and free of litter	2
114	No operations in living or sleeping quarters	2
115	Floors and walls cleaned after closing or between meals by dustless methods	2
116	Laundered clothes and napkins stored in clean place	2
117	Soiled linen and clothing stored in proper containers	1
118	No live birds or animals other than guide dogs	2

DEMERIT SCORE OF THE ESTABLISHMENT _____

REMARKS

Date _____   Health Authority _____

Fig. 8-11. *The inspection report for foodservice departments used by the U. S. Public Health Service.*

FOOD ADMINISTRATORS SANITATION INSPECTION REPORT

Date_____

Sanitation Inspection Report

Answer questions with a "✓" in space provided for a "YES", or Circle "O" for a "NO".

Facility_____

DISHROOM

(1) Are the following items clean?

Walls_____, Ceiling_____, Lights_____, Machine Wash Arms_____, Machine Rinse Arms_____, Floors_____, Floor Drains_____, Corners_____, Hood_____, Fan_____, Disposal_____, Dispenser_____, Windows_____, Screens_____, Racks_____, Shelves_____, Under equipment_____, Glasswasher_____, Dish Carts_____, Trays_____.

(2) Are the following items satisfactory?

Machine Wash Temperature_____, Machine Rinse Temperature_____, Machine Final Rinse Temperature_____, China_____, Glasses_____, Silver_____, Dish Racks_____, Glass Racks_____, Cup Racks_____, Dispenser_____.

SPECIAL DIET SECTION

(1) Are the following items clean?

Walls_____, Ceiling_____, Floors_____, Floor Drains_____, Lights_____, Corners_____, Hood_____, Fan_____, Filters_____, Tables_____, Drawers_____, Blender_____, Stoves_____, Windows_____, Screens_____, Ledges_____. Blender_____, Stoves_____, Utensils_____.

(2) Are the following items satisfactory?

MAIN COOK SECTION

(1) Are the following items clean?

Walls_____, Ceiling_____, Lights_____, Floors_____, Floor Drains_____, Corners_____, Hood_____, Fan_____, Filters_____, Racks_____, Shelves_____, Tables_____, Drawers_____, Cutting Board_____, Slicer_____, Mixer_____, Can Opener_____, Steam Kettle_____, Steam Cooker_____, Fry Kettle: Bowl & Element_____, Base_____, Underneath_____; Griddle_____, Stoves_____, Brailer_____, Windows_____, Screens_____, Ledges_____. Gaskets_____, Fry Kettle Oil_____, Fry Kettle Syphon_____, Syphon Bags_____, Oven Doors_____.

(2) Are the following items satisfactory?

POT SINK

(1) Are the following items clean?

Wash Water_____, Rinse Water_____, Final Rinse Water_____, Pots_____, Pans_____, Racks_____, Shelves_____, Disposal_____, Walls_____, Floors_____, Floor Drains_____, Ceiling_____, Lights_____, Tables_____, Under Equipment_____, Garbage Cans_____, Windows_____, Screens_____, Ledges_____. Temperature of Water_____, Faucets_____, Absence of Carbon_____, Disposal_____.

(2) Are the following items satisfactory?

BAKE SHOP

(1) Are the following items clean?

Floors_____, Floor Drains_____, Corners_____, Walls_____, Ceiling_____, Lights_____, Candy Stove_____, Oven Floors_____, Oven Heating Units_____, Oven Doors_____, Bakers Table_____, Scales_____, Mixers_____, Refrigerator_____, Proof Box_____, Steam Kettle_____, Windows_____, Screens_____, Ledges_____, Can Opener_____. Candy Stove_____, Thermostats_____, Scales_____, Mixers_____, Steam Kettle_____.

(2) Are the following items satisfactory?

(cont.)

FOOD ADMINISTRATORS SANITATION INSPECTION REPORT (cont.)

PANTRY & VEGETABLE PREPARATION   (1) Are the following items clean?

Floors____, Floor Drains____, Corners____, Walls____, Ceiling____, Lights____, Fan____, Shelves____, Tables____, Windows____,
Screens____, Ledges____, Drawers____, Potato Peeler____, Food Chopper____, Reach-In Coolers____,

(2) Are the following items satisfactory?   Potato Peeler Open to Air-Dry____, Condition of Reach-In Coolers____, Food Chopper____

PATIENT SERVICE   (1) Are the following items clean?

Food Carts____, Conveyor Belt____, Hot Food Tables____, Trays____,

(2) Are the following items satisfactory?   Food Carts____, Conveyor Belt____, Hot Food Tables____, Trays____,

STOREROOM   (1) Are the following items clean?

DAY STORAGE   Floors____, Floor Drains____, Corners____, Walls____, Ceiling____, Lights____, Fan____, Shelves____, Storage Cans____,
Can Dollies____, Platform Scales____, Other Scales____, Tables____, Potato Bin____, Onion Bin____, Meat Saw____, Meat Block____,
Grinder____, Windows____, Screens____, Ledges____.

BULK STORAGE   Floors____, Floor Drains____, Corners____, Walls____, Ceiling____, Lights____, Fan____, Shelves____, Floats____,
Tables____, Windows____, Screens____, Ledges____.

REFRIGERATION   Produce Walk-In: Floors____, Corners____, Walls____, Ceiling____, Lights____, Unit____, Shelves____, Floats____,
Dairy Walk-In: Floors____, Corners____, Walls____, Ceiling____, Lights____, Unit____, Shelves____, Floats____,
Meat Walk-In: Floors____, Corners____, Walls____, Ceiling____, Lights____, Unit____, Shelves____, Floats____,
Freezer Walk-In: Floors____, Corners____, Walls____, Ceiling____, Lights____, Unit____, Shelves____, Floats____.

(2) Are the following items satisfactory?

DAY STORAGE   Distance from Floor____, Pricing of Merchandise____, Scales____, Meat Saw____, Grinder____, Lids an Storage ·Cans____.

REFRIGERATION   Temperature of Produce Walk-In____, Temperature of Dairy Walk-In____, Temperature of Meat Walk-In____, Temperature of
Freezer Walk-In____, Covering of Left-Over Food____.

REST ROOMS   (1) Are the following items clean?

WOMEN'S ROOM   Floors____, Floor Drains____, Corners____, Walls____, Ceiling____, Lights____, Windows____, Screens____, Ledges____,
Wash Basin____, Toilet Bowls____, Shower Stall____, Mirror____.

MEN'S ROOM   Floors____, Floor Drains____, Corners____, Walls____, Ceiling____, Lights____, Windows____, Screens____, Ledges____,
Wash Basin____, Toilet Bowls____, Shower Stall____, Mirror____.

(2) Are the following items satisfactory?

WOMEN'S ROOM   Presence of Soap____, Towels____, Tissue____, Repairs____, "Wash Hands" Poster____.

MEN'S ROOM   Presence of: Soap____, Towels____, Tissue____, Repairs____, "Wash Hands" Poster____.

GARBAGE

(1) Are the following items clean?

Can Washing Area_____, Refrigerated Garbage Room_____, Can Storage Area_____, Cans_____, Mops_____, Mop Buckets_____.

(2) Are the following items satisfactory?

Absence of flies_____, Absence of other pests_____, Storage of Mops & Brooms_____, Supply of Mops & Brooms_____, Lids on Cans_____.

CAFETERIA OR DINING ROOM

(1) Are the following items clean?

Floors_____, Floor Drains_____, Corners_____, Walls_____, Ceiling_____, Windows_____, Screens_____, Ledges_____, Table Tops_____, Table Legs_____, Chair Seats_____, Chair Legs_____, Salt & Pepper Shakers_____, Sugar Bowls_____, Tray Stands_____, Ash Trays_____, Condiment Stands_____, Salad Counter_____, Pastry Counter_____, Milk Machine_____, Tea Urns_____, Coffee Urns_____, Beverage Counter_____, Hot Food Counter_____, Steam Table_____, Wells_____, Refrigerators_____, Toasters_____, Steam Table Pans_____, Kitchen Doors_____, Air Conditioner Grills_____, Telephone_____.

(2) Are the following items satisfactory?

Supply of Salt & Pepper Shakers_____, Fullness of Salt & Pepper Shakers_____, Supply of Sugar Bowls_____, Fullness of Sugar Bowls_____, Supply of Ash Trays_____, Temperature of Steam Table_____, Supply of Coffee Urn Cleaner_____, Supply of Steam Table Pans_____, Condition of Steam Table Pans_____.

OFFICE

(1) Are the following items clean?

Floors_____, Corners_____, Walls_____, Ceiling_____, Lights_____, Windows_____, Screens_____, Ledges_____, Desk_____, Office Equipment_____.

(2) Are the following items satisfactory? Office Equipment_____, Neatness_____, Orderliness_____.

After analyzing the answers to the above questions, I have

awarded to this Facility a rating of _____

_____ Supervisor

(Mark EXCELLENT, GOOD, FAIR, OR POOR)

_____ Food Service Director

BRAHCO—743—0411

Fig. 8-12. *An inspection check list used for checking foodservice departments in health facilities. Courtesy Mrs. Iris Lochner, Food Systems Design, Oklahoma City, Okla.*

IX: SAFETY

INTRODUCTION

Safety means freedom from danger; this means freedom from harm from an accident, food poisoning or other injury. Foodservice departments do not have good records for being free from danger to workers or patrons. Perhaps this is because there are so many chances for accidents. If this is true, it emphasizes the need for the extra precautions and better safety measures that assure an effective safety program. These measures will pay off, not only in reducing injury to and suffering of personnel but in reducing breakage, insurance and repair costs, creating better working conditions and improving worker morale.

A recent study has shown 90% of the foodservice accidents are caused by inattention, often because the worker is hurrying to get work done or has failed to obtain proper information before beginning his work. The National Safety Council found that 34% of the accidents occur during the time food is being served; 21% during preparation before cooking; 16% in handling food, equipment or supplies, etc. and 12% during cooking.

MANAGEMENT RESPONSIBILITY   It is said that a foodservice will be as sanitary as management wants it to be. It will also be safe to the same degree because the primary responsibility for safety also rests with management. Even though others in the operation may wish for a more safe or sanitary operation, little can be done unless the full co-operation of management is obtained, with management taking the initiative in seeing that a good safety program is implemented.

All individuals in the department should be assigned definite safety responsibilities. Management should also establish safety plans and procedures and spend time in instructing and training others in safety. Drills and emergency plans should be established by management.

The proper kind of equipment and tools must be provided and the facility should be maintained in a safe condition. The safety program should be co-ordinated with that of the entire health facility and should also agree with local regulations and codes. Advice on what the program should encompass can be obtained from competent authorities. Frequent inspections for hazards, deficiencies, the adequacy of safety measures and the safety of equipment or operating procedures should be made by management. Inspection results should be checked periodically with the fire department, insurance representatives and top management of the health facility or other responsible authorities. The suggestions of outside officials for improvement should be reported to top management. Employees should be encouraged to make suggestions and these should be followed by action from management. The co-operation of workers must be sought.

To set up a safety program:

1. Inspect the premises to ascertain the needs; utilize competent authorities in doing this.

2. Set up a safety committee to work on problems, to study them and to make recommendations.

3. Set up procedures and assign responsibilities.

4. Set up a record maintenance system.

5. Establish a training program, including setting up motivation for safety.

6. Establish a schedule for routine check-ups and reporting.

7. Set up procedures for investigation and analysis of hazard problems.

8. Set up procedures for follow-up.

If an accident or safety incident occurs, the management of the foodservice, or other responsible individual, should submit a report verbally to be followed by a written report on the nature of the incident. This should be done no matter how minor the mishap. (See suggested form). This not only helps to inform top management, but can help to pinpoint responsibility and lead to establishment of adequate measures to prevent recurrence.

SAFETY IN
PHYSICAL FACILITIES

The first step in establishing a good safety program is to see that the physical facilities of the foodservice department are properly planned and constructed. Building materials should be those that do not generate accidents or present other hazards. They should be fire-retardant.

Floors should be non-slip type, solid and even, with no jutting tiles, boards or other hazards. Stairs should be sufficiently wide to allow required passage; landings and handrails should be at the proper places.

Aisles should also be wide enough to provide adequate passage. The National Safety Council, engineering organizations and others concerned with safety can indicate satisfactory standards for aisles. Federal, state and municipal authorities have also set such standards. Avoid aisles with blind turns or those that lead into main work areas. Entrance and egress should be by the shortest route through the foodservice area. Emergency unlock devices or alarm systems should be installed on walk-in refrigerators, freezers or storage areas. Storage should be located away from areas where trash, garbage or rubbish may accumulate.

Accidents happen if doors open into corridors or aisles; if they must, provide sliding doors. All doors leading into work areas should have glass windows. Doors should open out to outside areas and adequate lighting should be provided around all entrances.

If it comes under their jurisdiction, equipment should bear the mark of approval of The Underwriters Laboratory or the National Sanitation Foundation. Installation should meet local or other code requirements and fixed equipment should be securely fastened to floors, walls or other supporting equipment. Sufficient working space should be allowed around equipment. Heavy mobile equipment should be equipped with locking wheels.

Heating equipment should be properly insulated. Insulate steam lines and provide adequate controls for them and the equipment they service. Adequate fusing and wiring should be provided for electrical equipment. See that line sizes and amperage are sufficient to cover expected loads. Gas equipment should be properly vented.

Main leads for water, gas, steam, electricity and ventilation should be near the foodservice area and easily accessible for quick turnoff. Provide wrenches and other equipment needed to turn services off and do not enclose these in a locked cabinet. If they must be in a locked cabinet, provide keys nearby.

See that adequate water at proper temperatures is furnished and that all lines over 160°F are coded so employees know there is danger of scalding.

Gears, chains and belts of mechanical equipment should be properly housed and guarded. Guards should be placed at those points on equipment where workers can make contact with moving parts. Interlocks or switches on machines with moving parts should be provided so power can be quickly shut off. Ventilation should be adequate in work and storage areas.

Many times we fail to recognize the need for safety in the use of small equipment. Grasps for knives and other cutting equipment should be adequate to give a good grip and not fatigue the muscles. Watch equipment that might tip easily.

CLEANING AND MAINTENANCE

Proper cleaning and proper maintenance are each a part of the safety program. Set up a schedule for cleaning and maintenance and see that individual employees are assigned responsibility for the schedule. (For information on setting up maintenance program, see p. 445.) Employees should immediately report evidence of soil, trash or safety hazards. Trash, clutter and packaging materials should be cleaned up and put into containers as soon as they are emptied.

Needs for repairs should also be reported. Floors should be maintained in good condition and kept clean so they are not slippery. All spillage should be wiped up immediately. Broken parts on mats and duckboards should be repaired immediately. Non-slip floor polishes and waxes should be used.

STORAGE AREAS

Accidents are common in the storage areas because heavy items may cause injury either when they fall or during handling. Good shelving, of adequate strength and size to hold the materials stored there, should be installed. Three cases of No. 10 cans will have a bearing weight of 125 to 150 lb/sq ft.

The shelf width should be such that items can be moved in and out without pinching the hands or crowding. About 1½ to 2 in. free space is desirable for this. A No. 10 case is about 14 in. wide and 18 in. long. Heavy or bulky items should be stored in lower areas. Stacks should not be over 7 ft high and materials in the stacks should be arranged alternately to bind materials into the stack.

Stores should be accessible from all points; over-reaching can result in strains or falls. The storage area should be free of clutter and organized so employees know where to go to find items. Provide enough space for lifting crates and packages. Workers should be instructed, when opening boxes, cartons or other items, to remove nails and not to bend them down; and to remove packing around glass carefully, at the same time looking for broken glass.

See that heavy items are moved with hand carts, trucks, etc. Sliding doors should be installed on storage areas for dishes, glassware and small cooking equipment. It is recommended that foods be stored in refrigerators in plastic containers and not in breakable ones. Blowers in refrigerators should be guarded by screens.

THE WORKER AND SAFETY   A majority of accidents occur because of human error. Workers should be taught to be constantly alert and should know how to avoid accidents.

Workers should dress for safety, working in comfortable work shoes that fit the feet well and are not the type held to the foot by straps, etc. Shoes should have good soles, with shock-cushioning material if the floor is hard. Shoes with open-toed or open-heeled areas are not suitable.

Safety shoes should be provided for workers who must lift heavy objects regularly. Safety shoes are equipped with toe guards or a strap to protect the toes from falling objects. Laces should be tightly tied to prevent tripping or slipping. Heels should be in good repair.

Workers should not wear loose, open sleeves or aprons. String, unguarded wiping cloths or aprons should be held close to the body and not be free to catch on things or in moving equipment. The hair should be worn under a hair net or under a work cap; since men now wear long hair, this rule should apply to them also. Workers should wear gloves when opening crates or handling items that might injure them.

If possible, men should not lift loads heavier than 50 lb and women loads heavier than 35 lb. If a heavier load must be lifted, they should ask for help and, if possible, use a cart or other equipment to move it. Before moving a heavy object, the worker should know where it is to be placed and that a clear avenue to that place exists.

Before lifting an object, the worker should size up the load and tilt it to ascertain its weight. Then, taking a firm stance with feet one shoe length apart, the worker should crouch down, bending his knees, keep his back straight and put his arms around the object, getting his hands securely under or on it. He should relax a little and then lift, bringing the load up with the strong leg muscles and not the back muscles. As he lifts, the legs should be straightened. The arms should hold the load close to the body. If the load to be lifted is at shoulder level or higher, it should first be lifted down to a shelf or a table and then handled as instructed.

To lower an object, estimate its weight—a rule to follow is that if the object is too heavy to lift, it is too heavy to lower. The lifter should get up close to the object and take a firm footing, again keeping the feet slightly apart. Tilt the object to get a firm grip around and under it. Keep the back straight and the head erect. Then lift, holding the load close to the body. Bend the knees, holding the back straight and, using the powerful leg muscles, lower the load, setting it a bit away from his body first and then removing the hands carefully while letting the load down.

Remind workers, that when lifting they should not lift too much at one time and to rest frequently. Tiring and overworking can cause a sudden strain or injury just as a sudden shock or jolt can.

To do a job, the worker should know how to do it and see that he has the right equipment and tools. The work area should be organized and free of clutter. Drawers and bins should be closed. Storage of small tools should be organized for convenient use. Workers should give some time to studying their work place and how they can best work in it. *Mise en place* (put in place) is a term used by professional culinary workers to indicate that things should be kept organized, in their places and that clutter should be cleaned up as they work.

A professional worker works rapidly, accurately and without endangering himself or others because he watches for and removes hazards as he works. He also knows how accidents can happen and where they might happen. Rhythmic, steady, even motions are used. Professionals seldom work in haste, never run and avoid horseplay. Some workers are accident-prone because they fail to follow simple rules for safety; however, most accidents occur when workers are tired.

Accidents frequently occur because workers do not follow the proper sequences in doing work. It is not the person who works at frantic speed who gets the most work done but the one who sets an even pace and works at this pace all day. Many workers who need glasses fail to wear them; over 25% of workers studied in foodservice work were found to have uncorrected sight problems.

Experienced workers automatically work safely. They never leave handles of pots sticking out but turn them in, taking care not to leave the handle over a hot burner or pilot light. If a handle is hot, they will put a cloth on it or even sprinkle a bit of salt on the handle to warn themselves and others that it is hot.

Safety conscious workers use a dry cloth, not a wet one, to pick up hot items. They avoid filling pots and pans so full they boil over. They watch to see that their clothing is not exposed to open flames. Any spill is immediately wiped up and a greasy spot may have common salt put on it to prevent others from slipping.

These workers use warning words to signal to the unwary that they are approaching with a heavy load or a hot one. In some establishments, the phrase "man with a baby" is used to warn others of such an approach so they will yield the right of way. If such a phrase is not in keeping with the atmosphere of your establishment, select a warning that is, so all will know instantly there is danger.

Experienced workers do not allow combustible or flammable items near the cooking area. Hot grease is handled gingerly. The danger of sharp objects or broken glass or crockery is known. Many operations do not use glass or china in the work area but use plastic or paper cups, etc.

Knife Handling

Knives should be kept sharp and the proper one selected for the job to be done. A dull knife takes more force and, therefore, can slip more easily. When working with a knife, a safe worker keeps his mind on his job and does not carry on a running conversation with others. Train workers to wash, rinse and sanitize knives and other sharp objects in one process. A knife should never be dropped into water and left to be cleaned later. When cleaning or drying the knife blade, the worker should always keep the sharp edge away from him.

Knives and other sharp items should be kept in racks (magnetic ones are easier to maintain than those with slots) or in drawers separate from other tools. If knives are kept in a drawer, they can be securely rolled in a clean cloth and set at the side of the drawer. Knives should be kept in the same place so the surprise factor of coming on a knife unexpectedly does not lead to an injury. Set up a time for sharpening knives and check to see that metal burrs are removed after grinding.

When using a knife, the worker should grip it firmly, keeping the sharp edge away from him, and cut away from his body and from others. To slice or chop with a French knife, ride the point, never lifting it from the cutting board. Use an up and down motion, letting the cutting edge riding the point cut through items. With the other hand, slowly push the item being cut under the cutting edge. Keep the fingers of this hand folded under the knuckles so the knife cannot cut them.

It is a joy to watch a good worker use a knife correctly. He does not leave knives on counters, tables or chopping blocks. If a knife falls, he won't grab for it but moves out of the way. He does not use knives or cleavers as can openers or hold a knife when transporting other things and never puts anything on top of a knife when it is lying on a flat surface.

Cutting Equipment

Slicers or choppers are frequently responsible for serious accidents; therefore, workers should be given detailed operating instructions like the following: Check slicers, choppers and similar equipment before turning on to be sure they are properly assembled and ready to use. Do not operate the equipment with wet hands. Keep the hands away from the blades and other moving parts when operating the machine. Before making any adjustments, turn the switch off and pull the plug or disconnect switch. With a slicer, turn the gauge to zero to close the blade and make the adjustment. Do not touch or wipe the edge of the blade. After adjusting, reset the blade and turn the machine on.

Choppers with rotating blades should have guards and feeding devices and these should be used. Feed these and the grinder types with a plastic or wooden mallet, *never with the hands.* Do not attempt to dislodge items in them when they are operating.

To adjust the machine, turn off the switch, unplug or disconnect and allow it to stop. Then, do what is required. Be sure you have reassembled the unit correctly and locked all parts into position. Be sure to do this before restarting the machine.

To clean a slicer blade without removing it, the worker can stop the machine and move a moistened cloth from the center to the edge of the blade without touching the cutting edge. A special swab or stick wrapped with a cloth is more desirable for this task than just a cloth. It is preferable, however, to shut the machine down, disassemble and take the blade to the sink for cleaning. In reassembling, set the gauge at zero, replace the guard and reset the gauge. Never leave a slicer running when it is not being used.

Garbage grinders should also be treated with respect. Do not feed them too rapidly or put in items the machine cannot handle. Also, if the machine must be stopped and examined, put it into an OFF position, disconnect the power and wait for it to stop. Examine the inside. If something is caught, remove it, using tongs, if possible. Metal trap catchers should be cleaned daily as instructed by the manufacturer. The unit should be allowed to run again for about a minute before reusing.

Cooking Equipment

Heating equipment can be dangerous. Before lighting gas equipment, the professional worker checks to see that the equipment is in good condition and the unit is in working order. He checks for the odor of gas and turns burners for gas or other fuels on slowly. A lighted match is struck away from the body and kept away from clothing, hair, etc.

The worker should not bend near the match in lighting burners. He should open oven doors and turn on the burner before lighting the match; then strike the match and set it at the lighting vent or proper location for lighting. He should make sure lighting occurs before closing the door and that the burner is working properly. If burner does not light, the worker should turn it off, check to find out what the problem is and correct it; then wait for accumulated gas or other fumes to dissipate before trying to light it again.

If pilots are used for lighting, before leaving the unit workers should check to see that they are on, that the burner lights and is operating correctly. Other instructions should include: clean pilot lights as frequently as burners are cleaned. Burners should not be lit with pots or pans over them. Gas and other fuels should burn with a blue flame. This indicates that the proper mixture of air and fuel is present. Burners should be free of soil which can interfere with proper burning. Ceramic broiler burners that crack should be replaced. It is recommended that all heating equipment be thermostatically controlled.

Electrical heating units should also be checked before using. Water should never be poured on electrical equipment. Before cleaning units, a worker should disconnect or unplug them and no attempt should ever be made to remove a jammed object from a toaster or similar unit with a metal knife, fork or other object; instead the unit should be unplugged and the object released with a wooden skewer.

Other important directions for those responsible for operating electrical equipment follow:

Do not wipe down electrical equipment with a damp cloth without first disconnecting. Keep metal objects away from wiring and electrical connections. Do not leave electrical or other cooking equipment unattended when it is on. Keep hands away from mechanical electrical equipment when operating. Let it stop first. Before plugging in electrical equipment see that the switch is in an OFF position.

Multiple connectors should not be allowed at receptacles and a large number of cords (called octopus connecting) should not be allowed to come from one receptacle. Cords should not be allowed to run under mats, rugs or equipment and both cords and plugs should be examined frequently; connections should be firm and solid. Look for frayed areas in cords or points where breaks may occur.

If circuit breakers or fuses blow, ascertain the cause and correct it. Do not bypass fusing by putting metal or copper pennies into fuse units. If a sudden increase in the use of electrical current occurs, check to ascertain the cause, since this might indicate open grounding with a heavy drain of electrical current.

Keep electrical motors dry. Plugs should be out of sockets when not in use. Do not touch connected electrical equipment with wet hands or plug it in when hands are wet. Switches should be recessed or otherwise guarded so they cannot be turned on by brushing against them. Switches should be of non-conducting material. They should be located for rapid emergency cutoff. Have electrical equipment inspected periodically by an electrician.

Hot grease is usually at higher temperatures than boiling water and can give dangerous burns. Never leave a deep fry kettle or other container holding hot cooking fat on the fire unattended. Do not put too much fat into the kettle or too much food into hot deep fat, especially wet food. As fat gets older, watch to see that it does not foam rather than bubble. When foaming is evident, discard the fat as it will not produce quality items.

Treat electrical fry kettles as electrical equipment and gas-fired ones as gas equipment. Check thermostats frequently. It is advisable, both in gas and electrical as well as old-fashioned "on-the-stove" types of deep fat fryers, to keep fat levels 3 in. or more below the top of the kettle.

Do not allow grease to accumulate on griddles or ranges or in hoods, ducts or filters. In case of a grease fire, smother; do not use water or a fire extinguisher with a water base solution; instead use carbon dioxide or a dry chemical.

The coffee urns should be treated like steam-jacketed kettles and other steam equipment. Always see that the water in the jacket is kept at least as high as the coffee. A stool should be used when cleaning an urn. An urn should never be left unattended when the operator is drawing water or coffee. Spigots and valves should be checked to be sure they are in closed position before filling.

Steam pressure equipment should be checked often to see that automatic valves, safety valves, drains, vents, door locks, safety locks, gaskets and other apparatus are in working order. Do not obstruct or tamper with safety. valves. Provide a steam close-off valve near the equipment in addition to the one at the equipment.

Sanitation Equipment

Safety in the sanitizing areas depends more on the handling of items than on equipment, although the latter should not be neglected. Accidents can happen when using steam, hot water or strong cleaning compounds. Steam pipes and steam are used to boost water to scalding temperatures. Pipes outside the equipment should be insulated and marked. Floors can be dangerous because of the large quantities of water that may spill in the area. Good organization will reduce hazards.

General Work Practices

Handling procedures for knives, other sharp objects and for loading and unloading trays should be checked for safety. The following are important instructions: When filling a tray, first load the center, placing the heaviest items there, then, load the area farthest away from the worker and, finally, put items on the area of the tray closest to the worker. This removes the danger of the tray tipping over and everything on it falling to the floor.

Unstack in the opposite manner, removing items first from the edge closest to the worker. Try to stack so items do not slip in transport. Use paper or cloth napkins on the bottom of trays to prevent slipping; moistened cloths are better than dry ones to prevent slipping.

Trays should not project over carts and be sure stacks of trays are not too high so they tip in transport. Do not stack items that do not stack well. If carrying a tray, carry it either waist high or at shoulder level, holding it off the shoulder on the palm of the hand so one can manipulate the tray and see from side to side as one walks.

Avoid the carrying of too many dishes at one time. Shelving should be deep and strong enough to handle china. Stacking, if not too high, may be permitted. Glasses should not be stacked inside each other. It is preferable that cups and glasses be washed and sanitized in racks, then stored upside down. If china or glass breaks, sweep broken particles together with a broom or brush into a dustpan. Dispose of broken pieces in a receptacle for broken glass, tin cans, etc. and not in regular garbage cans.

Never put hands in a waste receptacle to remove items. Dump the receptacle out onto clean papers and then sort items. Remove chipped or cracked items from service. Heavy china pieces break lighter ones as well as glassware, so separation is recommended as soon as possible.

If an item breaks, remove the pieces with care, preferably with tongs. If an item seems to have broken in a sink that has water in it, drain the sink and then carefully remove the broken pieces. If necessary, remove unbroken items first. Sometimes it is advisable to remove broken pieces from a tote box or sink by pushing them with an object into a dustpan or plate.

Use care in using moving equipment; do not overload and always be able to see where you are going. Watch, when pushing equipment in close quarters, that hands are not pinched. See that care is taken when turning corners so as not to collide with other carts. Check carts to see that they are operated correctly. After stopping a cart, set brakes before leaving it.

A professional worker is careful in opening cans, cutting completely around top with the can opener and then lifting the lid with a spoon or knife to remove it. Dispose of lid immediately in the proper waste receptacle. Do not use this lid as a cover.

To open a can for pouring, use a wedge type opener making two holes opposite each other. The caps on bottles or the lids on glass jars should be removed; otherwise, a sealed container, if thrown into an incinerator, explodes. Sudden changes in temperature also may fracture glass objects.

SAFETY IN SERVICE AND DINING AREAS
A double requirement for safety exists in the service and dining area because, in addition to employees of the foodservice department, the residents and staff may also be there. Many residents do not know how to perceive danger nor how to interpret danger warnings. When something happens, few will move away or know how to avoid the danger. They may not even realize that something is wrong. They may be weak, easily confused and may move irrationally and with difficulty. In emergency situations, they become much more susceptible to injury or accidents.

In an emergency, the welfare of the residents and their protection take precedence over all other factors. Usually, it is best to remove residents and then take steps to correct the problem. Frequently, the nursing staff assumes leadership for removing residents but the plan of action, i.e. what is to be done, should be discussed ahead of time with the foodservice staff.

The most usual accidents in the service or dining area are falls and burns from hot liquids. To prevent them workers should follow these procedures: Sharp items should not be left on the counter where residents can pick them up nor should dishes of hot foods be handed to them. Place hot dishes on underliners on the serving counter where they or the nursing staff can safely pick them up. Do not overfill dishes.

Do not allow mobile equipment, chairs or other equipment to stand in the aisles. See that things are always in the same place. Check tables, chairs and other equipment for splinters, broken legs, etc., removing any that are found for servicing or repair.

Check the floor for grease spots or other things that can cause slipping and a fall. Have spillage removed immediately. Place a chair or item over it while the worker gets a mop and other cleaning equipment. (Have these handy nearby for such emergencies.) Or, another worker can remain at the danger point until the equipment is brought in.

Residents and staff should not be allowed to congregate in the dining area prior to meal time. Non-dietary personnel should not be in food areas unless necessary or authorized.

Draperies, blinds, curtains, tables and chairs should be of fire-resistant materials. Items on walls or curtaining, etc. should be securely fastened. Tables should not be so close together that those serving have to carry food over the heads of those seated. Prompt clean up of "messy" eating areas should occur.

See that the help needed is available to residents while getting to their dining place, being seated and in eating. Provide help, also, in getting them up from the table. This is normally the responsibility of the nursing staff and not of foodservice employees. Crotch straps should be provided to keep some from slipping down while eating. If hot liquids are poured at the table, pour into the container while it is on the table and pour away from the resident, not over him. See that things are reachable. A lazy susan or rotating center may help to avoid dangers in passing. Check to see that the proper diet is given to each person. Color coding and naming of diets are recommended.

Work in the dining and service areas should be well organized and planned. Dishing-up there should be done with all things within reach. When putting counter pans into the steam table, the worker should tilt them slightly away and not have the pans too full. Hot foods should be transported on carts and protected with covers.

Clear dining areas only after residents have left or, if clearing is done while they are there, be sure they will not be subject to any hazards from the work. Keep soiled dish carts and other equipment out of main traffic aisles. Do not overload baskets or carts with soiled items. Separate glassware, silver and dishes when removing them from tables. Keep pieces of china from rubbing over or against each other. This wears away the glaze and reduces service life. Do not carry cups or bowls in stacks.

If foods on trays are transported by cart to residents' rooms, two people should work at the job, one taking the food into the resident while another is working at the cart. Do not block corridors or doorways with carts. See that cart wheels are in line so residents will not trip on them when walking by. Be sure before a tray is carried into a room that there is a place to put it down and that the resident is ready to receive it. Co-ordination with the nursing staff in such delivery is imperative.

FIRE*   The National Fire Protection Association reports
                                   that of 16,500 institutional fires from 1940 to
1950, 11% occurred in hospitals, 12% in penal institutions, 15% in mental institutions and 61% in nusring homes! Over 500 people died in these fires and there was a loss of $27 million. The causes of fires in foodservice departments were identified in another study as being caused 21% of the time by smoking or matches, 16% by electricity, 15% by defects in heating or cooking equipment, 9% from spontaneous combustion (heat build-up in greasy rags or cloths) and 7% from improper rubbish handling.

Three things are needed to start a fire: 1) some combustible material, 2) heat and 3) oxygen. If one or more is not present, a fire cannot start. This is the reason for the rules: Never allow burnable items nearer than 5 ft from an open flame. And: Stored flammable materials should not be in an area where there is apt to be enough heat to set them afire. Flammable materials should be stored in metal cans and on a shelf reserved for them. A metal locker with good ventilation from the outside used especially for such materials is recommended.

Oily wastes or greasy rags should be spread out so heat generated by oxidation of the grease or oil does not light the material. Some advise putting such materials in metal cans and closing thè cans. This is all right if no oxygen gets in; if it does, a fire can develop.

Check your foodservice facilities periodically to see that the three factors for a fire are avoided. A fire safety program should cover 1) safety factors needed to avoid fires; 2) inspections and reports needed; and 3) a training program for employees indicating: a) how to avoid fires; b) how to react to a fire, especially in protecting others; c) how to give the alarm; d) how to fight a fire; e) where fire fighting equipment is and how to use it; and, finally, 4) an evacuation plan.

Employees can be informed of their responsibilities in case of fire by

---

*Assistance in setting up a fire safety program can be obtained from The National Fire Protection Association, 60 Batterymarch St., Boston, Mass., or the National Board of Fire Underwriters, 85 John St., New York City, 10007. Information on fire fighting equipment can be obtained from the Underwriters Laboratories, Inc., 207 Ohio St., Chicago, Ill., 60607.

written instructions, through information posted on bulletin boards, in meetings and discussions and through drills. It is essential that they know what they are responsible for. Whether they are to move residents to a safer place or have them leave the building or whether the nursing staff should immediately take over and do this should be known.

The employees should be taught to identify the type of fire and how to fight it. They should understand how fire spreads and the dangers of smoke inhalation to themselves and others. Alternate plans of action should be established and all should know them.

Time is extremely important in fire prevention. A small fire uncontrolled for a short time can quickly become a raging inferno. It is important that avenues for the spread of fire and sources of air be cut off, if possible. Employees should demonstrate the technique of using a blanket to wrap around an employee whose clothing or hair is on fire. All should know where fire exits are. Check also to see that fire doors, stairs and other facilities for fire protection are usable and are sufficient to protect employees.

If a fire does break out, first be sure that unauthorized personnel are immediately moved out. Have someone sound the alarm or, after residents and others who may be endangered are safe, sound the alarm and call the fire department. All doors, windows, air ducts or other factors allowing fire to spread or acting as sources of air should be shut off. Ventilation systems should be shut down; utilities may have to be cut off as well. At this point, the fire should be evaluated and if there is reason to think it can be controlled by foodservice staff members, fire fighting equipment and measures to control the fire should be used. Individuals should be assigned to specific jobs or duties in case of fire so they are prepared to act. Train workers to identify gas or oil odors and to report them. Action should be taken calmly and without panic. Some responsible person should be in charge and should see that when a fire cannot be fought, all individuals leave the area. A census is recommended to see that all individuals have left the area.

Kinds of Fires

There are three kinds of fires and each must be fought differently. A Class A fire is the burning of ordinary combustible materials such as gas, wood, rubbish or rags; a Class B fire is the burning of grease, oil, gas or a petroleum substance and a Class C fire is one caused by electricity.

A Class A fire is fought with water-base extinguishing materials. These may be water pump tanks, air pressure tanks, gas cartridge tanks or foam type tanks. A tank is needed for every 1250 sq ft of floor space in the foodservice area.

A Class B fire should be smothered by keeping oxygen from it. This can be done with a blanket, the lid of a pot or with fire extinguishers that give off foam, dry chemicals or carbon dioxide. Some substances that smother may be dangerous in a grease fire, such as carbon tetrachloride which can break down from heat into a poisonous gas. Never try to beat out a grease fire. Soda and salt, if thrown on a grease fire, can be helpful in a minor way, but only in a minor way. It is better not to depend upon them since valuable time may be lost.

A Class C fire may start from an electrical short, an overheated electrical motor or from other electrical causes. Frequently, some combustible material, such as grease, is also present. It is important that the extinguishing material be non-conducting to electricity and, therefore, no water-base extinguisher should be used. Use, instead, a dry chemical or carbon dioxide type extinguisher. Carbon dioxide is an excellent fire deterrent as is evident from the above discussion. In addition, it is not harmful to food.

Small fire extinguishers holding 2½ gal or about 20 lb in weight should be installed so their tops are not over 5 ft above the floor. If they are larger, then the height of the top should not be more than 3½ ft above the floor. The fire department or fire insurance company can be helpful in indicating how often fire fighting equipment must be checked. Invite the fire department personnel or insurance company to inspect the foodservice department and make suggestions on how to improve the fire safety program.

Both an automatic sprinkler system and an automatic fire alarm system should be installed in the foodservice area. One should not be looked upon as a substitute for the other. The automatic alarm should not be expected to react as quickly as an individual might; therefore, see that emergency numbers to be used in case of fire are posted near telephones employees can reach. If there is a loud speaker system available, see that employees know how to use this to inform others of a fire.

Since grease fires are common in kitchens and these frequently occur in ventilating filters over cooking equipment, it is recommended that automatic closing doors be installed in ducts. These doors will close when the temperature rise becomes dangerous. It may also be advisable to install automatic dry chemical extinguishers which will activate in case of fire in hoods and ducts. Remember, however, that fire prevention is better than fire fighting. The best part of any fire program is the part that prevents a fire, not the plan for combatting fire.

NOTE: The bibliography cited for Sanitation, Chapter VIII, also applies to Chapter IX.

X: LAYOUT AND EQUIPMENT

INTRODUCTION

Food quality and cost are affected, to a considerable extent, by the design of the foodservice area and its equipment. A good layout does not come about by chance; it results from a great deal of effort and detailed planning.

Many factors need to be considered and none of these can safely be overlooked. It is too late after a foodservice goes into operation to correct errors, omissions or inadequacies. Too many foodservice operations are locked in the concrete of poor planning from which they never can remove themselves.

That too many foodservice operations are poorly planned becomes clear when we note the short period of time that elapses between the completion of these operations and the date when the need for "remodeling" is announced. Doing the job right in the first place pays off in an efficient operation that is able to meet the demands made upon it.

THE PLANNING TEAM Four areas of thinking and responsibility must be represented in planning a foodservice layout; those of 1) ownership, 2) operation; 3) planner and 4) builder. Each is dependent upon the other and participants from all four areas must work closely together to achieve a successful plan.

Ownership

In the beginning, someone must establish in detail the need for the facility, determine what it must do at what cost and indicate the essential factors or modes of operation. Allowances or limitations of space, money, location, etc. must also be established. This area of responsibility on the planning team is frequently called *management* or *ownership*. In many respects, it is the controlling member of the planning group since it establishes the basic criteria.

Operation

Management is usually unable to indicate in detail how the work should be done nor does it know the essentials required to do the job. A second viewpoint called *operation* must take this responsibility. The individual representing operation should know how to design the spaces and select the equipment to do the job. He must indicate the space, design and equipment required to fulfill ownership's criteria of need.

Requirements for operation need to be established as guidelines for planning. This may be done by a dietitian, foodservice consultant or other competent person. Some individuals may know how to operate a food facility extremely well after it is completed but may not be able to translate this ability into planning knowledge. Knowing how to produce a good meal is one thing, but knowing how to establish the essentials in layout and equipment to make such production possible is much different and requires a different kind of competency.

Planner

A third viewpoint or competence is needed and this comes from the professional planner or designer. This usually is an architect. It is his responsibility to interpret the ideas of the other two areas of responsibility and then create a material plan which adequately details all requirements, putting these into a professional plan drawn to scale. The planner should not overrule the recommendations of the other two viewpoints unless they are in error or cannot be translated into practical reality.

It is the planner's responsibility to indicate ways in which costs can be reduced, better facilities designed or other improvements made. Using his professional knowledge and experience, he should adapt the thinking of his teammates to conform to codes of construction, building and material requirements and other factors. He should indicate where new ideas or materials on the market can lead to an improved plan.

Builder

The fourth area of responsibility is the *builder* who should be able to take the plan and translate it into a building with its equipment ready to function in the manner intended. Advice based on his professional knowledge and experience should be sought but he should not seek to impose his ideas on the others, unless the ideas he is advancing help to improve the plan under discussion.

The Team

It is essential that representatives of all four areas of responsibility work together as a planning team. Co-operation and an appreciation of the viewpoints of the others are needed. There should be a willingness to compromise.

Establishing the plan too quickly may result in producing an inferior plan. Frequently, a plan evolves slowly. Originally there may be many gray areas where matters are not decided, requirements named or even a rough plan made; however, as each contributes his part, a workable plan begins to take shape. Time must be allowed so the ideas of the team members can be amalgamated and can mature.

Once a plan is decided on and construction is started, no changes should be made unless some gross error is discovered, an unexpected cost arises or some other major factor materializes. If a change is necessary, representatives of all viewpoints should be consulted to decide on the best course of action to follow.

PLANNING PRINCIPLES

The menu and the type of service will dictate design, the space, the equipment and other factors needed in the facility. To be sure that no detail is missed, requirements should be established by following through, in detail, the steps that will occur in planning, purchasing, receiving, storing, preparation, production, service and cleanup.

Flow

The flow of work should be continuous with no criss-crossing or backtracking. Storage spaces should be near the receiving area and preparation areas near storage spaces. If foods are moved through preparation to production and thence to service in a continuous process, quality is improved and efficiency gained; holding items between processing steps usually increases costs and lowers quality. Direct delivery from receiving to preparation, since it avoids storage, reduces time and labor requirements. Distances between sections in the layout should be minimized. Provisions should be made for good materials handling.

To make sure that the plan is right, use a pencil to trace the flow of work. Be constantly critical. Is the dishwashing section located so it is convenient to the point where soiled dishes arrive and is it also located conveniently close to the service area where the clean items must go? Most pots and pans come from the dishup area and from the cook's section but return to the cook's section.

Is waste and garbage moved with as little handling as possible and on equipment that eliminates heavy lifting?

Remember, also, that work flow revolves around record keeping; food purchasing; personnel management; coming to work; getting ready; finishing and leaving; eating and resting and many other things. All of these functions must be co-ordinated into the flow pattern to be sure a highly functional facility is obtained.

BUILDING BLOCKS OF PLANNING

A layout is composed of sections joined together in a closely integrated whole. Sections are composed of work centers similarly joined together.

The Work Center

The basic component of a layout is a work center. (See Fig. 10-1 and 10-2.) This is an area in which closely related jobs are done. For instance, in a cook's section there may be a mixing center where items are first processed before cooking. There will also be a cooking center and perhaps a roasting and slicing center.

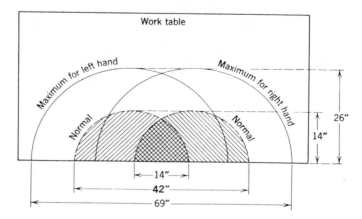

Fig. 10-1. *Chart of a maximum and normal work center for a sitting man of medium size. (10% less for a woman of medium size)*

In a small layout, work centers may be joined so mixing, baking and slicing may be done in one area and roasting and cooking in another work center. Work flow should move continuously and not back-track or criss-cross. Work is done best if one set of work activities utilizing repetition of motion occurs at the location and the job then moves on to another area for the next group of closely related work motions. Work should move in proper sequence from one work center to the other.

The Section

A section is an area in which work centers, doing very similar types of food production or work, are joined together. For instance, in a large food-service there may be a baking section, a pantry section, a cook's section, a pot and pan section, a dishwashing section, etc.; however, a smaller facility is apt to join several of these sections into one. The work centers joined together should be related. For instance, in a baking section there may be a mixing

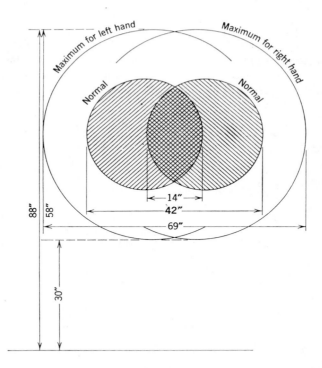

Fig. 10-2. *Chart of maximum and normal work center for a standing man of medium size. (10% less for a woman of medium size)*

and panning center, an oven center and a dishup and preparation center—a dishwashing center would not be included since such work is not related to the work done in the baking section. In this area, also, work flow should be continuous without criss-crossing or back-tracking.

The Layout

Sections joined together make a layout. Again, in joining sections, attention is paid to flow, criss-crossing and back-tracking; care is also taken to see that the sections are properly interrelated. Thus, the service area will be close to the cook's section so distance of travel is reduced.

Just as matter is composed of molecules and molecules are composed of atoms, a layout (matter) will be composed of sections (molecules) and sections will be composed of work centers (atoms). Good basic planning of work centers and later skillfully joining them into sections, then doing the same in joining sections into a layout is the secret of arriving at a successful plan.

Planning a Work Center

It is advisable in planning work centers, either physically or very carefully mentally, to go through the work procedures done in the center to see whether distances of reach are correct, whether tools, materials and equipment are located correctly and whether the work flow is right. Place pieces of newspaper on the floor or use chairs or other objects to indicate where equipment will be and then go through the work motions. Change locations and see if distances of travel are reduced or better work flow achieved. Then, draw the work center to scale; ¼ in. to 1 ft is advised.

Superimpose over your plan a transparency of a work center drawn to a similar scale. Does your work center come within the limits of the maximum reach shown on the transparency? Where are materials and tools located? Within or without the work center limits? (See Fig. 10-3.) Take a pencil and draw on the work center plan the paths the worker travels. A lot of lines indicates that more planning needs to be done to reduce travel.

Next, join the work centers together to make a section. Again draw lines to show travel and work flow. Change the arrangement and repeat the line drawing. When you have the best arrangement possible, join sections together, going through the same procedures. Perhaps, by the time you have finished working on the layout, the internal arrangement of work centers within a section may have to be changed or the work flow within a work center may have to be changed.

While such planning is time-consuming and requires a lot of work, it is worthwhile. Besides, it is a lot of fun. The reward for the effort and time comes when one sees how the actual fulfillment of the plan in operation gives a highly satisfactory food facility.

LOCATING THE FACILITY   The foodservice should be located where there is ready access to all parts of the building. Deliveries of food and supplies should be convenient and move short distances to storage or production or service. Prepared food should move in the shortest distance possible to patrons.

Plan good employee parking near the facility but not so close that it is

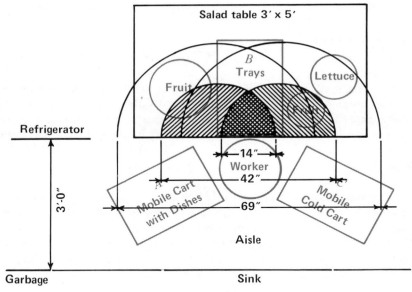

A Reach for plates at left.
B Construct salads.
C Store completed salads at right.

Fig. 10-3. *Chart of maximum and normal reach superimposed over a work center. This procedure is helpful in designing work centers and can also be used to set up work centers into sections.*

convenient to move unauthorized items from the facility into cars.

The facility should be where working conditions are pleasant. While we have gone a long way in reducing the need for sunlight with modern lighting, providing sunlight does help to improve working atmosphere. Locating the foodservice down in the basement with the "sewer pipes" usually reduces efficiency, increases costs and also lowers worker morale.

Frequently, separating storage from preparation and production and separating service from production increases costs and lowers food quality. The location of all sections on one level is recommended. If possible, avoid partitions. If properly planned, even the dishwashing section need not be enclosed. Partitioning is recommended only when privacy, security or other reasons require it. Enclose offices with glass enclosures as much as possible.

SPACE REQUIREMENTS

If the total space required by the equipment is known, multiplying this by 3 will give a quick approximation of total space needs. Many planners originally allow from 20 to 30 sq ft per bed for the food facility, not including the dining area, and later, as the plan evolves, reduce or increase this. Small operations will usually require 30 or more sq ft per bed. The final criteria in deciding on space needs will be:

1. Menu items required.
2. Type of foodservice.
3. Quantity prepared.
4. Service and distribution.
5. Storage needs.
6. Future expansion.

Dining space requirements must be added to this. Individual conditions may dictate different space needs; therefore, each operation must be planned to suit specific operating conditions. If the facility is located in a rural area where deliveries may not be as frequent as in an urban area, the storage space may have to be larger. If patrons are served in their rooms and not in a dining area, space needs will be reduced.

Plan at least 8 ft high ceilings and preferably higher. With the heat and moisture that develop in a food processing center, an 8 ft ceiling is often too low. Allow 5 to 6 ft for main aisles and 4 ft for secondary aisles. Work aisles in a work center between equipment are usually 42 in. wide but, if mobile equipment is moved in and out, 4 ft may be required. Oven or steam cooker doors that open out take up aisle space and planning must provide for this.

It is preferable to locate related equipment in a work center side by side, but if it cannot be located that way, then place pieces opposite each other, keeping the aisle between equipment 42 in. wide or, at minimum, 36 in. Minimum door width should be 42 in. but where mobile equipment is to be moved through, provide 48 in. or more.

UTILITY REQUIREMENTS   The importance of good lighting, good air, comfortable working conditions and similar factors in increasing the productivity of workers and improving the quality of work done is sometimes missed. Usually there is very little cost difference between adequate and poor planning for lighting. A facility may have an adequate number of lights of the right wattage but because of poor placement lighting will still be inadequate.

Lighting

Requirements for lighting in the various sections of a foodservice department are given, with the other requirements for these areas, in the following pages; these recommendations should be followed. In general, no area should have less than 20 ft candles and, where work is done, there should be 50 ft candles.

There should be no glare and workers should not have to stand in their own shadows or the shadows of equipment. Consult a competent authority on the final lighting plan.

Ventilating and Air Conditioning

Air from production centers should be exhausted at a rate that insures a complete change of air every 5 min during moderate weather and this should be increased in hot weather or in warmer climates to insure a complete air change every 3 min. Plans should exhaust air so drafts are not on workers. Either hoods over cooking equipment or individual exhaust units on equipment can be used.

Pulling air that is moist, hot or filled with cooking aromas out by individual pieces of exhaust equipment sometimes is preferred over exhausting from a general hood area. Fresh air should come from the outdoors. Where considerable heat, moisture or aroma build-up occurs, catching the air overhead in a dropped ceiling or hood and pulling it away helps to prevent its transfer to other kitchen areas.

Having 2 speeds on ventilating equipment makes it possible to operate at full speed in warmer weather and at lower speed during cooler weather. Exhaust ducts should be equipped with automatic closing vents to prevent drafts from going up them in case of fire. Filters should be easily removable from hoods and sized so they can be washed in a dishwasher.

If the air pressure in a production center is greater than that in the dining or other areas of the building, cooking aromas, heat and moisture will be carried out into these areas. In this case, the production center has a positive pressure and the outer areas a negative pressure. The negative pressures in the production center should be determined during the planning so that the air flow goes into this area and not out of it. A proper air exhaust system will do this.

Kitchens are seldom air-conditioned but some may have air conditioning in certain sections. Too much heat and moisture buildup occurs in many of the kitchen areas to make air conditioning feasible. It is frequently too difficult to provide an adequate amount of cooled air since so much air must be exhausted. If air conditioning in a dining or other area is brought into the kitchen, some cooling results. Such air should pass through a filter with 80% efficiency as judged by the National Bureau of Standards dust-spot method on atmospheric dust.

About 15 cu ft per min (cfm) is a desirable input of fresh, ventilated air into a dining area with perhaps slightly less needed if the room is air conditioned. Some air conditioning is operated through 2 units rather than 1 so 1 can be closed down when the load is less. This also assures that 1 unit will operate should the other break down. A competent authority should be consulted in planning ventilation and air conditioning needs.

Noise

Noise can reduce labor efficiency and worker harmony; it can also be transferred to other areas where it can cause resident or staff problems. Hard floors and walls, metal table and sink tops, large pots and pans and other factors in the foodservice area contributes to noise buildup and its transfer.

Isolate noisy equipment or install it where it will not bother workers or others. Use sound deadening equipment whenever possible. Dropped ceilings can be used to catch noise and, if sound deadening materials are used in them, ceilings can capture noise. Reducing the quantity of hard tile on walls can also help, so if a wall does not need tile, omit it. It is important that ceilings have sound deadening materials on them but not of the type that cannot be cleaned frequently or that absorbs moisture.

Water

Enough water at the proper temperature and proper pressure (20 to 30 lb/sq in. (psi)) is essential. Some authorities plan 4 gal/hr/meal at 180°F with heating capacity of 2 gal/hr/meal and a storage of 80% of total requirements. Thus, if 80 meals were to be served, 320 gal/hr would be needed with heating equipment able to heat 160 gal/hr; the storage tank should hold 250 gal.

Other authorities plan a total water requirement of 5 gal/meal, a third of which is cold and the remainder hot. Of the hot water needed, 60% should be 160°F to be supplied to equipment such as sinks, steam-jacketed kettles and the other 40% should be 180°F at equipment. This can be accomplished by having all hot water at 160°F and using boosters at equipment where needed to raise water temperature to 180°F.

Of the total requirement of 5 gal/meal, 55% will be needed at peak service, 28% before and 17% after. Providing a lead of about 25% of requirements in a storage tank is a good guide for establishing storage requirements. In some instances, instant heaters are being installed at some equipment to provide water at the proper temperature. Hot water should be circulated by a continuous pump so hot water is immediately available when the water tap is turned on.

Steam

A central boiler can provide steam for the food facility's needs. If it is at a higher pressure than required, steam pressure reducers will provide the right pressure. If such steam is not available, equipment that manufactures its own steam can be purchased.

For steam cleaning purposes, etc., a steam boiler can be installed in the food facility so garbage cans, carts and other equipment can be steam cleaned. If such steam comes from a central boiler, reduce it to the right pressure if need be. For cleaning, use a vacuum breaker type steam hose mounted about 54 in. above the floor and equipped with a suitable squeeze valve.

Steam equipment capacity is rated on the boiler horsepower required. For instance, a steam-jacketed kettle requires about 0.08 HP/gal of its capacity. One boiler HP provides 34½ lb of steam per hr.

Plumbing

A good plumbing plan will be required. See that 2 in. pipes running from the sink and other drains are connected at the closest point possible to larger piping. Good pitch should be provided. Pipes 4 or 6 in. in diam should be used to move wastes to main sewer connections. Easily accessible cleanout areas will be needed.

Check areas on the plan where water is apt to collect and see that a floor drain is put there. Floor drains should be directly in front of walk-in doors or nearby on the side. Do not put them inside refrigerated spaces and especially not in freezers, since water in them will freeze and clog drains.

Electricity

Consult your local electrical company or equipment manufacturers on electrical requirements. On the plan, check to see that sufficiently heavy wiring is specified to carry electrical loads. Even on 120-volt (v) equipment, 3-prong wiring is used. The third prong in such wiring grounds the equipment so, should a short* develop, the danger of electrical shock is reduced.

Watch amperage of circuits. Normally, 15 to 20 or even 30-ampere (amp) circuits are provided for 120-v lighting or light equipment. Heavy equipment circuits, as used in ovens, ranges and fans, will have higher amperage and higher voltage.

One can calculate amperage by dividing volts into wattage (W ÷ V). Thus, a 150-watt light on a 120-v circuit pulls 1.25 amps (150 ÷ 120). A range pulling 10,000 watts (10 Kw) on a 240-v line uses over 40 amps (10,000 ÷ 240). Most equipment tags will give volts and wattages; some even give amperages. Equipment manufacturers also list these factors for their equipment in their brochures.

A circuit is never loaded to capacity; see that a sufficient number of branch circuits are installed to meet needs. Provide overload fusing at equipment so, if a short develops or an overload of electricity flows through the

*A "short" is a term used to indicate when electricity does not flow in a planned manner through equipment or wiring. For instance, should a bare positive and a bare negative wire be crossed, the flow of electricity changes at this point, shortening the distance of flow. When this happens, an extra load of electricity with high heat buildup occurs. This trips a circuit breaker, stopping the flow. If it does not, a fire is apt to occur.

wire, the fuse at the equipment will burn out before harm is done to the equipment. Circuit breakers at the panel (fuse) box will also trip when this happens but, to play safe, fusing should be added at the equipment.

Watch the electrical installation, noting how wiring is insulated and connected to equipment. Heavy equipment on high voltages also should be grounded at the site even though it is 3-prong. This extra precaution may save a life. It is less costly to run equipment on higher voltages than on lower ones. Motors or other equipment operating on the wrong voltage have a short operating life.

Almost all electrical current today is *alternating* which means that the flow is not in one but, rather, in two directions with positive and negative currents alternating very rapidly. If it alternates 60 times per sec, the current is called 60-cycle current. Microwave units operate on a frequency of alternation of 2450 megacycles (2450 million cycles per sec.) In this case, the unit takes 60-cycle current and changes it into the higher cycle frequency.

Gas

Gas supply lines into the building and thence to equipment should be adequately sized to meet requirements. Check with equipment manufacturers to ascertain the gas load required for equipment. Check the total load to see that enough gas is delivered to keep pressures up. Venting is required for gas equipment. The American Gas Association, 605 Third Ave., New York City ments. The local gas company can also be helpful. Your local electrical company can be helpful on electrical problems.

Floors, Walls and Ceilings

Good floors are essential. They should be non-slippery, durable and impervious to moisture. Quarry tile is an excellent flooring; terrazzo is also very good, except that it may pit and it can be slippery. Concrete is inexpensive but breaks, cracks and is not attractive. All three are hard on the feet, legs and bodies of workers.

Wood is good but it is not impervious to moisture and soil. Cork or rubber will not be found to be durable in heavy work areas. Vinyl is durable, resilient and attractive, but may be slippery.

Asphalt is similar to vinyl, but less expensive and not quite as durable. Use grease-resistant asphalt. Install asphalt instead of vinyl or other composition coverings on floors that are on-grade; that is, where the cement or basic floor is on the ground. Asphalt and some other types of flooring prevent a moisture transfer when the floor is on-grade. Good installation is required to obtain a satisfactory floor.

Walls should be smooth plaster and covered with tile in areas where considerable cleaning will have to be done. Painted plaster is satisfactory in other areas. Make sure that paints used are durable, washable and do not mold, if they are to be used in areas of high heat and moisture. Special paints are available for damp areas or where other problems arise that damage paint. To reduce wall damage from mobile equipment, install corner and wall guards, specify sufficiently wide doors and aisles and provide a storage area for mobile equipment.

Ceilings should be of materials that reduce noise but still can be cleaned easily and do not absorb moisture. Dropped ceilings with a space above usually make for cooler work areas, providing the ceiling is not dropped too low. (Also check ceiling information in section on noise, p. 427.)

SECTION REQUIREMENTS

Each section in the food facility requires specific space and equipment plus proper arrangement of the equipment in the space to meet essential needs. While these needs may vary between large and small operations, most requirements mentioned here will be common to both.

Receiving

The receiving area should be located where there is easy access in and out of the health facility but not where it is in open view of the main entrance. Proper screening may help to avoid this.

The receiving platform should be 2-1/2 to 3 ft high and 8 ft deep, with a length sufficient to receive and temporarily hold deliveries as well as garbage, cartons and other items requiring removal. There should be a cover or roof over this section.

Some planners allow 1/2 to 2/3 sq ft of space per person served per day when making early estimates of space for the receiving area. If this area provides a refrigerated garbage area and a can washing area, there must be additional space. Sometimes an incinerator is located close to this area; if so, provide a work area near it and also a space to hold items awaiting disposal.

If mobile equipment is used to bring in items, there should be steel frames and doors as well as bumpers on walls and corners. The main door should be double and about 6 ft or more wide. The floors should have a bearing weight of 250 to 300 lb/sq ft, should be of concrete or some other durable, hard, impermeable material and be sloped to a drain. A water and possibly a steam hose connection should be nearby. Small equipment needed to handle deliveries, such as scales, conveyors, elevators, skids, dollies, hand trucks, etc., should be specified. About 25 to 35 ft-candles of light are required.

Storage

About 4½ sq ft/bed or person served gives a broad estimate of storage space needed. Shelving should be movable or mobile, easily cleaned with adjustable shelves; it should also be durable enough to hold bearing weights. Shelving should be at least 8 in. off the floor and the top shelf should not be over 72 in. above the floor. Provide 20 to 30 ft-candles of light in the general storage areas but from 40 to 50 in areas where records are maintained or items checked or weighed.

The dry storage area should be well ventilated and lighted and have a constant temperature of 70°F. This area will store canned goods, flour, beans, sugar and general grocery items. Specify bins or other storage for sacked foods that must be portioned out to production in smaller quantities. These bins should be on rollers and can be stored under shelving installed for light items. Allow 4 ft for aisle space.

A separate storage area should be provided for cleaning supplies, reserve linens, dishes, equipment, mops, buckets and other items. Dish and utensil storage should be protected from contamination by insects, rodents and other vermin in the general work areas.

In larger facilities, a vegetable room may be needed for holding squash, firm tomatoes, potatoes, tropical fruits and similar items. Temperatures in this area should not be below 50°F and not above 70°F, but preferably lower.

The floors in these three storage areas should carry a bearing weight of 250 to 300 lb/sq ft and planners often allow ½ sq ft per person served per day for the three.

A walk-in refrigerator is feasible when 300 to 400 meals/day are served. In larger facilities, 2 walk-ins may be feasible, 1 for meats and dairy products and 1 for general use. About 40% of the total refrigeration space of the operation will be needed for meats; 20% for dairy and 40% for fruits, vegetables and other foods.

A walk-in should have shelving that is 2 ft deep and aisles should be 42 in. The minimum width for a walk-in is 8 ft and depth of about 10 ft is minimum. A 42 in. wide door is needed with provision for emergency opening from the inside. Flooring in the walk-in should be even with the outside floors so mobile equipment can be moved in and out.

From 20 to 35 lb of food per cu ft can be stored in a refrigerator. Provide about 20 to 35 cu ft of refrigeration, including reach-ins, for every 100 meals served.

See that walk-in insulation is water-proof, non-absorbent and vermin-proof, of 4 in. deep cork or equal. Walls should be lined with non-absorbent, sanitary, hard-surfaced materials, impervious to moisture and soil. Refrigerants should be non-toxic, non-irritating and non-flammable. The meat and dairy box should be at an even 35°F under normal use and 40°F should be maintained in the general storage box. Compressors should be automatically controlled.

Select reach-in refrigerators made by reliable manufacturers. They should be easily cleaned, meet the National Sanitation Foundation (NSF) requirements and have strong doors and shelving that is removable and adjustable. Provide a drain under each unit. If the refrigerator is to take 18 x 26 in. or 14 x 18 in. or other size trays and pans, check to see that it will do so.

Some foodservice operations find mobile reach-in refrigerators useful. They allow for better work center arrangement and flexibility and also can be moved to deliver cold items to points where they are needed.

Low temperature storage (freezer) units in small facilities can either be the chest or upright type. If they are required, walk-in freezers should usually open into a refrigerator so lost cold air will be utilized in the refrigerated area. Temperatures should be 0 to -10°F. About 45 lb of food/cu ft can be stored, providing food is contained in cases.

The walls, floors and other factors in a walk-in freezer should be about the same as for a walk-in refrigerator, except the ice melt capacity must be greater and 6 in. or more of cork insulation, or equal, is needed. Some facilities plan 6 in. for both refrigeration and freezer units so if a refrigeration unit must be changed to a freezer, all that is needed is that the refrigeration equipment (ice melt capacity) be increased to establish the freezing temperature required.

The Ingredient Room

Larger facilities may need an ingredient room where items can be pre-weighed or portioned before sending them to production. Usually a space 10 ft wide and 6 ft deep is required, although more space may be needed if the operation is larger.

The ingredient room actually can be part of the dry storage area but it is more convenient if located close to dry storage and other storage areas, so items can be easily assembled for delivery to the production units. Proper weighing equipment, packaging materials, tables, shelving and delivery equipment must be provided.

Preparation

The preparation unit should be located near the storage and production centers. The space and equipment required will depend upon the quantity of food processed there. If ready-to-use meats, fish and poultry are purchased and only minimum amounts of fruits and vegetables have to be prepared for production, the area can be omitted.

If vegetables are to be prepared in quantity, provide a double sink large enough to hold bulky or leafy products. See that adequate drain board space, sloped to give good runoff of water, is provided. Also, specify an overhead spray. In larger units, a work table is needed. Some mechanical equipment, such as peelers and choppers, may be desirable. There should be mobile bins and carts.

The floors should be non-slip type and a good floor drain should be installed. In larger operations, a separate meat preparation unit may be needed but in most operations vegetables, fruits, meats and all other foods can be prepared for production in one small area.

Thick cutting boards make it possible to avoid the need for a meat block. Few foodservices, even larger ones, will need a meat saw, etc. Sometimes the preparation unit can be combined with the pantry section where salads, sandwiches, juicing of fruits, etc. are scheduled. In this case, meat preparation may be transferred to the cook's section.

In the preparation section, as in all others, planners should be sure that mechanical and other equipment requirements are not in excess of needs; in this country more facilities are over-equipped than are under-equipped. Efficiency can be lost in over-equipping as well as under-equipping.

Where the volume of work is small, buying special attachments for a mixer is usually recommended rather than buying a separate food chopper, slicer, etc. Small facilities may find that hand work does the job much more quickly with less labor than using mechanical equipment. For instance, if 10 lb of potatoes are to be pared, it may be more efficient to hand peel them than to get the parer ready, do the job and then clean the equipment.

The Cook's Section

In small facilities, more than just cooking may be done in the cook's section; baking, pantry work, preparation and even serving may also be done there. As the number to be served increases, separate sections are added and then the cook's unit may become a highly specialized cooking section only.*

Since a number of different production needs may be met here, planning must take all of them into consideration and should provide flexibility. It should be possible to change work centers easily, using mobile equipment to assist in this. Dual-purpose equipment should be specified wherever possible.

Space allocations should include: at least 4 to 6 ft of linear space for the work table—10 ft is normal; it should be 30 in. deep or 36 in. deep if items are stored in the back area. If workers work across from each other on such a table, make it 42 or 48 in. wide. Since ranges are about 30 in. wide, and work aisles usually 42 in., with a table 30 in. wide, the area at a minimum has to be 8½ ft wide; however, 10 ft is usually required.

The sink should provide good drainage and there should be adequate storage space for pots and pans, small equipment and other items. Pot and pan and utensil storage can be located over the work table on a utensil rack. Where space limitations make it necessary, shelving over the work table or under or on the back of the range can be planned. Don't forget to specify a good, heavy duty, commercial can opener.

---

*Few foodservices for small health facilities will require a special dietary preparation unit. The cook's section can usually do the work required.

Minimum equipment will be a range with oven space, refrigeration, a work table, a sink and, perhaps, a mixing machine. If the facility has over 75 beds, other desirable equipment might be a steam kettle, compartment steamer, a broiler and several small trunnion kettles. Water should be available over the range and the steam kettle. There should be a lavatory nearby for washing hands.

If the above cooking equipment is not provided for a unit over 75 beds, an additional range top may be needed. Even smaller units may find the need for additional oven space beside that provided in a range. All equipment should be of the heavy duty, commercial type. Home or light duty equipment does not perform adequately.

Lighting should be 50 ft-candles, with a minimum of 20 in non-work areas. Allow about 2 sq ft of space in this section per bed or person served; however, this may vary if sections are combined.

In this section, as well as in all others, see that equipment provides correct working heights. The normal working height is 34 in. for tables and sinks although, frequently, this is too low, especially for those over normal height. However, in some areas, such as New York City, where small statured Puerto Ricans may be employed, work heights may have to be dropped. Many sinks and work tables today are specified at 37 in. high or more. Sink bottoms are specified as being 16 in. from the floor rather than 12 in.

Baking Section

It may be that so few desserts and bakery items need preparation that a baking section is not needed. However, if volume warrants a baking section, it should contain a work table, sink facilities (or the possibility of using the cook's), mixer (or, again the cook's), oven space, refrigeration (or, cook's) and storage for breads, desserts, etc. Storage space will be needed for pots and pans and equipment. Bins for holding sugar, flour and other loose items may be needed. In larger operations, a hot plate and even a small trunnion kettle may be required.

Some planners specify a 2-deck oven with decks 38 in. wide and 28 in. deep equipped with an additional removable baking shelf, so baking and roasting can both be done without an additional oven. Or, a convection oven is installed in the baking unit. In larger facilities, provide a cooling rack. A good baker's scale will also be needed.

Pantry

Only in larger facilities will a pantry section be needed. In most operations, this can be combined with the cook's or preparation section or the baking and pantry sections can be combined.

A mixer may be needed and the cook's mixer may be used by pantry workers. If various workers use a mixer, provide individual mixing bowls, reducers and other equipment for each section or worker, since jurisdiction over such equipment may become a problem. A 10 or 20 qt mobile mixer may find good use where several people working in different sections share it.

In larger facilities, a separate refrigerator may be needed to hold the dressings, perishable foods and beverages, juices, salads, relishes, fruit, fruit cups, cold plates and other foods that need to go from the pantry section into storage. If any cooking must take place in producing pantry items, see that the cook's section is conveniently located so cooking can be done there or specify a small hot plate for the pantry. Provide 50 ft-candles of light.

An ice machine may be located in the pantry. Where it is to provide ice for the nursing staff as well as the food production services, it should be located where it can be used without entry into the foodservice area by the nursing staff. See that ice needs for food preparation and service as well as nursing services are adequately estimated. Consult manufacturers of such equipment on the size of equipment needed to furnish the ice needed. Proper drains should be installed for the ice equipment; also, to be sure that ice is handled in a sanitary manner, the right equipment should be at hand.

Serving

A separate serving area is desirable even in small facilities but, if space is not available, the cook's section can be used for this, with hot food being held on the range or in the oven, dishes heated in the oven and cold foods brought over at the last minute for dishup.

Concentrate on rapid, neat dishup with fast movement out after foods are plated. Dishes should be at a proper temperature when dishup occurs; hot—not warm—for hot foods and chilled—not room temperature—for cold foods. Find the right answers for these questions: Where will ice cream storage be? Hot beverages are prepared and served in what manner? How are chilled and hot foods kept at their *proper* temperatures? The following dishup and patron receipt temperatures should be achieved:

	Dishup °F	Patron Receipt °F
Gravies, soups, coffee, tea, etc.	180-190	160
Entree foods and some meat dishes	160	140
Rare meats	140	140
Vegetables, etc.	160	145-150
Chilled foods	30-40	40-45
Frozen foods	20 or lower	24

In this area, a serving counter with 3 hot compartments can be used. It may be mobile or fixed and should be at least 8 ft long. A moving belt is helpful but not necessary; storage should be available above it. Move in dishes and additional foods in mobile units, so workers can have all things required within easy reach. Fast, rapid, neat service should be sought. It is frustrating to see good food lose its acceptability because it becomes cold or warm or is unattractively served.

Many factors need consideration in the service unit; for instance, where will flatware, napkins, salts, sugars, peppers, card identification holders be stored. Because service must proceed at a rapid rate, every motion counts. Plan for the most efficient dishup procedures possible. It will pay in enhanced food quality.

Locate the serving section close to the cook's section but also convenient to where other foods can be delivered and to the dishwashing unit from which clean utensils, dishes and flatware must come. Allow space for food trucks. If a dumbwaiter or conveyor is used, locate it so service moves directly into it. Dumbwaiters should not be less than 24 in. x 24 in. x 36 in. and when loaded with 100 lb or more should move at a speed of 50 ft/min or more; if it is to serve a basement and four floors, provide a speed of 100 ft/min.

If elevators are used for transporting food in trucks or carts, see that an elevator is available *exclusively* for use of the dietary department during both delivery and return. The HUD (FHA 4514.1) requirement for nursing homes and small extended care facilities requires 2 elevators for every 60 to 200 patrons bedded and served above the first floor and a minimum of 3 elevators for every 200 to 350 on upper floors.

Food distribution may be decentralized (away from.the production area on the floors) or centralized (in the production area). Central distribution is preferable for small facilities. Some central distribution systems dish food on hot or cold dishes, putting hot foods into a warming receptacle and cold foods into a room temperature or chilled one. Coding indicates to serving personnel on the floors which warm and cold foods go together.

A hot pellet system can be used to keep foods warm and both hot and cold foods can then be put on the same tray with fair temperature control assured. Such a system is more practical for large than small units.

If food is delivered from the food production center within 3 min after dishup, no temperature control devices are required, providing the dishes and the food are at the proper temperature upon dishup. However, this time factor, while often considered feasible in planning, is seldom achieved in practice.

A new unit is on the market that permits dishup of hot and cold foods on a plastic server that, when stacked and held after dishup, holds food temperatures, both hot and cold—even frozen, for several hours. This equipment reduces the need for expensive food delivery carts and has worked well in many small or large health facilities. It is always wise to select a delivery system that holds food temperatures well and also provides some sanitation, i. e. delivery in enclosed carts.

In a decentralized system, the food is sent in bulk to service areas on the floors or into the dining rooms on the respective floors and dished there. In such cases, dishes and utensils may be washed on the floor or sent back to the production center for processing.

Sanitizing Sections
Four sanitizing jobs must be performed: dishwashing, pot and pan washing, waste disposal and general cleanup. Each needs its own special facilities and equipment to do the job. Location is important. Provide 30 to 40 ft-candles in these areas.

The dishwashing area should be located where soiled dishes come from service and also close to the serving area, to provide easy return of dishes from the patrons of the facility as well as for employees. A window and landing table may provide the required facilities for the latter and there should be ample room near the section for trucks returning from the patron's floors to stand until unloaded and cleaned. Employees may also put their trays into mobile carts which can then be moved into the dishwashing section. Space for holding carts is essential.

In small facilities, a single-tank machine that washes, rinses and sanitizes will be required. It should also hold trays used for service. A small sink for soaking is recommended. For a moderately large facility—about 100 beds —specify a single-tank, vertical sliding door machine that can process about 20 to 30 racks/hr.

For hand washing, provide a 3-compartment sink with the third compartment deep enough to hold baskets of dishes in 170°F water for 2 min or for the same period of time in a sanitizing solution. The first compartment is for washing and the second for rinsing. It is preferable to use this sink only for dishes, but, in smaller institutions, it may also have to be used for pots and pans and, in addition, as a general utility sink; however, this is undesirable. Pre-rinsing with an overhead spray into a small indented trough, having a removable drainer to catch soil, is recommended before washing. Provide adequate drain space. Do not towel dry but let items air dry after sanitizing.

Normally, a dish table 24 to 30 in. wide is needed; of total linear length, 60% should be for soiled dishes and 40% for clean dishes to dry in racks. Three or more 20 x 20 in. racks are usually held for drying; thus, about the minimum length for the soiled dish table would be 7½ to 8 ft. If less space than this is available or if more space is needed, put a shelf slanted toward the worker where glasses, cups, and other items awaiting washing or to be held for drying, can be put. There should be a soak bin for flatware. Normally, flatware is washed prongs up in perforated cups, given a quick dip in a hot despotting-destaining solution and allowed to air dry.

If additional space is needed at the clean dish section, put another slightly slanted shelf above. Space should be available for cleaning supplies. Check to see that there are hot and cold water hose connections, a grease trap, perhaps a garbage disposal unit (½ HP or more) by-passing the grease trap and enough space to do the job if carts and trucks are to be cleaned there. This area requires about 1 sq ft/person served/day.

Provide adequate ventilation for steam and moisture removal. Sound proofing is advised. Noise can be abated by providing a partial partition drop from the ceiling making an area in which the noise is captured. The area can be separated from the dining area by partitions but preferably not from the other work areas, unless noise is a problem. It is best, where possible, to locate the dishmachine away from the wall so cleaning around it is easy. Work tables located against the wall should have free space underneath so cleaning is facilitated under them.

The pot and pan section should be as close as possible to the serving, cook's and baking sections. It should contain a 3- or 4-compartment sink with compartments large enough to hold the utensils. Provision should be made for scrapping, soaking, washing, rinsing and sanitizing with adequate drain areas in the soiled and clean sections to hold items in process. Additional space can be obtained by positioning mobile carts at an angle, either loaded with soiled items or available for holding items after they have been sanitized and drained.

A spray at the soiled side will remove loose and scrapped soil before washing. A trough and removable strainer are recommended on the soiled drain side to catch such soil. Most specify that the sink should be 37 or 38 in. high but this should be determined after considering the heights of the workers that will use it. Work flow is usually best from right to left. Pots and pans should be stored at work centers in the sections at points of first use. An easy method of transporting soiled and clean items should be planned. Adequate grease trap facilities are essential and can be those used for the dishwashing section.

A gas, oil or electrically fired incinerator may be used to get rid of combustible waste. The type chosen should not give off polluting gas into the atmosphere. Compactors may handle non-combustible wastes and even garbage or a centralized 1-HP garbage disposal unit may be installed. Garbage may also be stored (preferably in a refrigerated unit) and hauled away. Soiled cans will need cleaning and this necessitates installation of a non-slippery cement or other suitable floor with a 3-in. coping, a drain, cold and hot water hose connections and steam.

The fourth cleaning unit that may be needed is a janitor's cleaning closet. This may or may not be enclosed. It should be near the food production areas. A slop sink is needed; one installed into the floor and 8 in. deep is recommended. Space is needed for hanging mops and brooms and should offer good ventilation for drying. There should also be storage space for buckets, cleaning supplies and other items stored there. Hot and cold water faucets to which a hose can be connected will be needed.

Office Space

A minimum of 60 sq ft should be allocated for an office but more usually can be used. Close off for privacy and security. Installing a window opening into the kitchen makes it easy for employees to come for information or instructions without having to enter into the office. There should be window space for supervision as well. It is desirable to have the door opening into the office located away from the kitchen so salesmen and others do not have to pass through the kitchen to get to the office. The office should have a desk, files, bookcases, typewriter table and perhaps another work table and several chairs.

Employee Space

Separate locker space and toilets should be available for men and women. This can be combined with locker space set aside for other employees in the health facility but, preferably, should be separate and near the kitchen. This unit should be close to the time clock and bulletin board. Employees should pass by the office area when leaving work and punching out.

A toilet should be provided for each 12 to 15 employees and, in larger installations, a urinal for every 15 men. A lavatory will be needed for every 8 to 10 employees with adequate soap and paper towel dispensers at hand. Showers and toilets should be enclosed in separate stalls and about 8 sq ft per employee will be needed for this area. It is desirable not to have this unit open into the food production area but into a hall or corridor. There should be 40 to 50 ft-candles of light. In addition, be sure there are drinking fountains for employees in the work area and also locate lavatories there so employees can conveniently wash their hands while at work.

Dining Areas

Two types of dining areas will usually be needed, one for employees and another for patrons. Keep them pleasant, light, airy and of suitable decor. Patrons and workers alike should find the dining area a place for relaxation and enjoyment of the foods prepared for them. Eating should be a social pleasure.

In small facilities, employee meals can be dished in the cook's section and handed to employees who can take them to the area provided for dining. If it is desirable to keep non-dietary personnel out of the food production area, a small service window between the dining area and kitchen or a service unit in the dining area can be installed.

In larger facilities, a service area for serving food can be installed in the dining area, composed of a small mobile hot cart and mobile table rolled there; in addition, some cabinets and shelving may be needed to hold dishes and other items. Some planners of serving areas allow 1-1/3 sq ft for each person in a group that will be seated at one time. Others say 15 to 18 sq ft per person should be allowed for dining, with from 1/5 to 1/7 of the space set aside for service. A minimum of 12 sq ft per person seated is recommended just for dining space. A service area will usually be about 10 ft deep and contain an 8 ft counter (minimum).

Calculate 2 ft for each person who must stand in line to be served. A 12 in. wide rail will hold a 14 in. tray. Unless 75 or more people are served, a cafeteria line is not set up for a meal; a simpler method of serving is used instead. It may be necessary to provide a lavatory and perhaps toilets near the dining area. Drinking water should also be available.

A central dining area may be provided for ambulatory residents even if they are housed on different floors. If they are not able to get to this, then each floor must have a dining area. From 15 to 18 sq ft per person seated at one time should be allowed. If the dining room and recreation room are combined, it is recommended that there be about 30 sq ft/bed for the first 100 beds and 27 sq ft for each bed in excess of 100. Drinking water should also be available here.

Durable, stable tables and chairs should be specified, but chairs should not be so heavy that they are difficult for many patrons to handle. If foods are sent from the kitchen and dished in the dining area, there should be adequate dishup facilities that can be sealed off from the patrons who might become a nuisance before or during dishup or who might try to take food they like but should not have. Allow 1½ sq ft in the serving area per person to be seated at one time.

EQUIPMENT SELECTION

Today the equipment in a foodservice will cost about as much as it costs to build the area into which it is placed. However, equipment selection is not only important from the standpoint of cost, but it is also of vital importance in achieving good food quality and in obtaining an efficient, smoothly operating unit. The best equipment selection occurs when adequate answers are provided for the following:

1. Is it essential?
2. What is the true cost?
3. Is it easily maintained, serviced and repaired?
4. Is it safe and sanitary?
5. Does it have good appearance and design?
6. Does it have general utility values?
7. Can it be suitably located?
8. What size or number is required?

1. Essentiality

A cooking unit is essential if we are to cook food. It might be a range, although the range could be omitted and all cooking done in steam equipment or ovens as some school foodservices and institutions now operate. If a range is planned, steam cooking equipment, fryers, griddles and other cooking equipment may also be considered although these may or may not be essential, since the cooking these additional units do could be done on a range top. Perhaps a dishwasher is considered essential but, if a suitable sink is available, it may not be. Is a potato peeler essential in a small facility? Is a baking section? These are questions that operation must decide.

In working out equipment requirements, a decision must be made whether equipment for a facility is absolutely essential—Category A—or extremely useful—Category B—or merely useful—Category C. All the equipment in Category A, or suitable alternatives, *must be* installed; perhaps most in Category B and some of Category C may be considered sufficiently useful to be selected, but equipment that does not fall into one of these categories should be eliminated. All alternatives should be studied. There are many new market forms of foods available, the use of which would change or reduce equipment needs. Consider whether another piece of equipment could do the job or if the job could be done in a different way. Be sure to consider quality in establishing needs.

2. True Cost

The original cost is not the true cost. Installation cost must be added. Then, over the operating life of the equipment, other costs will occur such as repair and maintenance, operating, interest, insurance, parts replacement and others. Cheap equipment may be expensive equipment in the long run when all costs are considered, while equipment that originally seems to be expensive may be much less costly. Further, consideration should be given to the economic value of the quality of item that can be produced by a certain piece of equipment. Checking with others who use the same equipment will help in ascertaining what they have found in their experience on such costs and values.

It is recommended that an equipment card be maintained on each piece of major equipment showing the original cost, installation cost and subsequent costs. This file can be an extremely valuable source of information and record of equipment performance and cost. When repair, maintenance and other costs add up, it can be an excellent argument for replacement of that piece of equipment.

	Equipment Record (front of card)	

Equipment Item   Inventory No.
Trade Name   Manufacturer
Model No.   Serial No.
Capacity   Attachments
Purchased from   Purchase date
New   Used   Cost $ Operation: Electric Gas Steam Hand
Utility Consumption/hr Operation
Guarantee Period   Free Service Period

	Equipment Record (back of card)	
	Cost of Repair, Maintenance, Servicing, Parts	
Date	Description of Work	Cost

Fig. 10-4. *The front and back of an equipment record card that could be used to keep track of the cost of equipment.*

Maintenance, repair and servicing costs can be reduced by establishing a good preventive maintenance and repair program. This is done by establishing a schedule for maintenance and repair. In a loose leaf file, devote a page to each piece of equipment on the schedule. Indicate the job to be done, who should do it and how frequently (daily, weekly, monthly, yearly or as required). Have squares that can be checked to show when the job is done, with the worker putting in his initials. Allow a space for notes or comments with the date and worker's initials.

Some maintenance jobs can be done by foodservice workers, others by the janitors or the maintenance department while some may have to be done by outside servicemen or contract service companies. Management should check the schedule frequently to see that it is being followed. If necessary, neatly post operating and maintenance instructions at the equipment, using those of the manufacturer if they are adequate. Such a program can save money and reduce the annoyance and extra expense of having equipment out of working order because of a breakdown.

Equipment is usually depreciated in 10 years in accounting records but many foodservices keep equipment operating longer than this. In many cases, the equipment is highly satisfactory, however, sometimes it is not and should be replaced. Even equipment that is still giving good service may be replaced to good advantage by new equipment if it saves money by reducing labor or doing a better job.

One of the most critical questions to ask in regard to cost is whether a piece of equipment will reduce labor requirements or not. The cost of labor is becoming such a significant factor today in quantity food production that replacement of it by equipment is becoming more and more feasible, even though the equipment may cost a substantial amount. Unless a major piece of equipment will save on labor, it may not be practical to purchase it. The following may be used to estimate whether a piece of equipment should be purchased or not:

A = savings in labor during equipment life
B = cost of equipment installed less salvage value of equipment at the end of lifetime use
C = operation, maintenance and other costs during equipment life
D = interest on investment

$$\frac{A}{B + C + D} = E$$

If E is 1.0 or more, the equipment probably should be purchased but, if 1.5 or more, the savings are so great purchase is strongly recommended.

Is gas less expensive than electricity? On the basis that it takes 1.8 cu ft of natural gas or .33 kilowatts of electricity to cook a meal, we can use the factor .0054 x cost of 1000 cu ft of gas to get the competitive cost in cents of a kilowatt of electricity or 184 x cost of a kilowatt of electricity to get the competitive cost in dollars for 1000 cu ft of gas. For example: gas costs $2.22/1000 cu ft, so .0054 x $2.22 = 1.2¢ per Kwh of electricity or electricity costs 1.2¢/Kwh, so 184 x 1.2¢ = $2.21 per 1000 cu ft of gas.*

_____
*The unit of sale for gas is 1000 cu ft.

If one multiplies the cost of a Kwh of electricity times 185 and compares this with the cost of 1000 cu ft of gas, one can estimate roughly which is the least expensive. However, employees usually waste more fuel than they use in cooking. Even if electricity is more costly, if employees would turn off electrical equipment when not in use, not permit items to boil hard while cooking, etc., electricity would not be an expensive fuel to use. The use of proper procedures also keeps the cost of gas at the minimum level.

3. Maintenance, Service and Repair

There is another factor beside cost to consider in the maintenance, service, repair and similar jobs associated with equipment. That is, "How easy is it to do?" Equipment may be hard to clean, or laborious to assemble and disassemble and clean or difficult to maintain, service or repair.

Employees will avoid cleaning such equipment, using it or doing the proper job of maintenance; thus, the equipment becomes a liability instead of an asset, a source of frustration and annoyance and frequently an eye-sore. Avoid buying such equipment. Look at equipment and see how easily motors, mechanical units or parts can be removed and replaced. Today some units come so that the entire mechanical system can be removed easily and another put in with dispatch so the equipment can continue to be used while the element is sent to the factory for repair.

4. Safety and Sanitation

Although it is said that sanitation problems in foodservices are caused 95% by human error and 5% by equipment error, nevertheless, the 5% is important. The surface areas of equipment should be smooth and hard surfaced and easily cleaned; all corners should be rounded.

There should be few places for soil to collect. Drawers and bins should pull out so they can be taken to the sink for washing. Shelving should be removable and bottom shelves that are fixed should be easily wiped clean. Gaskets should be cleanable and easily removable. Reject equipment in which insects, vermin or rodents can hide. Mechanical equipment should not create slop or soil. Equipment required to hold certain temperatures should consistently do so. Refrigerators should hold at an even 35°F, if set for this; a dishwasher should adequately maintain a 160°F temperature for washing and a 180°F temperature for rinsing.

It is said that a foodservice department is a more dangerous place to work than a coal mine. Perhaps the reason is that workers frequently handle sharp tools, knives and other items that can injure. Water and grease on floors are common hazards. Hot food, hot equipment, steam or hot fat can cause burns. Heavy roasting pans or pots must be lifted and carried from one place to the other. Therefore, there is no need to add to these dangers by purchasing equipment that may cause an accident.

See that equipment has the approval stamp of underwriter or other agencies certifying that it meets standards for safety and sanitation. Some of these may be the National Sanitation Foundation (NSF), Underwriter's Laboratory (UL), American Gas Association (AGA), etc. Reject equipment with sharp edges. Be sure that moving parts are guarded. Look for surprise factors such as a door that is hard to close, closes suddenly or one that locks loosely. Avoid a motor that has a switch that could easily catch as a worker walked by and so start up unexpectedly. What about fires? Wooden shelving may not be desirable because of this. What about toxic fumes? What about electrical shock? Every piece of equipment has its own potential hazards. Seek these out and reject the equipment that cannot meet standards for safety.

5. Appearance and Design

Some equipment can be downright ugly. It is out of proportion or unwieldy. Some can be quite garish looking, resembling a jukebox or peddlers cart more than it does equipment one would want in one's operation. Select equipment with symmetry, design or proportions that blend well. Use some care in mixing finishes. A huge black iron baking oven, standing prominently in the foodservice, destroys the appearance of the beautiful stainless steel.

Tastefully done, however, different finishes, metals and materials can be attractive. Equipment with enameled panels, such as the side of an oven, and black iron, stainless steel, aluminum, plastic or formica can be mixed and still maintain a good appearance. An excess of one kind can, however, overwhelm the rest.

The design of equipment should stress function, simplicity and the efficient use of space. Watch proportion in the design of sinks, tables or other similar units. It takes experience to design fabricated equipment that has excellent utility and good appearance.

6. Utility Values

Equipment may do an excellent job, be economical to operate and otherwise conform to all the tests suggested here, yet still be unsuitable. A noisy fan can reduce labor efficiency and be a source of annoyance and frustration. Excessive heat build-up from poorly insulated equipment can make a work area unpleasant.

A dishmachine that allows too much steam and moisture to escape may lower worker productivity. Frequently, in selecting equipment, we concentrate on certain factors, forgetting others and in doing so wind up with equipment which, while performing excellently, may not be entirely satisfactory because some value important to the total operation was missed.

7. Locating It

Will the piece of equipment fit into the space allowed for it? Can workers work around it and equipment be moved around it? Does it have the right utility requirements for those available at the location—does it take 240-v when there is only a 120-v circuit there? Does its placement violate principles for work center distances and work flow?

8. Size and Number

One of the most frequent mistakes in equipment selection is the failure to properly balance production capacities of various pieces of equipment with each other. One piece of equipment may produce a large quantity of food in a short time while a related piece of equipment cannot. A bottleneck develops and food quality and efficiency of production may suffer. There can be a related failure when equipment is planned to produce a specified quantity in a given time but, after installation, fails to meet these production requirements.

To get a fairly good estimate of how many pieces of equipment are required and/or what size will be needed, the following checks can be helpful:

The number of portions needed times the portion size will give the quantity required. This equated to the time available for production will indicate the number of pieces of equipment or the size required. For example: a planner wishes to know if one or two ranges will be required for a 75-bed facility with an average of 10 employee meals to be produced per meal. Hotcakes are on the menu being checked through by this planner and the portion is an average of 2/patron and 2½/employee, or 175 will be needed. Production will occur from 10 min ahead of service through the 30 min serving period. A batch of 12 hotcakes can be prepared in a cycle of 5 min on two 12- x 24-in. plates. Thus, in 40 min, 8 batches of 12 hotcakes can be produced on the range—it has 2 plates. This is 96. To get 175 hotcakes in this period, 2 range tops will be needed.

When fried eggs were considered, however, the necessary portions could be produced on one range top because an average of only 1¼ eggs per portion both for patron and employee would be needed and the cycle time to put on the plate, fry and remove, for a batch of 12, would be 4½ min. The planner's calculation was 85 x 1¼ = 106 ÷ 12/batch = 9 batches x 4½ min/batch = 40 min approximately, close enough to the time available for production.

After a number of checks for breakfast dishes, the planner decided that one range top would do but that a supplemental griddle, that could be connected up at the cook's work table and used by another worker, would be required when hotcakes and some other items were required. Of course, a large number of checks would have to be made on lunch and dinner requirements before it could be decided precisely whether one range top was enough.

This same planner wanted to know what size trunnion kettle would be needed. One check showed that 85 portions or 3 gal of a fresh vegetable would be required in a serving time lasting 45 min. It was desired, as an operational standard, that no vegetable would be served if it was held for service over 30 min. Therefore, two batches would be needed. Also, in this serving period 2/3 of the vegetables were required in the first 20 min of service and the remainder during the last 25 min. The trunnion could cook the vegetables in 20 min but an additional 10 min would be required to load, bring the vegetables to a boil, unload the trunnion and deliver the vegetables to the serving section.

These vegetable requirements could be met if a 2 gal batch were ready for service at 5:05, 10 min ahead of serving time, and another smaller batch of 1 gal ready 30 min later to finish the service, but the planner thought that 2 6-qt trunnions would be more suitable than 1 12-qt one—a trunnion or steam-jacketed kettle can be filled to 75% of capacity so the 12-qt kettle could hold 2 gal of vegetables and the 6-qt,1 gal. With the 2 6-qt trunnions, the production plan was:

1. Start the first gal of vegetables at 4:35 to be ready at 5:05.
2. Start the second gal of vegetables at 4:55; ready at 5:25.
3. Start the last gal of vegetables in the first trunnion, now free for use, at 5:05; ready at 5:35.

This also improved the quality of the vegetables served during the last part of the first serving period since they were fresher. As noted here, because production requirements for equipment may vary from meal to meal, it is sometimes better to install two smaller units rather than one large one. If this is done, one unit can be shut down and not operated when production requirements are small. This will depend upon the equipment but, frequently, with ovens, deep fryers and others, two or more units rather than one may be preferable.

EQUIPMENT MATERIALS

Metal is the material most commonly used in equipment, but plastics and other materials are being used more and more frequently. Equipment bodies, for example a mixer frame, are usually cast iron. Plate and sheet metal are lighter. Plate is from 3/8 to 3/16 in. thick and used for heavy equipment construction. Sheet is less than 3/16 in. thick and will be used for fabricated equipment.*

Thickness of metal is indicated by gauge; the U. S. Standards for stainless steel gauge are:

No. 8 11/64 in.   No. 12 7/64 in.   No. 16 1/16 in.   No. 20 1/32 in.
No. 10 9/64 in.   No. 14 5/64 in.   No. 18 3/64 in.   No. 24 1/40 in.

No. 8 sheet metal is usually too heavy for fabricated equipment, but No. 10 may be used for legs and some bodies and for tops of sinks, tables and other units where considerable strength is needed. Table tops, sinks and other equipment are usually made of No. 12 or No. 14 gauge metal while doors and shelving will be specified to be made from No. 16 or No. 18 gauge. Bodies, canopies or hoods are usually No. 20 gauge. If the metal is not stainless steel, the recommended gauge is usually larger. The cost in fabricated equipment is not as much in the material as it is in the workmanship. A galvaneal (galvanized iron) sink will cost almost as much as a stainless steel one, although the material in the latter is more costly than galvaneal.

It is not necessary to obtain all the strength required in equipment in the gauge of the covering metal. If a strong frame is designed, the gauge of the covering metal can be lighter because it will not have to support the equipment. Putting channeling (strips of metal, tubing, etc.) under a table top or sink drain gives added strength; it will do the same for a mobile cart and a lighter gauge can then be used for the covering surface. Shelving helps to give strength. A turndown on a top such as a bull-nosed bend adds strength. Extra legs will help to reduce the weight needed for load bearing. The support construction for drawers or bins under table tops helps add strength. In many instances, by utilizing one or more of these strength-giving factors, the gauge required can be reduced while the necessary durability is still assured.

While there can be a choice of materials for equipment, sinks, table tops
_____
*Fabricated equipment, as used here, means equipment made to special order.

and other units are best made from stainless steel. This is a high grade steel (approx 75%) combined with 18% chromium and 8% nickel, usually designated as 18-8 metal or No. 302 stainless. It is highly ductile; that is, it stretches, molds or shapes easily. It does not rust, is strong, wears well and is attractive in appearance. It is non-reactive to most food compounds although it can be tarnished and scratched by careless use. It is a poor heat conductor and, for this reason, cooking in stainless steel pots and pans is not recommended but stainless steel is satisfactory for steam table units, steam-jacketed kettles, and similar equipment.

If a metal, such as iron, is put between two sheets of stainless steel or stainless cooking units have copper clad bottoms, then heat is more evenly distributed and stainless can be used for cooking utensils. Because of its poor heat conductivity, stainless is difficult to weld and buyers should take care to see that buckled or discolored areas are not evident and that welds are evenly and carefully ground down so they are not evident. There should be no spot or tack welding, as spacing the welding solder apart does not give a strong joint.

Monel, about 75% high grade steel, 8% copper and 17% nickel, reacts to some food acids and is, therefore, not generally recommended for foodservice equipment. Aluminum is a soft metal that can be attacked by some foods and tarnished by others but it is light, inexpensive and an excellent conductor of heat. It is good for cooking utensils, legs of equipment, siding, furniture, etc. Mixtures of metals with aluminum give a harder, more durable metal; cold-rolling aluminum under high pressures does the same since this gives it better life where surface wear may occur. Copper formerly was used extensively for cooking equipment but it is expensive and reacts with food acids and so is used less frequently now. Copper is an excellent conductor of heat but it also tarnishes easily.

Cold-rolled steel is used where strength is required but appearance is not important. Black iron sheet is used for baking pans and other items and can be also used for bodies, canopies or other pieces of equipment.

There are a number of covered metals in use. Chrome covered metal is used for many small items such as coffee pots, toasters, etc. It has good luster and beauty. Galvaneal is galvanized iron or iron covered with a zinc layer which protects the iron from rust and attack from other compounds. Steel may have enamel baked on it and this may be used for refrigerator bodies, oven bodies, etc. Steel cleans well and has beauty, is durable but will chip under a strong blow or crack and sometimes when exposed to high heat or when handled too roughly during use.

Plastics are being used more and more. They are excellent for drawers, doors, bins, tote carts, etc., and are inexpensive. Plywood covered with formica can be used for doors, bodies and even tops if the wear is not too great. Plastics and formica may add color which may help to give a more attractive piece of equipment.

CONSTRUCTION FACTORS

Watch construction carefully. Inspect wiring to see how well wiring and connections are insulated. Check equipment frames for strength and how well metal parts are attached to them. Check for sharp raw edges of metal. Make sure that the following points are checked out: Do the tops of nuts, screws or bolts protrude so they can act as potential dirt catchers? Are shelves removable, door stops open so soil drops through, corners and junctures rounded, drains sloped for drainage, cleanable parts easily removable, equipment easily maintained and serviced, spare parts available, service available and good sanitation features incorporated. Does the equipment have the seal of approval of the National Sanitation Foundation?

Will the equipment take the required wear and strain? Mobile carts may become bowed because weights, heavier than planned, are put on them. Check the channeling, shelving, gauge, etc. to ascertain durability. Is welding strong? Welding is preferred to bolted equipment. Be sure surfaces are smooth and even. Can insects, vermin or rodents be harbored in the equipment? Watch for sharp edges or unrounded corners that can cause injury. Other items that might be checked would be:

Freedom from vibration.
Cleanable, removable gaskets.
Glass plate, ¼ in. and firmly set in strong metal frames.
Depressed door openings.
Strong hinges.
Removable doors, drawers, bins and shelving.
Welded or seamless type tubing.

Doors and drawers on rollers.
Good casters or wheels.
Two lockable casters or wheels on some pieces of equipment.
Protected heating strips.
Limit stops or safety-catches on doors, bins and drawers.
Soil-catching trim.
Good insulation.

EQUIPMENT SPECIFICATIONS

There are two types of equipment available: 1) standard stock and 2) fabricated or custom-built. The specifications for each differ.

Standard Stock Specifications

Many manufacturers make a standard item, such as a range, refrigerator, steam-jacketed kettle, and these are available as standard items. They are obtained by specifying catalog or brochure information identifying the equipment. The buyer should specify the name of the equipment, its catalog or order number, model number, type of utility connections needed, capacity or size and other factors needed to give a complete identification. Remember to completely indicate electrical requirements such as AC or DC voltage, single or three phase, cycles, etc.

Sometimes the mention of a proprietary or trade name is not possible in a specification. Getting the equipment required may be difficult, but usually restricting bidders to a selected list that includes only manufacturers of an acceptable product helps or adding the words "or equal" after the trade name of the equipment desired may be acceptable. What is equal should be decided by the buyer and equipment rejected if, in his opinion, it is not equal to the item specified.

Specify that standard stock equipment shall come with at least 3 operating manuals and 3 spare parts lists. Keep 1 of each of these in the files at the office, another in the maintenance and repair manual or schedule and another with the maintenance or janitor's department, if that department is responsible for maintenance and repair.

Fabricated Equipment Specifications

Custom-built equipment is made according to the buyer's specifications which should describe in writing what is needed. Sometimes this must be done in considerable detail and all construction factors must be covered. To assist in understanding what is wanted, a drawing, usually to a scale of ¼ in. = 1 ft, is presented. This drawing may be two-dimensional so the detail is more accurately presented. Accompany such a drawing with the plumbing, electrical and layout plans, if required, so the manufacturer will have all the information needed to indicate utilities and space occupancy.

In all specifications, require that the equipment conform to the National Sanitation Foundation standards. Some published specifications used by the General Services Administration, Federal Supply Service, may be helpful in showing what must be covered in specifications for individual pieces of equipment. Good, accurate, precise specifications and drawings have been shown to reduce custom-built equipment costs.

After the manufacturer has been selected, he will present to the buyer a shop drawing. This may be to a scale of ½ in. = 1 ft or even 1 in. = 1 ft. The buyer must study this carefully, checking every detail, because this drawing gives what the manufacturer has interpreted as wanted from the written specification and the drawing presented. The drawing should be corrected in red pencil and returned.

EQUIPMENT INSTALLATION

Good planning must precede installation. What is done in the installation, what is to be used and other pertinent matters must be decided and specified when the equipment is selected. The equipment must be right for the spot in which it will be placed; this involves size, utilities, use intended, etc. Specify that top grade workmanship is required, but also check during installation to see that it is provided by finding out: Do 2-in. drain pipes lead from a sink and connect in as short a distance as possible to a 4-in. one? Does the garbage grinder connection by-pass the grease trap? Are plumbing, electrical and other connections adequate? Do bolts or straps project so as to be hazards to workers walking by? Is the equipment located correctly? (A deep fryer at the end of a work area close to where workers walk by can be a hazard. Installing it between a tall oven and a proof box makes it difficult to work into.) Is work flow facilitated or hampered? Etc.

The sanitation requirements should also be checked out. If possible, equipment should be away from the wall so cleaning is easy or it should be mobile so it can be rolled away. Flexible cables are available for electricity and gas so ranges, grills, ovens and other equipment can be moved out for cleaning. Equipment placed against the wall can be suspended from it so cleaning underneath it is easy.

Equipment should be sealed closely to the wall so vermin and insects are kept out and the flat surface of equipment placed on the floor should be sealed with a mastic cement to keep out undesirable intruders. Watch for empty, enclosed dark areas and see that these are sealed off. See that pipes are buried in the wall or are enclosed so they do not have to be cleaned constantly. Piping over the food production, serving, storage or other critical areas should be kept at a minimum and not be exposed. Are steam and hot water lines properly insulated?

The way it is installed should insure that equipment is safe to operate, easy to clean, maintain and repair. Do not allow a piece of equipment to be installed so access into it is blocked by a wall or by other pieces of equipment.

Normally, the installation is done by the purveyor selling the equipment and this should be specified in the bid. Of course, equipment that is moved in and then put into place, such as a work table, will not have such a requirement.

At times, the builder may be responsible for installation and the general bid will state this. Or, installation may be unspecified and, in this case, the buyer has the responsibility of seeing that the equipment is installed and of selecting the workmen to do it. It is usually wise to specify installation with purchase because the purveyor knows his equipment and how it should be installed to give best performance. Check guarantees and free service periods carefully and do not hesitate to require the manufacturer or installer to correct installations that are functioning improperly or that are faulty.

EQUIPMENT CHECK LIST The amount of equipment required will vary with the size of the operation, type of food production and service used as well as other conditions within the facility. However, it is sometimes helpful to use an equipment check list as a guide in indicating equipment requirements. But, it should only be a guide. Too many variations can occur that will change requirements. One could add a griddle, as was indicated in the earlier discussion on equipment selection, and use 1 and not 2 range tops or perhaps a convection oven rather than a deck oven would be preferable.

Lists of suggested equipment for extended care facilities appear on the following pages.

SUGGESTED EQUIPMENT REQUIREMENTS FOR SMALL NURSING HOMES AND EXTENDED CARE FACILITIES

Equipment and Type	Bed Capacity			
	25	50	75	100
Range, commercial, 4 burner or 2 plate, 1 oven	1	1		
Range, commercial, 8 burner or 4 plate, 2 ovens			1	1
Griddle, 18 x 30 in., portable		1		1
Deck Oven, 2-deck (bake and roast) with additional removable shelf for baking, 38 x 38 in.		1	1	1
Convection Oven to hold 18 x 26 baking sheets	1	*	*	1
Steamer, small high pressure	1	1		1
Steamer, regular, 2-bu capacity		*	1	1
Kettle, trunnion, 6 qt		1	1	2
Kettle, 20-gal, tilt (steam)				1
Mixer, mobile, bench-type, 10-qt, 3-qt bowl and adapter, food chopper and slicer attachments	1			
Mixer, mobile, bench-type, 20-qt, 12 qt bowl and adapter, food chopper and slicer attachments		1	1	1
Dishwasher, single tank, floor model, vertical sliding doors, automatic wash and rinse		1	1	1
Dishwasher, double tank, floor model, vertical sliding doors, automatic wash and rinse				1
Soiled and Clean Dish Tables	1	1	1	1
Sink, single compartment, 24 x 24 x 13 in.	1	1	2	2
Sink, pot and pan, 3-compartment, 28 x 28 x 16 in., 2 drainboards		1	1	1
Sink, dishwashing, 3-compartment, 24 x 24 x 13 in., 2 drainboards	1	*		
Sink, 2-compartment, 24 x 24 x 13 in., 1 drainboard			1	1
Lavatory with knee or elbow control	1	1	1	2
Drinking Fountain	1	1	1	2
Garbage Grinder with pre-rinse at dishwashing section, 1/2 HP	1	1		
Garbage Grinder with pre-rinse at dishwashing section, 3/4 HP			1	1
Exhaust Fan, preferably at dishwashing section if 1 and add the other at the cooking section	1	1	1	2
Refrigerator, reach-in, self-contained, 45 cu ft	1	2	2	2

*If added, change requirements elsewhere.

**This facility is almost large enough to warrant a walk-in.

(cont.)

SUGGESTED EQUIPMENT REQUIREMENTS FOR SMALL NURSING HOMES AND EXTENDED CARE FACILITIES (cont.)

Equipment Type	Bed Capacity			
	25	50	75	100
Refrigerator, reach-in, self-contained, 70 cu ft			1	1**
Freezer, reach-in, self-contained, 68 cu ft		1	1	1
Freezer, reach-in, self-contained, 20 cu ft				1
Refrigerator, mobile, 12 cu ft			1	1
Peeler, 15 lb		1	1	
Peeler, 30 lb				1
Deep Fryer, gas or electric. table model, 15 lb or		1	2	2
Deep Fryer, gas or electric, standing, 30 lb			1	1
Broiler, single, 20 x 20 in. or equal in size (400 sq in.)		1	1	
Broiler, single, 475 sq in.				1
Toaster, 4- slice	1	2	2	
Toaster, 8-slice			2	2
Toaster, 18 x 16 x 30 in. high, chain-driven type				1
Tables, 6 to 8 ft long, 2 drawers, shelf under	2	3 .	3	4
Tables, work, approx 8 ft in length	1	1	2	3
Mobile carts, 36 x 30 in. (angle frame 1-1/2 x 1-1/2 x 1/8 in.), 2-shelf	1	1	2	2
Mobile carts, 60 x 30 in. (angle frame 1-1/2 x 1-1/2 x 1/8 in.), 3-shelf			1	1	2
Scales, 50 lb, table	1			
Scales, 100 lb, regular		1	1	1
Scales, baker	1	1	1	1
Food cart, 25-tray, non-heated	1	2		
Food cart, 25-tray, heated			3	4
Mobile serving counter, heated, 3-compartment	1	1		
Mobile serving counter, heated, 5-compartment			1	1
Can openers, commercial type	1	1	2	2
Slicer, mechanical			1	1

In addition, each facility will need dollies for holding garbage cans, racks for cups and glasses, hoods over equipment skids for storing items, platform trucks, hand trucks, shelving on which to store items, mobile shelving for the larger operations, mobile bins and fire extinguishers. Thus, the list presented here is only partial or more suggestive than complete. Some authorities might disagree considerably with the above list. For instance, some would question the use of deep fryers, especially a 30-lb unit in a 75 bed-facility, but experience has shown that they are extremely useful in giving a greater variety and a well liked type of food.

HEW HOSPITAL EQUIPMENT CHECKLIST

	Suggested Quantity No. of Beds			Local Requirements			
	50-75	100-150	200-225	Unit	No.	Unit Price	Total Cost
DIETARY*	**A**	**B**	**C**				
A—80 to 125 meals at peak (noon) period							
B—180 to 280 meals at peak (noon) period							
C—380 to 430 meals at peak (noon) period							
Centralized Service							
Receiving	1	1	1				
Fixed Equipment							
Counter, standup desk or shelf, 21 in. long, 18 in. wide, 42-46 in. high	1	1	1				
Major-Movable Equipment							
Scale, platform, portable, beam type, capacity 1000 lb with 8 oz graduations	1	1	1				
Stool, adjustable, with back 22-33 in.	1	1	1				
Table, utility, 1 under-shelf, locking casters, 30 x 24 in.	1	1	1				
Truck, platform, 4 wheels, 48 in. long, 24 in. wide, 12 to 14 in. high	1	1	1				
Storage							
Day Storage	1	1	1				
Fixed Equipment							
Cabinet	1	1	1				
Ventilator at ceiling	1	1	1				
Major Movable Equipment							
Can, 20 gal with cover	3	3	3				
Dolly for can	1	1	1				
Ladder, 2 step with rails	1	1	1				
Shelves metal, adjustable locking casters	1	2	1				
Truck, shelf type	1	1	1				

*For more detailed information in planning this department, see Public Health Service Publication No. 930-C-11, *Hospital Dietary Services, A Planning Guide.*

(cont.)

HEW HOSPITAL EQUIPMENT CHECKLIST (cont.)

	Suggested Quantity No. of Beds			Local Requirements		
	50-75	100-150	200-225	Unit No.	Unit Price	Total Cost
	A	**B**	**C**			
Nonfood Storage	1	1	3			
Fixed Equipment						
Ventilator at ceiling	1	1	1			
Major-Movable Equipment						
Shelving, metal, adjustable,						
locking casters	1	1	2			
Refrigeration (frozen and chilled foods for 7-day term storage)						
Dairy, fruit and vegetable, and meat						
Fixed Equipment	—	—	—			
Major-Movable Equipment						
Cabinet, frozen food storage, reach-in, 40-45 cu ft,						
net capacity	1	2	4			
Refrigerator						
Reach-in, 40-45 cu ft,						
net capacity	2	3	3			
Shelving, metal, adjustable,						
locking casters	—	—	4			
Walk-in, 150 cu ft,						
net capacity	—	—	1			
Food Production						
Vegetable and Salad						
Preparation	1	1	1			
Fixed Equipment						
Disposer, waste, institutional size with pre-rinse spray	1	1	1			
Sink, 2 drainboards each, compartment 24 x 24 x 12 in.						
1 compartment	1	—	—			
2 compartments	—	1	1			

	Suggested Quantity No. of Beds			Local Requirements			
	50-75	100-150	200-225	Unit	Unit No.	Price	Total Cost
	A	**B**	**C**				
Major-Movable Equipment							
Blender, electric	1	1	1				
Can, waste, with cover, 20 gal	1	2	2				
Cutter, food, bowl diam 14 in. with stand	—	1	1				
Dolly for can with cover	1	1	1				
Extractor, juice, electric	1	1	1				
Opener, can, electric, heavy duty	1	1	1				
Peeler, portable, capacity 15 lb per min	1	1	1				
Rack, tool	1	1	1				
Scale, portion	1	1	1				
Stool, adjustable, with back, 22-23 in.	1	1	1				
Table, preparation, undershelf, locking casters, 30 x 72 in.	1	2	2				
Modified Diet and/or Nourishment Preparation	—	—	1				
Fixed Equipment							
Sink, 2 drainboards, 2 compartment 24 x 24 x 14 in.	—	—	1				
Major-Movable Equipment							
Bin on casters	—	—	1				
Table, undershelf, locking casters							
30 x 48 in.	—	—	1				
30 x 60 in.	—	—	1				
Cooking and Baking	1	1	1				
Fixed Equipment							
Board, bulletin, 26 x 24 in.	1	1	1				
Extinguisher system for grease fires in hoods, ducts	1	1	1				

(cont.)

HEW HOSPITAL EQUIPMENT CHECKLIST (cont.)

	Suggested Quantity No. of Beds			Local Requirements			
	50-75	100-150	200-225	Unit	No.	Unit Price	Total Cost
	A	B	C				
Fountain, drinking	2	2	2				
Grease trap or interceptor	1	1	1				
Hood and fan, ventilating, with removable filters	1	1	1				
Kettle, steam-jacketed, tilt types swinging water spout							
Floor mounted or canti-levered, capacity 20 gal	—	1	2				
Table or counter mount-ed, capacity 20 qt	2	1	1				
Lavatory, spout mounted 5 in. above flood rim, wrist control	2	2	2				
Mixer, food, floor-mounted, capacity 30 to 60 qt, 12-qt bowl, meat grinder, chopper and other attachments, interchangeable hubs	—	1	1				
Oven, capacity two 18 x 26 in. pans							
Bake, single deck	2	2	1				
Roast, double deck, one removable shelf	1	1	2				
Range, fry, hot and open top 1 section	1	1	2				
Shelf above lavatory	2	2	2				
Spreader, plate	1	2	2				
Steamer							
1 compartment, 100-150 meals per hr	1	—	—				
2 compartment, 200-500 meals per hr	—	1	1				
Table, cook's, 2 drawers, sink and undershelf							
30 x 60 in.	—	1	1				
30 x 90 in.	1	—	—				

	Suggested Quantity No. of Beds			Local Requirements			
	50-75	100-150	200-225	Unit	No.	Unit Price	Total Cost
	A	**B**	**C**				

Major-Movable Equipment

Bin, roll under, for baker's table — 3, 3, 3

	A	**B**	**C**
Major-Movable Equipment			
Bin, roll under, for baker's table	3	3	3
Broiler			
1 deck	1	—	—
2 deck	—	1	1
Cabinet, frozen food storage, reach-in			
25-30 cu ft, net capacity	1	2	1
70-75 cu ft, net capacity	—	—	1
Crusher, can-bottle	1	1	1
Extinguisher, fire, CO_2	1	1	1
Fryer, deep fat			
15 lb capacity	1	—	—
25-38 lb capacity	—	1	2
Mixer, food, bench type, 20 qt capacity, 12 qt bowl on open shelf, stand, locking casters, meat grinder, chopper and other attachments, interchangeable hubs	1	1	1
Rack			
Bread, storage	1	1	2
Cooling, with casters, 24 x 18 x 72 in.	1	1	2
Utensil, storage	—	—	1
Receptacle, waste, foot operated, closed top for lavatory	2	2	2
Refrigerator, reach-in, bake, cook and salad			
20 cu ft, net capacity	2	—	—
40 cu ft, net capacity	—	2	4
Scale, baker's, tare beam, capacity 16 lb	1	1	1
Shelving, food file and roll out and gravity feed	(as needed)		
Slicer, food, electric, with stand	1	1	1

(cont.)

HEW HOSPITAL EQUIPMENT CHECKLIST (cont.)

	Suggested Quantity No. of Beds			Local Requirements			
	50-75 **A**	100-150 **B**	200-225 **C**	Unit	No.	Unit Price	Total Cost
Stand for broiler, open below	1	1	1				
Table							
Baker, 2 drawers, 1 shelf above, open below for bins							
30 x 72 in.	1	—	—				
30 x 90 in.		1	1				
Cook, under-shelf, 36 x 60 in.	—	1	1				
Utility, 1 under-shelf, locking casters, 30 x 24 in.	2	3	3				
Truck, shelf type	1	1	2				
Tray Set-Up, Serving and Distribution	1	1	1				
Fixed Equipment							
Clock, electric	1	1	1				
Coffee maker, stand							
Twin urn, 3 gal capacity each, water chamber 6 gal capacity	1	1	—				
Twin urn, 8 gal capacity each, water chamber 12 gal capacity	—	—	1				
Conveyor, tray							
Horizontal, assembly, open type	—	1	1				
Vertical, ascending-descending type	—	—	2				
Dumbwaiter	—	1	1				
Intercommunication system to patient floors	1	1	1				
Machine, icemaking and dispensing	1	1	1				
Major-Movable Equipment							
Cabinet, ice cream, upright							
10 gal capacity	1	—	—				
20 gal capacity	—	1	1				
Conveyor, tray, unheated, enclosed, capacity 20-24 trays	2	4	—				

	Suggested Quantity No. of Beds			Local Requirements		
	50-75	100-150	200-225	Unit No.	Unit Price	Total Cost
	<u>A</u>	<u>B</u>	<u>C</u>			
Dispenser						
Flatware, 4 compartment	1	2	4			
Self-leveling with locking						
casters						
Heated						
Bowl						
2 compartment, capacity 6 doz	1	—	—			
4 compartment, capacity 12 doz	—	1	2			
Cup-saucer						
2 compartment, capacity 6 doz	1	—	—			
2 compartment, capacity 12 doz	—	1	2			
Dish, vegetable						
1 compartment, capacity 6 doz	1	—	—			
2 compartment, capacity 12 doz	—	1	2			
Plate						
1 compartment, capacity 6 doz	1	—	—			
2 compartment, capacity 12 doz	—	1	—			
4 compartment, capacity 24 doz	—	—	1			
Unheated						
Dish, dessert						
1 compartment, capacity 6 doz	1	—	—			
2 compartment, capacity 12 doz	—	1	2			
Glass, rack 20 x 20 in. capacity to 16 doz	1	1	1			
Plate, bread-salad, 2 compartment, capacity 12 doz	2	2	4			

(cont.)

HEW HOSPITAL EQUIPMENT CHECKLIST (cont.)

	Suggested Quantity No. of Beds			Local Requirements			
	50-75	100-150	200-225	Unit	No.	Unit Price	Total Cost
	A	**B**	**C**				
Tray, 14 x 18 in., capacity 7½ to 12½ doz	1	1	2				
Holding units, food, electric table type with inserts and locking casters							
Cold food, refrigerated section	1	1	2				
Hot food, heated section	1	1	2				
Oven, heated disc with dispenser	—	1	1				
Refrigerator, 20 cu ft	—	1	1				
Table							
Tray assembly	1 or	—	—				
Tray set-up	1	1	1				
Utility, 1 undershelf, locking casters, 30 x 24 in.	2	3	5				
Toaster, electric, heavy duty, 4 slice	1	2	2				
Cafeteria-Dining Areas	—	1	1				
Fixed Equipment							
Back bar, open shelves below	1	1	2				
Board, menu	1	1	1				
Clock, electric	1	1	1				
Cold pan unit	—	1	2				
Conveyor, to Dishwashing room, gravity type with trough	1	1	1				
Counter, serving table type with open base below	1	1	1				
Fountain, drinking, electric cafeteria type	1	1	1				
Griddle, flush with counter top, with exhaust fan	—	1	1				

	Suggested Quantity No. of Beds			Local Requirements			
	50-75	100-150	200-225	Unit	Unit No.	Price	Total Cost
	A	**B**	**C**				
Panel, glass	1	2	2				
Partition, folding			2				
Railing		1	1				
Shelf, serving, panel and							
glass protector	1	1	2				
Shelves, glass, display	3	3	3				
Sink, counter, open							
shelves below	1	1	2				
Slide, tray	1	1	1				
Table, hot food, waterless							
with interchangeable inserts,							
24 x 48 x 30 in.	—	1	2				
Warmer, food, pass-through							
to cooking area	—	1	1				
Major-Movable Equipment							
Cabinet, ice cream, upright							
10 gal	—	1	—				
20 gal	—	—	1				
Case, pastry, stand	—	—	1				
Cash register	—	1	1				
Chair, dining	24	48	96				
Coffee maker, vacuum type,							
5 elements	1	1	2				
Dispenser							
Cream, capacity 2 qt	—	1	2				
Flatware, 4 compartment	1	1	2				
Self-leveling							
Heated							
Bowl, 2 compartment							
capacity 6 doz	—	1	2				
Dish, vegetable or dessert							
1 compartment,							
capacity 6 doz	1	1	—				
2 compartment,							
capacity 12 doz	—	—	1				

(cont.)

HEW HOSPITAL EQUIPMENT CHECKLIST (cont.)

	Suggested Quantity No. of Beds			Local Requirements			
	50-75	100-150	200-225	Unit	No.	Unit Price	Total Cost
	A	B	C				
Plate							
1 compartment, capacity 6 doz	1	1	—				
2 compartment, capacity 12 doz	—	—	1				
Unheated							
Dish, vegetable or dessert							
1 compartment, capacity 6 doz	1	1	—				
2 compartment, capacity 12 doz	—	—	1				
Plate, bread-salad, 2 compartment capacity 12 doz	—	1	2				
Dolly							
Cup	1	1	1				
Glass	1	1	1				
Tray racks	1	1	2				
Rack, coat, shelf above	1	1	2				
Refrigerator, reach-in							
20 cu ft, net capacity	—	1	1				
40 cu ft, net capacity	—	—	1				
Serving unit, hot-cold food	1	—	—				
Stand, folding tray	1	2	3				
Table, dining, 48 x 48 in.	6	12	24				
Toaster, electric, heavy duty, 4 slice	1	1	2				
Dishwashing	1	1	1				
Fixed Equipment							
Conveyor, tray							
Horizontal, tray-dish rack handling from soiled dish table	1	1	1				

	Suggested Quantity No. of Beds			Local Requirements			
	50-75	100-150	200-225	Unit	No.	Unit Price	Total Cost
	A	**B**	**C**				
Vertical descending type	—	—	1				
Dishwashing machine, automatic, floor model, 20 x 20 in. racks with booster heater, detergent dispenser, rack return conveyor, rinse injector and splash guard, wash and rinse thermometer							
Conveyor type, single tank, capacity 150-216 racks per hr	—	1	—				
Door type, automatic single tank, capacity 35-50 racks per hr	1	—	—				
Rackless type	—	—	1				
Disposer, waste, removable adjustable, flatware guards, pre-flush assembly, institutional size, in soiled dish table	1	1	1				
Hood and fan, ventilating	1	1	1				
Lavatory, spout outlet mounted 5 in. above flood rim, foot, knee or elbow control	1	1	1				
Partition, glass above wainscot	2	2	5				
Shelf above lavatory	1	1	2				
Sink, utility	—	—	1				
Table, dish							
Clean, rolled rim edge, shelf above, 4-5 racks	1	1	—				
Soiled, sink type, shelf above and below	1	1	1				
Major-Movable Equipment							
Can, with cover							
capacity 20 gal	1	1	1				

(cont.)

HEW HOSPITAL EQUIPMENT CHECKLIST (cont.)

	Suggested Quantity No. of Beds			Local Requirements			
	50-75	100-150	200-225		Unit	Unit Price	Total Cost
	A	**B**	**C**	Unit	No.	Price	Cost
Dolly							
Can	1	2	2				
Cup	1	1	2				
Glass	1	1	1				
Tray rack	1	2	2				
Rack, dishwashing machine							
Bowl, 20 x 20 in., open	2	4	—				
Creamer, 6 x 10 in., 24 compartment	2	4	8				
Cup, 20 x 20 in., 20 compartment	6	10	17				
Flatware, 12¾ x 6 in., 8 compartment	1	2	3				
Glass, 20 x 20 in., 36 compartment	4	6	12				
Plate, 20 x 20 in., 9 compartment	3	6	—				
Tray, 20 x 20 in., 8 compartment	3	6	—				
Sink, soak, 2 compartment, locking casters	1	2	2				
Truck, metal, adjustable shelves, locking casters	—	1	1				
Potwashing							
Fixed Equipment	1	1	1				
Disposer, waste, institutional size, pre-rinse spray	1	1	1				
Heater, booster, hot water line attachment	1	1	1				
Partition, glass above wainscot	1	1	2				
Shelf above sink	1	1	1				

	Suggested Quantity No. of Beds			Local Requirements			
	50-75	100-150	200-225	Unit	No.	Unit Price	Total Cost
	A	**B**	**C**				

	A	B	C	Unit	No.	Unit Price	Total Cost
Sink, 2 drainboards, 3 compartments 30 x 24 in. and 12-16 in. deep, 1 with dial thermometer	1	1	1				
Washer, automatic, pot and pan, rack type, single compartment	1	1	1				
Major-Movable Equipment							
Can, with cover, capacity 20 gal	1	2	2				
Dolly for can	1	1	1				
Rack, pot, shelving, metal adjustable shelves, locking casters							
24 x 32 x 60 in.	1	—	—				
60 x 30 x 60 in.	1	2	3				
Washer, pot and pan, mechanical brush	1	1	1				
Janitors Area	1	1	1				
Fixed Equipment							
Basin, mop service with floor drain	1	1	1				
Holder, mop handle	2	2	2				
Shelf, supply	1	1	1				
Major-Movable Equipment							
Truck mopping, 2 buckets wringer	1	1	1				
Vacuum cleaner, wet-dry, 10 gal capacity	—	1	1				
Linen Storage	1	1	1				
Clean							
Fixed Equipment	—	—	—				

(cont.)

HEW HOSPITAL EQUIPMENT CHECKLIST (cont.)

	Suggested Quantity No. of Beds			Local Requirements			
	50-75	100-150	200-225	Unit	No.	Unit Price	Total Cost
	A	B	C				
Major-Movable Equipment							
Cart, utility, 20 x 36 in.	1	1	2				
Soiled							
Fixed Equipment	—	—	—				
Major-Movable Equipment							
Receptacle, foot operated, closed top	1	2	2				
Trash and Can Wash Room	1	1	1				
Fixed Equipment							
Washer, can	1	1	1				
Major-Movable Equipment							
Can with cover, capacity 20 gal	2	4	8				
Dolly for can	1	1	1				
Rack, can, locking casters	1	1	1				
Cart Wash Room	1	1	1				
Fixed Equipment							
Outlet, steam and hot water	1	1	1				
Major-Movable Equipment							
Ice Manufacture							
Fixed Equipment	1	1	1				
Ice making machine, automatic, self-dispensing							
500 lb capacity	1	—	—				
1000 lb capacity	—	1	—				
2000 lb capacity	—	—	1				
Major-Movable Equipment	—	—	—				
Office	1	1	2				
Fixed Equipment							
Board, bulletin, 26 x 24 in.	1	1	1				
Counter, open below	1	1	1				

	Suggested Quantity No. of Beds			Local Requirements			
	50-75	100-150	200-225	Unit	Unit No.	Unit Price	Total Cost
	<u>A</u>	<u>B</u>	<u>C</u>				
Locker, clothes, steel,							
15 x 18 x 60 in.	1	1	2				
Panel, glass	2	2	2				
Pneumatic tube station	—	1	1				
Major-Movable Equipment							
Bookcase	1	1	1				
Cabinet, filing							
Card size, 2 drawers, 5 x 8 in.	1	1	1				
Letter size, 5 drawer	1	1	2				
Calculator, listing	1	1	1				
Case, map for holding large							
educational material	1	1	1				
Chair							
Office, swivel, with arms	1	1	2				
Straight	2	3	4				
Desk, office, single pedestal	1	2	3				
Lamp, desk	1	1	3				
Stand, typewriter	1	1	1				
Table, 24 x 42 in.	1	1	1				
Typewriter	1	1	1				

PERSONNEL FACILITIES

Men's Toilet	1	1	1				
Fixed Equipment							
Lavatory	1	1	1				
Light above lavatory	1	1	1				
Mirror above lavatory	1	1	1				
Partition, metal 1 ft above floor	3	3	3				
Shelf above lavatory	1	1	1				
Urinal	1	1	1				
Water closet							
Major-Movable Equipment	1	1	1				
Receptacle, waste, foot operated, closed top,							
paper towel	1	1	1				

(cont.)

HEW HOSPITAL EQUIPMENT CHECKLIST (cont.)

	Suggested Quantity No. of Beds			Local Requirements		
	50- 75	100- 150	200- 225	Unit No.	Unit Price	Total Cost
	A	**B**	**C**			
Women's Toilet						
Fixed Equipment						
Counter 30 in. high, open below	1	1	1			
Lavatory, counter	1	1	1			
Light above lavatory	1	1	1			
Mirror above lavatory	1	1	1			
Partition, metal, 1 ft above floor	2	2	3			
Water closet	1	1	2			
Major-Movable Equipment						
Receptacle, waste, foot operated, closed top, paper towel	2	2	3			
Dietary						
Minor Equipment						
Beater, rotary, manual, commercial type	1	2	4 ea			
Board, cutting, hardwood or synthetic material 10 x 16 x ¼ in.	1	2	2 ea			
Brush						
Pastry	1	1	1 ea			
Pot	2	2	3 ea			
Urn	1	2	3 ea			
Vegetable	6	6	6 ea			
Canister, assorted sizes	1	2	4 set			
Casserole, individual	9	18	25 doz			
Chopper						
Food, hand	1	1	1 ea			
Meat, manual, capacity 3 lb	1	1	1 ea			
Colander, metal, 16 in.	1	1	1 ea			
Corer, peeler	2	2	2 ea			

	Suggested Quantity No. of Beds			Local Requirements			
	50-75	100-150	200-225	Unit	No.	Unit Price	Total Cost
	A	**B**	**C**				
Cup							
Custard	10	15	25 doz				
Measure, metal							
1 cup	4	6	6 ea				
1 pt	2	3	4 ea				
1 qt	4	6	6 ea				
Cutter, metal							
Biscuit	2	2	3 ea				
Doughnut	1	1	2 ea				
Salad, manual, slicing, shredding or grating cone, rotary type	1	1	1 ea				
Dispenser							
Flatware, counter type, 4 compartment	1	—	— ea				
Napkin	1	1	2 ea				
Extractor, juice, manual	1	1	1 ea				
Fork, cook							
12 in.	2	2	2 ea				
14 in.	1	1	2 ea				
20 in.	—	1	1 ea				
Funnel, metal, capacity 1 qt	2	4	4 ea				
Holder, tray card	5	10	20 doz				
Knife							
Boning, blade 6 in.	1	1	2 ea				
Bread, serrated, blade 10 in.	1	1	1 ea				
Butcher, blade 12 in.	1	2	2 ea				
Chopping or mincing, double blades	1	1	1 ea				
French, blade 10 in.	2	2	2 ea				
Grapefruit	2	2	2 ea				
Paring	6	12	18 ea				
Sabatier, heavy, blade 14 in.	1	1	1 ea				

(cont.)

HEW HOSPITAL EQUIPMENT CHECKLIST (cont.)

	Suggested Quantity No. of Beds			Local Requirements			
	50-75	100-150	200-225	Unit	No.	Unit Price	Total Cost
	A	**B**	**C**				
Slicing							
12 in. blade, electric 1	1	1	1 ea				
14 in. blade	1	1	1 ea				
Ladle, stainless steel							
2 oz	2	2	2 ea				
4 oz	3	4	4 ea				
6 oz	2	2	3 ea				
8 oz	2	2	3 ea				
16 oz	2	2	3 ea				
Machine, patty, manual	1	1	1 ea				
Masher, heavy duty							
Mold, small, diam 3 in.	10	20	30 doz				
Opener							
Bottle, manual	2	2	2 ea				
Can, manual	3	4	6 ea				
Table model, heavy duty, adjustable	1	2	3 ea				
Pin, rolling, hardwood heavy duty, revolving handle	1	2	2 ea				
Pitcher, metal, capacity 3 qt	6	6	6 ea				
Scoop, metal with handle, 32 oz	1	1	2 ea				
Disher, spring type							
No. 6, capacity 2/3 c	1	2	2 ea				
No. 8, capacity 1/2 c							
No. 10, capacity 2/5 c	1	2	2 ea				
No. 12, capacity 1/3 c	1	2	2 ea				
No. 16, capacity 1/4 c	1	2	2 ea				
No. 20	1	2	2 ea				
No. 24	1	2	2 ea				
No. 30	6	12	18 ea				
Scraper, bowl, flexible non-metallic blade, 7 in. wide	1	2	2 ea				

	Suggested Quantity No. of Beds			Local Requirements			
	50-75	100-150	200-225	Unit	No.	Unit Price	Total Cost
	A	B	C				
Shaker	1	2	2 ea				
Pepper	3	6	12 ea				
Salt	3	6	12 ea				
Shears, steel, 8 in.	1	2	2 ea				
Slicer, egg	1	1	1 ea				
Spatula, baker, 10 in.	3	4	6 ea				
Spoon							
Measuring, graduated							
¼ t–1 T sets	2	2	2 set				
Mixing, 15 in.	2	3	4 ea				
Serving, stainless steel							
Perforated or slotted, 13¼ in.	4	4	6 ea				
Solid, 11-13 in.	2	2	3 ea				
Thermometer, food, stainless steel	2	2	2 ea				
Tongs, serving, 9-12 in.	2	4	4 ea				
Turner, pancake	2	4	4 ea				
Whip, wire	1	1	2 ea				
Utensils, Cooking and Baking and Serving							
Boiler, double with cover							
7 qt	1	1	2 ea				
11 qt	1	2	2 ea				
Bowl, mixing, metal							
1½ qt	2	2	2 ea				
3 qt	3	4	4 ea				
5 qt	2	3	4 ea				
11 qt	1	2	3 ea				
30 qt	1	1	1 ea				
Pan							
Bake							
3½ x 18 x 26 in.	6	12	16 ea				
4 x 12 x 20 in.	3	6	9 ea				

(cont.)

HEW HOSPITAL EQUIPMENT CHECKLIST (cont.)

	Suggested Quantity No. of Beds			Local Requirements		
	50-75	100-150	200-225	Unit No.	Unit Price	Total Cost
	A	**B**	**C**			
Bun						
1 x 18 x 26 in.	4	6	8 ea			
Cake						
2-1/8 x 18 x 26 in.	16	24	36 ea			
Tubed, diam 9 in.	6	12	16 ea			
Dish, 20-30 qt	1	2	2 ea			
Fry						
12 in. diam	2	3	4 ea			
14 in. diam	2	3	4 ea			
Loaf, 10 x 5 x 4 in.	3	4	6 ea			
Muffin, 12 cups	10	15	30 ea			
Pie, diam 9 x 1 or 1¼ in.	18	24	36 ea			
Sauce, with cover						
2 qt	2	4	6 ea			
6 qt	2	3	4 ea			
8 qt	1	2	2 ea			
Service, food holding, standard sizes						

Tableware: Patient Tray Service

Dinnerware

Bowl, cereal, 10 oz	6	12	24 doz			
Cup, tea, 6 oz	9	18	36 doz			
Dish, vegetable-dessert	9	18	36 doz			
Plate						
Bread and butter, diam 6 in.	9	18	36 doz			
Dinner, diam 9 in.	6	12	24 doz			
Salad, diam 7 in.	7½	15	30 doz			
Saucer, tea, 5 in.	6	12	24 doz			

Flatware

Fork, dinner	9	18	36 doz			
Knife, dinner	5	10	20 doz			

	Suggested Quantity No. of Beds			Local Requirements			
	50-75	100-150	200-225	Unit	No.	Unit Price	Total Cost
	A	**B**	**C**				
Spoon							
Soup	5	10	20 doz				
Teaspoon	10	20	40 doz				
Glassware							
Creamer, ¾-1 oz	7	12	25 doz				
Fruit juice, 4-5 oz	6	12	24 doz				
Sherbet	6	12	24 doz				
Tumbler, 10 oz	12	22	30 doz				
Carafe, water, individual	5	10	20 doz				
Containers, beverage, metal, insulated	50	100	200 ea				
Cover, metal plate	50	100	200 ea				
Shell for heated metal disc	—	100	200 ea				
Tray, serving, 14 x 18 in.	7½	12½	25 doz				

Tableware: Personnel and Visitors Service

Dinnerware							
Bowl, cereal, 10 oz	6	12	24 doz				
Cup, tea, 6 oz	9	18	36 doz				
Dish, vegetable-dessert	9	18	36 doz				
Plate							
Bread and butter, diam 6 in.	9	18	36 doz				
Dinner, diam 9 in.	6	12	24 doz				
Salad, diam 7 in.	7½	15	30 doz				
Saucer, tea, 5 in.	6	12	24 doz				
Flatware							
Fork, dinner	9	18	36 doz				
Knife, dinner	5	10	20 doz				
Spoon							
Soup	5	10	20 doz				
Teaspoon	10	20	40 doz				

(cont.)

HEW HOSPITAL EQUIPMENT CHECKLIST (cont.)

	Suggested Quantity No. of Beds			Local Requirements			
	50-75	100-150	200-225	Unit	No.	Unit Price	Total Cost
	A	**B**	**C**				
Glassware							
Creamer, ¾-1 oz	7	12	25 doz				
Fruit juice, 4-5 oz	6	12	24 doz				
Sherbet	6	12	24 doz				
Tumbler, 10 oz	12	22	30 doz				
Tray, serving, 14 x 18 in.	4	8	12½ doz				
Supplies							

Based on individual requirements

NOTE: *This table is based on one published by the U. S. Dept. of HEW for small hospitals.*

Additional Bibliography

Donovan, Anne C., and Ives, Orville B. *Hospital Dietary Services: A Planning Guide.* Washington, D. C.: U. S. Dept. of Health, Education and Welfare, 1966.

Frolich, Louise. *Planning and Equipping a Hospital Foodservice Facility.* St. Louis, Mo.: Koch Refrigerators, n. d.

Iowa State Board of Health. *Planning Food Facilities on a Small Scale,* Des Moines, Iowa, 1964.

Jernigan, Anna K. "Guide to Kitchen Equipment for Small Hospitals," *Hospitals, XVIII,* (October 1964)

Kotschevar, Lendal H., and Terrell, Margaret E. *Food Service Planning.* New York: John S. Wiley, 1961.

Rundquist, Ardyce, and Callahan, Mary. "Kitchen Equipment for Smaller Institutions," *Hospitals, XXXVI.* (October 1962)

Schneider, N. F.; John, E. A.; and Smith, A. Q. *Commercial Kitchens.* New York: American Gas Assn., 1963.

Stokes, John W. *Food Service in Industry and Institutions.* Wm. C Brown Co., Dubuque, Iowa: 1960.

U. S. Dept. of Health, Education and Welfare. *Programming and Equipping Hospital Departments.* Washington, D. C.: Government Printing Office, 1963.

U. S. Dept. of Health, Education and Welfare. *Hospital Equipment Checklist.* Washington, D. C.: Government Printing Office, 1963.

U. S. Dept. of Health, Education and Welfare. *Public Health Service Regulations, Part 53.* Washington, D. C.: Government Printing Office, 1963.

U. S. Dept. of Housing and Urban Development. *Minimum Property Standards for Nursing Homes,* PHA 4514.1. Washington, D. C.: Government Printing Office, May 1970.

APPENDIX

CONDITIONS OF PARTICIPATION:
EXTENDED CARE FACILITIES–REGULATIONS, U. S. DEPT. OF HEW[1]

405.1025 Condition of Participation–Dietary Department.—The hospital has an organized dietary department directed by qualified personnel. However, a hospital which has a contract with an outside food management company may be found to meet this condition of participation if the company has a therapeutic dietitian who serves, as required by scope and complexity of the service, on a full-time, part-time, or consultant basis to the hospital, provided the company maintains the minimum standards as listed herein and provides for constant liaison with the hospital medical staff for recommendations on dietetic policies affecting patient treatment.

(a) Standard; Organization.—There is an organized department directed by qualified personnel and integrated with other departments of the hospital. There is a qualified dietitian, full-time or on a consultation basis, and, in addition, administrative and technical personnel competent in their respective duties. The factors explaining the standard are as follows:

(1) There are written policies and procedures for food storage, preparation, and service developed by a qualified dietitian (preferably meeting the American Dietetic Association's standards for qualification).

(2) The department is under the supervision of a qualified dietitian who is responsible for quality food production, service, and staff education. The dietitian serves on a full-time basis if possible or, in smaller hospitals, on a regular part-time supervising or consulting basis.

(3) In the absence of a full-time dietitian, there is a qualified person serving as full-time director of the department who is responsible for the daily management aspects of the department and a dietitian visits the hospital at intervals to supervise and instruct personnel.

(4) The number of professional dietitians is adequate considering the size of the facility and the scope and complexity of dietary functions.

(5) Supervisors, other than dietitians, are assigned in numbers and with ability to provide a satisfactory span of control to meet the needs of the physical facilities and the organization as well as coverage for all hours of departmental operation.

(6) The number of personnel, such as cooks, bakers, dishwashers, and clerks, is adequate to perform effectively all defined functions.

(7) Written job descriptions of all dietary employees are available.

(8) There is an inservice training program for dietary employees which includes the proper handling of food and personal grooming.

(b) Standard; Facilities. —Facilities are provided for the general dietary needs of the hospital. These include facilities for the preparation of special diets. Sanitary conditions are maintained in the storage, preparation, and distribution of food. The factors explaining the standard are as follows:

(1) All dietary areas are appropriately located, adequate in size, well lighted, ventilated and maintained.

(2) The type, size, and layout of equipment provides for ease of cleaning, optimal work-flow and adequate food production to meet the scope and complexity of the regular and therapeutic diet requirements of the patients.

(3) Equipment and work areas are clean and orderly. Effective procedures for cleaning all equipment and work areas are followed consistently to safeguard the health of the patient.

(4) Lavatories specifically for handwashing, with hot and cold running water, soap and approved disposable towels, are conveniently located throughout the department for use by food handlers.

(5) There are procedures to control dietary employees with infections and open lesions. Routine health examinations at least meet local, State, or Federal codes for foodservice personnel.

(6) The dietary department is routinely inspected and approved by State or local health agencies as a food handling establishment. Written reports of the inspection are on file at the hospital with notation made by the hospital of action taken to comply with recommendations.

(7) Dry or staple food items are stored at least 12 inches off the floor in a ventilated room which is not subject to sewage or waste water back-flow, or contamination by condensation, leakage, rodents or vermin.

(8) All perishable foods are refrigerated at the appropriate temperature and in an orderly and sanitary manner.

(9) Foods being displayed or transported are protected from contamination and held at proper temperatures in clean containers, cabinets or serving carts.

(10) Dishwashing procedures and techniques are well developed, understood and carried out in compliance with the State and local health codes and with periodic check on:

(i) Detergent dispenser operation;
(ii) Washing, rinsing, and sanitizing temperatures and cleanliness of machine and jets;
(iii) Routine bacterial counts on dishes, flatware, glasses, utensils and equipment; and
(iv) Thermostatic controls.

(11) All garbage and kitchen refuse which is not disposed of through a disposal is kept in leakproof nonabsorbent containers with close fitting covers and is disposed of daily in a manner that will not permit transmission of disease, a nuisance, or a breeding place for flies. All garbage containers are thoroughly cleaned inside and out each time emptied.

(c) Standard; Diets. — There is a systematic record of diets, correlated, when appropriate, with the medical records. The factors explaining the standard are as follows:

(1) Therapeutic diets are prescribed in written orders on the chart by the physician and are instructive, accurate, and complete as possible; for example, bland low residue diet or, if a diabetic diet is ordered, the exact amounts of carbohydrates, protein, and fat allowed are noted.

(2) Nutrition needs are met in accordance with the current Recommended Dietary Allowances of the Food and Nutrition Board, National Research Council, and in accordance with physician's orders.

(3) The dietitian has available an up-to-date manual of regimens for all therapeutic diets, approved jointly by the dietitian and medical staff, which is available to dietary supervisory personnel. Diets served to patients are in compliance with these established diet principles.

(4) The dietitian correlates and integrates the dietary aspects of patient care with the patient and patient's chart through such methods as patient instruction and recording diet histories and participates appropriately in ward rounds and conferences, sharing specialized knowledge with others of the medical team.

(d) Standard; Conferences.—Departmental and interdepartmental conferences are held periodically. The factors explaining the standard are as follows:

(1) The director of dietetics attends and participates in meetings of heads of departments and functions as a key member of the hospital staff.

(2) The director of dietetics has regularly scheduled conferences with the administrator or his designee to keep him informed, seek his counsel, and present program plans for mutual consideration and solution.

(3) Conferences are held regularly within the department at all levels of responsibility to disseminate information, interpret policy, solve problems, and develop procedures and program plans.

[1]U. S. Dept. of HEW, Social Security Administration. "Conditions of Participation: Extended Care Facilities—Regulations," *Federal Health Insurance for the Aged* HIR-11. (Washington, D. C.: Government Printing Office. February, 1968)

CONTRACT AGREEMENT

Date_____

The undersigned parties agree to the following:

This agreement is between _____
(hospital or nursing home)

represented by_____, Administrator,

and _____, Registered Dietitian.

It is mutually agreed that_____

_____
(hospital or nursing home)

will use services of_____,R.D.,

as a dietary consultant beginning on _____

at_____dollars per month retaining fee,

(minimum of____hours per month).

It is also mutually agreed that the dietitian will provide written evidence of length of time spent in facility, a report of activities, recommendations for future action, other services to be rendered, including telephone consultation, and time of next visit.

The above agreement can be terminated by either party upon written notice of thirty days to the other party.

This contract will be renewed yearly.

_____
ADMINISTRATOR

_____
CONSULTANT

A.D.A. Registration No._____

DIETARY IN-SERVICE TRAINING REPORT

DATE_____

FACILITY_____   TIME STARTING _____

INSTRUCTOR_____ TIME ENDING_____

SUBJECT_____

Brief Outline of Subject Matter:

TOPIC OF DISCUSSION FOR NEXT VISIT ON _____

Date

THOSE ATTENDING: (Signed by those attending)

_____   _____

_____   _____

_____   _____

_____   _____

_____   _____

_____   _____

_____

CONSULTANT DIETITIAN

Registration No. _____

HOW TO HANDLE DIETARY RECORDS

The following "Guidelines for Therapeutic Dietitians on Recording in Patient's Medical Records"[1] are recommended by the American Hospital Association:

As the care of patients continues to become more and more complex, each person involved in the patient's care needs to have current information as to what others are doing for him, how he is reacting to the treatment or diet, his progress, and any treatment or diet changes recommended. The dietitian, like other members of the health care team, works under the direction of the attending physician, but usually when he is not present. By promptly recording all pertinent information concerning the patient's food habits and information related to his diet in the patient's medical record, the dietitian uses the only reliable means of regular communication with the physician and also with the other professional staff members involved in the patient's total therapeutic regime.

This kind of communication among members of the health care team is necessary for patients under short-term care and is of even greater importance when prolonged care is involved. The patient's record should also include summaries of evaluation and therapeutic planning conferences. Chronological recording of all this information in the patient's record is the method best designed to facilitate good medical care.

What to record

Information that should be recorded by the dietitian concerns patient progress (1) toward desired dietary intake and (2) toward understanding of nutrition instruction given to him. Other information representing a therapeutic factor may also be included. Some examples of significant information to chart are:

A. *Patient's daily food intake.*
1. Calculated nutrient intake as requested or indicated.
2. Observations, such as:
    a. Quality of appetite and its gross effect on food intake.
    b. Patient's food habits as they affect intake.
    c. Any gross inadequacy in one or more nutrients.

Use of graphs gives the physician a quick picture of the patient's daily food intake.

---

[1] Reprinted with permission, from *Guidelines for Therapeutic Dietitians on Recording in Patients' Medical Records,* published by the American Hospital Association, S31, 1966.

HOW TO HANDLE DIETARY RECORDS (cont.)

B. Reasons for patient's acceptance or rejection of food.

The dietitian is frequently able to assess the reason for the patient's acceptance or rejection of food, such as dislike of certain foods, intolerance for certain foods, loss of appetite, reaction to quality of foods presented, environmental factors, and so forth. This type of information may be helpful to the physician in prescribing further diet therapy for the patient.

C. Information related to diet order, such as:

1. Diet pattern, when distribution and type of food are of significance (for example, in diabetes).

2. Suggestions on how diet order might be altered to better meet patient's therapeutic needs, to be more acceptable, or to be adapted to home and working situation.

3. Explanation or interpretation of a prescription that is unusual in terms of amounts and types of food. This may be accompanied by an outline of the diet, an estimate of the daily food intake, and any other pertinent information.

4. Comments on multiple restrictions (for example, low sodium, high protein, no milk or milk products) that are impossible, undesirable, or unacceptable to the patient.

5. The composition of a tube feeding if it was not ordered by specific prescription.

D. Information related to diet instruction (concerning diet during hospitalization and for home or nursing home use), such as:

1. Record of initial diet instructions and the patient's response and progress, and, if necessary, a recommendation for making the diet realistic.

2. Information regarding day-to-day diet instruction and, if appropriate, a suggestion that an appointment be made with the clinic dietitian, or that the patient attend group diet instruction.

3. Information about the patient's ability to follow the diet after discharge, including his understanding, financial ability, eating facilities at home and at work, and so forth. (For instance, a factory worker may have difficulty adhering to a discharge diet providing 500 mg. sodium in six feedings.)

4. Request, if needed, for referral of the patient to the proper community agency for help in following the diet at home.

E. Diet history, including the facts and an interpretation of them, plus information about the patient's diet pattern habits, deficiencies as related to recommended allowances, and so forth.

F. Other pertinent information: for example, a notation that the patient has been chosen for a case study.

For patients in a psychiatric unit, the same items of information should be recorded, but special attention should be given to the patient's food associations and relationships.

Where to record

The American Hospital Association has recommended that the progress notes sheet is the most appropriate place in the patient's medical record for recording diet therapy information and dietary consultation reports.

How to record

Brevity without the sacrifice of necessary facts is the essence of effective recording. The dietary progress notes and summaries should be as brief as is consistent with good communication, should avoid professional jargon, and should have meaning for all responsible members of the health team. Remarks that are critical of the treatment carried out by others, that are undignified, or that indicate bias against the patient should never appear in the records. Facts are preferable to opinions. When opinions are expressed, they should be phrased to indicate clearly that they are the views of the individual doing the recording. Opinions requiring medical judgment should be written only by physicians.

A "Department of Dietetics" stamp is a good way to identify the dietitian's contribution to the patient's record for easy reference. The use of colored ink is not recommended because it will not be reproduced as color when the records are microfilmed or photocopied.

Comments or notations should be signed by the dietitian, with her name and title. When dietary notes are not made daily, a "flag" may be inserted to advise the physician that pertinent nutritional information has been added to the progress notes.

HOW TO HANDLE DIETARY RECORDS (cont.)

Standard IV, Dietetic Services, Accreditation Manual for Hospitals, 1970* states:

Standard IV

The administration of the nutritional aspects of patient care shall be under the direction of a qualified dietitian.

Interpretation
The nutritional aspects of patient care shall be directed by a qualified dietitian or by other appropriate persons who are supervised and guided by the dietitian. Duties shall include:

- Recording dietary histories of patients such as those with food allergies and those unable to accept a limiting diet regimen;

- Interviewing patients regarding their food habits;

- Counseling patients and their families concerning normal or modified regimens, and encouraging patients to participate in planning their own normal or modified regimens; and

- Participating in appropriate ward rounds and conferences.

Observations and information pertinent to dietetic treatment shall be recorded in the patient's medical record by the dietitian.[1]

All hospital menus must be approved by the dietitian. There shall be an up-to-date manual that is approved by the dietitian and the medical staff. The ordering of diets should be standardized by the use of this diet manual. The nutritional deficiencies of any diet in the manual must be indicated.

[1]For further assistance refer to *Guidelines for Medical Records.* (Chicago: American Hospital Association, 1966).

*Reproduced from *Accreditation Manual for Hospitals* 1970 with permission from Joint Commission on Accreditation of Hospitals, 645 North Michigan Avenue, Chicago, Illinois 60611.

The following policies and procedures are oftentimes followed in recording dietary information in some hospitals and other health facilities; they should appear in the policy and procedures manual of the dietary department:

I.   Diet Procedures:

A.   A facility should have a systematic record of diets, correlated, when appropriate, with the medical records. The standard procedures for following this are:

   (1)   Therapeutic diets are prescribed in written orders on the chart by the physician and are instructive, accurate and complete as possible, for example, bland low residue diets or, if a diabetic diet is ordered, the exact amounts of carbohydrates, protein and fat allowed are noted.

   (2)   Nutrition needs are met in accordance with the current Recommended Dietary Allowances of the Food and Nutrition Board, National Research Council, and in accordance with the physician's orders.

   (3)   The dietitian has available an up-to-date manual of regimens for all therapeutic diets, approved jointly by the dietitian and medical staff which is available to dietary supervisory personnel. Diets served to patients are in compliance with these established diet principles.

   (4)   The dietitian correlates and integrates the dietary aspects of patient care with the patient and patient's chart through such methods as patient instruction and recording diet histories and participates appropriately in ward rounds and conferences, sharing specialized knowledge with others of the medical team.

B.   Therapeutic diets are prescribed by the attending physician. Therapeutic menus are planned in writing, prepared and served as orders with supervision or consultation from the dietitian and advice of the physician whenever necessary. The following are considered standard procedures:

HOW TO HANDLE DIETARY RECORDS (cont.)

(1)   Therapeutic diet orders are written by the attending physician in the patient's medical record.

(2)   A system is established for written transmittal of diet orders to the dietetic services.

(3)   A current therapeutic diet manual, approved jointly by the dietitian and the medical staff, is readily available to attending physicians, nursing and dietetic personnel. A copy is maintained at each nurses' station.

(4)   An identification system is established to ensure that each patient receives his diet as ordered.

(5)   All therapeutic diet menus are in writing and are approved by the dietitian.

(6)   All persons responsible for preparation and service of therapeutic diets have sufficient knowledge to make appropriate and safe substitutions when necessary.

(7)   The dietetic service maintains a written record for each patient for whom a therapeutic diet is ordered.

(8)   The dietitian contributes pertinent information to the written patient care plan.

(9)   The dietitian records in the patient's medical record significant information relating to the patient's response to his diet to inform the attending physician and nursing personnel of the patient on a therapeutic diet.

See also (c) in the federal government's 1966 Conditions of Participation in Extended Care Facilities, p. 483 in this Appendix.

Table 5-8A—A LIBERAL DIABETIC DIET*
(1800 calories, carbohydrate 180 grams, protein 80 grams, fat 80 grams)

Breakfast
Broiled Pink Grapefruit
French toast (2 slices)
Low calorie jam
Ham slice (2 oz)
Butter or margarine (1)
Coffee**

Lunch
Consomme a la Printanier
Saltines (2)
Fresh fruit plate with ½ c cottage cheese
Dietetic lime sherbet
Milk

Dinner
Oyster cocktail, chili sauce
Melba toast (1)
Broiled steak, fresh mushrooms
Buttered asparagus tips
Baked tomato
Tossed salad, no-cal dressing
Hard roll, butter (1)
Orange Spanish Cream (dietetic)
Vanilla wafer
Tea with lemon**

Casaba melon, lime wedge
Poached egg on whole wheat toast
Bacon strips (2)
Coffee**

Tomato bouillon
Shredded wheat wafer
Cheese souffle, low-cal crushed strawberry topping
Baked artichoke hearts and broccoli
Steamed rice (½ c)
Delicious apple
Milk

Orange juice
Baked pork chop stuffed with apples
Zucchini squash, Italian
Celery sticks stuffed with cream cheese, radishes
Corn muffin, butter
Baked ½ banana with low-cal custard sauce
Tea with lemon**

Tomato juice
Broiled lamb chops
Hash brown potatoes
Toast (1), butter
Coffee**

Cream of watercress soup
Whole wheat wafer
Crab salad in tomato cup
Spinach timbale
½ toasted hard roll
Papaya with lime wedge
Milk

Stuffed egg with caviar on toast round
Braised veal bird, sausage stuffing
Boiled Belgium chicory
Broccoli with mock hollandaise
Parkerhouse roll, butter
Baked cherry souffle, dietetic
Tea with lemon**

*See page 495 for explanation of asterisks.

(cont.)

Table 5-8A–A LIBERAL DIABETIC DIET* (cont.)

Breakfast	Lunch	Dinner
Prunes Scrambled eggs with chicken livers Toast (2), butter Coffee**	Lobster bisque, wafer Broiled veal loin chop Carrots, buttered Double baked potato Slice bread, butter Pineapple sherbet (dietetic) Milk	Fresh fruit cup, saltine Baked ham Mashed hubbard squash Eggplant and mushroom creole Watercress salad, no-cal dressing Hot biscuit, butter Cantaloupe a la mode, (dietetic vanilla ice cream) Tea with lemon**
Nectarine juice Eggs benedict Coffee**	Chicken broth, saltines (2) Cold plate: 1 oz Swiss cheese, 2 oz rare roast beef, 1 oz ham Sliced tomatoes and cucumbers Raspberry whip (dietetic) Milk	Pate de foie gras on wafer Roast rib of beef, au jus Yorkshire pudding Deep-fried cauliflower String beans, buttered Hard roll, butter Heart of lettuce salad, no-cal dressing Baked pear in 1 T grenadine Tea with lemon**
Fresh sliced peach, 1 t sugar, cream Broiled salmon, lemon Steamed potato Toast (1), butter Coffee**	Beef broth with barley Saltine Broiled chicken leg Buttered string beans with toasted almonds Sliced cucumbers, vinaigrette Orange sherbet (dietetic) Milk	Shrimp cocktail, chili sauce, saltine Broiled shish-kabob (beef tips, cherry tomato, mushroom, bud onions alternated) Fresh boiled spinach, buttered ½ toasted hard roll, butter Shaggy mane peaches (dietetic) Tea with lemon**
Blended orange and grapefruit juice Broiled sirloin steak Fried egg Toast (2), butter	Oyster stew, saltine Braised sweetbreads and mushrooms Fresh fruit salad, no-cal dressing Hot cornbread, butter	Crab legs with ravigote sauce, wafer Broiled trout, lemon butter Deep-fried green tomato slices Green peas and tiny onions

Coffee**

Fresh strawberries, 1 t sugar, cream
Shirred egg with cheddar cheese
Canadian bacon (1)
Blueberry muffins (2)
Butter
Coffee**

Cantaloupe
Poached egg on toast
Broiled ham
Toast (1)
Coffee**

Chocolate pudding (dietetic)
Milk

Consomme with watercress
Saltines (2)
Cold boiled salmon, mayonnaise
Mixed buttered vegetables
Hearts of palm, no-cal dressing
Poppyseed roll, butter
Fresh pineapple slice
Milk

Borscht with sour cream, wafer
Fruit and cheese plate
Bran, nut and date muffins (2), butter
Sliced tomatoes
Orange slices with coconut
Milk

Tossed green salad, vinegar and oil
Orange cup filled with fresh fruit
Tea with lemon**

Clams on the half shell, chili sauce, melba toast
Broiled calves liver, bacon
Sauteed onions
Baked rice croquette
Creamed salsify and lima beans
Relish plate
Peach melba (dietetic peach, raspberry sauce and ice cream)
Tea with lemon**

Jellied consomme, lemon wedge
Saltine (1)
Deep-fried shrimp, tartar sauce
Glazed carrots
Fresh asparagus, buttered
French endive salad, no-cal dressing
Broiled angelfood cake with fresh raspberries
Tea with lemon**

*For late evening snack, serve diabetic eggnog with two graham crackers, or a diabetic milk shake with crackers, or milk with a lo-cal cookie, etc. to bring the milk intake to a pint a day and bring bread exchanges up to 7 or 8. Where a day has less than 7 or 8 bread exchanges, allow a cereal for breakfast or additional bread where desired.

**Artificial sweeteners, if allowed by the physician; all desserts prepared without sugar; for some diabetics the physician may allow 2 oz of a dry dinner wine with the evening meal.

INDEX